**CORE TAX ANNUALS**

# Corporation Tax 2006/07

## CORE TAX ANNUALS

# Corporation Tax 2006/07

**Juliana Watterston** MSc FCA CTA (Fellow)

**General Editor:**
**Mark McLaughlin** CTA (Fellow) ATT TEP

**Tottel Publishing Ltd, Maxwelton House, 41–43 Boltro Road, Haywards Heath, West Sussex, RH16 1BJ**



A CIP Catalogue record for this book is available from the British Library.

ISBN 13 978 1 84592 320 4

ISBN 10 1 84592 320 0

Typeset by Kerrypress Ltd, Luton, Beds

Printed and bound in Great Britain by CPI Antony Rowe, Chippenham, Wiltshire

# Preface

This book aims to provide a useful guide to the law and application of corporation tax at 31 August 2006 and forms one of the six books included in Tottel's Core Tax Annuals series.

There are many active companies in the UK at any one time. A UK limited company has a separate legal status. The legal structure has the protection of creditors in mind and therefore supports a trading status. The companies vary in size from the largest multi-glomerate to a one-person service company

Corporation tax was introduced to the UK in 1965. Prior to this companies paid income tax on their total income. They were also liable to profits tax. As companies develop more sophisticated transactions in a global economy the corporation tax rules follow suit. The same corporation tax rules apply to all companies, regardless of size or activity, with important modifications for small- and medium-sized companies and non-trading companies. Self-assessment shifts the onus of corporation tax reporting, assessment and payment to company officials.

The book's objective is to provide the reader with a practical illustrated commentary. Although, not always definitive, the book's general outline is to follow the issues affecting the 'life' and 'activity' of a limited company from 'small' single company to group member. Wherever possible, legislative references to facilitate further reader research have been given in the text. There may be areas or issues not covered in this book that readers would like to see in a later edition. If so, please let me know.

I would like to thank Mark McLaughlin for his informed technical comment as General Editor especially; and the Tottel staff for their assistance in producing this book, including Heather Saward for her editorial support and Sarah Blair who expedited the project from start to finish with foresight and enthusiasm. In addition, I would like to thank the tax team at Simmons Gainsford LLP for their encouragement and acknowledgement of my commitment.

This book is dedicated to Peter my husband and to Anastasia our daughter in grateful thanks for their enduring support throughout!

Juliana Watterston

watterston@mac.com

September 2006

# Contents

# Table of Statutes

[*All references are to paragraph number*]

# Table of Statutory Instruments and Codes of Guidance

*[All references are to paragraph number]*

# Table of European Legislation

*[All references are to paragraph number]*

# Table of Cases

# List of Abbreviations

| | |
|---|---|
| ACT | advance corporation tax |
| ADP | acceptable distribution policy |
| AIM | alternative investment market |
| APA | advance pricing agreement |
| APR | agricultural property relief |
| ARC | Accounting Regulatory Committee |
| ASB | Accounting Standards Board |
| BA | balancing allowance |
| BPR | business property relief |
| CA 1985 | Companies Act 1985 |
| CAA 2001 | Capital Allowances Act 2001 |
| CFC | controlled foreign company |
| CIHC | close investment holding company |
| CTO | Capital Taxes Office |
| EBT | employee benefit trust |
| EEA | European Economic Area |
| EIS | enterprise investment scheme |
| ESC | Extra-statutory Concession |
| ESOP | employee share ownership plan |
| ESOT | employee share ownership trust |
| EUFT | eligible unrelieved foreign tax |
| FA | Finance Act |
| FII | franked investment income |
| FRS | Financial Reporting Standard |
| FRSEE | Financial Reporting Standard for Smaller Entities |
| FYA | first year allowance |
| GWR | gift with reservation |
| HMRC | HM Revenue and Customs |
| IA | initial allowance |
| IA 1986 | Insolvency Act 1986 |
| IAS | International Accounting Standards |
| IASB | International Accounting Standards Board |
| IBA | industrial buildings allowance |
| ICTA 1988 | Income and Corporation Taxes Act 1988 |
| IFRS | International Financial Reporting Standards |
| IHT | inheritance tax |

| | |
|---|---|
| ACT | advance corporation tax |
| IHTA 1984 | Inheritance Tax Act 1984 |
| IHTM | Inheritance Tax Manual |
| ITEPA 2003 | Income Tax (Earnings and Pensions) Act 2003 |
| ITTOIA 2005 | Income Tax (Trading and Other Income) Act 2005 |
| LLP | limited liability partnership |
| OECD | Organisation for European Co-operation and Development |
| PCTCT | profits chargeable to corporation tax |
| PET | potentially exempt transfer |
| POA | pre-owned asset |
| R & D | research and development |
| SDLT | stamp duty land tax |
| SE | small enterprise |
| SI | Statutory Instrument |
| SME | small and medium-sized enterprise |
| SSAP | Statement of Standard Accounting Practice |
| SSCBA 1992 | Social Security Contributions and Benefits Act 1992 |
| TAAR | targeted anti-avoidance rule |
| TCGA 1992 | Taxation of Chargeable Gains Act 1992 |
| TMA 1970 | Taxes Management Act 1970 |
| UITF | Urgent Issues Task Force |
| UK GAAP | UK Generally Accepted Accounting Principles |
| UTR | Unique Taxpayer Reference |
| VCT | venture capital trust |
| VOA | Valuation Office Agency |
| WDA | writing down allowance |
| WDV | written down value |

*Chapter 1*

# Introduction to Corporation Tax

## THE BASIS OF CORPORATION TAX

**1.1** A UK company is formed by providing Companies House with details of its Memorandum and Articles of Association, directors, company secretary and members and registered office. The registrar of companies checks the documents and if approved retains them for public inspection. The members subscribe to the company's share capital, which forms their investment in the company. The company has a separate legal personality to its members. A company is required to maintain statutory books to record its constitution and structure and books of account to record its transactions. Documents notifying changes in structure must be filed at Companies House. Statutory accounts must be prepared annually and filed at Companies House. A company is also required to file an annual return with the Registrar of Companies every year.

The UK operates a free enterprise economy and any person or persons can subscribe to a company. The shareholder reward for his, her or their investment in the company is a distribution of profits, commonly known as a dividend.

The profits of a company are brought to charge to tax under the corporation tax regime. Corporation tax is directly levied on the profits of companies and is payable by the company. Profits are the company's income less expenses, together with its chargeable gains. A dividend payment is not an expense of the company, it is a distribution payment. There is no relief for corporation tax. Instead, each qualifying distribution to a shareholder who is an individual carries a tax credit of 1/9 of the distribution; which effectively satisfies the liability of a basic rate taxpayer, but not a higher rate taxpayer. Company shareholders are not chargeable to corporation tax on distributions from other UK companies.

Corporation tax rates have varied over the years but generally speaking current UK corporation tax rates are at their lowest. This does not mean that the corporation tax paid by companies is at its lowest as the tax base is subject to characteristic annual *Finance Act* changes to target avoidance or to provide incentives.

## LIABILITY TO CORPORATION TAX

### Definition of a company

**1.2** A company is not the only 'person' that is liable to corporation tax. This is because a company is defined as 'any body corporate or unincorporated association' (*ICTA 1988, s 832*(*1*)). Therefore members' clubs, societies and trade and voluntary associations will find themselves within the ambit of corporation tax (see 5.40–5.52). The *s 832* definition of a company excludes a partnership, a local authority or a local authority association. Therefore partnerships, trustees, local authorities and local authority associations are not chargeable to corporation tax. Please see *Tottel's Income Tax 2006/07* for partnerships and *Tottel's Trusts and Estates 2006/07* for trustees. Local authorities and local authority associations are exempt from corporation tax, income tax and capital gains tax (*ICTA 1988, s 519*(2) and *TCGA 1992, s 271*(*3*)).

### The extent of the corporation tax charge

**1.3** It is immaterial where and how a UK company earns its profits because all UK resident companies are liable to corporation tax on their profits wherever they arise and whether or not they are received or transmitted to the UK (*ICTA 1988, s 6*(*1*)).

The UK (United Kingdom) for these purposes includes Great Britain and Northern Ireland but not the Irish Republic, the Isle of Man or the Channel Islands.

A company is UK resident if it is incorporated in the UK, ie registered at Companies House. If it is not incorporated in the UK but is managed and controlled from the UK it will most likely be resident in the UK for corporation tax purposes. These concepts are discussed in Chapter 13.

If a non-UK resident company carries on a trade in the UK through a permanent establishment, it will be liable to corporation tax on the profits directly attributable to the permanent establishment. A permanent establishment could amount to an overseas company's UK branch, UK office or UK agency. Such profits may emanate directly or indirectly from the permanent establishment and will include income from trades, property, intangibles and gains (*ICTA 1988, s 11*(*2A*)).

### Taxation of company profits

**1.4** *Section 6*(*4*)(*a*) of the *Taxes Act 1988* brings a company's profits into charge to corporation tax by stating that the profits that are chargeable to corporation tax consist of income and chargeable gains. Dividends and distributions received from UK resident companies are excluded (*ICTA 1988, s 208*). The profits for each accounting period are then chargeable to corporation tax at the appropriate rate (*ICTA 1988, s 12*). Corporation tax rates are fixed for financial years. The financial year (for corporation tax) commences on 1 April in one year and ends on 31 March in the next year and is known as the calendar year of commencement.

In principle, company income and gains are calculated using income tax and capital gains tax principles (*ICTA 1988, s 9(1)* and *TCGA 1992, s 8*). The rules of Schedule A and the cases of Schedule D apply to corporation tax unless modified elsewhere in the legislation (*ICTA 1988, s 9(3)*).

# COMPANY ACCOUNTS

## Duty to prepare accounts

**1.5** A company's profit emanates from its accounts. Preparation of accounts is a duty of the directors. The *Companies Act 1985, s 226* (derived from previous *Companies Acts* and recently amended by *SI 2004/2947*) states that the directors of every company shall prepare accounts for the company for each of its financial years. Either 'Companies Act individual accounts' or 'IAS individual accounts' may be prepared. Clauses 400 and 401 of the proposed *Companies Bill* also state these requirements.

## Companies Act accounts

**1.6** *Companies Act* individual accounts comprise a balance sheet and a profit and loss account for each financial year, which are known as individual accounts. The balance sheet must give a true and fair view of the state of the company's affairs and the profit and loss must give a true and fair view of the profit or loss of the company for the financial year. The accounts are required to state by note whether they comply with UK Generally Accepted Accounting Principles (UK GAAP) and whether there are any departures (*CA 1985, Sch 4, para 36A*).

IAS individual accounts are accounts that comply with international accounting standards. If IAS are used the notes to the accounts must state that the accounts have been prepared in accordance with international standards.

Group accounts may be prepared on a similar basis, either *Companies Act* group accounts or 'IAS group accounts', which are in accordance with international accounting standards. Listed companies, as required by European law, must use IAS when preparing their consolidated accounts.

## Accounting standards

**1.7** The Accounting Standards Board (ASB), an independent body, sets the accounting standards that apply to all UK and Republic of Ireland entities that have not chosen to use International Financial Reporting Standards (IFRS). The Board has adopted a strategy of convergence with international standards.

The International Accounting Standards Board (IASB) sets the accounting standards to be used, with effect from 1 January 2005, by all listed groups. The standards are referred to as International Accounting Standards (IAS) or International Financial Reporting Standards (IFRS). UK companies may not use a standard as written by the IASB unless it has been adopted by the European Union. The European Commission set up the Accounting Regulatory Committee (ARC), which is chaired by the Commission and composed of representatives from member states. The ARC provides an opinion on Commission proposals of whether or not to endorse an international accounting standard (see 17.5–17.6).

## UK GAAP

**1.8** UK GAAP is applied by the vast majority of UK companies. Over the past few years there have been many changes to UK GAAP. This is largely due to the ASB's focus to bring the UK's accounting standards in line with the international standards.

UK GAAP includes accounting standards, Urgent Issues Task Force (UITF) abstracts, the Companies Act and Stock Exchange requirements and other accepted industry practices. Until 1970 the *Companies Act* was the only regulatory force that governed the preparation of companies' financial statements. Since then accounting standards have developed commencing with statements of standard accounting practice (SSAPs), Financial Reporting Standards (FRSs) and latterly International Accounting Standards and International Financial Reporting Standards. The purpose of the accounting standards is to give an authority as to how a certain type of transaction should be recorded in the accounts to reflect a 'true and fair view'.

Smaller companies may adopt the Financial Reporting Standard for Smaller Entities (FRSSE), which is within UK GAAP. The FRSSE may be applied to small companies and groups as defined in the *Companies Act* (see 3.6). Large or medium-sized groups cannot use the FRSSE. The FRSSE exempts the small company from complying with other accounting standards and UITF abstracts unless the company is preparing consolidated accounts. FRSSE embodies FRS 5 *Reporting the Substance of Transactions* and FRS 18 *Accounting Policies* principles amongst others. An International Standard for smaller entities is currently being discussed but no standard has been finalised as yet.

# TAXATION AND ACCOUNTS

## Legislation

**1.9** A company may have many sources of income but the vast majority of UK companies carry on a trade of some sort. Over the years, the courts have generally accepted accounting principles and practice as the rationale for determining the profits of a trade for taxation purposes. Accounts are treated as prepared according to GAAP for tax purposes even if they have not been so prepared: see *Threlfall v Jones* (*HM Inspector of Taxes*); *Gallagher v Jones* (*HM Inspector of Taxes*) (1993) 66 TC 77, [1993] STC 537, [1994] 2 WLR 160, [1994] Ch 107 and *Tapemaze Ltd v Melluish* (*HM Inspector of Taxes*) (2000) 73 TC 167, [2000] STC 189. HMRC acknowledge that profits computed in accordance with UK generally accepted accounting practice, subject to adjustments, form the starting point for the computation of taxable profits (HMRC Business Income Manual BIM 31019). The accounts could be prepared under international GAAP but the occurrence is not as common as UK GAAP. Also, small companies are within the realms of UK GAAP if they choose to adopt the FRSSE.

The accounting basis was first embodied into statute by the *Finance Act 1998, s 42*(*2*) that introduced the principle that the profits of a trade must be prepared on an accounting basis that gives a true and fair view. *Finance Act 2002, s 103*(*5*) amended the *s 42* requirement so that now the profits of a trade must be computed in accordance with GAAP. The inference is of course that by using GAAP the accounts will continue to show a true and fair view. UK GAAP or international GAAP may be used. The principle is then extended to say that this is subject to any adjustment required or authorised by law in computing profits for those purposes.

## HMRC practice

**1.10** HMRC discuss FRS 18 *Accounting Policies* in HMRC Business Income Manual BIM 31032.

FRS 18 sets the framework for GAAP. The standard provides definitions of accounting policies, estimation techniques and measurement bases. Accounting policies are the manner in which certain types of transaction should be presented. Estimation techniques are the methods used to arrive at an estimated monetary amount. Measurement bases are the monetary attributes that are reflected in the accounts.

For example, if a company changed its method of stock valuation from average cost to FIFO, this would be a change of accounting policy. If, on the other hand, the company changed its method of ascertaining the cost of stock from a percentage of selling price to actual invoiced cost, this would only be a change in estimation techniques.

FRS 18, para 14 states that 'an entity should adopt accounting policies that enable its financial statements to give a true and fair view. Those accounting policies should be consistent with the requirements of accounting standards, Urgent Issues Task Force (UITF) Abstracts and companies legislation'.

The standard also states that a business must select those policies that 'are judged by the entity to be most appropriate to its particular circumstances for the purpose of giving a true and fair view'. What is 'appropriate' is left to each business to determine and is not defined in the standard. Instead the standard provides guidance on how the appropriateness of the accounting policies is to be judged. There are four objectives:

- relevance,
- reliability,
- comparability, and
- understandability (FRS 18, para 30).

Balancing the four objectives and the cost/benefit balance of providing the information constrains the four objectives. There are two bases of accounting in the preparation of financial statements and these are going concern and accruals. A going concern basis is always used unless the entity concerned has ceased trading or is to be liquidated. The accruals concept determines that transactions should be reflected in the accounts in the period they are incurred as opposed to the period in which they are received or paid. However, a deferral of costs under FRS 18 is not permitted unless the corresponding debit on the balance sheet meets the definition criteria of an asset under FRS 5 *Reporting the Substance of Transactions* (FRS 18, para 27).

HMRC particularly note that FRS 18 states that that prudence requires accounting policies to take account of uncertainty about the existence of assets, liabilities, gains, losses and changes to shareholders' funds or the amount at which they should be measured. FRS 18 also states that there is no need to exercise prudence where there is no uncertainty, nor should prudence be used as a reason to create, for example, hidden reserves or excessive provisions, deliberately understating assets or gains, or deliberately overstating liabilities or losses. To do that would mean that the financial statements are not neutral and therefore not reliable.

In Business Income Manual BIM 31040, HMRC acknowledge the importance of SSAP 17 *Accounting for post balance sheet events*, by referring to comments in *Symons v Weeks* (*as personal representative of Lord Llewelyn-Davies*) (1982) 56 TC 630, [1983] STC 195. In this case it was commented that 'where facts are available they are preferable to speculative estimates'. For tax purposes it is not acceptable to ignore facts if by so doing an unreal loss is provided for. SSAP 17 has now been replaced by FRS 21 Events after the Balance Sheet Date (see 17.7).

Although HMRC recognizes that accounts are to be drawn up in accordance with GAAP, it seems uneasy with the notion of materiality. Materiality is closely related to the relevance objective. Accounting practice considers that an item would be material to the financial statements if its misstatement or omission might reasonably be expected to influence the economic decisions of the users of the statements. As such it acknowledges materiality as an accountancy concept and not as a taxation concept (HMRC Business Income Manual BIM 31047). Materiality is a judgment to be made in the light of the circumstances and the event. They suggest that the factual accuracy of any item in the accounts is not for the company, nor its accountants, nor indeed HMRC, but for the Commissioners to decide. Appeals before the Commissioners are discussed in Chapter 2 (see 2.14–2.16).

The objective of FRS 5 *Reporting the substance of transactions* is to ensure that the substance of any transaction is reported in the financial statements. The commercial effect of all transactions is therefore recorded in the financial statements. The standard predisposes that economic substance takes precedence over legal form. HMRC consider that by and large FRS 5 is a sound basis for the preparation of accounts for taxation purposes (HMRC Business Income Manual BIM 31055).

**1.11** The basic premise is that the accounting profits form the taxable profits, unless overridden by taxation law (*FA 1998, s 42(1)*). It is the overriding taxation law that we seek to examine in the following chapters. A further discussion of accounting and taxation is given in Chapter 17 together with a list of the UK and International Reporting Standards. Application of the accounting standards in relation to directors' remuneration and the valuation of work in progress is discussed in 5.15 and 5.31–5.36.

*Chapter 2*

# Self-Assessment

## INTRODUCTION

**2.1** Companies report their liability to corporation tax to HMRC through the self-assessment procedures. Any notices served on the company should be served on the 'proper officer', which is the company secretary or the person acting as the company secretary (*TMA 1970, s 108(3)*). In cases of liquidation, the liquidator is responsible or any other person with implied or apparent authority. The treasurer or person acting as treasurer is responsible in the case of unincorporated associations. A company tax return includes a declaration by the person making the return that to the best of his knowledge and belief the return is correct and complete (*FA 1998, Sch 18, para 3(3)*).

Companies are also required to deliver a copy of their statutory accounts to HMRC (*FA 1998, Sch 18, para 11*). The company must also calculate its own 'self-assessment' (*FA 1998, Sch 18, para 7*). Companies will prepare a corporation tax computation to calculate the corporation tax due and submit this together with the corporation tax return including the supplementary pages and the statutory accounts to HMRC. A return is strictly not 'delivered' to HMRC unless it is accompanied by 'all the information, accounts, statements and reports' (*FA 1998, Sch 18, para 4*). The CT600 asks the company to confirm that the accounts and computations are included. HMRC reject returns where delivery is incomplete.

A complete company tax return should include:

- a completed form CT600;
- any appropriate supplementary pages;
- a set of accounts, appropriate to the type of company (if registered at Companies House the statutory accounts required under the *Companies Acts*); and
- a tax computation showing how the figures on the CT600 have been derived from the accounts (detailed trading and profit and loss accounts are usually included).

If a company or a company's agent sends a CT600 without supporting accounts and tax computations, HMRC will return the CT600 to the company or the agent because it does not meet the legal return requirement (Working Together, Issue 18, November 2004).

HMRC has the power to request any documents relevant to the tax liability (*FA 1998, Sch 18, para 3*(*1*)).

The accuracy of the preparation of the corporation tax return and the completion of the Company Tax return is a prime management responsibility. Company Tax Return CT600 (2005) Version 2 and CT600 (Short) Version 2 are reproduced by kind permission of HMRC as Appendices. A 'model' corporation tax computation is included in 20.3, which can be adapted to a company's requirements.

## CONTACTING HMRC

**2.2** A company or an organisation must inform HMRC within three months in writing when it comes within the charge to corporation tax (*FA 2004, s 55*). The information required is as follows:

- the company's name and registered number;
- the address of the company's registered office;
- the address of the company's principal place of business;
- the nature of the business being carried on by the company;
- the date to which the company intends to prepare accounts;
- the full name and home address of each of the directors of the company;
- if the company has taken over any business, including any trade, profession or vocation formerly carried out by another;
- the name and address of that former business;
- the name and address of the person from whom that business was acquired;
- the name and registered office of the parent company (if any); and
- the date that the company is required to register for PAYE.

(*Corporation Tax* (*Notice of Coming within Charge—Information*) *Regulations 2004, SI 2004/2502.*)

In practice Companies House will inform HMRC of the formation of a new company and as a result HMRC will contact the company requesting information shown on form CT41G, which requests identical information as shown above. However, if HMRC does not contact the company for this information it is still the company's responsibility to supply the information and CT41G may be completed and submitted independently. The penalty for non-compliance is £300. There is also a £60 daily penalty (*TMA 1970, s 98*(*1*)). A false return can incur a penalty of £3,000 (*TMA 1970, s 98*(2)). Penalties cannot be imposed after the failure is rectified (*TMA 1970, s 98*(*3*)).

If a company fails to inform HMRC, HMRC will assume that the first accounting period runs for 12 months from the date of incorporation.

HMRC will maintain the company's details on their database. It is important to keep HMRC informed of any changes in the company's accounting period or address. HMRC use the database to issue returns and other communications to corporate taxpayers.

## COMPANY RECORDS

**2.3** A company has a requirement to keep and preserve records together with supporting documents to enable it to deliver a complete and correct corporation tax return for each relevant accounting period.

If a company complies with *Companies Act 1985, s 221* it will maintain sufficient records to prepare its statutory accounts. Good accounting records should in most cases form good records for corporation tax purposes. Under self-assessment a company is specifically required to keep records of:

> '(a) all receipts and expenses in the course of a company's activities and the matters in respect of which they arise and
>
> (b) in the case of a trade involving dealing in goods, all sales and purchases made in the course of the trade.'

(*FA 1998, Sch 18, para 21*(*5*).)

The type of records retained will vary with the industry, but it is important to bear in mind that information must be available on how a matter arises. Current legislation and HMRC often look behind a transaction and it can be important to demonstrate how a business decision or transaction was actioned at the time. When self-assessment was first introduced, HMRC commented that if a company satisfied *CA 1985, s 221* it will have satisfied the requirements to keep and preserve records for corporation tax self-assessment (*Revenue Tax Bulletin*, October 1998, p 587). Although that was some time ago, the article is still current.

In recent years, examinations of supporting vouchers by professionals acting for the company may have reduced due to the relaxation in the criteria for a statutory audit and also where the statutory audit concentrates on a risk-based approach. The onus for maintaining the supporting vouchers rests with the company and the supporting documents required are identified as 'accounts, books, deeds, contracts, vouchers and receipts' (*FA 1998, Sch 18, para 21*(*6*)).

HMRC will accept alternative forms of records such as optical imaging systems. This is admissible evidence in Commissioner hearings (*FA 1998, Sch 18, para 22*(2)).

The records must be kept for six years from the end of the relevant accounting period. Records should be kept longer if a return is under enquiry more than six years after the end of the accounting period, if the company makes its return late or the records relate to a continuing transaction that may affect current years (*FA 1998, Sch 18, para 21*(*3*)).

The maximum penalty for failing to preserve records is £3,000 (*FA 1998, Sch 18, para 23*(*1*)). There is no penalty for failing to keep or preserve records, which might have been needed, only for the purposes of claims, elections or notices not included in the return (*FA 1998, Sch 18, para 23*(*3*)).

Additional documentary evidence may be required to support arm's-length dealings under transfer pricing legislation. This is discussed in 14.23.

## COMPANY TAX RETURN

### Corporation tax accounting periods

**2.4** Under the *Companies Act 1985*, directors of UK companies are required to prepare and file statutory accounts for every 12-month accounting period. Usually, from three to seven weeks after the end of the accounting period from information held in its database, HMRC will send the company a 'Form CT603 Notice to deliver its company tax return by the due date'. The notice will specify a 12-month period for which HMRC consider that a return is due (*FA 1998, Sch 18, para 5*(*1*)). In general the corporation tax accounting period follows the statutory accounting period but for corporation tax purposes there are specific points at which an accounting period will begin or end.

A corporation tax accounting period first begins when a company comes within the scope of corporation tax by acquiring a source of income or becoming UK resident.

An accounting period ends on the earliest of the following events:

- 12 months from the beginning of the accounting period;
- the date on which the company draws up its accounts;
- the company begins or ceases to trade or ceases to be within the charge to corporation tax in respect of its trade or trades if more than one;
- the company begins or ceases to be UK resident;
- the company begins or ceases to be in administration; or
- the company goes into liquidation or winds up.

(*ICTA 1988, s 12.*)

Therefore, an accounting period will generally last for 12 months and will usually coincide with the period for which the company draws up accounts. If the statutory period of account exceeds 12 months, it is divided for corporation tax purposes into one or more accounting periods of 12 months, with a further accounting period covering the remainder of the period of account.

Each event will require the preparation of a separate company tax return.

---

**Example 2.1—Commencement to trade**

A Ltd incorporated on 1 January 2006. It completes form CT41G and commences trading on 1 April 2006. Form CT603 is issued on 1 April 2007. The company prepares accounts for the three months to 31 March 2006 and for the 12 months to 31 March 2007 and then to 31 March each year.

A Ltd is required to prepare company tax returns from 1 January 2006 to 31 March 2006 and from 1 April 2006 to 31 March 2007. The latest filing date for the 31 March 2006 return will be 30 June 2007 being three months after receipt of the Form CT603. The latest filing date for the 31 March 2007 return will be 31 March 2008 being 12 months after the year end (see 2.9).

---

---

**Example 2.2—Change in accounting date**

B Ltd has always prepared accounts to 30 September each year. In January 2006 it changes its accounting date to 31 December and prepares accounts for the 15 months to 31 December 2006.

B Ltd is required to prepare company tax returns from 1 October 2005 to 30 September 2006 and from 1 October 2006 to 31 December 2006. The filing date for both returns is 31 December 2007 being 12 months after the end of the period of accounts.

---

**2.5** An accounting period of more or less than 12 months may result in profits being apportioned. As a general rule these should be apportioned on a time basis, according to the number of days in the accounting period (*ICTA 1988, s 834(4)*). Chargeable gains are apportioned to the period in which they occur (*TCGA 1992, s 8(3)*).

---

**Example 2.3**

| | Days |
|---|---|
| A company prepares statutory accounts for the period 1 January 2005 to 31 March 2007. The company is trading throughout the whole period. Its total profits chargeable to corporation tax amount to £500,000 | 455 |
| Its corporation tax accounting periods are: | |
| First accounting period (12 months) from 1 January 2005 to 31 December 2005 | 365 |
| Second accounting period (balance) from 1 January 2006 to 31 March 2006 | 90 |

The total profit is apportioned to accounting periods as follows:

| | £ |
|---|---|
| First accounting period profit is (£500,000 ÷ 455) × 365 | 401,099 |
| Second accounting period profit is (£500,000 ÷ 455) × 90 | 98,901 |

(Working Together, Issue 18, August 2004 – Company Tax Return Helpful Hints Example adapted).

---

**2.6** Profits may be apportioned on a time basis if this gives more of an accurate result. This occurred in the case of *Marshall Hus & Partners Ltd v Bolton* (1980) 55 TC 539, [1981] STC 18. Marshall Hus & Partners Ltd was a property company that had not prepared accounts for six years. The time came for the company to fulfil its corporation tax requirements. In order to allocate its profits to the corporation tax accounting periods it averaged the profits over the entire period. The Inland Revenue objected because they had discovered that the first five accounting periods resulted in profits and the last in a substantial loss. The taxation legislation restricts the carry back of loss relief against profits of earlier periods (see 9.11). The judges upheld the Inland Revenue's contention commenting that it was not obligatory for the Inland

Revenue to divide and apportion profits where a 'more accurate and a fairer estimate of profit or loss' of the chargeable periods was available.

HMRC consider that transactions can only be matched with accounting periods where there are a few easily identifiable transactions (HMRC Company Taxation Manual 01405).

## CT600

**2.7** HMRC will issue the company with a company tax return CT600 (2006) Version 2.

Companies may also use the shorter version of the form CT600 (Short) (2005) Version 2 if this is sufficient to cover their activities (both forms are reproduced in the appendices). The shorter version omits overseas income, tonnage tax profits, intra-group activities and management expenses for companies with investment business. Additional or replacement copies may be obtained from the HMRC Orderline (telephone: 0845 300 6555 or fax: 0845 300 6777) or from the HMRC website (www.hmrc.gov.uk). HMRC also accept an HMRC approved substitute version.

If relevant to the company's activities the following supplementary pages must also be submitted together with the main return:

## Supplementary pages

| | | |
|---|---|---|
| CT600A | Loans to participators by close companies | See Chapter 4 |
| CT600B | Controlled foreign companies | See Chapter 13 |
| CT600C | Group and Consortium | See Chapter 10 |
| CT600D | Insurance | |
| CT600E | Charities and Community Amateur Sports Clubs (CASCs) | See Chapter 5 |
| CT600F | Tonnage Tax | |
| CT600G | Corporate Venturing Scheme | See Chapter 15 |
| CT600H | Cross-border royalties | See Chapter 13 |
| CT600I | Supplementary charge in respect of ring fence trade | See Chapter 15 |
| CT600J | Disclosure of tax avoidance schemes | See Chapter 18 |

## FILING DATE

**2.9** The company tax return must be filed on the last day of whichever of the following periods is last to end:

- within 12 months of the end of the accounting period for which it is made;
- if the company's statutory accounting period is longer than 12 months but no longer than 18 months, 12 months from the beginning of the accounting period;
- if the company's statutory accounts are for a period longer than 18 months then 30 months from the beginning of that period;
- alternatively if the notice to deliver a return is given late then three months after the notice was served (*FA 1998, Sch 18, para 14*).

A company may amend its company tax return within 12 months of the filing date. Therefore if a company's accounting period is 31 December 2007, its filing date is 31 December 2008 and it is able to file an amendment to the return anytime up to 31 December 2009. If a company makes a return for a wrong period it can correct the position any time up to 12 months after the filing date on the assumption that the return had been made for the correct period (*FA 1998, Sch 18, para 15*).

HMRC also has the power to amend returns for errors and omissions, but can only do so for up to nine months after the return was filed or nine months after an amendment was made if the correction follows an amendment. The company can in turn reject the correction within its amendment period or within three months of receipt of HMRC's amendment if later (*FA 1998, Sch 18, para 16*).

## ONLINE FILING

**2.10** Corporation tax returns can be filed online with HMRC by using the 'do it online facility' at www.hmrc.gov.uk/businesses. The company tax return (CT600), supplementary pages A to J, the statutory accounts and computations can be filed with HMRC over the internet. Attachments should be sent in PDF format.

Taxpayers registering for the first time will be asked to enter their name and to select a password. After successful registration a username will be displayed on screen. The company will then receive confirmation by post of the company's User ID and Activation PIN(s) to the address that HMRC have on their database within seven days of registering. The User ID is required together with the password every time the company logs in. The service must be activated within 28 days of the Activation PIN letter date.

Taxpayers will need a computer with an internet connection. HMRC have given the following information on their frequently asked questions on their website.

*To use our Online Services, you will require access to a computer with an Internet connection*

***Operating system and browser requirements***

*PC users:*

- *Operating system: Windows 98 or above (ie Windows ME/NT/2000/XP).*
- *Internet browsers: Internet Explorer 5.0 or above; Netscape 4.75; Opera 6.0.*

*Mac users:*

- *Operating system: Mac OS9 or above.*
- *Internet browsers: Internet Explorer 5.1; Netscape 4.77.*

*Please also note that your Internet browser must have JavaScript and cookies enabled and be capable of supporting 128-bit SSL.*

***Other operating systems and browsers***

*Although our Online Services are designed and tested for use with the above system requirements, you may be able to access the services using other operating systems and browser combinations. However the appearance of the pages and performance may be affected. Please also note that our Helpdesk cannot deal with any difficulties arising through their use.*

(*Frequently asked questions HMRC Website.*)

Any company with a CT Unique Taxpayer Reference can register and use corporation tax online filing. The Unique Taxpayer Reference (UTR) is made up of ten numbers and is shown on the company tax return, a notice to complete a company tax return or on the statement of account. It may also be on other documents from HMRC. Depending on the document or piece of correspondence, it may be printed next to the heading 'Tax Reference', 'UTR', or 'Official Use'.

Taxpayers may use HMRC's free online tax return – CT or any of the available third party products, which have successfully passed HMRC testing procedures.

Only the full company tax return may be filed online. The short return is a paper only option. The corporation tax software guides the user to the relevant sections of the full return. Questions are posed relating to the circumstances. It is important to understand the meaning of these questions and the consequences of the response. The software will perform the calculation. After successful submission the software will display an online message indicating that the return has been received and accepted. HMRC will also send an email confirming that the return has been received and accepted if an email address has been given. Taxpayers have the facility to print out a copy of the return from the online return software.

An agent may submit an online return on behalf of a client and complete the declaration if the following are met:

- Authorisation is in place with a form 64–8 signed by a proper officer of the company.
- The agent must make a copy of the relevant information before it is sent.
- A proper officer of the company, (or other person authorised to make the return on behalf of the company) must confirm that the information is correct to the best of his knowledge and belief before the information is sent by the agent. The officer must approve and sign the copy approved as such.

This does not apply where the agent is a person authorised by the company to make the return on its behalf (*Income and Corporation Tax* (*Electronic Communications*) *Regulations 2003, SI 2003/282*).

## PAYMENT

**2.11** Electronically coded payslips are included within form CT603 notice to deliver a company tax return. Payment can be made electronically by BACS or CHAPS, or by cheque to HMRC accounts office. It is important to use the payslip that corresponds to the relevant accounting period, otherwise the company's cheque may be misallocated.

Interest is charged on any corporation tax paid late. The interest paid is tax deductible (*TMA 1970, s 90*(*2*)). Interest earned on overpaid tax is taxable (*FA 1998, s 34*). The interest receivable calculations are based on the premise that the tax paid last is repaid first (see 3.11).

## PENALTIES

**2.12** Failure to deliver a return on time incurs a flat rate penalty of £100 if the return is up to three months late and £200 in any other case. These penalties are increased to £500 and £1000 where failure occurs for a third successive time (*FA 1998, Sch 18, para 17*). These penalties are not tax-related and will not reduce if the tax liability reduces. If an accounting period is longer than 12 months and HMRC has not been advised of the change, an automatic late filing penalty will be issued to meet the 12-month deadline. Companies should inform HMRC of any changes in accounting periods without delay.

If a company fails to deliver a return within 18 months of the end of an accounting period or by the later filing date then, in addition to the flat rate penalty, it will be liable to a tax-related penalty. The penalty is 10% of the unpaid tax if the return is delivered within two years after the end of the period for which the return is required or 20% of the unpaid tax in any other case (*FA 1998, Sch 18, para 18*).

There is no flat rate penalty where accounts are required under the *Companies Act* and the return is delivered no later than those accounts are required at Companies House (*FA 1998, Sch 18, para 19*). This would happen where a company extends its accounting period beyond 12 months.

---

**Example 2.4**

Renaldo Ltd, a small private company, prepares accounts to 31 March each year. However, the 2007 accounting period is extended to 30 September 2007. Renaldo Ltd prepares two corporation tax returns; the first to 31 March 2007 and the second to 30 September 2007. The two returns are submitted to HMRC on 30 April 2008. Provided Renaldo Ltd submits the accounts to 30 September 2007 to Companies House by 30 June 2008 no penalty will ensue. If HMRC raise a penalty notice, the company should appeal under *FA 1998, Sch 18, para 19*.

---

HMRC's computer system (COTAX) automatically issues flat rate and tax-related penalty notices shortly after the date the penalty is incurred. Additionally, tax-related penalty determinations are automatically amended when the amount of tax payable recorded on COTAX is revised. A further flat rate penalty notice will be issued automatically when incurred after three months unless the initial flat rate penalty is under appeal (Working Together, Issue 13, June 2003).

A company is liable to a tax-related penalty if it makes a fraudulent or negligent return, which is incorrect. It is also liable to a tax-related penalty if it discovers that it has made an incorrect return, which was not made fraudulently or negligently, but which it does not correct without unreasonable delay (*FA 1988, Sch 18, para 20*). Such penalties are normally negotiated with HMRC: see 2.19. All penalties carry interest. The rates are the same as for interest on unpaid tax: see 3.10 (*TMA 1970, s 103A*).

# ENQUIRY

## Time

**2.13** HMRC may by notice enquire into a company tax return any time within 12 months of the filing date, if the return was filed on or before the filing date. If the return was delivered late the enquiry time is extended to 12 months after the next 31 January, 30 April, 31 July or 31 October following the date the return was delivered. Similarly, if the company has made any amendments to the return, the enquiry time is extended to 12 months after the next 31 January, 30 April, 31 July or 31 October following the date the amendment was made (*FA 1998, Sch 18, para 24*). If the time limit has expired for enquiry into the main return but not the company amendments, then HMRC may only enquire into those amendments (*FA 1998, Sch 18, para 25*).

## Manner

**2.14** Where fraud is not suspected, HMRC conducts its enquiries according to set practices, which are set out in its Codes of Practice. COP14 Corporation tax self-assessment enquiries details the procedures regarding a corporation tax enquiry.

To begin an enquiry HMRC will issue notice, copied to an appointed agent, in the form of a letter that they intend to enquire into the company tax return (*TMA 1970, s 9A(1)*). Copies of these letters are reproduced in Working Together, Issue 12, February 2003.

The scope of the enquiry can extend to any item included in the return, any amount that affects the tax payable by the company for another accounting period and the tax liability of another company for any accounting period together with all claims and elections. The enquiry may also extend to the transfer pricing information. See Chapter 14 for a discussion on transfer pricing. If a return is made for the wrong period, HMRC may enquire into the period for which it should have been made (*FA 1998, Sch 18, para 26*).

HMRC expect and encourage the taxpayer's co-operation with the enquiry. They warn that if an offence has been committed and tax geared penalties result, they will take into account in calculating the amount of the penalty the extent to which the taxpayer has been helpful and has freely and fully volunteered any information about income or gains that were omitted or understated. Information on tax-geared penalties is given in IR 160 (enquiries under self- assessment) and is discussed below at 2.19.

Overall the company is responsible for its affairs, even if it has appointed a professional adviser, who should be fully informed of the facts of the case. HMRC will deal with a professional adviser if one has been appointed. If matters are not progressing with the adviser with sufficient speed HMRC will advise the company and may then deal with the company direct.

In most cases enquiries take the form of an aspect enquiry; in other words just dealing with one or two issues on a claim or return. In-depth enquiries do occur with HMRC conducting a wide-ranging examination into some companies' tax affairs. In such an event HMRC will undoubtedly require to see the records from which the return was prepared. Thus the importance of keeping good accounting records (see 2.3) manifests itself. Good accounting records are the company's only real defence in disputing HMRC claims. HMRC may ask to examine the records at the business premises or they may ask for them to be sent. With the withdrawal of the company statutory audit requirement and the influx of effective electronic systems into business life, the supporting evidence and vouchers are often ignored. The astute director/shareholder will ensure that he maintains good systems and company records.

Whether or not a professional adviser can be sued by a client in the wake of a full-scale HMRC enquiry for not warning him to keep better records is a case in point. Companies must realise that maintaining good records is not just an administration function but also a statutory function. HMRC's enquiries can stretch to opening separate enquiries into the directors' personal tax affairs. Even if there is nothing untoward the inconvenience of the scenario can be very unpleasant for those involved.

HMRC may by notice require the company to produce documents and to supply information in connection with their enquiry. The company must be given at least 30 days to comply with the notice. The time limit must be specified on the notice. Copies of documents may be supplied, but HMRC may, by notice, inspect the original documents. HMRC have the right to take copies of, or make extracts from any document produced (*FA 1998, Sch 18, para 27*).

The company has the right of appeal to the Commissioners against the notice to supply the documents. The appeal must be given in writing and within 30 days after the notice was given to the company. The Commissioners' decision will be final.

Failure to comply with a notice to supply documents will result in a £50 penalty. If the failure continues after the penalty has been imposed there is a daily penalty of £30 under *TMA 1970, s 100* if imposed by an HMRC officer or a daily penalty of £150 if imposed by the Commissioners under *TMA 1970, s 100C* (*FA 1998, Sch 18, para 29*).

## Enquiries into the affairs of the directors and their companies

**2.15** In the case of many small and medium-sized companies the affairs of the company are closely linked with those of the directors. HMRC may consider enquiring into the directors' affairs when they enquire into the company's affairs (HMRC Enquiry Manual EM 8205). If the Revenue officer discovers or suspects an omission or understatement of income in the company directors' returns or the returns indicate a build-up of private capital inconsistent with known income, he will refer the matter to the Revenue company case owner. If the company case owner decides to enquire into the company's tax return and the directors' returns he will co-ordinate and take responsibility for all enquiries. The company case owner will take a risk-based approach to the enquiry and in so doing will work closely with the case owners responsible for the individual director's affairs (HMRC Enquiry Manual EM 8210). If the individual case owner of the director's affairs wishes to enquire into a director's affairs because of some known or suspected inaccuracy they will look to the company first of all to ensure that all matters and therefore all sources of income are brought into account (HMRC Enquiry Manual EM 8207). If enquiries are made into the directors', as well as the company's, affairs the directors must be issued with their own *TMA 1970, s 9(A)* letters from HMRC addressed to each individual director.

## Enquiries into the directors' self-assessment returns

**2.16** HMRC's opening enquiry letter into a director's return will refer to the matters into which they wish to enquire and will include a request for documents and/or information about the areas of the returns that are to be enquired into. If there is a concern about the probable close link between the company's and the directors' private finances, HMRC should mention this at the outset (HMRC Enquiry Manual EM 8211). A close link is understood to mean the director's use of company funds for private purposes, without any charge to taxation arising. HMRC will not be in a position to know for sure whether there is a linkage between the two unless both the company's and the director's private records are cohesively examined.

The director's private papers, such as income statements and bank statements, are his own private property. If HMRC is carrying out an enquiry into the company's affairs alone the case worker concerned cannot compel either the company or the director to provide this information. Corporation tax document requests under *FA 1998, Sch 18, para 27* do not grant these powers. HMRC are aware of this and so, in the event, their procedure in their opening letter to the company is to ask the director to provide them voluntarily with all their private account statements. Whether or not to adhere to this request depends upon each individual director and company concerned. The situation is not made easy because HMRC correspondence, as this is a company enquiry, is sent to the company or the professional agent. The company may have no knowledge of the director's personal affairs and the agent may not even act for the director concerned. When faced with such a problem, careful consideration must be given to all factors involved by the director, the agent and the company.

If the director declines to give this information voluntarily to HMRC, HMRC may feel compelled to open an enquiry under *TMA 1970, s 9A* into the director's personal self-assessment tax return. Documents will then be requested from the director under *TMA 1970, s 19A*. This will also enable HMRC to obtain information regarding *TA 1988, s 419* in respect of loans to directors and overdrawn loan accounts (see 4.14–4.22). *TMA 1970, s 19A(2)* requires the director to submit this information within 30 days of the request.

If HMRC considers that a full enquiry into the director's return is not warranted they may issue a request to the director under *TMA 1970, s 20(3)* for the director to supply his private bank account statements to HMRC. HMRC may also make a request under *TMA 1970, s 20(3)* if the time limit for enquiring into the director's personal tax return has expired. For example, the enquiry window for self-assessment tax returns for the year ended 5 April 2006 will close on 31 January 2008.

If HMRC's concerns are justified the closure of the enquiry may result in a beneficial loan assessment under *ITEPA 2003, s 175* for the director and or a *TA 1988, s 419* liability for the company. In some cases the director's extraction of funds may be treated as employment income and, unless a PAYE direction transferring liability from the employer to the employee has been made, credit will be give in the income tax self-assessment for the PAYE that the company should have deducted.

## Course of enquiry

**2.17** Normally the course of enquiry involves the company and/or the professional agent supplying information and documents to HMRC in response to their queries. There is a period of time over which this happens and replies to the Revenue should be given accurately and in good time. In any event, if any enquiry is in progress it should not hold up the submission of the next year's tax return even if best estimated entries are included when preparing the return.

In addition HMRC may call a meeting with the directors, company secretary or even the employees to discuss the company's business affairs. Many indeed will feel nervous and intimidated in such a situation. HMRC cannot compel those involved to attend a meeting. A professional adviser may attend as well as or instead of the company attendees. In all circumstances, whether or not a meeting takes place, HMRC must be provided with all the information necessary to answer their enquiries.

If a meeting takes place HMRC have formal procedures, which they must follow.

They require the company representatives to bring the necessary records either to answer HMRC's questions or to support their own queries. HMRC will make a written record of what is said at the meeting. The company may ask to see the notes.

HMRC may even go as far as requesting the company to sign a copy of their notes to signify agreement. HMRC cannot compel the company to do so. The company, of course, may comment on the notes if it wishes. The worth of attendance at a meeting from the taxpayer's perspective must be judged on its own merits in each and every case.

## Corporation tax return amendment

**2.18** HMRC may by notice amend the self-assessment calculation during the course of the enquiry if it considers it insufficient. The company has a 30-day time limit to lodge an appeal against the amendment (*FA 1998, Sch 18, para 30*). Similarly, the company may amend its return during the course of the enquiry. This will not restrict the scope of the enquiry, but it may be taken into account. The amendment will not take effect until the enquiry is finished (*FA 1998, Sch 18, para 31*). During the course of the enquiry, if the company considers that it may have additional tax to pay it can make an additional payment to reduce any interest charges that might arise. Overpayments are always repaid if incorrect. If, during the course of the enquiry, it is discovered that there is a period for which a return is required but for which none has been submitted, then such a return is required to be submitted within 30 days of the final determination (*FA 1998, Sch 18, para 35*).

## COMPLETION OF ENQUIRY

**2.19** The enquiry is complete when HMRC issues their closure notice to the company stating their conclusions (*FA 1998, Sch 18, para 32*). The company must then amend its return within 30 days of the notice (*FA 1998, Sch 18, para 34*). Failing this HMRC will amend the return. The outcome of the enquiry may lead to an adjustment to the tax return or an additional payment.

HMRC will give written notification of the amendment required to the company tax return. The company should make these amendments within a 30-day period. If the company fails to do so, HMRC will make the amendments.

The additional corporation tax payments will most likely include interest on overdue tax and may include a penalty of up to 100% of the tax due under *FA 1998, Sch 18, para 20*. This is a situation whereby a company fraudulently or negligently delivers an incorrect company tax return to HMRC. It also covers the situation whereby a company, which discovering it had erroneously, as opposed to purposefully, delivered an incorrect company tax return to HMRC, failed to correct the error swiftly.

HMRC calculates the penalties and the agreed settlement as set out in IR 160 (enquiries under self-assessment). The procedure involves HMRC suggesting a pecuniary offer that the company should make to clear its corporation tax liabilities.

HMRC will calculate the amount of the offer based on tax, interest and penalty.

Tax and interest fall due under normal regulations and are non-negotiable. Penalties can amount to 100% of the tax underpaid or paid late and are negotiable.

HMRC commence their calculations with a 100% penalty. This can be reduced depending on how well or badly the company has co-operated with HMRC and its enquiries. Reductions are based on disclosure, co-operation and seriousness. The maximum reductions are shown in the chart below. In practice each situation will be viewed on its merits and the percentage reduction amended accordingly.

## HMRC penalty reduction percentages

| *% reduction* | *Reason* |
|---|---|
| 20% | Full disclosure after HMRC enquiries commenced |
| 30% | Full voluntary disclosure with no HMRC enquiry |
| 40% | Co-operation |
| 40% | Seriousness |

**2.20** Disclosure is distinguished by disclosure after HMRC enquiries commenced and a full voluntary disclosure prior to enquiry. Co-operation is determined by the speed with which questions are answered and information is truthfully and honestly supplied. Seriousness depends on the grievousness of the offence, be it slovenly accounting or a fraud.

# APPEALS PROCEDURES

## Lodging an appeal

**2.23** The company must lodge its appeal with the Commissioners within 30 days from the date that an assessment was issued (*FA 1998, Sch 18, para 48*). Normally cases are heard by the General Commissioners. If the appeal is more complex HMRC or the company may request that it be heard by the Special Commissioners. The prime difference between the two types of Commissioners is that the General Commissioners work voluntarily and are usually involved in cases of fact whereas Special Commissioners are remunerated and are involved in cases of law. Hearings are held in public unless the company requests a private hearing.

The company must make its appeal in writing to HMRC at the address shown on the appeal decision. The appeal should indicate whether the case is to be heard by either the General or the Special Commissioners. Grounds for the appeal must also be included and the location for the hearing. The choice of location cannot be altered once made. No charges are involved. The company pays its own professional costs such as tax advisers' fees and legal fees. The General Commissioners have no power to award costs to either party once a decision has been given. Attendance and travelling costs cannot be claimed. Professional fees and costs of the appeal are not an allowable deduction for corporation tax purposes: see 5.16 – legal expenses.

On receipt of the appeal HMRC procedure is to try to resolve matters by mutual agreement (HMRC Code of Practice COP 14). If this fails they will pass the case to the Clerk to the Commissioners for a formal appeal hearing.

## Preparing for a Commissioners hearing

**2.24** In due course the company and its professional agent will receive details of the arrangements for the hearing. There is no compulsion for a company representative to attend the hearing, but it is expedient. The company may be represented by a director or company secretary or by its professional agent.

Prior to the hearing some preparatory work should be undertaken. HMRC advise that the company should assume that the tribunal is totally ignorant of the facts and nature of the hearing before them and that the company must provide them with all the necessary facts and information. Therefore, in preparation for the case, the company should consider the precise facts of the case, the evidence to support the company's case and the evidence against HMRC.

The company should also consider whether there are any witnesses and whether they and their representatives will be attending the hearing.

HMRC requires that the following documents should be brought to the hearing:

- a copy of the HMRC decision against which an appeal is lodged;
- copies of correspondence with, and any other papers received from, HMRC;
- notes of the date and content of any relevant telephone conversations with HMRC, and the names of the people spoken to; and
- any other relevant documents, eg accounts, invoices, receipts or bank statements.

At the hearing the company will be invited to state its case first of all. HMRC will then state their case. The company can request a reverse order. Questions from all parties will follow and then the Commissioners adjourn to make their decision.

If either the company or HMRC disagrees with the decision they can ask for a review by the Commissioners. A review request must be made within 14 days from when the court's determination was sent to the company. The parties must be able to substantiate their claim.

## Appeal to the High Court

**2.25** A company dissatisfied with a reasonable claim may decide to take its case to the High Court. An appeal to the High Court must be made within 30 days of the date of the decision against the company. An appeal can only be made on a point of law. The High Court can award costs. An appeal against a General Commissioners' decision is made by firstly writing to the Clerk to the General Commissioners and identifying the point of law at issue. A £25 statutory fee must be enclosed. The Clerk to the General Commissioners will then prepare the case stated: a final draft of the case to be signed by the Commissioners and the company. The second stage in the appeal application process is for the company to send the case stated with form N161 (available from any county court office or downloadable from the court service website) known as the appellant's notice to HMRC's Solicitor's Office and any other party to the proceedings.

An appeal against a Special Commissioners' decision can be made by sending the appellants notice, together with a copy of the decision, to arrive within 56 days of the date of the decision. The case will then be heard at a fixed date by the High Court who can award costs (See *Tax Appeals – A guide to appealing against decisions of the Inland Revenue on tax and other matters*, Department for Constitutional Affairs).

## DETERMINATIONS AND DISCOVERY ASSESSMENTS

**2.26** HMRC have the power to make an estimation of the tax due for the accounting period if no return is submitted in response to a notice requiring a return. The company has no right of appeal against a determination assessment. If no return is due for the accounting period or the company can show that it has delivered a return for the period then the determination has no effect (*FA 1998, Sch 18, para 36*). The determination replaces the company's self-assessment.

If HMRC discovers that the amount assessed on a company tax return is insufficient or the relief has become excessive they may make a discovery assessment. They may also make a discovery assessment if there has been fraudulent or negligent conduct. A discovery assessment may be made at any time, even if the enquiry time had elapsed or they had completed their enquiries into the return, if they could not be reasonably expected, on the basis of the information made available to them, to be aware of the errors in the return.

Information is regarded as being made available to HMRC if:

(i) it is included in a company tax return or in the documents accompanying the return;

(ii) it is contained in a relevant claim made by the company or in any accounts, statements or documents accompanying any such claim; or

(iii) it is contained in any documents, accounts or information produced or provided by the company to HMRC for the purposes of an enquiry into a return or claim; or

(iv) it is information, the existence and relevance of which could reasonably be expected to be inferred by HMRC from the information supplied in circumstance (i), (ii) or (iii) above or is notified to HMRC (*FA 1998, Sch 18, para 44*).

It is therefore important to supply clear information to HMRC to support the return or the queries raised in order to avoid a discovery assessment.

In general an assessment may be made no longer than six years after the end of the accounting period to which it relates. However, in the case of fraud or negligence an assessment may be made up to 21 years after the end of the accounting period to which it relates (*FA 1998, Sch 18, para 46*). The company has a 30-day time period right of appeal against any assessment.

## FRAUD

**2.27** HMRC conducts its investigations into cases of suspected fraud under Code of Practice COP 9 (2005) – Cases of Suspected Serious Fraud.

This new Civil Investigation of Fraud procedure came into effect on 1 September 2005. Code of Practice COP 9 (2005) is applied to all new cases. Existing cases are worked to a conclusion under the old Hansard procedures (Code of Practice COP 9). The procedure covers both direct and indirect taxes. The Hansard procedure implied that, if a taxpayer made a full statement and co-operated with the Revenue during their investigation, he could expect that case to be dealt with on a civil basis rather than a criminal basis. There was of course no guarantee. Under Code of Practice COP 9 (2005) HMRC has decided that a criminal prosecution regarding a particular matter will not follow the civil investigation.

### Civil investigation fraud procedures

**2.28** In cases of suspected serious tax fraud where HMRC opt for a civil rather than a criminal investigation, the company (and the directors) being investigated will be given one opportunity to secure maximum benefit by making a full disclosure of all tax irregularities. It is envisaged that a full declaration will speed the outcome and efficiency of the enquiry. Disclosure reports are expected to cover direct and indirect taxes.

If the company does not co-operate, HMRC will institute its own enquiry and penalties are likely to be higher. Under this code of practice HMRC will be investigating direct and indirect tax fraud. The same penalty reduction percentages apply as detailed in 2.19 above.

### Prosecution for tax fraud

**2.29** Under the new code if HMRC has made a decision to follow a civil investigation route then further criminal investigations for that offence will not follow. However, HMRC may still carry out criminal investigations into the company and its directors for other alleged offences. HMRC is considering its criminal investigation powers and issued the Technical Consultation document 'Modernising Powers, Deterrents and Safeguards' on 9 August 2006 for response by 1 November 2006. It is anticipated that further legislation will ensue.

*Chapter 3*

# Rates and Payment of Corporation Tax

## RATES OF CORPORATION TAX

**3.1** The corporation tax chargeable is calculated by applying the applicable corporation tax rate to the company's profits chargeable to corporation tax (PCTCT). The main rate of corporation tax for the financial year 2006 remains at 30% (*FA 2006, s 24*). The corporation tax starting rate (which was 0% for the first £10,000 of chargeable profits) has been abolished with effect from 1 April 2006 (*FA 2006, s 26(1)*). The non-corporate distribution rate has also been abolished with effect from 1 April 2006 (*FA 2006, s 26*(2)).

The rates of corporation tax for the financial years 2006 and 2005 are:

| | *Financial Year 2006 Commencing 1 April 2006* | *Financial Year 2005 Commencing 1 April 2005* |
|---|---|---|
| Full rate | 30% | 30% |
| Small companies' rate | 19% | 19% |
| Starting rate | Not applicable | 0% |
| Profit limit for lower rate | Not applicable | £10,000 |
| Profit limit for lower marginal rate | Not applicable | £50,000 |
| Profit limit for small companies' rate | £300,000 | £300,000 |
| Profit limit for small companies' marginal relief | £1,500,000 | £1,500,000 |
| Marginal relief fraction for profits between £10,000 and £50,000 | Not applicable | 19/400 |
| Marginal relief fraction for profits between £300,000 and £1,500,000 | 11/400 | 11/400 |
| Non-corporate dividend minimum charge | Not applicable | 19% |

In addition, loans to participators attract *s 419* tax at 25% on the outstanding amount: see 4.14–4.22.

## Marginal rates of corporation tax

**3.2** The 19% small companies rate of corporation tax is applied to profits chargeable to corporation tax (PCTCT) if company profits for a financial year are £300,000 or less. Profits above £300,000 are chargeable at the full rate of corporation tax subject to the company's claim for marginal relief. Profits for this purpose are measured as PCTCT plus non-group FII. FII is the net dividend plus the 10/90 tax credit. A group for this purpose is the parent and any of the 51% subsidiaries (*ICTA 1988, s 13*).

A company may claim marginal relief by completing box 64 of the company tax return (*ICTA 1988, s 13*(2)).

Marginal relief is calculated as follows:

Fraction × (Upper relevant amount – profits) × (PCTCT ÷ profits)

---

**Example 3.1**

Apple Ltd's profits chargeable to corporation tax for the accounting period ended 31 March 2007 amount to £350,000. The company received a dividend of £9,000 from Pear Ltd a non-group company during the year. No dividends were paid during the year and there are no associated companies.

Corporation tax payable is calculated as follows:

| | £ |
|---|---|
| 350,000 @ 30% | 105,000 |
| Less marginal relief: | |
| 11/400 × (1,500,000 – 360,000) × (350,000 ÷ 360,000) | 30,479 |
| | 74,521 |

FII = £(9,000 × 100/90)

---

**Example 3.2**

Apple Ltd's profits chargeable to corporation tax for the accounting period ended 31 March 2006 amounted to £30,000. The company received a dividend of £9,000 from Pear Ltd, a non-group company, during the year. No dividends were paid during the year and there are no associated companies.

Corporation tax payable is calculated as follows:

| | £ |
|---|---|
| 30,000 @ 19% | 5,700 |
| Less marginal relief: | |
| 19/400 × (50,000 – 40,000) × (30,000 ÷ 40,000) | 356 |
| | 5,344 |

FII = £(9,000 × 100/90)

## Starting rate

**3.3** Until 31 March 2006 the 0% starting rate of corporation tax applied to PCTCT.

Profits are chargeable to corporation tax on a financial year basis. If an accounting period straddles two financial years, profits are apportioned on a time basis.

### Example 3.3

Blackberry Ltd's profits chargeable to corporation tax for the accounting period ended 31 December 2006 amount to £9,000. No dividends were paid during the year and there are no associated companies.

Corporation tax payable will be:

| | £ | £ |
|---|---|---|
| **Financial year 2005** | | |
| Profits £9,000 × 90/365 | 2,219 | |
| Corporation tax payable: £2,219 @ 0% | | Nil |
| **Financial year 2006** | | |
| Profits £9,000 × 275/365 | 6,781 | |
| Corporation tax payable: £6,781 @ 19% | | 1,288 |
| | | 1,288 |

**3.4** The marginal rate is also apportioned on a time basis.

**Example 3.4**

Gooseberry Ltd's profits chargeable to corporation tax for the accounting period ended 31 December 2006 amount to £15,000. No dividends were during the year and there are no associated companies. The company received a dividend of £900 during the year.

Corporation tax payable will be:

| | £ | £ |
|---|---|---|
| **Financial year 2005** | | |
| Profits £15,000 × 90/365 | 3,699 | |
| Corporation tax payable: £3,699 @ 19% | 703 | |
| Less marginal relief: | | |
| 19/400 × (50,000 – 15,000) × (15,000 ÷ 16,000) × 90/365 | 384 | |
| | | 319 |
| **Financial year 2006** | | |
| Profits £15,000 × 275/365 | 11,301 | |
| Corporation tax payable: £11,301 @ 19% | | 2,147 |
| | | 2,466 |

## Effective rates of corporation tax

**3.5** In cases where no dividends are received corporation tax payable where marginal relief is involved may be more simply calculated by applying the following effective rates of corporation tax.

**Corporation tax rates**

| | *Financial year 2006* | | *Financial year 2005* | |
|---|---|---|---|---|
| | *Rate of corporation tax* | *Maximum corporation tax payable* | *Rate of corporation tax* | *Maximum corporation tax payable* |
| £ | % | £ | % | £ |
| 0–10,000 | 19 | 1,900 | 0 | Nil |
| 10,001–50,000 | 19 | 7,600 | 23.75 | 9,500 |
| 50,001–300,000 | 19 | 47,500 | 19 | 47,500 |
| 300,001–1,500,000 | 32.75 | 393,000 | 32.75 | 393,000 |
| 1,500,001 | | 450,000 | 30 | 450,000 |

## Non-corporate distribution rate

**3.6** For the period 1 April 2004 until 31 March 2006 the non-corporate distribution 19% rate applied to dividends paid to a non-corporate recipient. In simple terms the 19% rate is applied in the accounting period in which there are sufficient basic profits to cover the non-corporate distribution. Non-distributed profits are chargeable to corporation tax at the underlying rate. The underlying rate is calculated as follows:

1. Calculate the basic profits or PCTCT following normal principles.
2. Calculate the corporation tax chargeable on those profits.
3. Apply the formula (Corporation tax ÷ Basic profits) × 100 to find the underlying rate.

---

**Example 3.5**

Strawberry Ltd has basic profits for the accounting period ended 31 March 2006 of £30,000. It makes a non-corporate distribution of £20,000 and a corporate distribution of £5,000. The underlying rate of corporation tax is calculated as follows. The corporate distribution is ignored for this purpose.

| *Basic profits £* | | % | £ |
|---|---|---|---|
| 10,000 | Starting rate | 0 | Nil |
| 20,000 | Marginal rate | 23.75 | 4.750 |
| 30,000 | | | 4,750 |
| | Underlying rate: | | |
| | (4,750/30,000) × 100 | 15.83 | 4,750 |

The corporation tax payable is calculated as follows.

| | £ | | £ |
|---|---|---|---|
| Non-corporate distribution | 20,000 | at 19% | 3,800 |
| Corporate distribution | 5,000 | at 15.83% | 791 |
| Retained profits | 5,000 | at 15.83% | 791 |
| Total | 30,000 | | 5,382 |

---

**3.7** The non-corporate dividend rate no longer applies from 1 April 2006. PCTCT for accounting periods that straddle financial years must be apportioned on a pro-rata basis.

**Example 3.6**

Raspberry Ltd has basic profits for the accounting period ended 31 December 2006 of £35,000. It makes non-corporate distributions of £5,000 on 1 March 2006 and on 1 September 2006.

The corporation tax payable is calculated as follows:

| **Financial year 2005** | **Basic profits** | | | |
|---|---|---|---|---|
| Basic profits £35,000 × 90/365 | £8,630 | | | |
| *Corporation tax due* | £ | | % | £ |
| 10,000 × 90/365 = | 2,466 | Starting rate | 0 | Nil |
| 25,000 × 90/365 = | 6,164 | Marginal rate | 23.75 | 1,464 |
| 35,000 × 90/365 = | 8,630 | | | 1,464 |
| | | Underlying rate: | | |
| | | (1,464/8,630) × 100 | 16.96 | 1,464 |
| Financial year 2005 profits matched to non-corporate dividends | | | | |
| | 5,000 | Non-corporate distribution | 19% | 950 |
| | 3,630 | Underlying rate | 16.96 | 616 |
| | 8,630 | | | |
| **Financial year 2006** | | | | |
| Basic profits £35,000 × 275/365 | 26,370 | | | |
| *Corporation tax due* | £ | | | |
| | 26,370 | Small companies rate | 19 | 5,010 |
| | | | | 6,576 |

The eventual corporation tax payable is corporation tax chargeable less marginal relief (if any) less CVS Investment Relief (see **12.38**), double taxation relief (see **13.19**), plus tax payable under *s 419* (see **4.14**), less research and development tax credit (see **8.20**), together with any income tax deducted at source (*FA 1998, Sch 18, para 8*).

## PAYMENT DATES

### Companies Act 1985 definition of size

**3.8** Payment dates are determined by the size of a company. The *Companies Act 1985* definition is used.

*Companies Act 1985, s 247(3)* defined a small and medium-sized company according to the following criteria:

| | *Small company* *Not more than* | *Medium-sized company* *Not more than* |
|---|---|---|
| Turnover | £5.6 million | £22.8 million |
| Balance sheet total | £2.8 million | £11.4 million |
| Number of employees | 50 | 250 |

A company is a small or medium-sized company for its first financial year if it meets two or more of the requirements in that financial year. Once a company has qualified as a small or medium-sized company it will remain so unless it fails to meet two or more of the requirements for two years in a row. When a large company reduces in size to become a small or medium-sized company it must meet two or more of the requirements for two successive years.

### Small and medium-sized companies

**3.9** A small or medium-sized company's corporation tax is due and payable nine months and one day after the end of the accounting period (*TMA 1970, s 59D*).

### Large companies

**3.10** Large companies are charged to corporation tax at the 30% full rate. A company is large if its 'profits' plus franked investment income exceed the upper relevant amount, currently £1,500,000 for a year. Franked investment income is the company's UK dividends that it has received during the accounting period plus the corresponding tax credit. Dividends received from other group members are not included. Groups are discussed in Chapter 10. This limit is proportionately reduced where the company has one or more associated companies (by dividing it by one plus the number of associated companies) and for accounting periods of less than 12 months (see 4.27–4.29).

Hence a company with a large number of associates may be a 'large' company even though its profits are relatively small (*ICTA 1988, s 13AA(4)*).

## Quarterly instalments

**3.11** 'Large' companies are required to pay their corporation tax liabilities in up to four quarterly instalments, based on the company's estimated liability for that accounting period.

A company will not be required to pay by instalments in an accounting period where its taxable profits for that period do not exceed £10m (divided by one plus the number of associated companies) and it was not large for the previous year.

A company is not treated as large for an accounting period if its corporation tax liability does not exceed £10,000. This limit is proportionately reduced where the accounting period is shorter than 12 months (see the *Corporation Tax (Instalment Payments) Regulations 1998, SI 1998/3175*).

Corporation tax is payable in four quarterly instalments, which are due:

| *Instalment* | *Due* |
|---|---|
| First | Six months and 13 days after the start of the accounting period |
| Second | Three months after the first instalment |
| Third | Three months after the second instalment |
| Final | Three months and 14 days after the end of the accounting period. |

**Example 3.7**

12 month accounting period ended 31 December 2007.

| *Instalment* | *Due* |
|---|---|
| First | 14 July 2007 |
| Second | 14 October 2007 |
| Third | 14 January 2008 |
| Final | 14 April 2008 |

**3.12** If the accounting period is less than 12 month, the final instalment is due as normal three months and 14 days after the end of the accounting period.

The earlier instalments only fall due if the payment date falls before the due date for the final instalment.

---

**Example 3.8**

Six month accounting period ended 30 June 2007.

| *Instalment* | *Due* |
|---|---|
| First | 14 July 2007 |
| Final | 14 October 2007 |

---

## Calculation of tax due

**3.13** A company, which considers that it is large, should calculate its quarterly payment at each due date. If it considers that it has paid too much tax for a quarter it may deduct the overpayment from the next quarter's liability.

The liability is calculated as follows:

3 × (Company's total liability ÷ Number of months in the accounting period)

---

**Example 3.9**

Wood Ltd's corporation tax liability for the year ended 31 December 2007 is £1,000,000.

Instalments are 3 × (1,000,000 ÷ 12) = £250,000

The liability for the year is payable as follows:

| *Instalment* | *Due* | *Amount* |
|---|---|---|
| First | 14 July 2007 | £250,000 |
| Second | 14 October 2007 | £250,000 |
| Third | 14 January 2008 | £250,000 |
| Final | 14 April 2008 | £250,000 |

---

**3.14** Instalments paid late are charged on the late instalment rate, which is slightly lower than the late payment rate until nine months and one day after the year end (see 3.16). Late payment rate is charged from thereafter.

If a company should have made quarterly instalment payments, regardless of whether or not it made such payments a cross should be placed in box 95. HMRC regards electronic payments as more efficient than payments by post. www.inlandrevenue.gov.uk/howtopay gives more information on how to make electronic payments (Working Together, Issue 18, August 2004 – Company Tax Return – Helpful Hints). See HMRC leaflet 'A Modern System for Corporation Tax Payment. A Guide to Quarterly Instalment Payments' (CTSA/BK3) for more information on quarterly instalments.

## Transitional provisions

**3.15** The instalment system was gradually phased in over a transitional period, which ended on 1 July 2002. A company must pay 60% of its tax liability by instalments for accounting periods ending before 1 July 2000, 72% for periods ending before 1 July 2001 and 88% for periods ending before 1 July 2002. The balance was payable on the normal due date.

INTEREST

## Late payment interest

**3.16** If a company pays its corporation tax beyond the due date (nine months and one day after the end of the accounting period) it will be charged late payment interest under *TMA 1970, s 87A* on the corporation tax that it pays late. The company will not be charged interest on interest.

Late payment interest is calculated from the day after the normal due date until the effective date of payment. HMRC's computer is programmed to calculate the interest due. Situations not covered by the programmes are calculated manually by HMRC clerical staff.

The most current rates are:

**Corporation tax interest on unpaid tax**

| *From* | % |
|---|---|
| 6 September 2006 | 7.5 |
| 6 September 2005 | 6.5 |
| 6 September 2004 | 7.5 |
| 6 December 2003 | 6.5 |

# REPAYMENTS

**3.17** If a company has overpaid tax it may make a repayment claim. Normally a company is only able to ascertain whether it has made an overpayment when it prepares its corporation tax computation and company tax return. The repayment claim is made by placing a cross in the appropriate repayment claim box on the front of form CT600 and by completing the relevant repayment claim sections of CT600 or CT600 (Short). HMRC advise that a company will receive its repayment faster if it files online. The fastest and most secure repayment method is direct credit to the company bank account (by BACS). For this to take place the company must ensure that the 'Bank Details' section of the return is fully completed (page 12 of the main return and page 4 of the short return) (Working Together, Issue 18, August 2004 – Company Tax Return –Helpful Hints).

If a company does not consider the overpayment to be worth claiming, it may indicate on the return by completing the CT600 boxes 139 or 140 that small overpayments are to be set against future liabilities instead of being repaid.

## Income tax

**3.18** A company may claim an income tax repayment. This can arise if the company has received income from which tax has been deducted at source. The claim must be made on the company tax return or on an amended return (*FA 1998, Sch 18, para 9*). Box 142 is the requisite box for completion (see 3.25 and example 3.18 for an income tax calculation). Tax deduction vouchers are not required in support of the claim and will only be requested if the return is under enquiry.

## Repayment interest

**3.19** If a company overpays corporation tax it will be entitled to repayment interest. Repayment interest is calculated from the later of the day after the normal due date or the date the payment was made to the material date (*ICTA 1988, s 826*).

Repayment interest runs from the material date to either the date when the repayment was issued or the HMRC allocation. HMRC assumes that the tax paid last is repaid first. If there are no loss carry-backs for an accounting period the material date is the normal corporation tax due date. If losses are carried back to an accounting period wholly within the previous 12 months the material date is the due date for the accounting period in which the tax was over paid (*ICTA 1988, s 826(2)*).

If the accounting period against which the losses are set does not fall wholly within the previous 12 months the material date becomes the due date of the accounting period in which the losses arise (*ICTA 1988, s 826*(*7A*)).

When a non-trading loan relationship deficit or double tax relief is carried back to an earlier period the material date is the due date for the accounting period in which the deficit or the double tax arose (*ICTA 1988, s 826*(*7C*), (*7BB*)).

The most current rates are:

**Corporation tax repayment interest**

| *From* | % |
|---|---|
| 6 September 2006 | 4% |
| 6 September 2005 | 3% |
| 6 September 2004 | 4% |
| 6 December 2003 | 3% |

## Interest rate formulae

**3.20** The interest rates charged are calculated using the formula given in the *Taxes* (*Interest Rate*) *Regulations 1989*, SI 1989/1297, regs 3ZA and 3ZB (inserted by the *Taxes* (*Interest Rate*) (*Amendment No. 2*) *Regulations 1998*, SI 1998/3176, reg 6). This results in late payment interest being charged at approximately 2.5% above base rate and overpayment interest being credited at 1% less than base rate.

## Late payment interest where there is a carry back of losses or a non-trading deficit

**3.21** Companies that have incurred a trading loss or a non-trading deficit may elect to carry that loss back to be set against the total profits of the previous accounting period under *TA 1988, s 393A* and *FA 1996, s 83*(*2*)(*c*) respectively. In anticipation of so doing they may not pay the corporation tax due for the previous period. The company must be aware that the late payment interest will run from the normal due date to the due date of the later accounting period (*TMA 1970, s 87A*(*4A*)).

---

**Example 3.10**

Roquet Ltd anticipates a trading loss for the year ended 31 December 2006 of £200,000. For the accounting period ended 31 December 2005 it had a trading profit of £100,000. The company has no other source of income. On 1 October

2006 the directors consider that it is not worth paying the corporation tax due for the year ended 31 December 2005 because of the forthcoming loss.

Roquet Ltd will be charged interest on £100,000 for the period from 1 October 2006 until 1 October 2007.

---

# QUARTERLY INSTALMENTS

## Debit and credit interest

**3.22** A large company that pays corporation tax by instalments will be charged interest on late quarterly instalment payments and will receive interest on quarterly instalment payments paid in advance (*Corporation Tax (Instalment Payments) Regulations 1998, SI 1998/3175, regs 7, 8* and *TA 1988, s 826*). Interest paid is known as debit interest and interest received is known as credit interest. The interest rate formulae are similar to late payment interest but result in lower rates. Debit interest is approximately 1% above base rate and credit interest is approximately 0.25% below base rate.

Debit interest is charged from the quarterly instalment due date until the normal due date, being nine months and one day after the end of the accounting period.

The most current rates are:

**Debit interest charged on underpaid quarterly instalment payment**

| *From* | *To* | % |
|---|---|---|
| 14 August 2006 | | 5.75 |
| 15 August 2005 | 13 August 2006 | 5.5 |
| 16 August 2004 | 14 August 2005 | 5.75 |
| 21 June 2004 | 15 August 2004 | 5.5 |

Credit interest will accrue from the date on which the overpayment arises or from the due date for the first instalment payment, if later to the earlier of:

- the date the overpayment is removed by being utilized as payment for another quarter; and
- the normal due date, being nine months and one day after the end of the accounting period.

The earliest date that it is possible from which the company can receive interest.

The most recent rates are:

**Credit interest paid on overpaid quarterly instalment payments and on early payments of corporation tax not due by instalments**

| *From* | *To* | % |
|---|---|---|
| 14 August 2006 | | 4.5 |
| 15 August 2005 | 13 August 2006 | 4.25 |
| 16 August 2004 | 14 August 2005 | 4.5 |
| 21 June 2004 | 15 August 2004 | 4.25 |

## GROUP PAYMENT ARRANGEMENTS

**3.23** *FA 1998, s 36* allows a company to optionally enter into group payment arrangements. A group payment arrangement (GPA) forms a contract between the company and HMRC and can be downloaded from HMRC's website: 'The Group Payment Arrangement Document and Schedule'. In order to enter into a GPA, members of the group in question must have a 51% group relationship and be up to date with their filing and payment obligations. A company cannot be a member of more than one group payment arrangement. The payment arrangements can cover not only corporation tax but also interest and penalties.

GPAs enable the group to process all corporation tax liabilities through one company. It is an administrative arrangement. The paying company should enter into a standard contract at least two months prior to the due date for the first instalment payment, where at least one of the companies is liable to make quarterly instalment payments. Payment of tax must be by electronic funds transfer.

Each individual company still remains liable for its own corporation tax (See Application for a Group Payment Arrangement – Notes for Guidance and Working Together, Issue 20, February 2005).

## QUARTERLY ACCOUNTING

### CT61 procedures

**3.24** Companies are required to make a return to the Collector of Taxes of income tax deducted and claimed in respect of certain interest and charges on income, through the completion of form CT61, obtainable from HMRC.

There are normally four quarterly CT61 return periods, plus a fifth where the company's accounting period does not coincide with one of the quarter ends (*ICTA 1988, Sch 16, para 2*). The return periods are to 30 March, 30 June, 30 September and 31 December. The company's first return will run from the start of its accounting period to the end of the relevant quarter. Subsequent returns will follow a quarterly cycle, and a fifth return (where appropriate) will cover the period from the end of the previous quarter to the end of the company's accounting period, if it does not coincide with the end of a normal return period. The completed CT61 return and any tax liability is due 14 days after the end of the return period.

## Deduction of tax

**3.25** Income tax on annual interest is generally subject to deduction of lower rate tax of 20%, whereas annual payments (eg copyright royalties paid to an owner whose usual abode is outside the UK) are made net of basic rate tax (22%) (*ICTA 1988, s 349*). Charitable donations under gift aid or charitable deed are made without deduction of income tax. Companies are not required to deduct tax from interest, royalties, annuities and annual payments where the recipient is a company, which is chargeable to corporation tax in respect of that income (*FA 2004, s 101*).

Companies also have the option to pay royalties overseas without deduction of tax at source (or at a reduced rate) without the approval of HMRC in advance, provided that there is a reasonable belief that the non-resident is entitled to relief from UK tax on those royalties under a double tax treaty (*ITTOIA 2005, s 758*).

Interest and royalty payments between associated companies in the UK and other EU states are not subject to deduction of income tax at source if the companies are at least 25% associates. HMRC must have issued an exemption notice in relation to interest payments, and a company making royalty payments must have a reasonable belief that the recipient company is entitled to the exemption (*ITTOIA 2005, ss 761, 762*).

The CT61 return allows for the offset of income tax due on relevant payments against tax deducted from the company's income. Where such payments exceed income, income tax is due only on the excess. Where income exceeds payments for a return period, income tax paid in an earlier return period may be repaid. At the end of an accounting period, if total income exceeds total interest and/or annual payments, the balance of tax suffered is offset against the company's corporation tax liability; any excess tax suffered is repaid (*ICTA 1988, Sch 16*). No repayment interest will be paid.

**Example 3.11**

S Ltd prepares accounts each year to 31 October. During the year ending 31 October 2007, it pays the following interest:

| | | £ |
|---|---|---|
| 21 December 2006 | (net of tax @ 20%) | 8,000 |
| 4 January 2007 | (net of tax @ 20%) | 5,600 |
| 9 August 2007 | (net of tax @ 20%) | 8,000 |
| 21 October 2007 | (net of tax @ 20%) | 12,000 |

All the interest is paid to individuals.

S Ltd will enter the following figures into its CT61 returns and account for tax as follows:

| *Return periods* | *Payments* | *Income tax paid* |
|---|---|---|
| | £ | £ |
| 1 November 2006 to 31 December 2006 | 8,000 | 2,000 |
| 1 January 2007 to 31 March 2007 | 5,600 | 1,400 |
| 1 April 2007 to 30 June 2007 | (no return) | |
| 1 July 2007 to 30 September 2007 | 8,000 | 2,000 |
| 1 October 2007 to 31 October 2007 | 12,000 | 3,000 |
| Total income tax paid | | £8,400 |

*Chapter 4*

# Close Companies and Connected Issues

## INTRODUCTION

**4.1** Ownership of a company is vested in its shareholders. A share is a bundle of rights; namely voting rights, dividend rights and a right to assets in a winding-up. Companies owned by a small number of individuals are in a position to control a company to their advantage. The corporation tax legislation looks through these relationships and modifies the corporation tax rules in particular in relation to:

- close companies;
- close investment holding companies; and
- associated companies.

## CLOSE COMPANIES

### Consequences

**4.2** The 'close company' provisions were included within corporation tax provisions when they were first introduced in 1965 and similar legislation was in existence before then.

The effect of the provisions (and if all the related conditions apply) is to widen the scope of a distribution to include shareholder and shareholder family member benefits (see Chapter 16 for distributions). The provisions regard some loans to shareholders as an extraction of profits and seek to tax the loan. Close investment holding companies are prevented from applying the lower rate of corporation tax on their profits.

### Status

**4.3** A close company is defined as:

'a "close company" is one which is under the control of five or fewer participators, or of participators who are directors ...' (*TA 1988, s 414*(*1*))

## Control

**4.4** Control is the ability to exercise, or entitlement to acquire, direct or indirect control over the company's affairs, including the ownership of, or entitlement to acquire the greater part (over 50%) of the company's share capital; voting rights, distributable income or distributable assets (*ICTA 1988, s 416*(*1*)). If the rights and powers of two or more persons taken together amount to the greater part of the company's share capital etc, these two or more persons will control the company.

Rights and powers of a nominee, an associate and any company of which the person has control or he or she and or her associates (including nominees of associates but not associates of associates) have control are attributable to the person (*ICTA 1988, s 416*(*5*), (*6*)).

## Exceptions

**4.5** As with all definitions there are exceptions and a company with the following criteria is not close (or is open).

- a company not resident in the UK;
- a registered industrial and provident society or building society;
- a company controlled by or on behalf of the Crown;
- a UK resident company controlled by a non-resident company (unless the non-resident company would itself be close if resident in the UK);
- a company controlled by a non-close company or companies, where it cannot be treated as a close company except by including a non-close company as one of its five or fewer participators;
- a quoted company:
  - where 35% or more of the company's voting power is held by the 'public' (excluding shares entitled to a fixed rate of dividend); and
  - within the preceding 12 months those voting shares have been the subject of dealings on a recognised stock exchange unless the total voting power of the company's 'principal members' exceeds 85% (including shares entitled to a fixed rate of dividend) (*ICTA 1988, s 414*(*1*)).

## Public

**4.6** In this sense, the public excludes directors and their associates, any company controlled by them, any associated company, any fund for the benefit of past or present employees, directors or dependants of the company or associated companies, and the principal members (*ICTA 1988, s 415*(*5*)).

## Principal member

**4.7** A principal member is a person holding more than 5% of the company's voting power or where there are more than five such persons, one of the five possessing the greatest percentages. Where two or more persons hold equal percentages, so that the greatest percentages are held by more than five persons, a principal member is any one of that number (*ICTA 1988, s 415*(*6*)).

## Director

**4.8** A director includes any person who acts in that capacity whatever name is given to him. A director is also someone who gives directions upon which directors are accustomed to act or who is concerned in the management of the company's business and controls. A director is also someone who is able, either directly or indirectly, to control 20% or more of the company's ordinary share capital (*ICTA 1988, s 417*(*5*)).

## Close company tests

**4.9** In order to determine whether a company is close, HMRC apply five tests (HMRC Company Taxation Manual CTM 60102):

| | *Test* | *Answer* | *Result* |
|---|---|---|---|
| 1. | Is the company within one of the specific exceptions that exclude it from being a close company? | Yes | The company is not close. |
| | | No | Consider further tests. |
| 2. | Who are the participators in the company and what powers or rights do they possess or are they entitled to acquire? | | |

| | *Test* | *Answer* | *Result* |
|---|---|---|---|
| 3. | What rights and powers of other persons are attributable to the participators? | | |
| 4. | Having regard to the rights, etc, of each participator, and other persons' rights, etc, which are attributed to the participator, do: | | |
| | (i) five or fewer participators control the company, or | Yes | The company is close. |
| | | No | Consider further tests. |
| | (ii) participators who are directors control the company? | Yes | The company is close. |
| | | No | Consider further tests |
| 5. | Would more than half the assets of the company be ultimately distributed to five or fewer participators, or to | Yes | The company is close |
| | participators who are directors, in the event of the company being wound up? | No | The company is not close |

The result as to which participators control the company should always be inferred from the minimum controlling holding. X, Y and Z may each own 33.33% of the company. Therefore control in applying the tests is given to X and Y or Y and Z or X and Z but never X, Y and Z (*ICTA 1988, s 416*(*3*)).

## Participator

**4.10** Test 2 requires the identity of the participator to be determined. The full definition of a participator is given as:

> 'A participator is any person having a share or interest in the capital or income of the company … and includes:
>
> (a) any person who possesses or is entitled to acquire share capital or voting rights in the company;
>
> (b) any loan creditor of the company;
>
> (c) any person who possesses or is entitled to acquire a right to receive or participate in distributions of the company … or in any amounts payable by the company (in cash or kind) to loan creditors by way of premium or redemption;

(d) any person who is entitled to secure that income or assets (whether present or future) of the company will be applied directly or indirectly for his benefit' (*ICTA 1988, s 417(1)*)

Generally speaking a participator is anyone who has a financial interest in a close company, ie who has invested into share capital or who has provided loan finance. A participator is 'entitled to acquire' or 'entitled to secure' if he has a contractual right to do so (see *R v CIR, ex p Newfields Developments Ltd* (2001) 73 TC 532, [2001] STC 901, [2001] 1 WLR 1111, [2001] 4 All ER 400 on this point).

The definition of a participator can be extended through a company structure (*ICTA 1988, s 419(7)*).

---

**Example 4.1**

In the following circumstances all companies are close.

| *Fact* | *Result* |
|---|---|
| A is a shareholder of A Ltd. | A is a participator of A Ltd |
| A Ltd owns all the shares in B Ltd. | A is also a participator in B Ltd |
| If B Ltd makes a loan to A. | The loan is within *ICTA 1988, s 419* |

---

## Loan creditor

**4.11** A loan creditor is also a participator and is defined as;

' "loan creditor" means a creditor in respect of any debt incurred by the company:

(a) for any money borrowed or capital assets acquired by the company, or

(b) for any right to receive income created in favour of the company, or

(c) for consideration the value of which to the company was (at the time when the debt was incurred) substantially less than the amount of the debt (including any premium thereon),

or in respect of any redeemable loan capital issued by the company' (*ICTA 1988, s 417(7)*).

Normal company trade creditors are not included in the definition. Any holder of redeemable capital is a loan creditor. Hire purchase arrangements are not regarded as part of loan capital. Arrangements where a person makes annual payments to a company in exchange for a capital sum at some future date treats the person as a participator.

Loans in the normal course of banking business do not bring about a loan creditor relationship (HMRC Company Taxation Manual CTM 60130).

## Associate

**4.12** An associate of a participator includes the following:

- any 'relative': spouses or civil partners, parents or remoter forebear, children or remoter issue, brothers or sisters (but not aunts, uncles, nephews and nieces). Separated spouses and half-brothers or sisters are associated, but divorced spouses and step-brothers or sisters are not;
- any business partner;
- the trustee(s) of any settlement in which the participator (or any living or dead 'relatives') is or was the settlor; and
- the trustee(s) of a settlement or personal representatives of an estate holding company shares in which the participator has an interest (where the participator is a company, any other company interested in those shares is also an associate) (*ICTA 1988, s 417*(*3*), (*4*)).

## Benefits to participators

**4.13** Benefits or services provided to close company participators, who are also directors or other employees, will be treated as remuneration and will be assessed to income tax, as calculated under the taxable benefit rules for employments (*ICTA 1988, s 418*(*3*), (*4*)). Payments to a non-working participator or the non-working associate of a participator cannot be classed as employment income and will be treated as a distribution to the participator. Hence the 'distributions' will not be an allowable expense of the company (*ICTA 1988, s 418*(*2*)).

## Loans to participators

**4.14** The company must self-assess tax liabilities in respect of any loans not in the ordinary course of business to participators or associates, which can result in the requirement to make tax payments to HMRC equal to 25% of the outstanding loan or advance made during the accounting period. The tax need not be paid if the loan has been repaid, released or written off within nine months and one day following the end of the accounting period. Where the loan or advance is repaid, released or written off more than nine months after the end of an accounting period, the tax paid can be repaid nine months after the end of the accounting period in which the repayment, release, etc takes place.

## Self-assessment disclosure

**4.15** Loans to participators or their associates made during the accounting period must be disclosed on the corporation tax return. Supplementary page CT600A (2004) Version 2 (loans to participators by close companies) is used for this purpose and is reproduced in the Appendices. Details of the name of the participator or associate to whom the loan was made and the amount of the loan outstanding at the end of the accounting period for which the return has been made must be disclosed in Part 1.

If the loan has been repaid, released or written off within nine months and one day after the end of the accounting period, details of the name of the participator or associate whose loan has been repaid, released or written off, together with the amount and date repaid, released or written off, must be disclosed in Part 2.

The effect of completion of both Parts 1 and 2 will result in no liability to *s 419* tax at 25%. The practical implication is that HMRC will now have been informed of the amounts loaned to the participators and the associates and will be able to follow through the beneficial loan declarations on form P11D for directors, other employed participators and their associates.. A benefit in kind may arise on a participator who is an employee or director in respect of direct loans. A benefit in kind may also arise on a participator who is an employee or a director in respect of direct loans made to their associates.

Relief is given if the loan is repaid, released or written off (*ICTA 1988, s 419(4)*). If the loan has been repaid, released or written off later than nine months and one day after the end of the accounting period, details of the name of the participator or associate whose loan has been repaid, released or written off, together with the amount and date repaid, released or written off must be disclosed in Part 3. It follows that if the loan has not been repaid, released or written off at all then neither Part 2 nor Part 3 can be completed. The effect of completion of Part 3 or non-completion of Parts 2 and 3 is that the *s 419* liability will be shown in Box A13. This amount should be shown in Box 79 on CT600 (the corporation tax self-assessment return for the year). Corporation tax software and online filing will automatically make these calculations but manual completion following the step-by-step instructions on form CT600A should arrive at this result. The tax at 25% of the outstanding loan then becomes payable with the main corporation tax. Any late payment falls within the normal interest provisions. Interest is charged on any outstanding liability from the due date until the earlier of the payment of the *s 419* tax and the date that the loan or part is repaid, released or written off (*TMA 1970, ss 87A*(*1*)*, 109*(*3A*)). If the repayment, release or write-off of a loan takes place earlier then nine months and one day after the end of the accounting period in which the loan was made repayment interest will accrue from the later off nine months after the end of that accounting period and the date the tax was paid. If the loan is repaid, release or written-off more than nine months after the end of the accounting period in which the loan was made interest will accrue from the later of nine months after the end of the accounting period in which the loan was cleared and the date the tax was paid (*ICTA 1988, s 826*(*4*)). HMRC may make enquiries into the loan accounts as part of their corporation tax self-assessment enquiries.

## Loans within s 419(1)

**4.16** To be within *s 419*(*1*) the loan must have been made 'otherwise than in the ordinary course of a business carried on by it which includes the lending of money'. The principle of the lending of money was tested in *Brennan v Denby Investment Co Ltd* (2001) 73 TC 455, [2001] STC 536 and resulted in the comment that 'business requires some regularity of occurrence'. It would seem that without doubt a commercial lending bank's business includes lending money. HMRC state that they will look at the following characteristics to determine whether there is a money lending trade:

- Money lending advertisements aimed at the general public.
- Interest rate publication.
- Receipt of loan applications from the public.
- Commercial interest rate charge.
- In situ debt collection personnel and procedures.
- Legally enforceable written repayment term contracts.
- A reasonable number of existing loans (usually 200+) enabling inter alia loan set-off.
- Matched time period borrowing and lending.

If indeed there is a money lending business the loan to the participator must be made to the participator on the same commercial lending terms (HMRC Company Taxation Manual CTM 61520).

Loans to employee share schemes and employee benefit trusts are within *s 419*. *Section 419*(*1*) is applied at the time of the loan, if the trust is a shareholder or individual trustees are participators in the company. HMRC state that *ICTA 1988, s 419*(*5*) may apply when the trustees make payments to existing shareholders for their shares (HMRC Company Taxation Manual CTM 61525).

HMRC state that they will not apply *s 419* where money is lent to a partnership of which the company is a member where there is a genuine partnership with bona fide arrangements. However, HMRC may invoke *s 419*(*5*). This section enables HMTC to assess a loan not made by the close company but by arrangements not in the ordinary course of business to *s 419*(*1*) (HMRC Company Taxation Manual CTM 61515). Payments by a company to a director in respect of the directors private business were held to be within *s 419* in *Grant* (*Andrew*) *Services Ltd v Watton* (*Inspector of Taxes*) (*aka HCB Ltd v HM Inspector of Taxes*) (1999) 71 TC 333, [1999] STC 330.

## Loans not within s 419(1)

**4.17** Not only are loans and advances that a company makes to its participators and/or their associates, other than in the ordinary course of business, within *s 419*(*1*), but also:

- any debt due by the participator or associate to the company (*ICTA 1988, s 419*(2)(*a*));
- any debt due to a third party, which has been assigned by the third party to the company (*ICTA 1988, s 419*(2)(*b*)); or
- the provision of goods or services in the ordinary course of trade or business to a participator on credit terms that exceed six months or are longer than normally given to the company's customers (*ICTA 1988, s 420*(*1*)).

As regards debts due to a third party, HMRC acknowledge that a debt can only be assigned by the third party. If the debtor (the person to whom the money is lent) and the close company of which he is a participator agree that the close company will pay the debt on his behalf, *ICTA 1988, s 419*(2)(*b*) cannot apply. However, a debt due from the participator to the close company may arise when the close company pays the debt to the third party on the participator's behalf, which will fall under *ICTA 1988, s 419*(2)(*a*). Indeed, depending on the facts of the case, HMRC may treat the amount as remuneration or a distribution (HMRC Company Taxation Manual CTM 61535).

As regards the provision of goods or services, HMRC acknowledge that a credit period runs from the time that goods are delivered or services are performed until time of payment (*Grant (Andrew) Services Ltd v Watton* (1999) 71 TC 333, [1999] STC 330; HMRC Company Taxation Manual CTM 61535).

*Section 419* does not apply to loans less than £15,000, where the borrower is a full-time working director or employee of the close company or of an associated company with no material interest in the company (*ICTA 1988, s 420*(2)). No material interest means 5% or less direct or indirect control (associates included) of the ordinary share capital or the assets in winding-up (*ITEPA 2003, s 68*). HMRC interpret full-time as not less than three-quarters of the normal working hours of the close company (HMRC Company Taxation Manual CTM 61540). As soon as the conditions of *s 420*(*2*) are no longer met, for example, by the borrower acquiring an interest of more than 5% then *s 419* will apply from that time. Spouses and civil partners, if employees of the company, have their own £15,000 limit.

## Loan accounts

**4.18** For accounts purposes if a loan is made to a participator the company will record the loan in its nominal ledger as a 'loan account'. Director loan accounts are a common feature of owner-managed companies, which are invariably close companies. HMRC will not concur to the netting off of one loan account against another unless there is a genuine joint loan, for example, as between spouses, where a joint nominal ledger loan account would be operated. A participator or director may have more than one nominal ledger loan account with the company, where loans carrying different terms are recorded. The fact that one loan account may be in debit and another in credit has no avail with HMRC. This is because HMRC treat all loan accounts as separate loans. If a genuine posting is made to clear the two loan accounts then this is treated as though the loan had been repaid under *ICTA 1988, s 419*(*4*). The posting date is the repayment date (HMRC Company Taxation Manual CTM 61550).

Actual repayment by the participator or a third party takes place on the date that payment is made. A director's loan account may be cleared by a bonus payment. *ITEPA 2003, s18* onwards determines the date that the bonus is received by the director for income tax purposes. For *s 419* purposes the date of repayment is the date that the bonuses are voted or the date on which PAYE was operated if earlier (HMRC Company Taxation Manual CTM 61605).

The director/participator may wish to use a dividend payment to clear the loan account. In practice, the company's articles should be examined for any matters that may affect dividend payments. If, following Table A, final dividends may be declared by the company in general meeting (*Article 102*

*Table A 1985 Regulations*) and interim dividends may be paid by directors from time to time (*Article 103 Table A 1985 Regulations*). A dividend may only be declared if there are sufficient net realized profits. For accounts purposes a final dividend is due and payable on the date that it is declared. An interim dividend is due when paid.

A dividend is paid when it is due and payable (*ICTA 1988, s 834(3)*) but for *s 419(4)* purposes *s 834(3)* does not apply and until the dividend is paid the debt remains outstanding to the company (HMRC Company Taxation Manual CTM 61605). 'A dividend is not paid and there is no distribution, unless and until the shareholder receives money or the distribution is otherwise unreservedly put at their disposal, perhaps by being credited to a loan account on which the shareholder has the power to draw' (HMRC Company Taxation Manual CTM 20095). Evidence of the payment or credit should be shown in the company's books of account. If a dividend is paid unlawfully and the shareholder knew or was in a position to know of this fact he or she is liable to return the distribution to the company (*CA 1985, s 277*; *It's a Wrap (UK) Ltd (in liquidation) v Gula* [2006] EWCA Civ 544).

HMRC acknowledge that in many small private companies the directors and shareholders are one and the same, and dividends are often credited to the directors/shareholders' account with the company. In the case of a final dividend the dividend is 'due and payable' on the date of the resolution unless some future date for payment is specified. An interim dividend is only paid when the money is placed unreservedly at the disposal of the directors/shareholders as part of their current accounts with the company. So, payment is not made until such a right to draw on the dividend exists (presumably) when the appropriate entries are made in the company's books.

If, as may happen with a small company, such entries are not made until the annual audit, and this takes place after the end of the accounting period in which the directors resolved that an interim dividend be paid, then the 'due and payable' date is in the later rather than the earlier accounting period.

A director may clear the account shortly before the year end by borrowing from an external third party shortly before the year end only to reinstate the loan at the beginning of the accounting period. HMRC will regard the company as submitting a negligent or fraudulent return under *FA 1998, Sch 18, para 20*, which can attract a tax related penalty: see 2.12 (HMRC Enquiry Manual EM 8565).

## Section 419 tax repayment

**4.19** When the loan is actually repaid the company will be due the *s 419* tax that it has already paid. There is no facility for setting the repayable overpaid *s 419* tax against the corporation tax liability for the year in which the repayment is made. The company will need to complete an amended Part 3 CT600A for the accounting period in which the loan was made. If the loan is repaid in time to enable the amended CT600A to be completed and submitted within the 12-month enquiry period, this will act as an amended return and repayment will be issued. Alternatively, if submission is outside the enquiry period, the revised form will act as a separate claim under *TMA 1970, Sch 1A*.

## Section 419 loan released

**4.20** If the loan is released or written off, the same procedures apply to the company as for repayment but the individual participator will be treated as receiving a distribution net of the 10% tax credit (*ICTA 1988, s 421*). The *s 421* charge takes precedence over the employment income charge (HMRC Company Taxation Manual CTM 61630).

## Circuitous and indirect loans

**4.21** Circuitous and indirect loans are also caught by *s 419*. In particular, HMRC quote the situation whereby, for example, a close company makes a loan to an employee who is not a participator and that employee applies the loan in purchase of the shares from an existing shareholder. The existing shareholder is a 'deemed borrower' under *ICTA 1988, s 419(5)* and *s 419(1)* can apply (HMRC Company Taxation Manual CTM 61540).

This is because *s 419(5)* catches the situation where a close company makes a loan but no *s 419(1)* liability arises. A third party then makes a payment or transfers property to a participator or releases a participator's debt. HMRC give the following examples:

---

**Example 4.2**

Company D is a close company. Instead of making a loan directly to D, an individual participator, it makes it to an associated company, Company E. Company E then passes the loan to D. The loan by one company to the other is treated as if it had been made direct to D.

---

---

**Example 4.3**

Company T, a close company, makes a loan to A. A is an individual participator in Company W but not in Company T. Company W, acting in concert with Company T, then makes a loan to D, an individual participator in

Company T. Company T and Company W have swapped loans to participators and are treated as if they had made loans to their own participators.

Such loans should be assessed to *s 419(1)* in the normal way except where the amounts form assessable income receipts for the individual concerned (HMRC Company Taxation Manual 61670 and 61680).

---

## Anti-avoidance

**4.22** *TA 1988, s 422* (extension of *s 419* to loans by companies controlled by close companies) is an anti-avoidance clause. A loan to a participator by a third party, directly or indirectly financed by the participator's close company, is within *s 419(1)* by virtue of *TA 1988, s 422*. In addition, a loan to a participator by a company controlled by a close company is also within *s 419(1)*.

# CLOSE INVESTMENT HOLDING COMPANIES

## Consequences

**4.23** Trading uncommercially or letting property to connected parties may mean that a close company becomes a close investment holding company.

The small company corporation tax rate can be utilised by a close company, but not by a 'close investment holding company', which will pay corporation tax at the full rate, regardless of profit levels (*ICTA 1988, s 13(1)(b)*).

## Status

**4.24** A close company will *not* be a close investment holding company if throughout the period it exists wholly or mainly for one or more of the following purposes:

- carrying on a trade on a commercial basis;
- making investments in land or estates or interests in land and in cases where the land is or is intended to be let to persons other than:
  - any person connected with the close company, or
  - any person who is the wife or husband of an individual connected with the relevant company, or is a relative, or the wife or husband of a relative, of such an individual or of the husband or wife of such an individual,

- the purpose of holding shares in and securities of, or making loans to, one or more companies each of which is a qualifying company or a company which:
  - is under the control of the relevant company or of a company that has control of the relevant company, and
  - itself exists wholly or mainly for the purpose of holding shares in or securities of, or making loans to, one or more qualifying companies;
- the purpose of co-ordinating the administration of two or more qualifying companies;
- the purpose of a trade or trades carried on on a commercial basis by one or more qualifying companies or by a company that has control of the relevant company; and
- the purpose of the making, by one or more qualifying companies or by a company, which has control of the relevant company, of investments as mentioned in lands or estates as set out above (*ICTA 1988, s 13A*(*1*), (*2*)).

In general terms a 'qualifying company' is a trading company or a property investment company (*TA 1988, s 13A*(*3*)).

## Letting of land to a connected person

**4.25** Letting of land to a connected person may bring the company into the close investment holding company regime. Connection is defined here in *ICTA 1988, s 839*(*5*), (*6*).

### Connection to another company

'A company is connected with another company

(a) if the same person has control of both, or a person has control of one and persons connected with him, or he and persons connected with him, have control of the other, or

(b) if a group of two or more persons has control of each company, and the groups either consist of the same persons or could be regarded as consisting of the same persons by treating (in one or more cases) a member of either group as replaced by a person with whom he is connected.' (*TA 1988, s 839*(*5*))

**Connection with another person**

> 'A company is connected with another person if that person has control of it, or if that person and persons connected with him together have control of it.' (*TA 1988, s 839(6)*)

Control is given the same meaning as at **4.4** (*ICTA 1988, s 416*(2)).

## Letting of land

**4.26** Land let to a relative may also bring the company within the close investment holding company regime.

A relative includes a brother, sister, ancestor or lineal descendant (*ICTA 1988, s 839(8)*). Lettings to a relative of the individual's spouse, or the spouse of a relative of the individual will affect the close investment holding company status.

---

**Example 4.4**

*Facts*

Joe is married to Mary. Joe owns 100% of Joe Ltd, a building and construction company in the South of England. Joe would like to provide Mary's mother Mrs K with a home where she could reside independently of Joe and Mary.

On 1 January 2007, Joe forms Mrs K Ltd, a 100% subsidiary of Joe Ltd. The subsidiary buys a plot of land with development value on which stands Plum Cottage, a Victorian property. Mrs K moves into the cottage and pays her landlord Mrs K Ltd a full market rent for the property. Mrs K maintains her independence and pays for the upkeep of Plum Cottage herself.

*Comments*

The facts appear to fall under *TA 1988, s 13A*(2)(*b*)(*ii*).

This would bring the company within the close investment holding company regime. Corporation tax will be payable on profits at the full 30% rate.

Joe formed the company in order to buy a property suitable for his mother-in-law's occupation. The land on which the property stood had development value.

If the situation were reversed such that Joe bought land with development value (albeit through Mrs K Ltd) for use in his trade on which stood a vacant cottage, there may be an argument that the company had a trading 'purpose'.

This would mean that the company might fall out of the close investment holding company regime. There is also the possibility that the company would pay corporation tax at the full rates because of the associated company rules.

---

# ASSOCIATED COMPANIES

## Consequences

**4.27** Associated companies share the small companies rate band by dividing the lower relevant amount and the higher relevant amount equally between them.

A company is to be treated as an associated company of another at a given time if at that time one of the two has control of the other, or both are under the control of the same person or persons (*TA 1988, s 13*(*4*)).

## Status

**4.28** The same definition of control is used as for close companies (see **4.3** and **4.4**).

For these purposes not only are the rights of the person concerned taken into account but also the rights and powers of associates that can be attributed to that person (*ICTA 1988, s 416*(*6*)). Associates are as defined in **4.12**. HMRC expressly state that rights and powers of associates must not be attributed to the person concerned (HMRC Company Taxation Manual CTM 03750). However, rights and powers of the person's nominees must be attributed to the person (*ICTA 1988, s 416*(*5*)).

Associated companies share the £300,000 lower and £1,500,000 higher corporation tax profit limit bands between them. With the result that, if there are two associated companies, the 19% band for each will only reach £150,000 and the 30% band will commence at £750,000.

## Exceptions

**4.29** An associated company that has not carried on any trade or business during the accounting period in question is excluded from the count of associated companies (*TA 1988, s 13*(*4*)).

A trading company that ceased to trade and placed its surplus funds on a non-actively managed bank deposit account was regarded as dormant (*Jowett*

(*Inspector of Taxes*) *v O'Neill and Brennan Construction Ltd* (1998) 70 TC 566, [1998] STC 482). A company that ceased trading but continued to receive rent from an established source that required little administration was also excluded from the count of associated companies (*HMRC v Salaried Persons Postal Loans Ltd* [2006] EWHC 763 (Ch), [2006] STC 1315).

A close company, which merely holds a bank deposit account, will fall into the definition of a close investment holding company and will be liable to corporation tax at the full rate, but can still be included in the count of associated companies.

A non-trading holding company is excluded from the count of associated companies provided that throughout the accounting period all the following conditions apply:

- Its only assets are its shares in its 51% subsidiaries.
- There is no deduction entitlement for charges or management expenses.
- It has no income of gains other than dividends, which it has distributed to its shareholders and which amount to franked investment income if distributed to a company (SP 5/94).

## Rights of attribution

**4.30** In practice the rights of attribution are an important consideration for close companies. By concession HMRC, in cases where there is no substantial commercial interdependence between companies, will only treat spouses, civil partners and minor children as relatives. HMRC interpret companies' interdependence in the commercial sense as reliance upon one another for trade or services etc. HMRC amongst other things will look at common administration or joint directorships, use of staff and facilities, purchasing and selling arrangements, co-operation on joint projects and inter-company loans and guarantees. HMRC interpret substantial in relative terms as not being insubstantial and as a guide anything more than 10% will be substantial (HMRC Company Taxation Manual CTM 03770).

Neither will HMRC attribute shares held by a trustee company to the party concerned if there is no other past or present connection with the trustee company (ESC C9).

In *R v CIR, ex p Newfields Developments Ltd* (2001) 73 TC 532, [2001] STC 901, [2001] 1 WLR 1111, [2001] 4 All ER 400 the Revenue's power to exercise attribution under *ICTA 1988, s 416(6)* was taken to the House of Lords.

The facts of this case are briefly as follows. Before his death, Mr W created a will trust in favour of his wife, Mrs W. The trustees of W's trust (Trustees A) owned shares in N Ltd for which the small companies rate of corporation tax was claimed. In his lifetime Mr W had also created a discretionary trust and had appointed separate trustees (Trustees B). Trustees B controlled a separate company L Ltd. The point of issue was whether N Ltd was associated with L Ltd.

The result of the House of Lords decision was as follows:

Mrs W was a participator. Her husband (a relative of hers) was the settlor of both the will trust and the discretionary trust. Therefore by reason of *ICTA 1988, s 417(3)(b)*, Mrs W was an associate of Trustees A and Trustees B. The rights and powers of both Trustees A and Trustees B could be attributed to her, even though she personally, owned no shares in the companies concerned. Therefore, indirectly N Ltd and L Ltd were controlled by the same 'person' simply because of the rules of attribution and hence were associated companies.

In addition it was further decided that HMRC has neither discretion as to whether or not it should operate the rules of attribution nor indeed in deciding whether companies are associated.

In *Gascoignes Group Ltd v Inspector of Taxes* [2004] EWHC 640 (Ch), [2004] STC 844 the Revenue exercised the powers of attribution. In this case Mr D held 71% of the shares in G Ltd. Mr & Mrs G had created a settlement in favour of their three children. The settlement owned 99% of the shares in S Ltd. Mr D was a participator and therefore associated by reason of *ICTA 1988, s 417(3)(b)* with the trustees of the settlement. The rights and powers of the trustees must be attributed to him and hence he controls G Ltd and S Ltd and therefore these companies are associated companies for small companies rate purposes.

In HMRC Company Taxation Manual CTM 03750 the Revenue acknowledge that attribution rights in some cases are limited by ESC C9. However, even if ESC C9 applies, rights will always be attributed to:

- spouse (civil partner) and minor children;
- business partners;
- trustee or trustees of a settlement where that person is the settlor, or the settlor's spouse or minor child.

The following examples are given:

**Example 4.5**

F Ltd and C Ltd have the following shareholders. Mr F and Mrs F are married to each other. Mr B and Mr C have no connection at all.

| *F Ltd* | *Shares* | *C Ltd* | *Shares* |
|---|---|---|---|
| Mr F | 60 | Mrs F | 75 |
| Mr B | 40 | Mr C | 25 |
| Total issued shares | 100 | Total issued shares | 100 |

Neither B nor C is an associate of Mr F or Mrs F. Mr F controls Company F. Mr F is a participator and under *ICTA 1988, s 416(6)* Mrs F's rights may be attributed to him. He therefore controls C Ltd. The two companies are associated whether or not there is substantial commercial interdependence between them because ESC C9 does not ignore the interspousal relationship.

**Example 4.6**

The situation is the same as **Example 4.5** except that Mrs C is Mr F's sister.

| *F Ltd* | *Shares* | *C Ltd* | *Shares* |
|---|---|---|---|
| Mr F | 60 | Mrs C | 75 |
| Mr B | 40 | Mr C | 25 |
| Total issued shares | 100 | Total issued shares | 100 |

Neither Mr B nor Mr C is an associate of Mr F. Mrs C is an associate of Mr F. Mrs C's rights may be attributed to Mr F. However, this will only occur if there is substantial commercial interdependence between F Ltd and C Ltd.

**4.31** By concession, HMRC do not consider a company to be controlled by another (non-close) company if that control derives solely from preference shares or loans and that is the only connection (ESC C9). The loan in question must be a commercial loan. HMRC disregards fixed rate preference shares where the company takes no part in the management of the company and they have been subscribed for in the ordinary course of its business (HMRC Company Taxation Manual CTM 03810). In addition the fixed rate preference shares must be issued for new consideration, carry no conversion rights and have no rights to dividend other than the fixed dividend together with redemption rights at a reasonable commercial rate of return.

## Company tax return

**4.32** The corporation tax return form CT600 requires the number of associated companies to be entered in boxes 39, 40 and 41. This is necessary in order to determine the company's entitlement to small or marginal relief as appropriate, which must be the subject of a claim.

---

**Example 4.7**

*Facts*

The following companies are all wholly-owned by Bill. They each make up accounts to 31 March each year.

| A Ltd | B Ltd | C Ltd | D Ltd |
|---|---|---|---|
| £100,000 | (£220,000) | £390,000 | £20,000 |

Assessable profits and allowable losses for the year ended 31 March 2006 are shown.

*Comments*

The lower and upper relevant amounts of £300,000 and £1,500.000 are dividend by 4 resulting respectively to bands of £75,000 and £375,000.

The effective corporation tax paid by each company is as follows:

| | | *Tax* | | *Tax* | | *Tax* | | *Tax* |
|---|---|---|---|---|---|---|---|---|
| | *A Ltd* | | *B Ltd* | | *C Ltd* | | *D Ltd* | |
| | £ | | £ | | £ | | £ | |
| Profits | 100,000 | | Nil | | 390,000 | | 20,000 | |
| 19% | 75,000 | 14,250 | | | 75,000 | 14,250 | 20,000 | 3,800 |
| 32.75% | 25,000 | 8,188 | | | 300,000 | 98,250 | | |
| 30% | | | | | 15,000 | 4,500 | | |
| Total corporation tax | | 22,438 | | | | 117,000 | | 3,800 |

Although B Ltd has made a trading loss it must still be included in the count of associated companies.

The company's total results are below £300,000, being £290,000, but it is not possible to make full use of the small companies rate. Bill may wish to consider restructuring the group to either put all activities into one company or to form a group. (See **Chapter 9** regarding losses and **Chapter 10** regarding group relief). Bill may also wish to consider reducing A Ltd's profits that fall within the marginal rate band.

---

# Chapter 5

# Income

## RECEIPT OF INCOME AND BEING WITHIN THE CHARGE TO CORPORATION TAX

**5.1** Commencing or ceasing to trade (**5.5**) or the receipt of income from any source is a question of fact. However, whether or not a company is within the charge to corporation tax can often in practice be more difficult to ascertain where the company is not in receipt of any income. *ICTA 1988, s 832*(*1*) states that a source of income is 'within the charge to corporation tax' if corporation tax would be chargeable on that income were there to be any from that source. *The Centaur Clothes Group Ltd v Walker* (2000) 72 TC 379, [2000] STC 324, [2000] 1 WLR 799, [2000] 2 All ER 589 was not carrying on a trade but had potential sources of income from an inter-company debt and an agency agreement. The company was held to be within the charge to corporation tax. The case overturned the established principle in *National Provident Institution v Brown* (1921) 8 TC 57, [1921] 2 AC 222 whereby a company had to be in receipt of a source of income to be within the charge to corporation tax. If a company is not carrying on any activity whatsoever, it is a dormant company.

HMRC regards a company as dormant if it does not receive any profits or income and holds no assets capable of producing assets of gains (HMRC Revenue Manual COTAX). The rule is relaxed if a company holds chargeable assets that are unlikely to produce any profits, income or gains in the near future. *FA 2004, s 55* requires companies to inform HMRC wihin three months of the beginning of the accounting period that it becomes within the charge to corporation tax. Coming within the charge to corporation tax marks the beginning of a new accounting period for corporation tax purposes (see **2.4**). Companies are required to follow the CT41G notification procedures detailed in **2.2**.

## SOURCES OF INCOME

### Computation of income and gains

**5.2** Corporation tax is charged on income and chargeable gains but is not charged on dividends and distributions from UK resident companies.

Each source of income and each chargeable gain is computed separately, in accordance with income tax law and practice, but excluding provisions relating solely to individuals and subject to corporation tax provisions.

Thus the corporation tax computation and the corporation tax return bring together the company's total assessable income from trading and other sources, and chargeable gains. Deductions such as allowable losses and charges on income are taken into account in arriving at the company's profit chargeable to corporation tax (PCTCT).

An outline corporation tax computation is shown in **20.3**. The various sources of income reliefs are discussed as follows:

| *Source* | *Type of income* | *Chapter* |
|---|---|---|
| Schedule A | Profits from rents and other income from property in the UK | 12 |
| Schedule D | | |
| Case I | Profits from a trade | 5 |
| Case III | Interest | 11 |
| Case V | Income from foreign possessions | 13 |
| Case VI | Any income subject to tax but not taxed by any other Case or Schedule | 5 |
| Chargeable gains | Profits and losses arising from the disposal of capital assets | 5 and 7 |
| | *Type of relief* | |
| Management expenses | Expenses relating to investment business | 12 |
| Charges on income | Expenditure deducted from total income | 9 |
| Loss relief | Relief for excess of expenditure over income against other sources of income | 9 and 10 |

# TRADING INCOME

## Accounting principles

**5.3** Taxable profits must be computed in accordance with generally accepted accounting practice 'UK GAAP' (*FA 1998, s 42*(*1*); *FA 2002, s 103*(*5*)). See Chapter 17 Accounting and Taxation for the interaction of accounting standards and taxation law. Accounting principles do not apply where they conflict with the tax legislation and case law. As a result, a company's PCTCT will usually differ from the profit shown in the company's profit and loss account or income statement.

## Trading income

**5.4** Trading and professional profits are computed according to the principles of Schedule D Cases I and II respectively (*ICTA 1988, s 18(1)(ii)*). A trade is defined as 'every trade, manufacture, adventure or concern in the nature of trade' (*ICTA 1988, s 83(1)*). There is no statutory definition of profession. It is normally understood to mean a high degree of skill or competence attributed to an individual, for which he or she has undergone specialised training. Therefore, professional income for incorporated firms of architects, engineers, lawyers etc would fall under the rules of Schedule D Case II. The rules for the two cases are virtually interchangeable and are referred to collectively as Schedule D Case I.

## Trade

**5.5** As to whether a trade is being carried on is a statement of fact. The badges of trade established by the Royal Commission on the Taxation of Profits and Income in 1955 look to the subject matter of the transaction, the period of ownership, the frequency of the transactions, the supplementary work, the circumstances or method of realisation and the motive. In other words, has the company acquired products or services over a short space of time that had no use to the company, which it enhanced in some way or to which it added its own identity, which it has then sold in a strategic manner in order to make a profit.

### CASE LAW

**5.6** There is a substantial body of case law relating to trading activities, which confirms the 'badges of trade' of which the following are a selection:

**Subject matter of transaction**. In the case of *Rutledge v CIR* (1929) 14 TC 490 the taxpayer bought and sold a large quantity of toilet rolls in an isolated transaction. The subject matter of the transaction determined that this was a trading transaction.

**Period of ownership**. In the case of *Marin v Lowry* (1926) 11 TC 297, [1927] AC 312 an agricultural machinery merchant with no previous connection with the linen trade bought a surplus of government stock of 44,000,000 yards of linen. Negotiations for sale to the linen manufacturers fell through. The taxpayer advertised the linen and eventually all was sold within a year to numerous purchasers. The goods were sold swiftly at a profit. It was held that this was an adventure in the nature of trade.

**Frequency of transactions**. In *Pickford v Quirke* (1927) 13 TC 251 the taxpayer was a member of four different syndicates involved in buying and selling cotton spinning mills. It was held that the repetition of this transaction implied a trading intention. In *Leach v Pogson* (1962) 40 TC 585, [1962] TR 289 the taxpayer founded a driving school which he later sold at a profit. He then founded 30 more driving schools. Once the schools were operational he transferred them to companies, partly for shares and partly for cash. Because of the frequency of the transactions the taxpayer was found to be trading.

**Supplementary work**. In *Cape Brandy Syndicate v CIR* (1921) 12 TC 358, [1921] 2 KB 403 three wine merchants all from different firms bought a quantity of South African brandy. Most of the brandy was shipped to the UK where it was blended with French brandy, re-casked and sold in numerous lots. It was held that the transactions amounted to a trade.

**Circumstances or method of realisation**. In *West v Phillips* (1958) 38 TC 203, [1958] TR 267 a retired builder owned 2,495 houses, of which 2,208 had been built as investments and 287 for eventual sale. After a period of time the taxpayer began to sell the houses. It was held that 287 houses were sold as trading stock but the sale of the remainder held for investment purposes not a trade.

**Motive**. In *Wisdom v Chamberlain* (1968) 45 TC 92, [1969] 1 WLR 275, [1969] 1 All ER 332 the taxpayer made a profit on the purchase and sale of silver bullion. The bullion was bought to protect his wealth against the devaluation of sterling. It was held that this was a trading activity because the silver had been purchased for the specific purpose of realising a profit.

Of recent importance is the decision in *Marson v Morton* (1986) 59 TC 381, [1986] STC 463, [1986] 1 WLR 1343. In this case factors that should be considered as to whether a particular transaction was a trading transaction were summarised as follows:

| *Factor to consider* | *Comment* |
|---|---|
| Was the transaction a one-off transaction? | Frequency of transactions indicate a trade, but a one-off transaction may still constitute a trade depending on intention and other factors. |

| *Factor to consider* | *Comment* |
|---|---|
| Was the transaction in some way related to a trade carried on by the taxpayer? | If related to the trade this will point to a trading transaction. |
| Was the transaction in a commodity of a kind which is normally the subject matter of trade? | If yes, then again this will point to a trading transaction. |
| Was the transaction carried out in a manner typical of a trade in a commodity of that nature? | If yes, then again this will point to a trading transaction. |
| Has was the transaction financed? | If financed by borrowings, this often indicates that a trade is being carried on. |
| Was work done on the item before resale? | If yes it is more likely to be a trading transaction. |
| Was the item purchased broken down into several lots? | If so, there is an indication that a trading transaction has taken place. |
| What were the purchaser's intentions at the time of purchase? | Was it intended to hold the asset as an investment? |
| Did the asset purchased either provide enjoyment for the purchaser, or produce income? | If so, its resale is unlikely to be a trading transaction. |

The issues can be transferred to professional income but here more than likely the central issue is whether professional skills are sold and marketed for remunerative gain.

All these indications point to whether a trade is being carried on. Overall the company's activities must be looked at as a whole. A company may carry on a trade and an investment business. Transactions for each must be kept separate as the rules for each are different. See Chapter 11 for investment business.

**5.7** On the premise that a trade is being carried on, the company must establish whether its receipt is from the trade and whether it is a capital or a revenue item. It is an established principle that trading income is received when it is recognised in the trader's accounts (HMRC Business Income Manual BIM 40070). See Chapter 17 Accounting and Taxation. See **5.35–5.36** for recent developments.

## SELF-ASSESSMENT OF TRADING INCOME

### Company tax return

**5.8** On the assumption that a company is carrying on a trade or profession, the company is required to declare its trading or professional turnover in box 1 of the company tax return. This information should be available from the company's accounts. Box 2 is for use by financial concerns such as banks, building societies and insurance companies.

## Schedule D Case I and II profits

**5.9** The company must then compute its assessable Schedule D Case I and II profits, to enable it to complete box 3 of the company tax return. The profit for each trade must be computed on separate computations and a calculation of the capital allowances claimed should also be provided.

The accounting profits form the basis of the taxable profits and so the starting point for computing the Schedule D Case I assessable profit is the reported profits.

It is necessary to review the computation of profits to ensure that it is compliant with tax law. It will be necessary to review the specific Schedule D Case I computational provisions on which trading profits for income tax and corporation tax are based, as discussed below. It will also be necessary to review the more recent legislation that has direct relevance to corporation tax. This will encompass intangible assets, research and development expenditure, loan relationships and transfer pricing. In this respect please see the respective following chapters 7, 8, 11 and 13. Capital expenditure is not deductible for Schedule D Case I purposes.

## CAPITAL V REVENUE

**5.10** There is a body of case law, which established the revenue versus capital principles.

In general asset repair carried out during the course of trading activities is a revenue expense. Expenditure in order to put an asset into working order or the replacement of an entirety is not a revenue expense. In *Law Shipping Co Ltd v CIR* (1923) 12 TC 621, expenditure on repairs to a ship in order to make it seaworthy shortly after purchase was held to be capital expenditure. In contrast in *Odeon Associated Theatres Ltd v Jones* (1971) 48 TC 257, [1973] Ch 288, [1971] 1 WLR 442, [1972] 1 All ER 681 expenditure carried out on repairs to a useable cinema over a period of years was held to be revenue expenditure.

In *O'Grady v Bullcroft Main Collieries Ltd* (1932) 17 TC 93 a colliery company built a factory chimney at a cost of £3,067. After several years it became unsafe and was demolished. The company built another improved chimney near the site of the old one and claimed £287 of the cost as repairs. The whole of the cost was found to be capital expenditure because the new chimney was the replacement of an 'entirety'.

In *Samuel Jones & Co (Devondale) Ltd v CIR* (1951) 32 TC 513, [1951] TR 411 the company replaced a factory chimney and also incurred costs in respect of the removal of the old chimney. The expenditure was found to be an allowable revenue deduction because it was an integral part of the factory. The chimney was not an entirety as in the case of *O'Grady v Bullcroft Main Collieries Ltd.*

In *Brown v Burnley Football & Athletic Co Ltd* (1980) 53 TC 357, [1980] STC 424, [1980] 3 All ER 244 a stand at the football ground was found to be unsafe. It had been built in 1912 of wood and steel with a brick wall at the back. It was demolished and replaced with a new modern concrete stand. The new stand, with approximately the same capacity, was nearer the pitch but included office and other accommodation not provided by the old stand. The expenditure was held to be capital expenditure because the new stand was a replacement in its entirety.

Expenditure related in connection with enduring benefits to a trade is considered to be capital. In *Atherton v British Insulated & Helsby Cables Ltd* (1925) 10 TC 155, [1926] AC 205 a company set up a pension fund and made an initial lump sum contribution to enable the past service of existing staff to rank for pension. The expenditure was held to be capital. The principle was established that expenditure was normally capital if it was made not only once and for all but with a view to bringing into existence an asset or advantage for the enduring benefit of the trade.

In *Tucker v Granada Motorway Services Ltd* (1979) 53 TC 92, [1979] STC 393, [1979] 1 WLR 683, [1979] 2 All ER 801 the rent, which a company paid to the Ministry of Transport for a motorway service area, was calculated in part by reference to its gross takings. The gross takings included the duty on sales of tobacco. The lease was not assignable. In order to have the duty on sales of tobacco excluded from the gross takings, the company made a once and for all payment of £122,220 to the Ministry of Transport. The expenditure was held to be capital and therefore not deductible from profits. The expenditure related to an identifiable capital asset.

In *Beauchamp v F W Woolworth plc* (1989) 61 TC 542, [1989] STC 510, [1989] 3 WLR 1 a company entered into two loans, each for 50 million Swiss Francs, for five years but repayable earlier at the option of the company, subject to a payment of a graduated premium. The first loan was repaid six months early and the second on the due date, giving rise to losses of £11.4 million, due to currency exchange transactions.

It was held that the loss was incurred in relation to a capital transaction and was therefore not allowable as a revenue deduction. The company had increased its capital employed and thereby obtained an asset or advantage which endured for five years and as such was a capital asset. A loan is only a revenue transaction if it is part of the day-to-day incidence of carrying on the business, which was not the case in this situation. The loss was not deductible.

Often there is doubt as to whether an item of expenditure is capital or revenue. In the case of *Heather v P-E Consulting Group Ltd* (1972) 48 TC 293, [1973] Ch 189, [1973] 1 All ER 8 it was established that this is the court's decision. In this case a company undertook to pay 10% of its annual profits, subject to a minimum of £5,000 to a trust set up to enable its staff to acquire shares in the company and to prevent the company from coming under the control of outside shareholders. Accountancy evidence given at the time, which was accepted by the Commissioners, confirmed that the expenses were of a revenue nature. Although the Court of Appeal upheld the Commissioners' decision, it was made clear that whether the expenditure was capital or revenue was a matter of law for the court to decide and that accountancy evidence is not conclusive.

It was necessary to turn to the courts to establish whether the cost of airspace was capital or revenue. In *Rolfe v Wimpey Waste Management Ltd* (1989) 62 TC 399, [1989] STC 454 the company purchased several sites on which to tip waste under a contract with its customers. The company claimed that the purchases were revenue expenditure, on the grounds that it had acquired the land in order to use the airspace above it. The expenditure was held to relate to the land and was therefore capital.

Professional and other associated costs in connection with capital expenditure are also disallowed. See HMRC Business Income Manual BIM 35000 for a discussion on the capital/revenue divide.

## SCHEDULE D CASE I COMPUTATIONAL PROVISIONS

**5.11** As already mentioned, corporation tax is enshrined in income tax law and the reported profits.

The adjustments to the reported profit for taxation purposes follow four broad headings:

- Expenditure charged against profits in the accounts but not allowable as a deduction for tax purposes.
- Income that has not been included in profits in the accounts but that is taxable under Schedule D Case I.
- Income included in profits in the accounts but not taxable under Schedule D Case I.
- Expenditure that has not been charged against profits in the accounts but that is allowable under Schedule D Case I.

In particular it will be necessary to review the accounts for any capital items. Capital expenditure included within the profit and loss account for whatever reason is not an allowable deduction against profits for Schedule D Case I purposes.

## EXPENDITURE CHARGED AGAINST PROFITS IN THE ACCOUNTS BUT NOT ALLOWABLE AS A DEDUCTION FOR TAX PURPOSES

### Wholly and exclusively

**5.12** Expenditure is only allowed as a deduction if it has been incurred 'wholly and exclusively' for the purposes of the trade or profession (*ICTA 1988, s 74(1)*). Company expenditure must be reviewed from this prerogative. Expenditure on preserving a trade from destruction was treated as incurred wholly and exclusively for the purposes of the trade (*McKnight v Sheppard* (1999) 71 TC 410, [1999] STC 669, [1999] 1 WLR 1133, [1999] 3 All ER 491).

In the normal business environment, the types of expenditure often under consideration include entertaining and remuneration. A summarised but not exhaustive list of other allowable deductions is given in **5.16**.

### Entertaining

**5.13** Entertaining expenditure is disallowed by statute (*ICTA 1988, s 577*) except for staff entertainment. *Section 577* overrides the decision in *Bentleys, Stokes and Lowless v Beeson* (1952) 33 TC 491, [1952] WN 280, [1952] 2 All ER 82. Entertainment and gifts (excluding food and drink) that carry a conspicuous advertisement for the business, provided that the cost for the company is no more than £50 per donee in any one year, are also disallowed. Assets used for business entertainment do not qualify for capital allowances.

A number of relevant principles, based on VAT decisions involving business entertainment cases, indicate the like interpretation of *s 577*. Based on VAT decisions, the definition of business entertainment includes hospitality both free and subsidised (*Celtic Football and Athletic Club Ltd v Customs & Excise Commrs* [1983] STC 470). However, hospitality is not defined as business entertainment if it was given 'pursuant to a legal obligation in return for which it obtains proper and sufficient quid pro quo. The quid pro quo may be cash or it may be goods or services.' This also extends to a contractual obligation a company may have to provide hospitality (eg as part of a package).

Travel costs associated with business entertainment are not allowable expenses but exceptions exist such as employees travelling to meet a client.

*ICTA 1988, s 577(10)* allows the deduction of business entertainment expenses for the provision of items relevant to the trade and provided in the normal course of business, eg hospitality provided by restaurants and pubs (*Fleming v Associated Newspapers Ltd* (1972) 48 TC 382, [1973] AC 628, [1972] 2 All ER 574). Also, the cost of goods or services given away as an advertising promotion is allowable (*ICTA 1988, s 577(10)*).

Staff entertainment is allowable (*ICTA 1988, s 577(5)*) as long as it conforms to the wholly and exclusively for trade requirement and is not 'excessive'. Staff includes retired staff and partners. If an employee takes a client out for lunch *s 577(5)* does not apply and therefore the hospitality is not allowable. However, if the employee has an allowance, which is an expense of employment, such expenditure is allowable. The cost of subsistence for persons directly involved in the company's business or the conduct of the business are allowable expense.

Training costs for employees, which may include hospitality, are allowable. Hospitality is disallowed for persons not directly employed by the company who attend training courses paid by the company. The cost of sponsorship is not allowable in full if the company sponsoring receives other benefits for its sponsorship. Payments to specialist entertainment providers/organisers/arrangers are disallowed (HMRC Business Income Manual BIM 45047).

Advertising and promotion costs will normally be allowed. A company incurring costs on room hire and entertaining potential customers in order to gain firm orders found that the entertaining costs were disallowed but the room hire cost was allowable (*Netlogic Consulting Ltd v HMRC*).

## Remuneration

**5.14** **Employees.** Provided the remuneration charged is 'wholly and exclusively' for the purposes of the trade it should be an allowable deduction (*Copeman v Flood (William) & Sons Ltd* (1940) 24 TC 53, [1941] KB 202; *LG Berry Investments Ltd v Attwooll* (1964) 41 TC 547, [1964] 1 WLR 693, [1964] 2 All ER 126). An employee will normally have an employment contract with the company, which together with *ITEPA 2003* will determine the time that payment is due to the employee. The existence of a contractual obligation for the company will bring about the allowable deduction, normally at the same time that the remuneration is 'earnings' for the employee. In order to qualify as a deduction from profits, remuneration charged must be paid to the employee within nine months of the year end (*FA 1989, s 43(1)*).

**5.15 Directors' remuneration.** A director is any person occupying the position of director by whatever name called (*CA 1985, s 741*(*1*)). A shadow director is any person in accordance with whose instructions directors are accustomed to act with the exception of a professional adviser (*CA 1985, s 741*(2)). A similar definition is used within *ITEPA 2003, s 67*.

The time that remuneration is due and payable to a director is not only determined by *ITEPA 2003* and the director's contract of employment but also by company law.

Directors are treated as having received earnings at the time when they become entitled to be paid them. However, an entitlement to payment is not necessarily the same as the date on which the employee acquires a right to be paid (HMRC Employment Income Manual EIM 42290).

The terms of a service agreement may be written, verbal or implied and may give entitlement to a regular salary or a contractual bonus or other sums. The director would then enjoy rights to earnings under the agreement. The time at which entitlement to earnings under a service agreement arises will be governed by the terms of the agreement.

Under company law, a company may draft a special clause in its constitution regarding the directors' entitlement to directors' remuneration. Many companies adopt Table A of the *Companies* (*Tables A–F*) *Regulations 1985*.

Regulation 82 states:

> 'Remuneration of Directors
>
> The directors shall be entitled to such remuneration as the company may by ordinary resolution determine and unless the resolution provides otherwise the remuneration shall be deemed to accrue from day to day.'

The provision requires that directors' remuneration be voted in general meeting. This involves the members of the company passing a resolution that determines the amount payable to the directors.

In small private companies a meeting may not take place, but the directors would have agreed the remuneration anyway, possibly because they are a single director or because the company operates in that way. *CA 1985, s 382B* requires and *Companies Bill 2006, clause 364* proposes that the single member must provide the company with a written record of the decision. In some cases, particularly where no other person other than the member is entitled to attend the meeting, this requirement can be overridden by the *Duomatic* principle.

In *Re Duomatic Ltd* [1969] 2 Ch 365, [1969] 1 All ER 161 the directors, who were also the only ordinary shareholders having a right to attend and vote at a general meeting, had drawn remuneration, which was subsequently shown in accounts, which they had as directors approved. That was challenged in the subsequent liquidation on the ground that it had never been sanctioned by a general meeting. The court held that although the directors did not take the formal step of constituting themselves a general meeting of the company and passing a formal resolution approving the payment of directors' salaries at the time of approving the accounts, they did apply their minds to the question, and accordingly, their consent should be regarded as tantamount to a resolution of a general meeting.

HMRC accept the *Duomatic* principle. If there is no such specific resolution, but the directors' remuneration is approved by the shareholders entitled to attend and vote at a general meeting, without a meeting actually taking place, this has the same effect as a resolution passed by the company in general meeting (HMRC Employment Income Manual EIM 42300).

Also, a resolution of the members approving the company's accounts will be a sufficient authorisation of directors' remuneration if the members are aware that by approving the accounts, they are also approving the directors' remuneration (*Felix Hadley & Co v Hadley* (1897) 77 LT 131). The time at which entitlement to earnings arises is the time at which the resolution is passed, agreement reached or the accounts approved, unless specific provision otherwise is made at that time.

Although, these principles establish the time of payment to the individual they must be looked at carefully to establish whether they permit a deduction for corporation tax purposes. The time of passing a resolution is of particular importance if remuneration is unpaid and decided upon after the end of the accounting period.

In order to be acceptable for taxation purposes a company's accounts must be drawn up in accordance with GAAP. FRS 12 permits a provision if an entity has a present obligation as a result of a past event (see **17.16**). FRS 21 only permits adjustments to the accounts for events that occurred after the balance sheet date if they provided evidence of conditions that existed at the balance sheet date (see **17.11**). Unless a decision is made to vote additional remuneration or to pay a bonus before the year a corporation tax deduction appears to be prohibited (See *Taxation*, 20 April 2006, *Directors' remuneration – A not so simple question*, Tim Good).

Ideally a written service agreement between the company and the director should be put in place. In order to confirm the deductibility of payments when voted for corporation tax purposes, it is imperative that a formal decision be made before the end of the accounting period. A written record of any informal decision made by the members should be supplied to the company as soon as possible. Alternatively a separate written shareholder agreement outside of the memorandum and articles of association, granting an entitlement to remuneration for an accounting period but quantifying the amount after the end of accounting period, may be considered in order to satisfy the GAAP requirements.

## ALLOWABLE DEDUCTIONS

**5.16**

| *Item* | *Explanation* | *References* |
|---|---|---|
| General | Statutory rules on deductions under Schedule D Cases I and II are to be found in *ICTA 1988, ss 817, 74*(*1*), which operate in a negative way by stating what cannot be deducted rather than what is allowed. The Courts' interpretation of the Taxes Acts is based on the principle that if an item of expenditure is an allowable deduction in line with ordinary accounting rules then it should be allowed under the Acts unless expressly prohibited. The business purposes must be the sole purpose for the transaction. Where there is a 'mixed' purpose, say providing additional amounts to employees, the amounts are assessed on the individual through the PAYE and benefits system. The deduction is not restricted in the company, unless it is totally disallowed by statute or because the payment is not 'wholly and exclusively' for the purposes of the trade.<br>The following expenses are allowable where indicated unless capital or failing the wholly and exclusively test. | HMRC Business Income Manual BIM 42060 for prohibitions under *ICTA 1988, s 74*(*1*), (*2*) dealing with Schedule D Cases I and II. Specific rules for deductions including Schedule D Cases I and II are set out in HMRC Business Income Manual BIM 42070. |

| *Item* | *Explanation* | *References* |
|---|---|---|
| Administration | Costs a company occurs in ordinary annual expenditure on such matters as the keeping of the share register, the printing of annual accounts, and the holding of shareholders' AGMs are normally allowed as trading expenses. Also, the annual cost of a Stock Exchange quotation and the fees paid to newspapers for the inclusion of the company's shares in the newspaper's report of Stock Exchange prices and annual fees paid to trustees for debenture holders or mortgagees are treated as allowable expenses. The cost of valuations, normally of land and buildings, made for the purpose of inflation accounting. Valuation costs required by the Companies Act to be included in the director's report attached to the balance sheet are allowed. Costs incurred in maintaining historic business archives will generally be allowable expenses. Company expenditure on the provision of access to archives and on linked educational services is normally also usually allowable. | HMRC Business Income Manuals BIM 42501, BIM 42510, BIM 42540. |

| *Item* | *Explanation* | *References* |
|---|---|---|
| Advertising | Ordinary current expenditure on advertising a company's goods or services is normally allowable. Sponsorship costs are allowable in arriving at the profits of a company unless they are considered to be capital expenditure or the expenditure is not made wholly and exclusively for business purposes, in which case it is specifically disallowed. Sums paid as sponsorship to support the personal hobbies and pastimes of a shareholders family were held not to be deductible from trading profits.<br>A company may obtain relief in certain circumstances under the intangible assets regime (see Chapter 7). | HMRC Business Income Manuals BIM 42551, BIM 42555, BIM 42560, BIM 42565.<br>*Executive Network (Consultants) Ltd v O'Connor* [1996] STC (SCD) 29. |
| Annuities and annual payments | An annuity or an annual payment is disallowed as a business deduction in accounts under *ICTA 1988, s 74(1)(m)*. In general terms an annual payment will be (a) paid under a legal obligation, (b) annually recurring and (c) pure income profit in the hands of the recipient but may be allowed as a charge on income (see **9.8**, **9.15**). | HMRC Business Income Manual BIM 42601.<br>*Gresham Life Assurance Society v Styles* (1890) 2 TC 633, (1890) 3 TC 185, [1892] AC 309. |

| *Item* | *Explanation* | *References* |
|---|---|---|
| Bad and doubtful debts impairment losses | No deduction may be allowed for an impairment loss or a bad debt under *ICTA 1988, s 88D* except for any debts under *ICTA 1988, s 74(1)(j)*, except:<br>(a) A confirmed bad debt or a doubtful debt – amount estimated to be bad, ie the debt less any amount expected to be received on the debt.<br>(b) A debt or part of a debt released by the creditor wholly and exclusively for the purposes of his trade as a relevant arrangement or compromise (voluntary arrangement under the *Insolvency Act 1986* and compromise under *CA 1985, s 425*).<br>Accountancy practice accepts that events arising after the balance sheet date and before accounts are finalised may need to be reflected in the provision for bad and doubtful debts. See FRS 21 Chapter 17. HMRC interpretation requires that the debt existed at the balance sheet date and the creditor at that date had no reason to believe that payment would not be made, but before the accounts were finalised it was discovered that the financial position of the debtor at the balance sheet date was such that the amount due was unlikely to be paid in part or fully. | HMRC Business Income Manuals BIM 42701, BIM 42705, BIM 42710, BIM 42715, BIM 42720, BIM 42725, BIM 42730, BIM 42735, BIM 42740.<br>*Bristow v Dickson (William) & Co Ltd* (1946) 27 TC 157, [1946] KB 321, [1946] 1 All ER 448. |

| Item | Explanation | References |
|---|---|---|
| | Where an amount claimed as a deduction represents a waiver or partial waiver for reasons other than the financial position of the debtor, the deduction may not be allowable. It may, however, be admissible as a special discount or trade allowance. Likewise, habitual slow payers are inadmissible. | |
| | Where a deduction for a bad or doubtful debt has been made and the company recovers the debt or an amount of its written-down value. The amount recovered or the excess should be brought into the year of recovery. | |
| | Companies can accept assets in satisfaction of trading debts. Where the market value of the asset at the date of acceptance of the asset is less than the amount of the outstanding debt the shortfall may be allowable as a deduction. However, the company must agree to account as a trading receipt any excess as a result of the disposal of the asset. The excess is excluded from CGT (*TCGA 1992, s 251*(*3*)). | |
| Capital | Capital payments are disallowed. A company's initial contribution to a staff pension fund was a capital payment because it was made not only once and for all, but with a view to bringing into existence an asset or an advantage for the enduring benefit of trade. | *Atherton v British Insulated and Helsby Cables Ltd* (1925) 10 TC 155, [1926] AC 205. |

| *Item* | *Explanation* | *References* |
|---|---|---|
| Car or motor cycle hire | Where the retail price of new vehicle exceeds £12,000 and is hired for the purposes of the trade the hire charge is reduced for tax purposes by using the formula (12,000 + P) ÷ 2P where P is the retail price of the vehicle when new. | HMRC Business Income Manuals BIM 47715–47720. *Lloyds UDT Finance Ltd v Britax International GmBH* (2002) 74 TC 662, [2002] STC 956, [2002] EWCA Civ 806 (*ICTA 1988, s 578A*). |
| Compensa-tion and damages | Compensation and damages payments depend on the circumstances of the payment. A compensation payment may be reduced by the reimbursement of trading expenses allowable as a deduction. Compensation and damages payments require to be 'wholly and exclusively' for trade purposes and on 'revenue account'. Where compensation relates to normal trading activity and not an identifiable capital asset, it will be an allowable deduction. Compensation for termination of an agency was held to be a trading expense. | HMRC Business Income Manual BIM 42950+ *Anglo-Persian Oil Co Ltd v Dale* (1931) 16 TC 253, [1932] 1 KB 124. |
| Computer software | Expenditure may either be capital or revenue expenditure. See **6.14**. | CAA 2001, ss 71–73. |
| Counselling services | Expenditure on employee counselling and other outplacement services, which fall within the earnings exemption of *ITEPA 2003*, is deductible in computing profits. | *ICTA 1988, ss 589A, 589B* |
| Crime | 'No deduction shall be made for any expenditure incurred in making a payment, the making of which constitutes a criminal payment' | HMRC Business Income Manual BIM 43100 + *ICTA 1988, s 577A(1), (1)(a).* |

| *Item* | *Explanation* | *References* |
|---|---|---|
| Defalcations/ embezzlement | Funds misappropriated by a director then claimed as a remuneration payment on which PAYE was to be paid were held not to be an allowable deduction for corporation tax purposes. Losses are allowed as deductions but not misappropriations by a director. Defalcations made good are taxable. | *Bamford v ATA Advertising* (1972) 48 TC 359, [1972] 1 WLR 1261, [1972] 3 All ER 535; *Curtis v Oldfield (J & G) Ltd* (1925) 9 TC 319; *Gray v Penrhyn (Lord)* (1937) 21 TC 252, [1937] 3 All ER 468. |
| Dilapidations | Where the costs of repairs at the end of a lease, called dilapidations, would be the same if the repairs had been undertaken during the course of the lease period, and are not of a capital nature, then they should be allowable (*ICTA 1988, s 74*(*1*)(*d*)). At the expiry of the lease the lessee may agree to pay a sum, compensation in lieu of accrued repairs, to the lessor. This payment is allowable if it does not reflect capital costs. | HMRC Business Income Manuals BIM 43250, BIM 43251, BIM 43255, BIM 43260, BIM 43265. *Hyett v Lennard* (1940) 23 TC 346, [1940] 2 KB 180, [1940] 3 All ER 133. |
| Employees' or directors' remuneration | Remuneration wholly and exclusively for the purposes of trade is deductible. See **5.14**, **5.15**. Remuneration paid to connected parties, say to shareholder's family, must be on arm's-length terms. | *Stott and Ingham v Trehearne* (1924) 9 TC 69; *Earlspring Properties Ltd v Guest* (1995) 67 TC 259, [1995] STC 479; *Robinson v Scott Bader & Co Ltd* (1981) 54 TC 757, [1981] STC 436, [1981] 1 WLR 1135, [1981] 2 All ER 1116. |
| Employees seconded to charities and educational bodies | When an employee is seconded to a charity or an education body on a temporary basis, the expenditure attributable to the employment is deductible. | *ICTA 1988, s 86.* |

| *Item* | *Explanation* | *References* |
|---|---|---|
| Fines | Usually fines are disallowed, as they are not incurred wholly and exclusively for the purpose of trade – as confirmed in case law. Penalties for breaches of trading regulations are disallowed. Legal costs in defending a business were allowable. Costs of civil actions in connection with company formations were held to be allowable. In situations where the employer pays a fine (eg parking) that is in fact the liability of the employee, the cost to the employer will be allowable in determining his trading profit and the employee will be chargeable on the emolument arising. Fines resulting from civil actions arising out of trade may be allowed if not punitive. Interest payable on overseas tax may be deducted but not if it relates to a capital tax or overseas tax penalty. VAT penalties and repayment supplements are not deductible. | *CIR v Alexander von Glehn & Co Ltd* (1920) 12 TC 232, [1920] 2 KB 553; *McKnight v Sheppard* (1999) 71 TC 419, [1999] STC 669, [1999] 1 WLR 1133, [1999] 3 All ER 491; *Golder v Great Boulder Proprietary Gold Mines Ltd* (1952) 33 TC 75, [1952] 1 All ER 360. HMRC Business Income Manuals BIM 31610, BIM 45101, BIM 42515. |
| Franchise payments | An appropriate part of the initial franchise fee will be considered a revenue payment if the items it represents are revenue items and are not separately charged for in the continuing fees. | HMRC Business Income Manuals BIM 57600–57620. |

| *Item* | *Explanation* | *References* |
|---|---|---|
| Gifts | Business gifts are not allowed as a deduction against profits (*ICTA 1988, s 577*). Included in 'gifts' are goods and services supplied below cost. An exception is gifts with a value of less than £50, containing the company's advertisement and not related to food, drink or tobacco will be allowed as a deduction.<br>Free samples given to the public are not gifts.<br>Gifts to charities are not disallowed.<br>Sales promotion scheme gifts to customers are not disallowed provided the customer is obliged to do or give something in return. | HMRC Business Income Manuals BIM 45065, BIM 45070, BIM 45071, BIM 45072, BIM 45085. *ICTA 1988, s 577*(*9*). ESC B7 |
| Guarantee payments | A payment under a loan guarantee is deductible only if the 'wholly and exclusively for the purpose of trade' concept is met at the time it was made and a capital advantage is not secured. Guarantees between grouped and/or associated companies may not fulfil these conditions. It may fall within loan relationships see Chapter 11.<br>Payments under guarantee in respect of an associated company were held to be capital expenditure.<br>An exhibition guarantee payment made in order to secure work was considered to be an allowable deduction. | *Milnes v J Beam Group Ltd* (1975) 50 TC 675, [1975] STC 487; *Garforth v Tankard Carpets Ltd* (1980) 53 TC 342, [1980] STC 251; *Redkite v Inspector of Taxes* [1996] STC (SCD) 501; *Morley v Lawford & Co* (1928) 14 TC 229.<br>HMRC Business Income Manuals BIM 45301, BIM 45305. |

| *Item* | *Explanation* | *References* |
|---|---|---|
| Hire Purchase | Revenue payments for the hire of an asset are deductible but capital payments for the purchase of an asset are not.<br>Payments under a hire purchase agreement split between amounts for hire (allowable) and payments for the eventual purchase (capital).<br>If ownership of the equipment passes to the purchaser at the time of signing the agreement and payment is via an extra charge then these payments are capital expenditure.<br>Cost of repairs and renewal to hire purchase assets are allowable as a deduction.<br>Note: The accountancy treatment for hire-purchase contracts governed by SSAP 21. | HMRC Business Income Manual BIM 45351.<br>*Darngavil Coal Co Ltd v Francis* (1931) 7 TC 1.<br>Also HMRC Business Income Manuals BIM 45355, BIM 45360, BIM 45365 |
| Holding company formation expenses | This is treated as capital expenditure and is not deductible | *Kealy v O'Mara (Limerick) Ltd* [1942] 2 ITC 265; [1942] IR 616. |
| Incentive and reward schemes | Expenditure on performance related awards and incentive schemes, which satisfy all of the following conditions, may be allowable if (a) the award requires to be based on genuine performance achievement and (b) a formal scheme based on known rules is in place.<br>Suggestion scheme awards are treated in a similar manner provided the award is reasonable. | HMRC Business Income Manual BIM 45080. |

| *Item* | *Explanation* | *References* |
|---|---|---|
| Insurance | Policies, which provide indemnity for loss or damage to fixed or intangible assets, current assets, are allowable if the business purpose requirement is satisfied (*ICTA 1988, s 74(1)(a)*). Insurance proceeds for stock lost are assessable as trading income. Premiums for policies covering (a) fire at company's premises, (b) interruption or loss of use of income producing assets, (c) interruption or cessation of the supply of raw materials, or (d) events causing loss of profits for a temporary period, are allowable deductions from trading profits. Insurance receipts in connection with the trade are taxed as trading receipts. Insurance policy premiums to cover professional negligence and employee indemnity risks are usually allowable as a deduction. | HMRC Business Income Manuals BIM 45501, BIM 45505, BIM 45510, BIM 45515, BIM 45520, BIM 45525, BIM 45530. *Green v Gliksten (J) & Son Ltd* (1929) 14 TC 364, [1929] AC 381; *Mallandain Investments Ltd v Shadbolt* (1940) 23 TC 367. |
| Interest on director's property loan | Where interest is paid by a company on a loan (not overdraft) taken out by a director to purchase land or buildings occupied rent-free by the company and used for business purposes, it is considered that the company can obtain relief as a trading expense for the interest in the normal way and that the payments would not normally constitute either remuneration or a benefit of the director. | *ICTA 1988, s 74(1)(a)*. HMRC Business Income Manual BIM 45755 |

| *Item* | *Explanation* | *References* |
|---|---|---|
| Key employee insurance | Premiums on policies in favour of the employer insuring against death or critical illness of key employees are generally allowable, and the proceeds of any such policies are treated as trading receipts.<br>Keyman insurance proceeds were taxable as receipts of the trade.<br>Premiums on policies taken out as a condition of loan finance are not deductible. See **11.15** regarding loan relationship expenses.<br>Life assurance receipts paid to a company in respect of insurance taken out at the request of a shareholder to guarantee the company's bank overdraft were held not to be receipts of the trade and were not taxable. | HMRC Business Income Manuals BIM 45525, BIM 45530.<br>*Keir & Cawder Ltd v CIR* (1958) 38 TC 23;<br>*Greycon Ltd v Klaentschi* [2003] STC (SCD) 370. |

| *Item* | *Explanation* | *References* |
|---|---|---|
| Legal expenses | Legal expenses incurred in maintaining existing trading rights and assets are revenue expenses.<br>The legal costs of defending an overseas branch's title to land in the foreign courts, which it used for the purposes of its trade was deductible from profits.<br>Expenditure on defending a company from public ownership and thereby the prevention of the seizure of its business and assets was held to be an allowable business expense.<br>The cost of tax appeals even though successful is not deductible. Additional accountancy expenses incurred as a result of 'in-depth' examination by HMRC will be allowed if this results in no discrepancies. If there are discrepancies the costs are not allowable even if the investigation reveals no addition to profits.<br>Costs of an appeal before the Special Commissioners was disallowed.<br>A premium for insuring against the costs incurred in the case of a tax enquiry are allowable, only to the extent that the costs insured against would themselves be allowable. If the premium covers the cost of accountancy fees incurred in negotiating additional liabilities resulting from negligent or fraudulent conduct, it is not deductible. Apportionment is not permitted. | *Southern v Borax Consolidated* (1940) 23 TC 598, [1941] 1 KB 111, [1940] 4 All ER 412; *Morgan v Tate & Lyle Ltd* (1954) 35 TC 367, [1954] AC 21, [1954] 2 All ER 413; *Allen v Farquharson Bros & Co* (1932) 17 TC 59.<br>EM 9010.<br>Statement of Practice SP 16/91.<br>HMRC Business Income Manual BIM 46452 |
| Loan finance | See loan relationships Chapter 11 | |

| *Item* | *Explanation* | *References* |
|---|---|---|
| Losses | Losses arising in the normal course of trading are allowable. Losses arising from theft or misappropriation by directors are not allowable.<br>Note: Foreign exchange gains and losses are dealt under the loan relationship provisions see Chapter 11. | *Curtis v Oldfield (J & G) Ltd* (1925) 9 TC 319; *Bamford v ATA Advertising Ltd* (1972) 48 TC 359, [1972] 1 WLR 1261, [1972] 3 All ER 535.<br>HMRC Business Income Manual BIM 45850+ |
| Management expenses | HMRC will accept reasonable management expenses allocations to group companies of expenses incurred by a group service company on their behalf. HMRC will investigate arrangements where expenditure is incurred by one company for the purposes of the trade of another that is outside the scope of UK tax. However, expenses relating to the trade of one group company will not be allowable against the separate trade of another group member. | HMRC Business Income Manual BIM 42140 |
| National Insurance Contributions | Secondary Class 1 NICs are deductible in computing profits, as are Class 1A NICs and Class 1B NICs. | *ICTA 1988, s 617(3)–(5).* |
| Onerous contract | Payment of a sum of money to remove a company from an onerous trading contract was considered to be a trading expense.<br>A payment by a company to secure release of an option over a trade investment was held to be a trading expense. | *Vodafone Cellular v Shaw* (1997) 69 TC 376, [1997] STC 734 (see HMRC Business Income Manual BIM 38220 for details); *Walker v Cater Securities Ltd* (1974) 49 TC 625, [1974] STC 390, [1974] 1 WLR 1363, [1974] 3 All ER 63. |

| *Item* | *Explanation* | *References* |
|---|---|---|
| Overseas taxes | Tax of an overseas country charged on the profits arising in that country will be available for tax credit relief in most cases. A deduction may in certain circumstances arise for taxes of a capital nature. Interest payable on overseas tax may be admitted as a Schedule D Case I deduction – this does not extend to overseas tax penalties. (See Chapter 13 generally regarding overseas taxes.) | HMRC Business Income Manuals BIM 45901, BIM 45905. *Harrods* (*Buenos Aires*) *Ltd v Taylor-Gooby* (1964) 41 TC 450. |
| Patents and royalties | See Chapter 7 Intangible Assets. | |
| Payments in lieu of notice | Payments in lieu of notice on a cessation of trade were held to be an allowable deduction. | *O'Keefe v Southport Printers Ltd* (1984) 58 TC 88, [1984] STC 443; |
| Political expenses | No deductions are allowable for party political expenditure but propaganda costs to prevent the loss of business and protect assets may be allowable. | *Morgan v Tate and Lyle Ltd* (1954) 35 TC 367, [1955] AC 21, [1954] 2 All ER 413. HMRC Business Income Manual BIM 46210. |
| Premiums | Payment of premiums for premises used for trading purposes is an allowable deduction under Schedule D Cases I, II where the lessor is liable under *ICTA 1988, ss 34, 35*. | HMRC Business Income Manuals BIM 46251, BIM 46255, BIM 46260, BIM 46265. |

| *Item* | *Explanation* | *References* |
|---|---|---|
| Pre-trading expenditure | Relief is given under *ICTA 1988, s 401* for allowable business expenditure incurred in the seven years prior to the commencement of a trade. Relief is given in the accounting period in which trade commences, covers relief for pre-trading expenditure for certain revenue items, which satisfy the test under *ICTA 1988, s 74(1)(a)*. | HMRC Business Income Manual BIM 46351 |
| Procurement fees | Procuring others to enter into a tax avoidance scheme was not considered to be a trade | *Ransom v Higgs* (1974) 50 TC 1, [1974] STC 539, [1974] 1 WLR 1594, [1974] 3 All ER 949. |

| *Item* | *Explanation* | *References* |
|---|---|---|
| Professional fees | Professional fees are not allowable if they are of a capital nature or excluded by statute. Costs of an unsuccessful planning application were held to be capital expenditure. A company's in-house professional fees in relation to work involved with the company's capital assets are not allowed. Fees for the maintenance of a company's assets, facilities or trading rights are normally revenue expenses and allowable but fees in relation to rights or facilities of a capital nature are capital expenses. Costs in relation to renewal of a short lease (less than 50 years to run) are revenue and allowable. Otherwise the amounts are capital. A company's costs of promoting private Bills for the improvement of facilities was held not to be an allowable deduction. Fees in relation to raising equity finance including purchase of own shares are capital. Fees in relation to the preparation of business accounts and other accountancy services are normally allowable. Insurance charges to cover the risk of incurring additional costs are only allowable if the additional costs are of a revenue nature. The acquirer's fees in relation to take-overs are normally capital. The target's fees are capital if in relation to the structure, but revenue if in connection with protecting the trade. | *ECC Quarries Ltd v Watkis* (1975) 51 TC 153, [1975] STC 578, [1975] 3 All ER 843; *Moore (A & G) & Co v Hare* (1941) 6 TC 572. HMRC Business Income Manuals BIM 46405, BIM 46410, BIM 46415, BIM 46420, BIM 46425, BIM 46450, BIM 46452, BIM 46460. |

| *Item* | *Explanation* | *References* |
|---|---|---|
| Provisions | If a provision in the accounts satisfies the following requirements: (a) it has been estimated with reasonable accuracy, (b) it does not conflict with any statutory rules, (c) it relates to revenue and not capital expenditure and (d) agrees with UK GAAP and FRS 12 principles, it may be allowable. Case law has disallowed provision in accounts held to be capital expenditure and a company's provisions calculation as it was held to be insufficiently accurate. To comply with FRS 12 it may be necessary to discount the provision to present value if it is material. | *RTZ Oil & Gas Ltd v Ellis* (1987) 61 TC 132, [1987] STC 512, [1987] 1 WLR 1442; *Owen v Southern Railway of Peru Ltd* (1956) 36 TC 602, [1957] AC 334, [1956] 2 All ER 728. HMRC Business Income Manual BIM 46510+ |
| Redundancy payments | To be allowed under Schedule D Cases I, II redundancy payments are required to be wholly and exclusively for employer's trade and the company does not acquire capital assets or rights (eg restrictive covenants). Redundancy payments in connection with the discontinuance of a trade are not allowable. Statutory redundancy payments are permitted under *ICTA 1988, ss 90, 579*. However, in this case, redundancy payments were allowed because the company had a contractual requirement to make the payments. | *ICTA 1988, ss 579, 580, 90.* *CIR v Anglo Brewing Co Ltd* (1925) 12 TC 803; *Hong Kong Commissioner of Inland Revenue v Cosmotron Manufacturing Co* (1997) 70 TC 292, [1997] STC 1134, [1997] 1 WLR 1288. HMRC Business Income Manual BIM 47200 +. |

| *Item* | *Explanation* | *References* |
|---|---|---|
| Removal expenses | Reasonable employee removal costs due to an employee's change of residence at the employer's request are allowable. Profits arising from the purchase and sale of the employee's earlier residence are taxed as a trading receipt. | HMRC Business Income Manual BIM 42531 |
| Rent and rates | Costs associated with a company's premises including rent, rates, repairs, insurance will normally be allowed. | HMRC Business Income Manual BIM 46801+ |
| Repairs and renewals | Repair costs are normally regarded as revenue expenditure. Repair by replacement with a new asset is capital expenditure. Mere replacement of parts that are defective by the renewal of those parts is considered to be revenue expenditure<br>Note concept of 'entirety' used by courts. Any repair expenditure resulting in an improvement or upgrade to an asset, is capital expenditure. See **5.10**. | HMRC Business Income Manual BIM 46900<br>*Brown v Burnley Football & Athletic Co Ltd* (1980) 53 TC 357, [1980] STC 424, [1980] 3 All ER 244; *Transco plc v Dyall* [2002] STC (SCD) 199. |
| Restrictive covenants with employees | Where a business makes a restrictive covenant with an employee to protect its trade, if the employee leaves, then, under *FA 1988, s 73*(2), the employer may claim relief, only if the employee receives a payment as part of the agreement (which is taxable under *ITEPA 2003, s 225*). | HMRC Business Income Manuals BIM 47005, BIM 35595, BIM 35510. |

| *Item* | *Explanation* | *References* |
|---|---|---|
| Security expenditure | Where a company needs to protect its employee from a special security threat because of the nature of the company's business then the revenue expenditure incurred in providing the required security measures are likely to be allowed if all the qualifying conditions are met under *ITTOIA 2005, s 81.* | HMRC Business Income Manual BIM 47301+ |
| Subsidies, grants | Grants to a company under *Industrial Development Act 1982, s 7* or *s 8* are trading receipts unless grant is specifically capital expenditure or as compensation for loss of capital assets. | *ICTA 1988, s 93. ITTOIA 2005, Sch 1, para 72.* |
| Subscriptions | Generally, charitable and political subscriptions are not allowable. Small local or trade charity subscriptions with a trade connection may be allowed. Subscriptions paid by a company to a professional body, which is assessed under Schedule D Case I, may be allowable. | HMRC Business Income Manual BIM 47400+ |
| Tied licence premises | Receipts and expenses in respect of tied premises are accounted as trading receipts and expenses rather than under Schedule A. Improvements to tied premises are treated as capital. | *ICTA 1988, s 98. ITTOIA 2005, Sch 1, para 77. Usher's Wiltshire Brewery v Bruce* (1914) 6 TC 399, [1915] AC 433; *Mann Crossman & Paulin Ltd v Compton* (1947) 28 TC 410, [1947] 1 All ER 742. |

| *Item* | *Explanation* | *References* |
|---|---|---|
| Tied petrol stations | Exclusivity payments made to retailers by petroleum companies were allowed in computing the petroleum companies' profits. In the hands of the retailer they are either capital or revenue depending upon expenditure. Payments were held to be trading receipts rather than capital receipts. | *Bolam v Regent Oil Co Ltd* (1956) 37 TC 56, [1956] TR 403; *Tanfield Ltd v Carr* [1999] STC (SCD) 213. |
| Trade organisations | Company contributions to an industrial training board for its industry or trade are allowable. | HMRC Business Income Manual BIM 47600+ *ICTA 1988, ss 79, 79A, 79B.* |
| Training, education and welfare | A company's expenditure on training, education and welfare are normally allowed. | HMRC Business Income Manual BIM 47080 |
| Travel and subsistence | Reasonable expenses incurred by an employee on an occasional business journey (or overnight subsistence and accommodation when away from home on business) may be allowed. The allowable costs for hiring a car for business purposes are restricted under *ICTA 1988, s 578A.* | HMRC Business Income Manuals BIM 47705, BIM 47710, BIM 47715, BIM 47717, BIM 47720. |
| Unsuccessful applications | The expenses of unsuccessful applications for licences were held to be not allowable – the company accepted that expenses of successful applications are capital. Costs for variation of a licence were not an allowable deduction. | *Southwell v Savill Bros* (1901) 4 TC 430, [1901] 2 KB 349; *Pyrah v Annis & Co Ltd* (1956) 37 TC 163, [1957] 1 WLR 190, [1957] 1 All ER 196. |

## APPROPRIATIONS OF PROFIT

**5.17** Appropriations of profits, ie a distribution or dividend payment, are not deductible from profits. UK corporation tax payments themselves are not deductible and neither are payments from which tax has been deducted at source. Depreciation is disallowed but capital allowances are deductible as a trading expense (*CAA 2001, s 352*).

The full amount of depreciation must be added back in the corporation tax computation regardless of any other entry (*William Grant & Sons Distillers Ltd v CIR* [2004] STC (SCD) 253).

**5.18** Lease amortisation is given if a premium is paid on a short lease (less than 50 years) to a landlord assessable under Schedule A. The permitted deduction is the premium paid less 2% for every year of the lease except the first, spread over the duration of the lease. Capital expenditure is specifically disallowed. See **5.10**.

## Income that has not been included in profits in the accounts but which is taxable under Schedule D Case I

**5.19** If a company is operating GAAP correctly, there are unlikely to be any items not credited in the accounts, but circumstances vary between every company.

A transfer pricing adjustment increases taxable profits but never decreases chargeable profits. See **14.23**. Credits may arise under the intangible assets regime. See **7.17–7.20**.

## Income credited in the accounts but not taxable under Schedule D Case I

**5.20** In the main this will include items taxable under another schedule such as Rent – Schedule A, interest Schedule D Case III and sundry income Schedule D Case VI.

## Expenditure that has not been charged against profits in the accounts but which is allowable under Schedule D Case I

**5.21** If the company is operating GAAP there should not be too many expenses that fall into this category. As mentioned above capital allowances are not charged in the accounts but are allowed as a trading deduction.

# EMPLOYEE INCENTIVES

**5.22** Specific statutory deductions are given for the costs of setting up 'approved' employee share schemes known as SIP (share incentive plans), SAYE (savings-related share option schemes), CSOP (company share option plans) and APS (approved profit share schemes) (*ICTA 1988, s 84A, Sch 4AA, para 7*), QUEST (qualifying employee share ownership trusts) (*ICTA 1988, s 85A*). This is on the proviso that the share schemes are approved within nine months of the end of the accounting period in which they are charged and that the share ownership trust is executed within nine months of the end of the accounting period in which its expenditure is charged. If the criteria is not met in that accounting period the expenditure is carried forward to the next accounting period until it is met (*ICTA 1988, ss 84A(3ZA), 85A(3)*).

Normally a company's incidental running costs for an employee share scheme investing in 'qualifying shares', is a deduction under Schedule D. Shares that are not 'qualifying shares' under *FA 2003, Sch 23* do not qualify for relief (HMRC Business Income Manual BIM 44450). Relief under *FA 2003, Sch 23* is given under Schedule D Case I or Schedule A for trades and Schedule A businesses, *ICTA 1988, s 75* for companies with investment business and *ICTA 1988, s 76* for assurance companies. Qualifying shares must be fully paid-up, non redeemable ordinary shares (HMRC Business Income Manual BIM 44290). The employing company will qualify for a deduction for the costs of the shares except where the business is taken over by a successor company unless the companies are 51% members of the same group (*FA 2003, Sch 23, paras 16, 23*; HMRC Business Income Manual BIM 44295). Revenue-approved schemes and unapproved schemes, which satisfy the conditions previously mentioned, will be qualifying shares. It is also a requirement that the share options (or awards) are made by the employing company, which must be chargeable to corporation tax on the profits of its business.

In a group situation normally the employer will be able to claim the deduction. Under FRS 20 the reporting entity will typically measure the value of the services received in return for share-based payments by reference to the 'fair value' of the share-based payment. Intra group payments should represent arm's-length prices (Transfer-pricing and employee share plans – guidance for accounting periods beginning on or after 1 January 2005).

Relief is also given for the cost of providing employee share scheme shares (*FA 2003, Sch 23, para 8*). Full relief is given to a company offering EMI options by matching relief for the company with both the amount taxed on the employee and the amount on which income tax relief is given under the EMI scheme (*FA 2006, s 93*).

## Shares acquired under EMI option before FA 2006

**5.23** From 1 January 2003, an employer company receives corporation tax relief on an amount being the difference between the market value of the shares at the time the employee exercises an option and the price the employee pays. The relief is given in the accounting period in which the option is exercised and the shares acquired (*FA 2003, Sch 23, paras 15, 16*). The relief applies to enterprise management investment (EMI) scheme options, company share option plans (CSOP), unapproved share option plans and share acquisitions where the employee is subject to tax. The shares must be ordinary shares in a listed company, single company or holding company.

For share incentive plans (SIP) the company employer receives a corporation tax deduction for the market value of the shares in the accounting period in which they are awarded (*ITEPA 2003, s 488, Sch 2*).

---

**Example 5.1**

Longtemps Ltd granted its eligible employee Mr A EMI options over 1,000 shares, to be exercised at the current market price of £3 per share. Two years later when Mr A exercises the option the shares are worth £10 each.

As the option arrangement required Mr A to pay a price equal to the market value of the shares at the grant, there is no income tax on the exercise of this option. *ITEPA 2003, s 530* applies.

Longtemps Ltd can claim corporation tax deduction for the accounting period in which Mr A acquired ownership of the shares as follows:

| | £ |
|---|---|
| Value at exercise | 10,000 |
| Less amount paid | 3,000 |
| Corporation tax deduction (*FA 2003, Sch 23, para 8*) | 7,000 |

Without the EMI share option arrangement, Mr A would normally be charged to income tax on £7,000 (*ITEPA 2003, s 476*). The company may still claim a deduction under *FA 2003, Sch 23, para 8.*

---

**5.24** Relief for restricted shares has been introduced by *FA 2006, s 93(2)*, which is treated as applying to the acquisition of shares from the exercise of EMI options on or after 1 September 2003, the date on which the restricted and convertible shares income tax legislation in *Finance Act 2003* came into force. Prior to *FA 2006* no relief was available.

---

**Example 5.2—Pre *FA 2006***

B is granted EMI options over 1,000 shares, to be exercised at a discount of 50% to the current market value of £1, where the shares to be acquired are restricted. When B exercises his options, the unrestricted market value of the share is £5, but, because B has no voting rights for three years, the actual market value is only £3. As the options were granted at a discount *ITEPA 2003, s 531* rather than *s 530* applies.

The acquisition of shares is a chargeable event and the *ITEPA 2003, s 476* income tax charge on the employee is calculated as follows:

| | £ |
|---|---|
| Value at exercise | |
| Value of grant | 1,000 |
| Less consideration | nil |
| Amount paid for shares | 500 |
| Employee taxable amount | 500 |
| Corporation tax relief (*FA 2003, Sch 23, para 21*(3)) | 500 |

**Example 5.3—Post *FA 2006***

The employee has made an income tax saving being the difference between the exercise price and the amount paid for the shares. If an election were made under *ITEPA 2003, s 431* the unrestricted value can be taken as the exercise price, which will increase the potential savings. The same relief is now taken for corporation tax purposes.

| | *Income tax saved*<br>£ | *Income tax saved with an election under* ITEPA 2003, s 431<br>£ |
|---|---|---|
| Value at exercise | 3,000 | 5,000 |
| Value of grant | | |
| Less consideration | — | — |
| Amount paid for shares | 500 | 500 |
| Income tax saved on | 2,500 | 4,500 |
| Corporation tax relief (*FA 2003, Sch 23, para 21*(3)) | 2,500 | 4,500 |

**5.25** These changes apply to the acquisition of shares from the exercise of EMI options on or after 1 September 2003, the date on which the restricted and convertible shares income tax legislation in *FA 2003* came into force.

## Employee benefit trusts

**5.26** An employee benefit trust (EBT) is a discretionary trust set up by an employer for the benefit of its employees and directors. EBTs can be resident in the UK or offshore, and can be subject to UK or foreign law. An 'offshore' EBT is only liable to UK income tax on its UK source income and is not liable to UK capital gains tax. An EBT is managed by trustees, who are usually appointed by the company. The trust fund will comprise of: (a) the initial amount settled by the employer to establish the trust, (b) subsequent contributions from the employer, and (c) sums paid to the trustees by third parties. The beneficiaries and life of the EBT will be defined in the trust deed (HMRC Business Income Manual BIM 44501+). EBTs are used with employee share schemes, retirement benefit schemes, accident benefit schemes and healthcare trusts. EBTs set up with employee benefit schemes are called employee share ownership trusts (ESOT); they can also be known as employee share ownership plans (ESOP) trusts. ESOTs may be used by unquoted companies to provide a market for employees' shares (acquired through employee share schemes) that might otherwise not exist, maintain shareholder control and help with business planning and management buy-outs. Established case law has determined that where the trust is set up for the benefit of employees that the contributions meet the 'wholly and exclusively' test (*Heather v P-E Consulting Group Ltd* (1972) 48 TC 293, [1973] Ch 189, [1973] 1 All ER 8; *Rutter v Charles Sharpe & Co Ltd* (1979) 53 TC 163, [1979] STC 711, [1979] 1 WLR 1429; *Jeffs v Ringtons Ltd* (1985) 58 TC 680, [1985] STC 809, [1986] 1 WLR 266, [1986] 1 All ER 144; *E Bott Ltd v Price* (1986) 59 TC 437, [1987] STC 100). In *Mawsley Machinery Ltd v Robinson* [1998] SSCD 236 the 'wholly and exclusively' test was not met because the reason for the contributions was to facilitate a share purchase (HMRC Business Income Manual BIM 44155).

Providing healthcare benefits for employees is an allowable deduction in computing taxable profits of a company. However, there will be a liability to Class 1A NICs for the employer and income tax for the employee. General purpose EBTs can be set up for genuine business reasons and for use in avoidance, for example the payment of income tax by employees and Class 1A NICs by employers.

The timing of the employer's deduction and employee's liability to IT and employer's to NIC is governed by *FA 2003, Sch 24*.

If a close company settles assets in a discretionary trust for the benefit of shareholders in the company those deductions are disallowed and there may arise a lifetime IHT charge on the shareholders in proportion to their shareholdings. However, there are no IHT consequences if a close company makes a contribution to an EBT, which is allowed as a deduction in computing a company's taxable profits (*IHTA 1984, s 12*; HMRC Business Income Manual BIM 44550).There is no corporation tax deduction for amounts put into an EBT by an employer until the amount becomes taxable earnings of the employee (*FA 2003, Sch 23, para 1*). Pension and accident benefit schemes are excluded. With effect from 2 December 2004, securities and options are included as benefits (*FA(No2) 2005, s 12, Sch 2*; *MacDonald v Dextra Accessories Ltd* [2005] UKHL 47, [2005] STC 1111).

# PENSION CONTRIBUTIONS

**5.27** Payments to a pension scheme are a revenue expense and will be deductible from profits if the payment meets the wholly and exclusively for the purposes of the trade test. Staff pension contributions are allowable unless there is an identifiable non-trade purpose. Contributions in respect of a controlling director or an employee who is a close friend or relative of the controlling director or proprietor of the business may be queried by HMRC. In establishing whether a payment is for the purposes of the trade they will examine the company's intentions in making the payment (HMRC Business Income Manual BIM 46015).

## Pension contribution spreading rules

**5.28** Contributions paid by an employer to a registered pension scheme in respect of an individual are deductible for Schedule D Case I purposes if the company is carrying on a trade or are deductible as management expenses if the company has an investment activity (*FA 2004, s 196*). If the amount of the contribution for the current chargeable period (CCCP) exceeds 210% of the amount of the contributions paid in the previous chargeable period (CPCP) the payments made in the second period may have to be spread forward. In order to ascertain whether or not this is the case, the company must calculate its relevant excess contributions (REC). The REC is calculated by deducting 110% of the CPCP from the CCCP.

---

**Example 5.4**

Wishbone Ltd makes pension contributions of £250,000 in the year ended 31 December 2006. In the year ended 31 December 2007 it makes contributions of £775,000.

| | £ |
|---|---|
| CCCP | 775,000 |
| Less 110% × £250,000 | 275,000 |
| REC | 500,000 |

If the RECs are less than £500,000 there is no spreading. If the RECs are £500,000 or more but less than £1,000,000, one half of the RECs is spread into the following accounting period, in this case the year ended 31 December 2008. If the RECs are £1,000,000 or more but less than £2,000,000, one-third of the RECs is spread into each of the next two accounting periods. If the RECs are £2,000,000 or more, one-quarter of the RECs is spread into each of the next three accounting periods (*FA 2004, s 197*).

**Example 5.5**

Wishbone Ltd's pension contribution relief of £775,000 for the year ended 31 December 2007 is spread as follows:

| | £ |
|---|---|
| Year ending 31 December 2006 | 500,000 |
| Year ending 31 December 2007 | 275,000 |

## CAPITAL ALLOWANCES COMPUTATION

**5.29** A company may claim capital allowances on its expenditure on plant and machinery, industrial and related buildings, agricultural land and buildings, mineral extraction and research and development allowances (*CAA 2001, s 1*).

A company can also claim capital allowances on expenditure incurred prior to 1 April 2002 on patent rights and know-how. Capital allowances are discussed in Chapter 6 and the rates of capital allowances are shown in **6.17**.

Capital allowances are given by reference to accounting periods. Where an accounting period is less than 12 months, writing-down allowances are proportionately reduced. Where a trade starts part-way through an accounting period, capital allowances for plant and machinery, research and development etc are also proportionately restricted.

## Trading and professional profits

**5.30** On the assumption that all information is to hand the company can now calculate its trading and professional profits. If the result is positive this amount should be shown in box 3 of the company tax return. If the result is negative box 3 should be left blank.

# VALUATION OF STOCK AND WORK IN PROGRESS

## Statement of Standard Accounting Practice 9 (SSAP 9)

**5.31** According to GAAP, stocks should be valued at the lower of cost and net realisable value (SSAP 9). Net realisable value is used where there is no reasonable expectation of sufficient future revenue to cover cost incurred, for example, as a result of deterioration, obsolescence or 'change in demand'. Ideally stocks should be considered item by item but this may be impractical and groups of items may be considered. Provisions may be made on a justifiable basis and in consideration of age, past and future movements and estimated scrap values, to reduce valuation from cost to net realizable value. Long-term contracts are valued on a pro-rata completion stage basis.

## International Accounting Standard 2 (IAS 2) Inventories

**5.32** IAS 2 adopts the same basic principle that inventories should be measured at the lower of cost and net realisable value. Net realisable value is the estimated selling price in the ordinary course of business less the estimated costs of completion and the estimated costs necessary to make the sale. See also **17.24**.

## Lower of cost and net realisable value

**5.33** *Companies Act 1985, Sch 4, para 26* requires the addition of incidental costs of acquisition to the stock cost. The company may include production costs and interest on funds borrowed to finance the asset's production in the stock valuation. Overheads should be included if appropriate and for consistency.

## Professional work in progress

**5.34** Companies with professional work in progress will in particular need to consider the extent of the inclusion of 'production costs', ie staff remuneration and overheads etc in the light of Urgent Issues Task Force (UITF) Abstract 40, effective for accounting periods ended on or after 22 June 2005.

As a general rule, long-term contracts incomplete at the balance sheet date are valued in accordance with SSAP 9. Other work in progress is to be valued at cost plus attributable overheads, which are normally based on time costs.

## UITF 40

**5.35** A company, when applying GAAP (UK or International), may require to utilise SSAP 9 and Application Note G as interpreted by UITF 40. If the profits in the previous accounting period were calculated in accordance with GAAP but not as interpreted by UITF 40, this may result in a change of accounting approach from one period of account to the next in calculating the profits of a business for corporation tax purposes.

The adjustment may be spread over three accounting periods; the accounting period in which the adjustment is made, followed by the two subsequent accounting periods.

The lesser of the following amounts are chargeable either:

- one-third of the amount of the original adjustment, or
- one-sixth of the profits of the business for that period.

In the fourth and fifth accounting periods, if the whole of the adjustment has not been charged to tax in the previous periods, an amount equal to whichever is the least of:

- the amount remaining untaxed,
- one-third of the amount of the original adjustment, and
- one-sixth of the profits of the business for that period,

is treated as arising and charged to tax (*FA 2006, Sch 15, para 10*).

In the sixth accounting period so much (if any) of the adjustment as has not previously been charged to tax is treated as arising and is charged to tax.

For these purposes 'the profits of the business' means the profits of the business as calculated for corporation tax purposes leaving without taking into consideration any other change of accounting basis under *FA 2002, Sch 22* (see **17.1**) or any capital allowances or balancing charges. Special rules apply to 'short' accounting periods of less than 12 months that arise in certain circumstances. The particular short periods are those arising because of a change of accounting date, a company entering administration (see **19.6**), or an insurance business transfer scheme under *ICTA 1988, s 12(7A), (7B)*. The amounts chargeable substitute the profits for the short period instead of the normal 12-month accounting period.

If the company ceases to be within the charge to corporation tax, or winding-up proceedings have commenced the whole of the untaxed amount is chargeable in that year. If the company ceases to trade, but remains within the charge to corporation tax, the spreading adjustment continues. The spreading relief is restricted to one-third of the adjustment for each year concerned amount with a final adjustment in year four if necessary (*FA 2006, Sch 15, para 12*).

Within 12 months of the company tax return filing date the company may elect for an additional amount to be treated as arising in that period and thereby disapply the spreading relief. The company may wish to do this if it has particular losses that it wishes to utilise. Spreading relief will continue to be available on any remaining balance.

The spreading relief occurs in any type of business where the adjustment is made. This includes; a trade or vocation, a Schedule A business or overseas property business. It also applies where the business is carried on by the company in partnership in accordance with the normal profit-sharing arrangements.

---

**Example 5.6**

Nimrod Ltd's trade is the provision of management consultancy advice. The company prepares accounts to 31 May each year. The company calculates that its UITF taxable amount is £90,000. Taxable profits exclusive of capital allowances are £120,000 for the year ended 31 May 2006. The company estimates that taxable profits will grow at the rate of 10% per annum over the next five years.

The adjustment is calculated as follows:

| *Year ending 31 May* | *Profits* £ | *Calculation of taxable adjustment income* £ | *Adjustment income* £ |
|---|---|---|---|
| (1) 2006 | 120,000 | Lower of:<br>1/3 × 90,000 or<br>1/6 × 120,000 | 20,000 |
| (2) 2007 | 132,000 | Lower of:<br>1/3 × 90,000 or<br>1/6 × 132,000 | 22,000 |
| (3) 2008 | 145,200 | Lower of:<br>1/3 × 90,000 or<br>1/6 × 145,200 | 24,200 |
| (4) 2009 | 159,720 | Lower of:<br>[90,000 – (20,000 + 22,000 + 24,200)] or<br>1/3 × 90,000 or<br>1/6 × 159,720 | 23,800 |
| | | Total | 90,000 |

**5.36** UITF 40 requires revenue to be recognised to the extent that a business has obtained the right to consideration through its performance. IAS 18 Revenue requires revenue to be recognised by reference to the stage of completion of the transaction at the balance sheet date. Revenue accrued is valued at the sales value.

## SCHEDULE A INCOME

### Income from UK land and buildings

**5.37** Companies are charged to corporation tax on income arising from the letting of UK land and property under Schedule A (see **12.15–12.21**). Income from land and buildings is included in box 11 of the company tax return. Losses are recorded in box 26.

### Furnished holiday lettings

**5.38** Furnished holding lettings are treated as a trade. For this to occur certain conditions apply. The property must be:

- available for holiday letting to the public on a commercial basis for 140 days or more, and
- let commercially for 70 days or more, and
- not occupied for more than 31 days by the same person in any period of seven months (*ICTA 1988, s 503*).

As the income is treated as a trade, loss relief is available but group relief is not available.

## CAPITAL GAINS

**5.39** Gains on the disposal of a company's chargeable assets are included in box 16 of the corporation tax self-assessment return. The gain is computed according to normal capital gains principles.

The gross sale proceeds less the allowable items of expenditure and indexation results in the chargeable gain. Allowable items include the purchase cost and the costs of acquisition and disposal (*TCGA 1992, s 38*). Indexation based on purchase and acquisition costs is still available to companies from the date of purchase or 31 March 1982 if later until date of sale.

When preparing the capital gains computation the incidental costs of sale are deducted from sale proceeds and may include such items as valuation fees, auctioneers' or estate agency fees, costs of advertising or legal costs. These costs do not qualify for the indexation allowance. Allowable expenditure includes the original cost of the asset, any enhancement expenditure and the incidental costs of sale. All this expenditure qualifies for indexation allowance.

Enhancement expenditure is capital expenditure, which adds to, improves or enhances the value of the asset. Repairs, maintenance and insurance are excluded since such costs only maintain the value of an asset and are normally deductible for Schedule D Case I purposes. Conversely capital expenditure that has not qualified as a deduction for Schedule D Case I may be allowable for capital gains purposes.

Indexation allowance is calculated by multiplying the relevant allowable expenditure by the indexation factor. The indexation factor is computed by expressing the following fraction as a decimal (to three decimal places) (*TCGA 1992, s 54*).

(RD – RI) ÷ RI

Where RD is the retail prices index (RPI) for the month of disposal and RI is the RPI for the later of:

- March 1982; or
- the month in which the expenditure was incurred.

If there should be a decrease in RPI between the base month and the month of disposal, the indexation allowance is nil. If expenditure is incurred on two or more dates, separate indexation calculations are required for each. No indexation is available if proceeds less costs results in a loss before indexation is calculated (*TCGA 1992, s 53(2A)*). Neither can indexation allowance be deducted so as to turn a gain before indexation into a loss. Instead, the gain is reduced to nil (*TCGA 1992, s 53(1)(b)*).

Capital losses may only be set against capital gains of the current year or carried forward to set against future capital gains. Allowable capital losses including losses brought forward are recorded in box 17 of the company tax return.

---

**Example 5.7**

The West End Trading Co Ltd prepares accounts to 31 March each year. The company disposes of an office block on 3 December 2007 for £40m. The incidental costs of sale are £1m. The block was purchased in January 2002 for £15.5m. Costs of acquisition amounted to £0.5m. In January 2003 a new frontage at a cost of £2m was added to the building that was deemed to be capital expenditure. The chargeable gain to be included within the corporation tax computation for the year ended 31 March 2008 is calculated as follows:

| | | *£000* | *£000* |
|---|---|---|---|
| December 2007 | Gross sale proceeds | | 40,000 |
| | Less: Incidental costs of sale | | 1,000 |
| | Net sale proceeds | | 39,000 |
| | Less: Relevant allowable expenditure: | | |
| January 2002 | Acquisition cost | 15,500 | |
| January 2002 | Incidental costs of acquisition | 500 | |
| January 2003 | Enhancement expenditure | 2,000 | |
| | | | 18,000 |
| | Unindexed gain | | 21,000 |

| | | |
|---|---|---|
| Less: Indexation allowance | | |
| Cost 16,000 × 0.183 | 2,928 | |
| Enhancement 2,000 × 0.150 | 300 | |
| | | 3,228 |
| Chargeable gain | | 17,772 |

Workings: calculation of indexation factor

| | | |
|---|---|---|
| RPI | December 2007 | *205.1 |
| RPI | January 2002 | 173.3 |
| RPI | January 2003 | 178.4 |
| Factor | | |
| Cost | (RPI December 2007 – RPI January 2002) ÷ RPI January 2002 | 0.183 |
| Enhancement | (RPI December 2007 – RPI January 2003) ÷ RPI January 2003 | 0.150 |
| * assumed | | |

---

**Example 5.8**

Sebastian Ltd is a trading company with the following results. There are no associated companies:

**Profit and loss account for the year to 31 December 2006**

| | £000 | £000 |
|---|---|---|
| Gross profit | | 900 |
| Interest on bank deposit | 70 | |
| Schedule A | 30 | |
| Profit on sale of UK quoted shares | 10 | |
| | | 110 |
| | | 1,010 |
| Less: | | |
| Directors' remuneration | 100 | |
| Salaries | 80 | |
| Repairs | 90 | |

| | | |
|---|---|---|
| Advertising and promotion | 20 | |
| Depreciation | 100 | |
| Miscellaneous expenses | 50 | |
| Impairment loss | 2 | |
| | | 442 |
| Profit before taxation | | 568 |
| Miscellaneous expenses: | | |
| Payment to various charities | | 10 |
| Donation to political party | | 10 |
| Staff entertaining | | 14 |
| Christmas gifts: | | |
| 5,000 key rings with company name | | 5 |
| Cigars | | 1 |
| Other expenses (all allowable) | | 10 |
| | | 50 |
| Impairment provision | | |
| Impairment losses | | 5 |
| General provision (2% of debtors) on 31 December 2006 | | 2 |
| | | 7 |
| Less: General provision (2% of debtors) on 1 January 2006 | | 5 |
| | | 2 |

Capital allowances for the year amount to £10,000.

The chargeable gain on the sales of UK quoted shares is £8,000

**Adjusted profits for the year ended 31 December 2006.**

| | *£000* | *£000* |
|---|---|---|
| Schedule D Case I: | | |
| Net profit per accounts | | 568 |
| Add: | | |
| Depreciation | 100 | |
| Deed of covenant | 10 | |

| | | |
|---|---|---|
| Political donation | 10 | |
| Gifts – cigars | 1 | |
| | | 121 |
| | | 689 |
| Less: | | |
| Bank interest | 70 | |
| Profit on sale of shares | 30 | |
| Schedule A | 10 | |
| Reduction in general impairment provision | 3 | |
| Capital allowances | 10 | |
| | | 123 |
| Schedule D Case I | | 566 |

**Corporation tax computation for the year ended 31 December 2006**

| | *£000* |
|---|---|
| Schedule D Case I | 566 |
| Schedule D Case III income (£61 + £2,800) | 70 |
| Chargeable gains | 8 |
| | 644 |
| Less: | |
| Charges on income: | |
| Payments to charity | 10 |
| PCTCT | 634 |

**Corporation tax payable**

| | £ |
|---|---|
| £634,000 at 30% | 190,200 |
| Less: 11/400 × (1,500,000 – 634,000) | 23,815 |
| Corporation tax liability | 166,385 |

# BODIES GRANTED EXEMPTION FROM CORPORATION TAX ON TRADING INCOME

## Charities

**5.40** Various exemptions are available to a company that meets the charitable status criteria provided by the Charities Commission (*ICTA 1988, s 505*). Trading income will be exempt from corporation tax in limited circumstances. Exemption applies if the profits from the trade are applied solely for the purposes of the charity. The trade must be exercised in the course of carrying out a primary purpose of a charity and the work in connection with the trade is mainly carried out by the beneficiaries of the charity (*ICTA 1988, s 505*(*1*)(*e*)), eg exhibition profits of a local history society. If a charity franchises its trading activities and receives royalty payments these will be exempt from tax (*ICTA 1988, s 505*(*1*)*C*(*ii*)).

Often a charity will form a trading subsidiary for the purpose of carrying out all its trading activities that do not meet the exceptions tests. Such a company's income will be taxable but it can arrange to gift aid it to the charity and obtain relief as a non-trading charge on income. The payment to the charity can be made up to nine months after the end of the accounting period (*ICTA 1988, s 339*(*7AA*)).

**5.41** If the profits are not applied solely for the purposes of the charity, the profits are taxable. However, in respect of chargeable periods beginning on or after 22 March 2006, apportionment is available. Where a trade is exercised partly in the course of the actual carrying out of a primary purpose of the charity and partly otherwise, each part is treated as a separate trade. Expenses and receipts are to be apportioned on a reasonable basis (*FA 2006, s 56*).

The separate trade basis also applies where work in connection with the trade is carried out partly but not mainly by beneficiaries. Expenses and receipts are apportioned on a reasonable basis.

**5.42** If a charity has activities unrelated to its primary purpose, it may operate these through a subsidiary company. A company that is owned by a single charity company by making a charge on income under *ICTA1988, s 339* is able to gift aid its profits to its parent. With effect from 1 April 2006, this relief has been extended to companies that are owned by more than one charity (*FA 2006, s 57*). Previously such amounts were treated as distributions under *ICTA 1988, s 209*(*4*).

**5.43** HMRC announced on 25 August 2006 that they would continue their practice of not requiring corporation tax returns from clubs and unincorporated associations with very small tax liabilities. Small in this context means not expected to exceed £100. If a club is run exclusively for its members then HMRC will prevent the issue of notices to file returns and treat the club as dormant subject to review each year.

To be within the scope of this practice the body must not be a privately owned club run by its members as a commercial enterprise for personal profit, a housing or trade association, a thrift fund, holiday club, friendly society or company that is a subsidiary of, or wholly owned by, a charity and for each year of dormancy the body must have no anticipated allowable trading losses or chargeable assets likely to be disposed of. The exemption is also extended to non-profit making property management companies.

## Cash gifts to charities

**5.44** There is no requirement for the company to deduct basic rate income tax for the payment (unlike payments by individuals). The charity in turn does not recover any tax from the receipt (*ICTA 1988, s 349(1B)*).

## Benefits received

**5.45** Close company payments will not qualify as gift aid payments if they are subject to conditions that the company is to receive a repayment to the company or a connected party is to receive benefits in excess of £250 in total. The actual benefits receivable is based on the formula:

| *Total donations in year* | *De minimis limit of benefits* |
|---|---|
| £0–£100 | 25% of value of gift |
| £101–£1,000 | £25 |
| £1,000–£10,000 | 2.5% of value of gift |

(*ICTA 1988, Sch 20*)

## Non cash gift to charities

**5.46** Companies may make gifts of trading stock or plant and machinery to a charity. There is no requirement to show the trading stock disposal in the corporation tax computation nor the plant and machinery disposal in the capital allowances computation (*ICTA 1988, s 83A*).

# MUTUAL COMPANIES

## Mutual trading

**5.47** As a person cannot trade with themselves, a mutual trader is not liable to tax on any profits arising from their 'mutual' trade.

Mutual trading is a situation whereby an organisation is controlled by the people who use its services. Those in effect who contribute to an activity are its sole participators. Arrangements must be in place to ensure that any surplus ultimately finds its way back to the contributors, with no arrangements for it to go to anybody else. Rules that include a winding-up surplus to be gifted to charity will not support mutual trading. Donations to charity are permitted provided the gift is approved by all members.

In normal circumstances the *Companies Act* states that in the event of a winding up any surplus available to distribute to members will be distributed pro rata to shareholding.

The normal rules also provide that any such distribution will only be to the members on the register at that time.

For mutual trading purposes it will be necessary to amend the Articles of Association to state that on a winding up any surplus available for distribution will be returned to contributors in a reasonable proportion to their contribution to that surplus; and that any distribution will also need to include contributors who have left in the last five years.

# MEMBERS' SPORTS CLUBS

**5.48** Members' sports clubs would normally fall outside the scope of Schedule D Case I. This is because they are usually established by the members for their own social or recreational objects and any surplus is for distribution amongst the members. They are therefore not trading. Services provided commercially to non-members may constitute a trading activity within Schedule D Case I. Expenditure should be allocated on a reasonable basis, but costs specifically in relation to members are not deductible against the non-member related Schedule D Case I income. Other income received, such as interest or rents, will be taxed in the normal way.

# COMMUNITY AMATEUR SPORTS CLUBS (CASCS)

## CASC conditions

**5.49** Reliefs are available to a community sports club that may register as a CASC provided certain conditions are satisfied. Namely, that it is open to the whole community, it is organised on an amateur basis and its main purpose is the provision of facilities for and the promotion of participation in one or more eligible sports (*FA 2002, Sch 18, para 1*).

A club is open to the whole community if membership of the club is open to all without discrimination. Club facilities must be available to members without discrimination, and any fees are set at a level that does not pose a significant obstacle to membership or use of the club's facilities (*FA 2002, Sch 18, para* 2(*1*)).

A club is organised on an amateur basis if it is non-profit making and it provides for members and guests only the ordinary benefits of an amateur sports club. The constitution must provide for any net assets on dissolution to be applied for approved sporting or charitable purposes (*FA 2002, Sch 18, para 3*).

## CASC reliefs

**5.50** The CASC may apply for exemption from corporation tax on the following income provided that it is applied for a qualifying purpose. The qualifying purpose being 'providing facilities for and promoting participation in one or more eligible sports' (*FA 2002, Sch 18, para 16*(*b*)).

- Trading income not exceeding £30,000 (*FA 2002, Sch 18, para 4*).
- Interest income and gift aid income (*FA 2002, Sch 18, para 5*).
- Rental income not exceeding £20,000 (*FA 2002, Sch 18, para 6*).
- Chargeable gains (*FA 2002, Sch 18, para 7*).

Where any income or gains are spent for non-qualifying purposes the tax exemption is reduced proportionately (*FA 2002, Sch 18, para 8*).

## Donor reliefs

**5.51** Gifts to a CASC will constitute a charity for gift aid and inheritance tax purposes.

## CORPORATION TAX SELF-ASSESSMENT

**5.52** Clubs and mutual companies are required to self-assess themselves for corporation tax, unless in practice they have agreed otherwise with HMRC.

A CASC must give details of its income on supplementary pages CT600E (reproduced in the appendices), which also enables it to recover income tax on its gift aid receipts.

*Chapter 6*

# Tangible Fixed Assets

## ACCOUNTANCY TREATMENT

**6.1** A company's fixed assets are disclosed in the balance sheet according to the *Companies Act 1985, Sch 4, paras 17–21* and to Generally Accepted Accounting Principles (GAAP). The GAAP applied will either be FRSSE or FRS 15 (tangible fixed assets) when using UK GAAP or IAS 16 (property, plant & equipment). Investment properties are accounted for under the FRSSE SSAP 19 (accounting for investment properties) or IAS 40 (investment property).

FRS 15 defines tangible fixed assets as assets with physical substance that are held for use in the production or supply of goods or services for rental to others or for administrative purposes on a continuing basis in the activities of the reporting entity.

Tangible fixed assets are reported at cost less depreciation at a rate that reflects the economic consumption of the asset by the entity,

## TAXATION TREATMENT

**6.2** The taxation system maintains the capital/revenue divide for capital assets. Depreciation calculated for accounting purposes is not allowable deduction against income for taxation purposes. Instead, the taxation grants its own form of depreciation on qualifying assets through the capital allowance system.

## QUALIFYING EXPENDITURE

### Capital allowances claim

**6.3** A company may claim capital allowances on its qualifying capital expenditure (*CAA 2001, s 1*). For corporation tax purposes, relief is given in an accounting period (*CAA 2001, s 6(1)(b)*). The reliefs given are a first year allowance (FYA), a writing down allowance (WDA), an initial allowance (IA) and a balancing allowance (BA). Capital allowance charges are referred to as balancing charges. The relief must be claimed (otherwise no relief is given) (*CAA 2001, s 3(1)*).

The capital allowance claim is made by including the amount of the claim in boxes 105 to 121 of the company tax return or an amended return. The company need not claim the full amount available. A company may choose either to make a reduced claim or not to claim at all if it wished to maximise a loss in a future accounting period (see Chapter 9). The claim is within the normal self-assessment corporation tax return time limits, being two years after the end of the accounting period concerned (see **2.9**) (*FA 1998, Sch 18, para 82*). The normal time limit is extended in such circumstances where there is an enquiry, amendment or appeal to 30 days after the respected closure notice, amendment or determination. HMRC has the power to extend the statutory time limits in exceptional circumstances but has stated that it will not extend the time limits in respect of the following:

- A change of mind.
- Hindsight showing that a different combination of claims might be advantageous: for example, the group relief available may be lower than the company expected it to be when it claimed capital allowances. The company may then want to claim further capital allowances. But that is not a circumstance beyond the company's control. It could have claimed sooner.
- Oversight or error, whether on the part of the company or its advisers.
- Absence or indisposition of an officer or employee of the company unless:
  - the absence or illness arose at a critical time, which delayed the making of the claim;
  - in the case of absence, there was good reason why the person was unavailable at the critical time; or
  - there was no other person who could have made the claim on behalf of the company within the normal time limit (HMRC Capital Allowances Manual CA 11140).

Capital allowances given in respect of a trade are deducted from trading income as an adjustment (see **5.17**). Balancing charges are added to trading income. Capital allowances in respect of non-trading activities are generally deducted primarily from the source of income to which they relate, eg Schedule A. If the accounting period is less than 12 months, the WDA is time apportioned accordingly. If the accounting period is longer than 12 months, the chargeable period for capital allowance purposes is divided into 12-month periods and the remaining balance.

## Capital expenditure incurred – timing

**6.4** For the purposes of claiming capital allowances, capital expenditure is incurred on the date on which the obligation to pay becomes unconditional even if there is a later payment date (*CAA 2001, s 5(1)*). Delivery of the goods is normally the time when the obligation to pay becomes unconditional. For capital allowance purposes, if the contractual payment period is longer than four months the expenditure is treated as incurred on the payment due date (*CAA 2001, s 4(5)*).

For works under contract, expenditure is incurred upon the issue of a certificate of work to date. If a certificate is issued within one month of the end of the accounting period but the asset has become the company's property before the end of the accounting period, the expenditure is deemed to have been incurred on the last day of the accounting period concerned (*CAA 2001, s 5(4)*). However, expenditure incurred before a trade begins is treated as incurred on the first day of trading.

Expenditure still to be incurred under a hire purchase etc contract at the time when the asset is brought into use is treated as incurred on the date on which the asset is brought into use. Expenditure incurred on the purchase of an unused building or structure is deemed to be incurred on the date on which the purchase price becomes payable (HMRC Capital Allowances Manual CA 11800). If a company is not registered for VAT, any VAT paid on the cost of the asset is taken into account when calculating capital allowances. If an additional VAT liability is incurred or an additional VAT rebate arises this is treated as taking place on the last day of the relevant VAT interval.

Sales between connected parties are deemed to be made at market value (*CAA 2001, s 567*). Parties under common control may elect for the asset to be transferred at the lower of tax written down value or market value (*CAA 2001, s 569*).

## Assets on which capital allowances may be claimed

**6.5** The types of capital expenditure that attract a capital allowance claim are:

| *Para* | | *CAA 2001* |
|---|---|---|
| 6.04 | Plant and machinery | Part 2 |
| | The construction of industrial buildings, qualifying hotels, commercial buildings in enterprise zones | Part 3 |
| | The construction of agricultural buildings and works | Part 4 |
| | Flat conversion allowances | Part 4A |
| | Mineral extraction | Part 5 |
| | Research and development | Part 6 |
| | Know-how | Part 7 |
| | Patents | Part 8 |
| | Dredging | Part 9 |
| | Assured tenancies | Part 10 |

This chapter discusses plant and machinery (**6.6–6.36**) and industrial buildings (**6.37–6.50**). Research and development is discussed in Chapter 8. Agricultural buildings allowance, mineral extraction and dredging are not discussed. Capital allowances are no longer available on know-how and patents. These are dealt with under the intangible assets regime (see Chapter 7) with effect from 1 April 2002. Capital allowances on assured tenancies are no longer available. Capital allowances may also be claimed on other types of expenditure such as agricultural buildings, flat conversions, mineral extraction, dredging etc but these types of expenditure are not covered in this text.

## PLANT AND MACHINERY

### Qualifying expenditure

**6.6** In order to be able to claim capital allowances for plant and machinery the company must incur qualifying expenditure on a qualifying activity (*CAA 2001, s 11*(*1*)). Qualifying expenditure is capital expenditure incurred on the provision of plant and machinery, wholly or partly for the purposes of the qualifying activity carried on by the company that incurs the expenditure. As a result of incurring the expenditure, the company 'owns' the asset (*CAA 2001, s 11*(*4*)).

A qualifying activity may consist of:

- a trade;
- an ordinary property business;
- a furnished holiday letting business;

- an overseas property business;
- a profession or vocation;
- mines, quarry or canal or other concern giving rise to profits from land charged to tax as a trade under Case I Schedule D in accordance with *ICTA 1988, s 55*;
- management of an investment company;
- special leasing business (*CAA 2001, s 15*).

Specific provisions relating to property businesses and investment companies are discussed in Chapter 12. This chapter deals with trades as well as general capital allowance provisions.

**6.7** Capital allowances can only be claimed on the cost of the plant and machinery itself, not the additional costs of interest or commitment fees (*Ben-Odeco Ltd v Powlson* (1978) 52 TC 459, [1978] STC 460, [1978] 1 WLR 1093, [1978] 2 All ER 1111). HMRC only allow professional fees and preliminary fees to be included within the cost on an asset for capital allowance purposes if they relate directly to the acquisition, transport and installation of the plant and machinery (HMRC Capital Allowances Manual CA 20070).

## Expenditure on buildings and structures

**6.8** In general plant and machinery expenditure does not encompass expenditure on buildings and structures (*CAA 2001, s 21(1)*). Certain assets are not included in this general rule but, in order for a company to claim plant and machinery capital allowances, they still need to qualify as 'plant' in their own right.

The following assets are not regarded as part of the fabric of the building for capital allowance purposes. Therefore a claim for plant and machinery capital allowances may be made for the following:

- Thermal Insulation installed in industrial buildings.
- Fire safety.
- Safety at designated sports grounds.
- Safety at regulated stands at sports grounds.
- Safety at other sports grounds.
- Personal security.
- Software and software rights (*CAA 2001, s 23*(*2*)).

The following items in 'List C' are again not regarded as part of the fabric of the building:

1 Machinery (including devices for providing motive power) not within any other item in this list.

2 Electrical systems (including lighting systems) and cold water, gas and sewerage systems provided mainly:

   (a) to meet the particular requirements of the qualifying activity, or

   (b) to serve particular plant or machinery used for the purposes of the qualifying activity.

3 Space or water heating systems; powered systems of ventilation, air cooling or air purification; and any floor or ceiling comprised in such systems.

4 Manufacturing or processing equipment; storage equipment (including cold rooms); display equipment; and counters, checkouts and similar equipment.

5 Cookers, washing machines, dishwashers, refrigerators and similar equipment; washbasins, sinks, baths, showers, sanitary ware and similar equipment; and furniture and furnishings.

6 Lifts, hoists, escalators and moving walkways.

7 Sound insulation provided mainly to meet the particular requirements of the qualifying activity.

8 Computer, telecommunication and surveillance systems (including their wiring or other links).

9 Refrigeration or cooling equipment.

10 Fire alarm systems; sprinkler and other equipment for extinguishing or containing fires.

11 Burglar alarm systems.

12 Strong rooms in bank or building society premises; safes.

13 Partition walls, where moveable and intended to be moved in the course of the qualifying activity.

14 Decorative assets provided for the enjoyment of the public in hotel, restaurant or similar trades.

15 Advertising hoardings; signs, displays and similar assets.

16 Swimming pools (including diving boards, slides and structures on which such boards or slides are mounted).

17 Any glasshouse constructed so that the required environment (namely, air, heat, light, irrigation and temperature) for the growing of plants is provided automatically by means of devices forming an integral part of its structure.

18 Cold stores.

19 Caravans provided mainly for holiday lettings.

20 Buildings provided for testing aircraft engines run within the buildings.

21 Moveable buildings intended to be moved in the course of the qualifying activity.

22 The alteration of land for the purpose only of installing plant or machinery.

23 The provision of dry docks.

24 The provision of any jetty or similar structure provided mainly to carry plant or machinery.

25 The provision of pipelines or underground ducts or tunnels with a primary purpose of carrying utility conduits.

26 The provision of towers to support floodlights.

27 The provision of:

(a) any reservoir incorporated into a water treatment works, or

(b) any service reservoir of treated water for supply within any housing estate or other particular locality.

28 The provision of:

(a) silos provided for temporary storage, or

(b) storage tanks.

29 The provision of slurry pits or silage clamps.

30 The provision of fish tanks or fish ponds.

31 The provision of rails, sleepers and ballast for a railway or tramway.

32 The provision of structures and other assets for providing the setting for any ride at an amusement park or exhibition.

33 The provision of fixed zoo cages.

Items 1 to 16 do not include any asset whose principal purpose is to insulate or enclose the interior of a building or to provide an interior wall, floor or ceiling which, in each case, is intended to remain permanently in place.

The following assets are treated as part of the structure of the building and not plant and machinery (*CAA 2001, s 21(3)*). It is not possible to make a claim for plant and machinery capital allowances in their respect:

1 Walls, floors, ceilings, doors, gates, shutters, windows and stairs.

2 Mains services and systems, for water, electricity and gas.

3 Waste disposal systems.

4 Sewerage and drainage systems.

5 Shafts or other structures in which lifts, hoists, escalators and moving walkways are installed.

6 Fire safety systems.

## The meaning of plant

**6.9** Plant owes its meaning to the development of case law. Plant was first defined in the case of *Yarmouth v France* (1887) 19 QBD 647 as 'whatever apparatus is used by a businessman for carrying on his business – not his stock in trade which he buys or makes for sale but all goods and chattels, fixed or moveable, live or dead, which he keeps for permanent employment in his business'. In other words the assets that enable a business to be carried on. This was confirmed as the functional test in the case of *Benson v Yard Arm Club Ltd* (1979) 53 TC 67, [1979] STC 266, [1979] 1 WLR 347, [1979] 2 All ER 336. Capital allowances were refused on the cost of purchasing and adapting a floating restaurant on the grounds that this was the place where the business was carried on rather than the tools that enable it to be carried on. HMRC regard assets with a life of more than two years as falling within the definition of plant: *Hinton v Madden & Ireland Ltd* (1959) 38 TC 391, [1959] 1 WLR 875, [1959] 3 All ER 356 (HMRC Capital Allowances Manual CA 21100). Whether the setting in which the business is carried on is plant is a question of fact. Lighting that was part of the setting but performed no function was not held to be plant: *J Lyons and Co Ltd v Attorney-General* [1944] 1 All ER 477. Moveable office partitions in a shipping agents, which were often moved to enable the trade to be carried on, were held to be plant; the partitions performed a function (*Jarrold v John Good & Sons Ltd* (1962) 40 TC 681, [1963] 1 WLR 214, [1963] 1 All ER 141). The law has now been changed on this issue: see item 13 List C at **6.8**. HMRC comment that only moveable partitions that possess mobility as a matter of commercial necessity qualify as plant (HMRC Capital Allowances Manual CA 21120). The function test was also met in *Leeds Permanent Building Society v Proctor* (1982) 56 TC 293, [1982] STC 821, [1982] 3 All ER 925 whereby decorative screens in a building society window were held to be plant. *CIR v Scottish & Newcastle Breweries Ltd* (1982) 55 TC 252, [1982] STC 296, [1982] 1 WLR 322, [1982]

2 All ER 230 was a landmark case in its time. Decorative assets in a pub and restaurant were allowed as plant because they provided atmosphere and ambience, within that trade; proving that assets must be judged within the context of the trade. The law has now been changed on this issue: see item 14 List C at **6.8**. HMRC comment that decorative items only qualify as plant if:

- the trade involves the creation of atmosphere/ambience and in effect the sale of that ambience to its customers, and
- the items on which plant or machinery allowances are claimed were specially chosen to create the atmosphere that the taxpayer is trying to sell (HMRC Capital Allowances Manual CA 21130).

HMRC particularly give the example of a painting hanging in an accountant's office not qualifying as plant because selling atmosphere is not part of an accountant's business. The point of course is debatable.

## Lighting

**6.10** Lighting installed in a building in order to make that building useable was not considered to be plant; it is part of the building. Lighting installed into a useable building to enable a trade to be carried on more effectively was considered to be plant (*Cole Bros v Phillips* (1982) 55 TC 188, [1982] STC 307, [1982] 1 WLR 1450, [1982] 2 All ER 247).

*Wimpy International Ltd v Warland* (1988) 61 TC 51, [1989] STC 273 generally upheld the decision in *CIR v Scottish & Newcastle Breweries Ltd*. In particular the cost of lighting in a restaurant was allowed because it provided atmosphere and ambience. Since then case law has moved to the function test and whether the piece of equipment is used within the trade. The tests applied in this case which HMRC also apply are:

**Questions**

1. Is the item stock in trade?
2. Is the item the business premises or part of the business premises (the premises test)?
3. Is the item used for carrying on the business (the business use test)?

**Response**

If the answers to questions 1 and 2 are negative and the answer to question 3 is positive the item is plant (HMRC Capital Allowances Manuals CA 21010 and CA 21140).

In this case it was suggested in order to ascertain whether an asset was part of the premises the following four factors can be considered:

- Does the item appear visually to retain a separate identity?
- With what degree of permanence has it been attached to the building?
- To what extent is the structure complete without it?
- To what extent is it intended to be permanent or alternatively is it likely to be replaced within a short period?

HMRC accept that electrical installation is plant, if the installation is fully integrated, designed and adapted to meet the particular requirements of the trade, functions as apparatus of the trade and is essential for the functioning of the trade. If the installation fails to qualify as plant HMRC will adopt a piecemeal approach. The same general and then piecemeal approach is applied to cold water, sewerage and gas systems.

In particular, HMRC will accept that the following elements of an electrical installation are plant:

- the main switchboard, transformer and associated switchgear provided that a substantial part of the electrical installation – both the equipment and the ancillary wiring – qualifies as plant;
- a standby generator and the emergency lighting and power circuits it services;
- lighting in sales areas, if it is specifically designed to encourage the sale of goods on display;
- wiring, control panels and other equipment installed specifically to supply equipment that is plant or machinery.

Lighting in a sales area will qualify even if there is no other lighting. The public areas in banking businesses are treated as sales areas (HMRC Capital Allowances Manual CA 21180). HMRC also accept that central heating systems, hot water systems, air conditioning systems, alarm and sprinkler systems, ventilation systems, baths, wash basins and toilet suites qualify as plant. Flooring and ceilings are generally considered not to be plant (HMRC Capital Allowances Manuals CA 22070 and CA 22080).

## Buildings alterations connected with installations of plant or machinery

**6.11** Incidental capital expenditure on alterations to an existing building for the installation of plant and machinery for the purposes of the qualifying activity qualifies as plant (*CAA 2001, s 25*). A lift and its necessary wiring qualify as plant. Installation of a lift shaft in an existing building qualifies as plant. Installation of a lift shaft in a new building does not qualify as plant. Plant removal and re-erection costs qualify as plant if not allowable as a deduction from trading profits (HMRC Capital Allowances Manual CA 21190).

## Demolition costs

**6.12** Net demolition costs of plant and machinery that was last used for the purposes of a qualifying activity may either be added to the cost of the new plant if the plant is replaced, or added to other qualifying expenditure of the same chargeable period as the demolition if the plant is not replaced.

The net demolition costs are the costs of demolition less any money received for the remains of the asset or any insurance receipts (*CA 2001, s 26*).

## Fire safety expenditure

**6.13** Fire safety equipment expenditure incurred by law by a person carrying on a qualifying activity is plant (*CAA 2001, s 29*).

## Computer software

**6.14** Computer software is within the intangible assets regime. An election may be made under *FA 2002, Sch 29, para 83* for it to be treated as plant for capital allowance purposes within *CAA 2001, s 71*. The election must be made within two years from the end of an accounting period in which the expenditure was incurred.

## Case law

**6.15** There are a number of decided capital allowance cases, besides those mentioned above. A summary of which is given below:

| *Case* | *Asset* | *Held* |
|---|---|---|
| *Yarmouth v France* (1887) 19 QBD 647 | A horse | Plant |
| *Benson v Yard Arm Club Ltd* (1979) 53 TC 67, [1979] 1 WLR 347, [1979] 2 All ER 336 | A floating restaurant | Not plant |
| *J Lyons and Co Ltd v Attorney-General* [1944] 1 All ER 477 | Lighting – as part of the setting | Not plant |
| *Jarrold v John Good & Sons Ltd* (1962) 40 TC 681, [1963] 1 WLR 214, [1963] 1 All ER 141 | Moveable office partitions | Plant |
| *Leeds Permanent Building Society v Proctor* (1982) 56 TC 293, [1982] STC 821, [1982] 3 All ER 925 | Window screens – particular to the business | Plant |
| *CIR v Scottish & Newcastle Breweries Ltd* (1982) 55 TC 252, [1982] STC 296, [1982] 1 WLR 322, [1982] 2 All ER 230 | Lighting and décor providing 'an atmosphere' necessary for the trade | Plant |
| *Cole Bros v Phillips* (1982) 55 TC 188, [1982] STC 307, [1982] 1 WLR 1450, [1982] 2 All ER 247 | Certain electrical installations | Plant |
| | Others | Not plant |
| *Wimpy International Ltd v Warland* (1988) 61 TC 51, [1989] STC 273 | Decorative items and certain specialist lighting | Plant |
| | Shop fronts | Not plant |
| *Cooke v Beach Station Caravans Ltd* (1974) 49 TC 514, [1974] STC 402, [1974] 1 WLR 1398, [1974] 3 All ER 159 | Swimming pool used for a holiday caravan park | Plant |
| *Hampton v Fortes Autogrill Ltd* (1979) 53 TC 691, [1980] STC 80 | False ceilings in a restaurant to conceal pipes and wires etc | Not plant |
| *Grays v Seymours Garden Centre (Horticulture)* (1995) 67 TC 401, [1995] STC 706 | An unheated glass house – a planteria | Not plant |
| *St John's (Mountford) v Ward* (1974) 49 TC 524, [1975] STC 7 | A pre-fabricated fixed school building | Not plant |
| *Munby v Furlong* (1977) 50 TC 491, [1976] 1 WLR 410, [1976] 1 All ER 753 | A barrister's law books | Plant |
| *Schofied v R & H Hall Ltd* (1974) 49 TC 538, [1975] STC 353 | Grain silos | Plant |

| Case | Asset | Held |
|---|---|---|
| *Hinton v Maden & Ireland Ltd* (1959) 38 TC 391, [1959] 1 WLR 875, [1959] 3 All ER 356 | A shoe repairer's loose tools, knives and lasts – with an expected life of more than two years | Plant |
| *Dixon v Fitch's Garages Ltd* (1975) 50 TC 509, [1975] STC 480, [1976] 1 WLR 215, [1975] 3 All ER 455 | A garage canopy to protect customers whilst vehicle refueling | Not plant |
| *Rose & Co (Wallpapers & Paints) Ltd v Campbell* (1967) 44 TC 500, [1968] 1 WLR 346, [1968] 1 All ER 405 | Wallpaper pattern books | Not plant |

**6.16** The expenditure is deemed to be incurred at cost on the first day of trading (*CAA 2001, s 12*). Expenditure is deemed to be incurred at the lesser of market value or cost at the date of a change of use if a change of use occurs (*CAA 2001, s 13*).

## RATES OF ALLOWANCES

**6.17** Current capital allowance rates for plant and machinery are:

| *Incurred by* | *Expenditure incurred* | *Allowance* | *Rate* |
|---|---|---|---|
| All companies | Energy-saving plant or machinery | FYA | 100% |
| | Energy service providers | | |
| | Low carbon dioxide emission cars not exceeding 120gm C02/km driven | | |
| | Equipment for refuelling vehicles with natural gas or hydrogen fuel | | |
| | North Sea oil ring-fence plant and machinery | | |
| SMEs | All other plant and machinery | FYA | 40% |
| SEs | Year ended 31 March 2007 | FYA | 50% |
| | Year ended 31 March 2005 | FYA | 50% |
| All companies | All plant and machinery | WDA | 25% |

The FYA is distinguished either by size of company or by type of expenditure. Subject to the necessary conditions, SMEs (Small and Medium-Sized Enterprises) and SEs (Small Enterprises) may claim FYAs on all their plant and machinery purchases. Companies of any size may claim FYAs generally on energy efficient technologies or oil technology if in that area of business.

## FIRST YEAR ALLOWANCE

**6.18** An FYA can only be claimed during the chargeable period in which the expenditure is incurred (*CAA 2001, s 52*). (See **6.4** above for the date that expenditure is incurred.) If that is also the period in which the qualifying activity is discontinued, no claim is allowed.

## SMEs (Small and Medium-Sized Enterprises) and SEs (Small Enterprises)

**6.19** The current definition of SMEs and SEs for plant and machinery capital allowance purposes follows the *Companies Act 1985, s 247(3)* and *s 249(3)* definitions (as introduced by the *Companies Act 1985* (*Accounts of Small and Medium-Sized Enterprises and Audit Exemption*) (*Amendment*) *Regulations 2004, SI 2004/16*). (See HMRC Capital Allowances Manual CA 23170 for definitions for the financial years ending before 30 January 2004). The limiting criteria are turnover, assets and the number of employees. A company means a company incorporated in the UK or a company with a place of business in the UK. To claim the FYA the company must be an SME or SE at the time the expenditure is incurred and not a member of a large group.

The definitions are as follows:

| | *Small company*<br>*Not more than* | *Medium-sized company*<br>*Not more than* |
|---|---|---|
| Turnover | £5.6 million | £22.8 million |
| Balance sheet total | £2.8 million | £11.4 million |
| Number of employees | 50 | 250 |

The balance sheet total is the aggregate of the company's assets as shown on the balance sheet before both current and long-term liabilities. The amounts are reduced proportionately for accounting periods of less than 12 months.

For the first year that a company satisfies two or more of the above-mentioned requirements, it qualifies as an SME for that financial year. Once a company has qualified as an SME it will continue to be treated as such unless it fails to meet the requirements for two consecutive years. If a large company reduces in size to become an SME it will not be treated as such unless it has met the requirements for two successive years.

## Groups

**6.20** The definitions of a small and a medium-sized group are as follows:

| | *Small group* | | *Medium-sized group* | |
|---|---|---|---|---|
| | *Not more than* | *Not more than* | *Not more than* | *Not more than* |
| | Net | Gross | Net | Gross |
| Turnover | £5.6 million | £6.72 million | £22.8 million | £27.36 million |
| Balance sheet total | £2.8 million | £3.36 million | £11.4 million | £13.68 million |
| Number of employees | 50 | | 250 | |

The balance sheet total 'net' is the aggregate of the company's assets as shown on the balance sheet before both current and long-term liabilities, with inter-company balances 'netted' off.

The balance sheet total 'gross' is the aggregate of the company's assets as shown on the balance sheet before both current and long-term liabilities. Inter-company group balances are included.

A company may only claim an FYA if it is neither a parent undertaking nor a subsidiary undertaking of a large group (*CAA 2001, s 49*(2)). An undertaking is a corporate body, a partnership or an unincorporated association carrying on a trade of business with a view to profit. A parent undertaking is the body that exercises control either by votes or dominant influence (*CA 1985, ss 259, 258*). The definition of a group includes an overseas parent.

If arrangements existed at the time the expenditure was incurred, which if they had come into effect before the expenditure was incurred would have made the company or its successor a member of a large group, the expenditure will not qualify for an FYA (*CAA 2001, s 49(4)*). Arrangements can be of any kind and need not be in writing or legally enforceable. A successor company is a company that carries on the trade or part of the trade of the predecessor under the rules of *ICTA 1988, s 343* (company reconstructions without a change of ownership). (See Chapter 15).

---

**Example 6.1**

Garcia plc is a large business. It wants to buy a new lathe but if it does it will not be entitled to FYAs because it is not an SME. Terry Ltd, an SME, buys the lathe for a qualifying activity of operating the lathe, thus obtaining FYA, with fixed supply and sale contracts with Garcia plc. The lathe is installed in Garcia plc's factory and operated by its workforce on a subcontract basis. The tax saving is shared by Garcia plc and Terry Ltd through the contract price.

Terry Ltd is not entitled to FYA's by reason of *CAA 2001, s 49(4)* (HMRC Capital Allowances Manual CA 23110 – Adapted).

A partnership of which a company is a member cannot claim an FYA (*CAA 2001, s 48(2)(b)*).

---

## Environmentally beneficial plant and machinery

**6.21** Particular plant and machinery that meets environment criteria qualifies for 100% FYA, which may be claimed by companies of any size. This machinery can be found by logging on to www.eca.gov.uk . The technologies that are included are:

- boilers (including oil-fired boilers);
- pipe insulation;
- combined heat and power (CHP);
- radiant and warm air heaters;
- compressed air equipment;
- solar thermal systems;
- heat pumps for space heating;
- thermal screens;
- lighting;
- variable speed drives (VSD);
- motors;
- refrigeration equipment (including display cabinets and compressors);
- automatic monitoring and targeting equipment;
- air-to-air energy recovery equipment;
- compact heat exchangers; and
- heating, ventilation and air conditioning zone controls.

It is necessary for the government to certify that the equipment meets the required standards or that the machinery is a product specified on the product list.

**6.22** Certain water technologies and products also qualify for 100% FYA. These fall into classes of efficient taps, efficient toilets, flow controllers, leakage detection, meters and rainwater harvesting equipment. Information regarding these products can be found on www.water-eca.gov.uk. Component parts of an asset may meet the environmental criteria. If so, an FYA will be available in respect of these parts. A certificate issued to the buyer will indicate the cost of the environmental components, which should be used in calculating the FYA (*CAA 2001, ss 45H, 45J*). If the total expenditure incurred on the asset containing the qualifying component (or components) is less than the amount specified in the order for the component or components incorporated in that asset, the total expenditure qualifies for 100% FYA (HMRC Capital Allowances Manual CA 23135). If qualifying expenditure is incurred on an asset in stage payment, the payment is allocated pro-rata over the various payments.

If an environmental certificate is revoked, the company should withdraw the 100% FYA claim.

## Expenditure incurred by energy services provider

**6.23** If a company energy service provider of any size supplies energy efficient plant and machinery, which is on the technology list of products list to his client he may be able to claim an FYA. The provider must make an election with this client. The plant must not be for use in a dwelling house and the service provider or another organisation with which it is connected must carry out all or substantially all of the operation and maintenance of the plant and machinery (*CAA 2001, s 180A*).

## Expenditure on cars with low carbon dioxide emissions

**6.24** Expenditure by any size of company on cars with low carbon dioxide emissions qualifies for an FYA if incurred between 17 April 2002 and 31 March 2008. The car must be unused and not second hand. It can either be an electric car or a car with $C0_2$ emissions of not more than 120gm per km driven. Information regarding a car's carbon dioxide emissions figure can be found on the vehicle registration document (the 'V5') or on the Vehicle Certification Agency's website at www.vca.gov.uk. Neither the rules for cars costing more that £12,000 nor the car hire or leasing expenses restriction applies to these vehicles (*CAA 2001, s 45D*).

## Expenditure on natural gas and hydrogen refuelling equipment

**6.25** Expenditure incurred on natural gas and hydrogen refuelling equipment between 17 April 2002 and 31 March 2008 and installed in a refuelling station qualify for FYA. The stations can be private to the company or open to the public. Eligible expenditure includes storage tanks, compressors, controls and meters, gas connections, and filling equipment (*CAA 2001, s 45E*).

## Expenditure on North Sea oil ring-fence plant and machinery

**6.26** Extraction of gas or oil in the North Sea trades may claim a 100% FYA on equipment purchased for use in the 'ring-fence' trade. (A ring-fence trade is a trade subject to the supplementary charge). Long life assets qualify for 24% WDA (*CAA 2001, s 45G*).

# EXPENDITURE ON WHICH AN FYA MAY NOT BE CLAIMED

**6.27** No FYA is available on the purchase of a car unless it is a low-emission car (see **6.17**). No FYA is available on a gifted asset. This is because to qualify for FYA the entity must incur the expenditure (*CAA 2001, s 52*). Similarly, an FRA is not available if a company buys an asset for one purpose and then uses the asset for another purpose. An FYA may not be claimed on the provision of plant and machinery for leasing, unless the expenditure is on qualifying energy saving plant and machinery, cars with low CO2 emissions or natural gas or hydrogen refuelling equipment. HMRC take the view that the hire of machinery with an operative constitutes contract hire as in the non-tax case of *Baldwins Industrial Services plc v Barr Ltd* [2003] BLR 176. The expenditure is not within finance leasing and an FYA will be available (HMRC Capital Allowances Manual CA 23115). No capital allowances whatsoever are given on assets used for business entertainment (*CAA 2001, s 269*).

The general rule is that no FYA may be claimed on assets purchased from connected parties (*CAA 2001, s 217*). This rule does not apply where the asset is produced by the seller, un-used and sold in the ordinary course of the seller's business (*CAA 2001, s 230*). Connection for these purposes is determined by *ICTA 1988, s 839* (see **4.25**).

## COMPUTATION OF ALLOWANCES

### The pool

**6.28** All qualifying expenditure is pooled in a multi asset pool. Single asset pools are maintained for non low emission cars costing more than £12,000 (*CAA 2001, s 74*), and short life assets (*CAA 2001, s 86*). The writing down allowance on an expensive car is restricted to £3,000 per annum. A separate asset class pool is maintained for long life assets (*CAA 2001, s 101*). An outline plant and machinery capital allowance computation is given below.

### Allowances

**6.29** Three types of adjustment are made: first year allowance, writing down allowance and a balancing adjustment. A first year allowance can only be claimed in year of purchase in which case there is no writing down allowance. The first year allowance is deducted from the cost of the asset and the net result (if any) is added to the balance of pool expenditure and carried forward to the next chargeable period. Writing down allowances are claimed annually on a reducing balance basis. The unrelieved pool of qualifying expenditure at the beginning of the year adjusted for disposals and additions (but not additions on which FYA has been claimed) times 25% forms the writing down allowance for the year.

### Disposal proceeds

**6.30** When an asset is disposed of the disposal proceeds up to the amount of the original cost are deducted from the asset balance on the expenditure pool. If a positive balance remains after the deduction on a multi asset or long life asset pool the balance continues to be written off on a reducing balance basis, except in the final period of account when it becomes a balancing allowance that may be deducted from chargeable profits. If a negative balance remains on the pool after the deduction this forms a balancing charge, which must be added to the company's assessable profits. In the case of a single asset pool, a positive balance, after the deduction for sale proceeds, is allowed as a deduction from profits as a balance adjustment. A negative balance will become a taxable balancing charge (*CAA 2001, s 55*). If the assets concerned have not been the subject of a capital allowance claim it is not necessary to deduct the disposal proceeds from the pool. This is not the case if the asset was originally acquired from a connected person or by means of a series of transactions between connected persons and any one person has brought the disposal value into account (*CAA 2001, s 64*). Expenditure on an asset that is partly used for a qualifying activity and partly for other purposes is put into a separate pool. The expenditure is apportioned on a just and reasonable basis and the allowances are reduced accordingly. If the market value of the asset in the pool exceeds that actual pool value by more than £1 million and there is a significant reduction in the value of the asset, the asset is deemed to have been disposed of at market value for the notional trade and reacquired for the purposes of the separate notional trade (*CAA 2001, s 208*).

---

**Example 6.2**

The written down value of Sebastian Ltd's plant, after deduction of capital allowances for the year to 31 December 2005, was £6,660.

In July 2006 the company sold an asset for £300 on which capital allowances had been claimed. The company bought new plant and machinery that qualified for a first year allowance on 1 February 2006 for £4,500.

The capital allowance claim is as follows:

(b) Capital allowances – plant and machinery:

| | | | *Pool* | *Allowances* |
|---|---|---|---|---|
| | | | £ | £ |
| WDV b/f | | | 6,660 | |
| Sales proceeds – July 2006 | | | -300 | |
| | | | 6,360 | |
| WDA @ 25% | | | -1,590 | 1,590 |
| | | | 4,770 | |
| Additions (FYA) | | | | |
| | 1 February 2006 | 4,500 | | |
| | FYA (40%) | -1,800 | | 1,800 |
| | | | 2,700 | |
| WDV c/f | | | 7,470 | |
| ALLOWANCES | | | | 3,390 |

## Short life assets

**6.31** Assets that are continuously renewed, such as technology assets, may be placed in a separate short life pool. The company must make an irrevocable election for the asset to be treated as 'short life' within two years of the end of the chargeable period for which the expenditure was incurred (*CAA 2001, s 83(b)*). The asset then remains in the short life pool until the earlier of disposal or the fourth anniversary of the end of the chargeable period in which the asset was acquired. If the asset is disposed of, a balancing charge or a balancing allowance will arise. Alternatively, if unsold, the asset's net book value is transferred back to the main pool (*CAA 2001, s 86*).

## Long-life assets

**6.32** If the expected life of an asset is 25 years or more, it may be included in a separate pool (*CAA 2001, s 91*). The annual writing down allowance is 6%. Expenditure on plant, machinery and fixtures in a house, hotel, shop or showroom will not qualify. Nor will expenditure on cars or where the total expenditure on long-life assets for the year is £100,000 or less (*CAA 2001, ss 93, 96, 98*).

## Reduced allowances

**6.33** If the chargeable period is less than 12 months (ie if the accounting period is less that 12 months), the writing down allowance is reduced proportionately (but not the first year allowance). A company may reduce or disclaim the writing down allowance for any chargeable period. The tax written down value is carried forward to the next accounting period and will be written down accordingly (*CAA 2001, s 56*).

## Assets purchased under hire-purchaser

**6.34** The asset is treated as that of the hirer who may claim capital allowances (*CAA 2001, s 67*). The full contract cost is treated as expenditure incurred. The disposal value is the proceeds received together with any unpaid capital instalments (*CAA 2001, s 68*).

**6.35** A company may only claim capital allowances on plant and machinery if the assets belong to the company at some time (*CAA 2001, s 11(4)(b)*). HMRC consider that, if there is a contractual relationship that states that 'a company may become the owner of the plant or machinery on the performance of the contract' and the purchasing company pays a deposit for plant that is not supplied, it will be able to claim capital allowances under *CAA 2001,* *s 67(1)(a)*. When the beneficial period ends the company must bring a disposal value into account (HMRC Capital Allowances Manual CA 23350 and Tax Bulletin, Issue 2, February 1992).

## Finance leasing

**6.36** A finance lease is essentially a lending arrangement between two companies. The finance lessor company (the lender) retains ownership of the leased asset. The leased assets are not disclosed as fixed assets on the balance sheet but as a loan, which is normally the cost of the leased asset. The finance lessor's return is interest and loan repayment. Interest is recorded in the profit and loss account as income. Capital repayments reduce the amount of outstanding debt.

Although the finance lessee company (the borrower) does not own the asset it is recorded on the balance sheet as an asset under SSAP 21 (accounting for leases and hire purchase contracts) following the economic substance over form principle of FRS 5. Capital owed to the finance lessor is shown as a creditor. Interest payable is charged to the profit and loss account.

The finance lessee charges depreciation on the asset.

The taxation legislation regards the finance lessor as owner of the leased assets with entitlement to capital allowances. The lessor may only claim a 25% WDA. No FYA is available. Plant leased to companies not resident in the UK and whose activities are not charged exclusively to UK tax will only qualify for a 10% WDA during the designated period (*CAA 2001, s 105*). The designated period is ten years from the time that the plant and machinery is first brought into use. The equipment is placed in a separate pool.

With effect from 1 April 2006, or earlier if a written agreement was in place before 21 July 2005, new rules will apply to long leases; essentially those with a life of more than seven years. Companies will be able to choose to enter within the new regime. The effect being that the lessor brings the finance element of the rentals arising under the lease as income. The lessee deducts the finance element of the rentals payable over the life of the lease and will be entitled to capital allowances (*FA 2006, s 81, Sch 8*).

# INDUSTRIAL BUILDINGS ALLOWANCES

## Construction of an industrial building or structure

**6.37** A company may claim an industrial buildings allowance (IBA) if it has incurred expenditure on the construction of a building or structure. The company must actually incur the expenditure. The expenditure cannot be covered directly or indirectly by a third party. In order to qualify the building or structure must be:

- in use for the purposes of a qualifying trade;
- a qualifying hotel;
- a qualifying sports pavilion; or
- a commercial building in a qualifying enterprise zone,

and the expenditure must be qualifying (*CAA 2001, s 271*).

As a result of incurring the expenditure the company must have the relevant interest in the building (*CAA 2001, s 286*).

HMRC acknowledge that there is no definition of a building within the industrial buildings legislation and will treat anything with four walls and a roof as a building provided it is of a reasonably substantial size. Something that is too small or insubstantial will be a structure (HMRC Capital Allowances Manual CA 31050). A structure is artificially erected or constructed and is distinct from the earth surrounding it (HMRC Capital Allowances Manual CA 31110) and roads, car parks which have a hard concrete or asphalt surface, concrete surfacing, tunnels and culverts, walls, bridges, aqueducts, dams, hard tennis courts and fences would qualify as such.

## Qualifying trade

**6.38** A list of qualifying trades is given in Table A of *CAA 2001, s 274(1)* and consists of the following:

| | | |
|---|---|---|
| 1 | Manufacturing | A trade consisting of the manufacturing of goods or materials. |
| 2 | Processing | A trade consisting of subjecting goods or materials to a process. This includes subject to s 276(3) maintaining or repairing goods or materials. |
| 3 | Storage | A trade consisting of storing goods or materials:<br>(a) which are to be used in the manufacture of other goods or materials,<br>(b) which are to be subjected in the course of a trade to a process, |

| | | |
|---|---|---|
| 1 | Manufacturing | A trade consisting of the manufacturing of goods or materials.<br>(c) which having been manufactured or produced or subjected in the course of a trade to a process, have not yet been delivered to any purchaser, or<br>(d) on their arrival in the UK from a place outside the UK. |
| 4 | Agricultural contracting | (a) Ploughing or cultivating land occupied by another person, or<br>(b) carrying out any other agricultural operation on land occupied by another person, or<br>(c) threshing the crops or vegetables of another person. |
| 5 | Working foreign plantations | A trade consisting of working land outside the UK used for:<br>(a) growing and harvesting of crops and vegetables,<br>(b) husbandry, or<br>(c) forestry. |
| 6. | Fishing | A trade consisting of catching or taking fish or shellfish. |
| 7. | Mineral extraction | A trade consisting of working a source of mineral deposits. Mineral deposits include any natural deposits capable of being lifted or extracted from the earth and for this purpose geothermal energy is to be treated as a natural deposit.<br>'Source of mineral deposits' includes a mine, an oil well and a source of geothermal energy. |

## Manufacturing

**6.39** Manufacturing includes the making of articles and the assembly of component parts made elsewhere (HMRC Capital Allowances Manual CA 32210). Cold storage premises that contained ice-making machinery and plant were held to be an industrial building (*Ellerker v Union Cold Storage Co Ltd; Thomas Borthwick & Sons Ltd v Compton* (1938) 22 TC 195).

## Goods and materials

**6.40** Goods and materials are understood to be raw goods and materials. In *Girobank plc v Clarke* (1997) 70 TC 387, [1998] STC 182, [1998] 1 WLR 942, [1998] 4 All ER 312 the bank's processing of cheques and credit card slips was not a qualifying trade. Cheques and credit card slips are not within the definition of goods and services.

Similar decisions were made in *Buckingham v Securitas Properties Ltd* (1979) 53 TC 292, [1980] STC 166, [1980] 1 WLR 380 regarding coins or notes used as currency, in *Bourne v Norwich Crematorium Ltd* (1967) 44 TC 164, [1967] 1 WLR 691, [1967] 2 All ER 576 regarding human remains and in *Carr v Sayer & Sayer* (1992) 65 TC 15, [1992] STC 396 with respect to dogs and cats.

## Subject to a process

**6.41** In *Kilmarnock Equitable Co-Operative Society Ltd v CIR* (1966) 42 TC 675, [1966] TR 185 a building in which coal was screened and packed qualified as an industrial building. In *Vibroplant Ltd v Holland* (1981) 54 TC 658, [1982] 1 All ER 792 IBA was claimed on a building used to repair individual plant hire items when not being hired to customers. The activity was not considered to be a process because the items were treated individually. Repairing goods or materials is now treated as a process unless the person who repairs the goods or materials uses them in a non-qualifying trade (*CAA 2001, s 276(3)*).

*Bestway (Holdings) Ltd v Luff* (1998) 70 TC 512, [1998] STC 357 claimed IBA on its cash and carry wholesale store. The claim was refused because the checking, unpacking and labelling of goods was not considered to be a process and the goods were not retained for sufficient time to qualify for storage.

## Storage

**6.42** The trade of storage particularly refers to storage of goods for manufacture or process or goods manufactured or processed but not yet delivered to customers and includes imports (*CAA 2001, s 274*).

A company examined, selected and graded used tyre casings which it sold on for remoulding. It used a building for storage of the items that were only delivered to customers in small batches. The building qualified as an industrial building (*Crusabridge Investments Ltd v Casings International Ltd* (1979) 54 TC 246).

The storage of goods on their arrival in the UK refers to their immediate storage. In *Copol Clothing Ltd v Hindmarsh* (1983) 57 TC 575, [1984] STC 33, [1984] 1 WLR 411 an IBA claim on a Manchester warehouse was refused because the building was the goods' ultimate place of storage. HMRC considers that a building will qualify for an IBA for storage of goods when they first enter the country if the following conditions are satisfied:

- the goods have been imported;
- the goods are being stored for the first time since their arrival in the UK; and
- the goods are still in transit – that is they have not yet arrived at their final destination in the UK (HMRC Capital Allowances Manual CA 32224).

In *Revenue and Customs Comrs v Maco Door & Window Hardware (UK) Ltd* [2006] EWHC 1832 (Ch) the company, a UK subsidiary of an Austrian company, claimed industrial buildings allowance on a warehouse. The warehouse was used to house goods such as door locks and door handles, which were manufactured by the Austrian company and stored in the warehouse while awaiting sale to wholesalers and to manufacturers of doors and windows in the UK. The company contended that it carried on a trade of storage. The court held that the company's trade was that of import and sale of doors and windows hardware. Storage was part of that trade. The industrial buildings allowance claim was refused.

## Expenditure on which IBAs are available

**6.43** IBAs are not given on the cost of land. Where repairs to an industrial building qualify as capital expenditure IBAs are given to that part as if it were a new construction at that time (*CAA 2001, s 272*). IBAs are given on the preparation of a site for building or for the installation of plant and machinery (if not allowed elsewhere).

Qualifying expenditure consists of the following:

- capital expenditure on the construction of a building;
- the purchase of an unused building without developer involvement;
- the purchase of an unused building from a developer;
- the purchase of a used building from a developer (*CAA 2001, s 292*).

IBAs are based on the cost of construction if the company erects the building (*CAA 2001, s 294*). HMRC regards the following expenditure as forming part of the cost of the building on which an IBA is available:

- expenditure on capital repairs (*CAA 2001, s 272*(2), (*3*));
- demolition costs of the old building making way to erect a new building if these costs have not already been taken into account in calculating a balancing adjustment on the old building;
- professional fees relating to the design and construction of a building provided that the building is actually constructed (HMRC Capital Allowances Manual CA 31400).

Land preparation costs, including cutting, tunnelling or levelling land in readiness for the installation of plant and machinery, will qualify for an IBA if there are no other allowances available on that expenditure (*CAA 2001, s 273*).

HMRC does not consider that the following items of expenditure can be included within the cost of a building for IBA purposes:

- the cost of obtaining planning permission, except where included in the builder's quotation;
- capitalised interest;
- the cost of a public enquiry;
- the cost of land drainage and reclamation;
- landscaping;
- legal expenses;
- abortive expenditure.

These items do not qualify for IBA (HMRC Capital Allowances Manuals CA 31400 and CA 31410).

If the company decides to sell the building without bringing it into use the new purchaser can claim IBAs on the lower of purchase price and construction cost (*CAA 2001, s 295*). If the company buys an unused building from a property developer it can claim IBAs on the purchase price (*CAA 2001, s 296*).

If the company buys a used building from a developer, ie one on which IBAs have already been claimed, the company claims IBAs as the second user (*CAA 2001, s 297*). IBAs are not available on the cost of land (*CAA 2001, s 272*(*1*)). If the building is purchased with other assets the expenditure should be apportioned between the qualifying and non-qualifying assets on a just and reasonable basis (*CAA 2001, s 356*).

A dwelling house, a retail shop, or premises similar to a retail shop where retail trade or business (including repair work) is carried on, a showroom, a hotel or an office do not qualify for IBA (*CAA 2001, s 277*(*1*)). An office that forms part of the manufacturing process will qualify for IBA, such as a drawing office in the case of *CIR v Lambhill Ironworks Ltd* (1950) 31 TC 393. An 'industrial building' may have a non-industrial part such as an office. If the non-industrial part consists of 25% or less of the total cost of the building, allowances are given on the total cost of the building. If the non-industrial parts are more than 25% of the total cost, the allowances are only given on the industrial part. A drawing office in a factory qualifies as industrial usage. Staff welfare buildings in a qualifying trade will qualify for IBA (*CAA 2001, s 275*).

## Hotels

**6.44** A qualifying hotel has to be a permanent building, which is open during the year for at least four months during April to October. When the hotel is let during April to October:

- it must have ten or more letting bedrooms,
- the sleeping accommodation that it offers consists wholly or mainly of letting bedrooms, and
- the services provided for guests normally include the provision of breakfast and an evening meal, the making of beds and the cleaning of rooms (*CAA 2001, s 279*(*1*)).

## Initial allowance

**6.45** Initial allowances may no longer be claimed except on buildings in an enterprise zone where a 100% allowance is available. A list of enterprise zones can be found in HMRC Capital Allowances Manual CA 37600.

## IBAs writing down allowance (WDA)

**6.46** WDAs are given at 4% per annum straight line basis on the assumption that the building has a tax life of 25 years (*CAA 2001, s 310*). Buildings in an enterprise zone qualify for a straight line 25% WDA.

---

**Example 6.3**

Sebastian Ltd's factory was built in December 1999 at a cost of £75,000.

In December 2001 a new factory block was built, which cost £90,000, including offices, which cost £20,000.

Industrial buildings allowance:

| | | £ | | £ |
|---|---|---|---|---|
| December 1999 | Factory | 75,000 | × 4% | 3,000 |
| December 2001 | Factory | 90,000 | × 4% | 3,600 |
| | (No restriction for offices – not over 25% of cost) | | | |
| | Allowances given | | | 6,600 |

**6.47** For the allowance to be given the building must be in use as an industrial building at the end of the chargeable period (*CAA 2001, s 309*).

If the building is not in industrial use at the end of the year no WDA is given to the company. However a notional WDA reduces the tax written down value of the building, because in effect its 25-year life is expiring. If the chargeable period is more or less than one year the allowance is adjusted proportionately. No adjustment is made if the building was acquired during the chargeable period.

## Temporary disuse

**6.48** A period of temporary disuse is ignored (*CAA 2001, s 285*). Temporary disuse infers that the building is to be used for an industrial purpose but there has been a short break in activities and industrial use is to be resumed.

The building must have been in use as an industrial building immediately before the period of temporary disuse. The legislation states no time limit for the temporary disuse unless the building was a qualifying hotel. A qualifying hotel, which becomes temporarily disused, is treated as a qualifying hotel for two years after the end of the chargeable period in which the temporary disuse begins but for no longer.

HMRC will accept that a building is temporarily disused if it is capable of being used at all. It need not be capable of being used for a qualifying trade, but if it is not capable of further use for any purpose it is not temporarily disused. If a company breaks its manufacturing pattern and moves into another qualifying trade, this is clearly a period of temporary disuse.

If the building is left to deteriorate or left empty prior to development or demolition this is not a period of temporary disuse and any IBA claims will be rejected.

A claim made in good faith for a period of disuse may be made only to find that the disuse becomes permanent. Earlier claims will remain although no further claims can be made once it is known that the building has no further use (HMRC Capital Allowances Manual CA 32800).

---

**Example 6.4**

Marmaduke Ltd prepares accounts to 31 December each year. The company incurs expenditure on 1 June 2004 of £100,000, which qualifies for IBAs. The building is used throughout as an industrial building except for the period 1 June 2006 to 31 May 2007. The available industrial buildings allowances are as follows:

| | | £ | *Allow-ances* |
|---|---|---|---|
| **Year ending 31 December 2004** | | | |
| Expenditure | | 100,000 | |
| | WDA (4%) | 4,000 | 4,000 |
| | | 96,000 | |
| **Year ending 31 December 2005** | WDA (4%) | 4,000 | 4,000 |
| | | 92,000 | |
| **Year ending 31 December 2006** | Notional WDA (4%) | 4,000 | 0 |
| | | 88,000 | |
| **Year ending 31 December 2007** | WDA (4%) | 4,000 | 4,000 |
| | | 84,000 | |

---

## Disposal of an industrial building

**6.49** If the building is sold before the expiry of its 25-year life and it has been used as an industrial building throughout its life, the lesser of the sale proceeds and the cost for IBA purposes is deducted from the tax written down value that is known for these purposes as the 'residue before sale' to give rise to a balancing event. If the proceeds are less than the residue before sale a balancing allowance arises, which is deductible from profits. If the sale proceeds are more than the residue before sale a balancing charge arises that is added to profits chargeable to corporation tax. The balancing charge is restricted to the amount of the allowances actually given.

If a building is sold before the expiry of the 25-year life that has not been used throughout as an industrial building and it is sold for less than cost then the balancing allowance is the difference between the adjusted net cost of the building and the allowances actually given.

The adjusted net cost is calculated by the formula:

$(S - P) \times (I \div R)$

where:

S = original expenditure

P = sale proceeds

I = the period of industrial use

R = the total period of use

(*CAA 2001, s 323*)

If the building is sold for more than cost the balancing charge amounts to the allowances actually given (*CAA 2001, s 319(5)*).

The purchaser of the building is able to claim IBAs on the residue of qualifying expenditure for the remainder of the building's 25-year life according to the following formula:

$RQE \times (A \div B)$

where:

RQE = the amount of the residue of qualifying expenditure after sale.

A = length of chargeable period

B = length of the period from the date of sale to the end of the building's tax life

(*CAA 2001, s 311*)

---

**Example 6.5**

Herbert Ltd prepares accounts to 31 December each year. The company bought a new factory on 31 August 1997 for £100,000, which it sold to Maximillius Ltd on 1 October 2007. The sale price is assumed to be (i) £90,000, (ii) £3,000, (iii) £120,000. Maximillius Ltd prepares accounts to 31 March each year.

**Herbert Ltd**

| | | *(i)* £ | *(ii)* £ | *(iii)* £ |
|---|---|---|---|---|
| 1 September 1997 | Cost | 100,000 | 100,000 | 100,000 |
| Year ending 31 December 1997 to year ending 31 December 2006 | WDA (4%) = £4,000 per annum for 10 years | (40,000) | (40,000) | (40,000) |
| | Residue before sale | 60,000 | 60,000 | 60,000 |
| 1 October 2007 | Proceeds | (90,000) | (3,000) | (120,000) |
| Year ending 31 December 2007 | Balancing charge | (30,000) | | (60,000) |
| | Balancing allowance | | 57,000 | |
| | But restricted to allowances given | | | (40,000) |

**Maximillius Ltd**

| | | *(i)* £ | *(ii)* £ | *(iii)* £ |
|---|---|---|---|---|
| | Residue after sale (workings below) | 90,000 | 3,000 | 100,000 |
| Year ending 31 March 2008 (and also for a further 14 years) | WDA Residue × 1/15 | 6,000 | 200 | 6,667 |

At 31 August 2007 the building has a remaining life of 15 years.

**Calculation of residue after sale**

| | *(i)* £ | *(ii)* £ | *(iii)* £ |
|---|---|---|---|
| Residue before sale | 60,000 | 60,000 | 60,000 |
| + balancing charge | 30,000 | 0 | 40,000 |
| - balancing allowance | 0 | (57,000) | 0 |
| Residue after sale | 90,000 | 3,000 | 100,000 |

## Successions

**6.50** Where the whole of a trade is transferred to another company under *ICTA 1988, s 343* without a change of ownership, the successor takes over the predecessor's assets at tax written down value for capital allowance purposes.

# CHARGEABLE GAINS

## Roll-over relief

**6.51** Assets sold in excess of cost may bring about a chargeable gain, assessable upon the company. If the assets are of a certain class and if new assets have been purchased to replace them the gain may qualify for roll-over relief under *TCGA 1992, s 152*. This will enable the gain to be deferred within the cost of the new asset.

The assets that can qualify for relief are listed under *TCGA 1992, s 155*.

The relevant classes of assets are as follows:

**Class 1 Assets within heads A and B below**

*Head A*

1 Any building or part of a building and any permanent or semi-permanent structure in the nature of a building, occupied (as well as used) only for the purposes of the trade.

2 Any land occupied (as well as used) only for the purposes of the trade. Head A has effect subject to *s 156*.

*Head B*

Fixed plant or machinery which does not form part of a building or of a permanent or semi-permanent structure in the nature of a building.

**Class 2**

Ships, aircraft and hovercraft ('hovercraft' having the same meaning as in the *Hovercraft Act 1968*).

**Class 3**

Satellites, space stations and spacecraft (including launch vehicles).

**Class 4**

Goodwill. (But not applicable after 1 April 2002)

**Class 4**

Goodwill no longer qualifies after 1 April 2002 as it is included within the intangible assets regime. See Chapter 7 for intangible assets.

## Conditions affecting the old assets and the new assets

**6.52** The old assets must have been used solely for the purposes of the trade throughout the period of ownership. The consideration received must be used in acquiring new assets or an interest therein. Upon acquisition the new assets must also be used solely for the purposes of the trade. The new assets must not be acquired for the purposes of realising a gain, ie as an investment (*TCGA 1992, s 152(5)*).

The trading company can then claim that the consideration on the sale of the old assets is reduced up to the amount reinvested that produces neither a gain nor a loss on disposal. The acquisition cost of the new asset is reduced by the same amount. The relief is given after indexation.

The new assets must be acquired during the period commencing 12 months before and ending three years after the disposal of, or of the interest in, the old assets. A provisional claim may be made if the company enters into an unconditional contract for purchase.

Apportionment takes place if the old asset is not used throughout the period of ownership for the purposes of the trade or if only part of an asset is used for the purposes of a trade. Periods before 31 March 1982 are ignored in calculating the period of ownership.

## Assets only partly replaced

**6.53** If only part of the asset is replaced it follows that the gain on disposal of the old asset is limited to the amount of consideration reinvested with the balance of the gain being rolled over (*TCGA 1992, s 153*).

## New assets which are depreciating assets

**6.54** If the new assets are depreciating assets the chargeable gain is not deducted from the cost of the new asset but is held over and becomes chargeable at the earliest of the following events:

- the new asset is disposed of,
- the asset is no longer used for the purposes of the trade, or
- 10 years have elapsed since the acquisition of the new asset.

A depreciating asset is any asset that will become a wasting asset within 10 years of acquisition. A wasting asset is an asset with a predictable life of 50 years or less (*TCGA 1992, s 44*). Fixed plant and machinery installed in a building with a life of more than 60 years to run will not be a depreciating asset. A leasehold building with less that 60 years to run will be a depreciating asset (Tax Bulletin, Issue 7, May 1993).

## Land and buildings and roll-over relief

**6.55** Land and buildings are treated as separate assets for roll-over relief purposes. The Revenue wish to see separate computations to support a claim together with an appropriate apportionment of costs (HMRC Capital Gains Tax Manual CG 60990). No roll-over relief is available for land held or property dealt with in the course of trade by a property dealing or development company other than land and buildings that it used for the purposes of the trade. Lessors of tied premises are treated as occupying and using the premises for the purposes of their trade (*TCGA 1992, s 156*(*4*)).

## New assets not purchased

**6.56** By concession proceeds used from the disposal of old assets may be used to enhance the value of qualifying assets already held. The other assets must only have been used for the purposes of the company's trade and on completion of the work undertaken the assets are immediately taken back for use in the trade (ESC D22).

Similarly, by concession if proceeds from the sale of old assets are used to acquire a further interest in another asset that is already being used for the purposes of the trade that new interest is treated as a new asset if it is taken into use for the purposes of the trade (ESC D25).

## New asset not brought immediately into trading use

**6.57** If a new asset on acquisition is not taken immediately into use for the purposes of the trade, roll-over relief will still be available in the following circumstances:

- the owner proposes to incur capital expenditure for the purposes of enhancing its value;
- any work arising from such capital expenditure begins as soon as possible after acquisition and is completed within a reasonable time;
- on completion of the work the asset is taken into use for the purpose of the trade and for no other purpose; and
- the asset is neither let nor used for any non-trading purpose in the period between acquisition and taking into use for trade purposes (ESC D24).

## Assets owned personally but used for the purposes of the trade of a personal company

**6.58** If an individual exercises no less than 5% of the voting rights of a company, which uses an asset owned by that individual for the purposes of its trade, that individual will be entitled to roll-over relief if all other conditions apply (*TCGA 1992, s 157*).

*Chapter 7*

# Intangible Assets

## SCOPE PRE AND POST 1 APRIL 2002

**7.1** As the UK economy moves forward on technological fields the taxation system is forced to keep pace. The intangible assets regime introduced with effect from 1 April 2002 provides companies with tax relief on their intangible assets including their intellectual property. The previous rules brought intangible asset disposal within the chargeable gains regime and taxed royalties and patent sales as income.

### Existing assets

**7.2** The pre 1 April 2002 rules have been in existence for many years and continue to apply to assets in existence on that date (*FA 2002, Sch 29, para 117*).

The legislation terms these assets as 'existing asset' (*FA 2002, Sch 29, para 118*(*3*)).

### Chargeable intangible assets

**7.3** The new intangible asset regime rules apply to assets, which are:

- intangible assets created by the company after 1 April 2002; or
- intangible assets that the company acquired after 1 April 2002, from a third party who was unrelated to the company at the time of the acquisition (*FA 2002, Sch 29, para 118*(*1*)).

The legislation terms these assets as 'chargeable intangible assets' (*FA 2002, Sch 29, para 137*(*1*)(*a*)).

The new intangible asset regime rules also apply to post 1 April 2002 chargeable intangible assets acquired from related third parties in the following circumstances:

- the asset at the time of sale was a chargeable intangible asset of the vendor company;
- if the asset is acquired from an intermediary who acquired the asset post 1 April 2002 from a third person, at the time of acquisition, the third person was neither a related party of the intermediary, nor of the company; or
- the asset was created after 1 April 2002 either by the person from whom it was acquired or by any other person (*FA 2002, Sch 29, para 118*(2)).

## Transitional period

**7.4** Therefore, the intangible asset regime does not apply to existing assets; namely those held by the company on 1 April 2002 or those acquired from a related party who held them on 1 April 2002. If an asset was internally generated, eg goodwill, and the business was in existence prior to 1 April 2002, the asset is treated as an existing asset prior to 1 April 2002. That being the case, the goodwill arising on incorporation of a sole trader or partnership business will remain as an existing asset and remain subject to capital gains on disposal if it was in existence prior to 1 April 2002. HMRC Corporate Intangibles Research and Development Manual CIRD 10145 gives a useful key to manual references applying to pre 1 April 2002 assets (grand-fathered assets).

---

**Example 7.1**

Ted commenced trading as a sole trader on 1 January 1987. Over recent years his business has expanded and he incorporates the business on 1 January 2007. He transfers the tangible fixed assets for £50,000 and the goodwill professionally valued at £20,000 to Ted Ltd, his newly formed company. Although Ted transfers the goodwill to the company after 1 April 2002, it was in existence prior to 1 April 2002 and is not within the intangible assets regime.

This example is continued in **7.10**, Example 7.3.

---

---

**Example 7.2**

Bill commenced trading as a sole trader on 1 January 2003. His business has expanded and he incorporates the business on 1 January 2007. He transfers the tangible fixed assets for £100,000 and the goodwill professionally valued at

£40,000 to Bill Ltd his newly formed company. Bill's goodwill was not in existence prior to 1 April 2002 and is therefore within the intangible assets regime.

This example is continued in **7.10**, example 7.3.

---

## MEANING OF AN INTANGIBLE ASSET

**7.5** The legislation gives intangible assets their accountancy meaning and includes intellectual property within the meaning of an intangible asset.

### Accountancy definition

**7.6** FRS 10 (goodwill and intangible assets) defines intangible assets as:

> 'Non-financial fixed assets that do not have a physical substance but are identifiable and are controlled by the entity through custody or legal rights'.

*Companies Act 1985, Sch 4* includes intangible fixed assets under the following sub-headings:

- development costs;
- concessions, patents, licences, trade marks and similar rights and assets; and
- goodwill.

The assets may only be included in the balance sheet if they were acquired for valuable consideration and are not effectively part of goodwill, or the assets were created by the company itself, except for internally generated goodwill.

For example, a company may include intangible assets under the following headings within intangible assets:

- patents, trade marks and other product rights;
- brand names;
- goodwill;
- publishing copyrights, rights and titles;
- newspaper titles;
- programmes, film rights and scores;

- databases;
- know-how agreements;
- development costs;
- betting office licences;
- trade value of retail outlets;
- exhibition rights and other similar intangible assets.

For taxation purposes intellectual property includes UK and overseas patents, trademarks, registered designs, copyright or design rights, plant breeders' rights, together with rights under *s 7* of the *Plant Varieties Act 1997* and the overseas equivalent. Assets owned outright and by licence are included, as are assets that are not protected by a legal right but which have an industrial, commercial or other economic value. Options or rights to acquire or dispose of an intangible asset are also included (*FA 2002, Sch 29, paras 2, 3*).

The intangible assets regime applies to goodwill and the accounting meaning is adopted (*FA 2002, Sch 29, para 4*), which defines goodwill as:

> 'The difference between the cost of an acquired entity and the aggregate of the fair values of that entity's identifiable assets and liabilities. Positive goodwill arises when the acquisition cost exceeds the aggregate fair values of the identifiable assets and liabilities. Negative goodwill arises when the aggregate fair values of the identifiable assets and liabilities of the entity exceed the acquisition cost'.

If a company has not drawn up accounts on this basis it will be treated as having done so for the purposes of corporation tax. Therefore HMRC will adjust accounts if they do not comply with GAAP and in particular FRS 10 (goodwill and intangible assets) (*FA 2002, Sch 29, para 5*).

## Excluded assets

**7.7** Assets entirely excluded from the intangible assets regime comprise rights over land or tangible moveable property, oil licences, financial assets, shares in a company, trust and partnership rights and powers and assets neither held for a business nor a commercial purpose (*FA 2002, Sch 29, paras 72–77*).

The FRS 13 definition of financial assets FRS 13 (derivatives and other financial instruments: disclosure) is adopted namely:

> 'cash, a contractual right to receive cash or another financial asset from another entity, a contractual right to exchange financial instru-

ments with another entity under conditions that are potentially favourable or an equity instrument of another entity.' (*FA 2002, Sch 29, para 75*(2))

## Assets excluded in certain situations

**7.8** Apart from royalties all assets owned by a life assurance business and a mutual trade association are excluded from the definition of intangibles. Expenditure on films, sound recording and computer software expenditure (when accounted for with the hardware) is also excluded apart from expenditure on royalties (*FA 2002, Sch 29, para 76*). If the computer software is bought separately, the company may elect for the software to be removed from the intangible assets regime (*FA 2002, Sch 29, para 83*).

The valuation of the intangible assets if need be is made on a just and reasonable basis.

Royalties and licences granted over existing assets from related parties are themselves treated as existing assets for accounting periods ending on or after 5 December 2005 (*FA 2006, s 77*).

## Research and development expenditure

**7.9** Research and development expenditure has its own taxation regime (see Chapter 8). The proceeds from the sale of research and development are included within the intangible assets regime (*FA 2002, Sch 29, para 82*).

# CORPORATION TAX TREATMENT

## Debits and credits

**7.10** With effect from 1 April 2002, gains and losses relating to intangible assets bought or made for continuous use in a business are taxed generally as revenue items (*FA 2002, Sch 29, para 1*).

Expenditure within the legislation is known as 'debits' and income as 'credits'.

The treatment of the debits and credits in calculating the taxable profits will depend on whether the assets are held for the purposes of a trade, a property business or if the company is non-trading.

Debits and credits in respect of assets held for the purposes of a trade are treated as receipts and expenses of that particular trade and are brought into the Schedule D Case I computation. Likewise debits and credits held for a property business are treated as income and expenses of that property business. A property business includes normal Schedule A lettings, furnished holiday lets and an overseas property business.

Expenditure and the reversal of an earlier gain are deductible from profits as it is written off in the accounts. Depreciation is allowed on an accounting basis or on a Revenue fixed rate basis (*FA 2002, Sch 29, para 7(1)*).

HMRC will look to consistency with UK group accounting policies to determine whether the individual company's accounting treatment may be adopted for taxation purposes (*FA 2002, Sch 29, para 6*).

---

**Example 7.3**

Example continued from **7.4**, Examples 7.1 and 7.2.

Assuming the same facts as Examples 7.1 and 7.2 in **7.4**, Bill Ltd but not Ted Ltd will be able to write off the cost of the goodwill on incorporation in its books. Assuming Bill decides a 10% deprecation rate, the annual write off is £4,000 (10% × £40,000).

This example is continued in **7.26**, Example 7.3.

## Annual payments and patent royalties

**7.11** Irrespective of when the intangible assets were acquired, the related annual payments and patent royalties are no longer deducted from total income as a charge on income. Instead they are deducted as a 'debit' on an accruals basis (*FA 2002, Sch 29, para 8(3)*).

If the royalty is payable to a related party and the payment is not made within 12 months after the end of the accounting period it cannot be allowed as a deduction for that period (*FA 2002, Sch 29, para 94*). See **7.27** regarding related parties.

## Depreciation

**7.12** The company may select its own depreciation policy or it may adopt the legislation policy. If using the legislation policy, it must make a written irrevocable election to HMRC no later than two years after the end of the accounting period in which the asset is created or acquired. The asset is then depreciated at 4% per annum on a straight-line basis apportioned for accounting periods less than 12 months (*FA 2002, Sch 29, paras 10, 11*).

## Non-trading debits and credits

**7.13** Non-trading debits and credits are netted off against each other. A net gain is assessable under Schedule D Case VI. A net loss is relieved in the following way:

- By claim within two years of the end of the accounting period to which the loss relates to set the loss against the company's total profits for that accounting period.
- By claim within two years of the end of the accounting period to which the loss relates to surrender by group relief under *ICTA 1988, s 403*.
- Any unutilised loss is carried forward to the next accounting period as if it were a non-trading debit of that period (*FA 2002, Sch 29, para 35*).

# PRESCRIBED DEBIT AND CREDIT ADJUSTMENTS

**7.14** There are certain prescribed pro-rata debit and credit adjustments. These are summarised in the following paragraphs.

## Impairment review

**7.15** The acquisition of an asset may be part of FRS 7 (fair values *in acquisition accounting*) impairment review because the acquisition cost is more than fair value. This could happen if a subsidiary was acquired in stages and deferred values are obtained. The accounting loss pro rata the tax and accounting cost is an allowable deduction from profits. The following formula is used to calculate the deductible debit in the year of acquisition:

Accounting loss × (Tax cost ÷ Accounting cost)

where:

Accounting loss = the amount of the loss recognised for accounting purposes

Tax cost = the amount of expenditure on the asset that is recognised for tax purposes

Accounting cost = the amount capitalised in respect of expenditure on the asset

In subsequent periods of account the following adjustment is made:

Accounting loss × (Tax value ÷ Accounting value)

where:

Accounting loss = the amount of the loss recognised for accounting purposes

Tax value = the tax written down value of the asset immediately before the amortisation charge is made or, as the case may be, the impairment loss is recognised for accounting purposes

Accounting value = the value of the asset recognised for accounting purposes immediately before the amortisation charge or, as the case may be, the impairment review (*FA 2002, Sch 29, para 9*).

## Reversal of a previous accounting gain

**7.16** If an accounting loss is recognised, where the tax value and the accounting value of the asset differ, the amount of the loss is adjusted in accordance with the following formula:

Accounting loss × (Previous credit ÷ Accounting gain)

where:

Accounting loss = the amount of the loss recognised for accounting purposes

Accounting gain = the amount of the gain that is (in whole or in part) reversed

Previous credit = the amount of the credit previously brought into account for tax purposes in respect of the gain (*FA 2002, Sch 29, para 12*).

This could occur on a change in an accounting policy during an accounting period.

## Income taxable

**7.17** Receipts, revaluations, negative goodwill credits and reversals of any previous debits are all taxable as income on an accounting basis as they accrue (*FA 2002, Sch 29, para 13*). Apart from assets for which an election has been made for the 4% fixed rate depreciation, accounting adjustments brought about by a revaluation of intangible assets or the restoration of past losses are adjusted by the following formula:

Accounting adjustment × (Tax value ÷ Accounting value)

where:

Accounting adjustment = the amount of the increase in the accounting value of the asset

Tax value = the tax written down value of the asset immediately before the revaluation

Accounting value = the value of the asset by reference to which the revaluation is carried out (*FA 2002, Sch 29, para 15*).

Any gain recognised in calculating negative goodwill is apportioned to the intangible assets on a just and reasonable basis and included in income accordingly (*FA 2002, Sch 29, para 16*).

Accounting gain reversals of previous losses recognised in the company's accounts is adjusted as follows:

Accounting gain × (Tax debit ÷ Accounting loss)

where:

Accounting gain = the amount of the gain recognised for accounting purposes

Accounting loss = the amount of the loss that is (in whole or in part) reversed

Tax debit = the amount of the tax debit previously brought into account in respect of the loss (*FA 2002, Sch 29, para 17*).

## Realisation of intangible fixed assets

**7.18** Amounts arising from asset sale (proceeds less incidental costs of realisation) or balance sheet writing off are compared to the asset's tax written down value and the resultant net debit or credit is included in calculating profits chargeable to corporation tax. Abortive expenditure costs are allowed as a deduction (*FA 2002, Sch 29, para 26*).

In the case of a part realisation, the tax written down value is apportioned by the following formula:

Reduction in accounting value ÷ Previous accounting value

where:

Reduction in accounting value = the difference between the accounting value immediately before the realisation compared with that immediately after the realisation

Previous accounting value = the accounting value immediately before the realisation (*FA 2002, Sch 29, para 22*).

Cost is substituted for tax written down value if the asset has not been depreciated. Where there is no balance sheet valuation for the asset, possibly because it was created by the company, the full sale proceeds are brought into the profit and loss account as income.

Where the asset has been written down on an accounting basis, the tax written down value is calculated as follows:

Tax cost – Debits + Credits

where:

Tax cost = the cost of the asset recognised for tax purposes

Debits = the total amount of the depreciation debits previously brought into account for tax purposes

Credits = the total amount of any credits previously brought into account for tax purposes in respect of a revaluation (*FA 2002, Sch 29, para 15*).

The comparable adjustment for assets that have been written down on the fixed basis is as follows:

Tax cost – Debits

where:

Tax cost = the cost of the asset recognised for tax purposes

Debits = the total amount of the depreciation debits previously brought into account for tax purposes on the fixed rate basis (*FA 2002, Sch 29, para 28*).

## Part realisation of an asset

**7.19** If there has been a partial sale of an intangible asset, the tax written down value of the asset immediately after the part realisation is calculated as follows:

Previous tax value × (New accounting value ÷ Previous accounting value)

where:

Previous tax value = the tax written down value of the asset immediately before the part realisation

New accounting value = the accounting value of the asset immediately after the part realisation

Previous accounting value = the accounting value immediately before the part realisation (*FA 2002, Sch 29, para 29*).

An asset may cease to be a chargeable asset during its lifetime in which case there is a deemed disposal for the company (*FA 2002, Sch 29, para 108*).

## SALE OF AN INTANGIBLE ASSET

### Sale proceeds

**7.20** Sale proceeds arising from a sale of intangible assets are credited to the profit and loss account. Disposal costs are allowed as a deductible debit. Relief is also given for abortive costs of sale (*FA 2002, Sch 29, para 26*).

### Roll-over and reinvestment relief

**7.21** When a company sells an intangible asset it may, provided all conditions are met, be able to claim reinvestment relief. The effect being that it will avoid the credit (sale proceeds less incidental costs of sale) to its profits.

The conditions imposed are first that the asset disposed of must have been within the intangible assets regime throughout its ownership. Where the asset was within the intangible assets regime at the time of sale and for a substantial period of the ownership (but not the whole), it will be treated as a separate asset for the time that it so qualified. Sales proceeds are apportioned on a just and reasonable basis. Secondly, the sale proceeds must be greater than the original cost of the original asset or adjusted cost where there has been a part realisation.

The new assets acquired must be immediately chargeable intangible assets for the company as soon as they are acquired (as recognised for accounting purposes). The expenditure must be capitalised. The time limits for incurring the expenditure are 12 months before the sale of the old asset and three years thereafter (*FA 2002, Sch 29, para 39*).

Any claims to HMRC must be in writing, must specify the old assets, identify the expenditure on new assets and must state the amount of the relief claimed (*FA 2002, Sch 29, para 40*). A company may make a provisional claim for relief if it has sold an intangible asset and intends to replace it with new intangible assets. The provisional claim continues until the earlier of its being withdrawn, replaced by a new claim or the expiry of four years after the end of the accounting period in which the realisation took place. Adjustments are then accordingly made to the corporation tax returns or are assessed regardless of time limits (*FA 2002, Sch 29, para 43*).

The effect of the claim is to reduce the realisation proceeds and the tax cost of the new asset by the same amount.

The amount is calculated as follows:

- If the new expenditure on other assets is equal to or greater than the proceeds of realisation of the old asset, the amount available for relief is the amount by which the proceeds of realisation exceed the tax cost of the old asset.

- If the amount of the new expenditure on other assets is less than the proceeds of realisation of the old asset, the amount available for relief is the amount (if any) by which the new expenditure on other assets exceeds the tax cost of the old asset.

- If the new expenditure does not exceed the tax cost of the old asset no relief is given (*FA 2002, Sch 29, para 41*).

---

**Example 7.4**

P Ltd makes up accounts to 31 December each year. The following accounting transactions take place:

| *Year ended* | | *Sale proceeds* £000 | *Cost* £000 | *Profit and loss account* £000 | | *Net book value* £000 |
|---|---|---|---|---|---|---|
| 31 December 2006 | Bought copyright with an estimated life of five years | | 50 | 10 debit | Annual depreciation | 40 |
| 31 December 2007 | Sold | 70 | | 30 credit | Profit on sale | Nil |
| | Bought copyright with an estimated life of five years | | 75 | 15 debit | Annual depreciation | 60 |

For corporation tax purposes the company wishes to claim reinvestment relief on the first disposal. In order to do this it must first analyse the gain arising.

| *Year ended* | *Total gain* £000 | *Arising from depreciation* £000 | *Gain available for reinvestment relief* £000 | *Actual new chargeable intangible asset purchased* £000 | *Tax cost of new asset purchased* £000 |
|---|---|---|---|---|---|
| 31 December 2007 | 30 | 10 | 20 | 75 | 55 |

The corporation tax deductions on these transactions are as follows:

| *Year ended 31 December* | | *Purchase and sale transactions* £000 | *Reinvestment relief* £000 | *Opening tax value* £000 | *Adjustment to profits for corporation tax* £000 | *Closing tax value* £000 |
|---|---|---|---|---|---|---|
| 2006 | Bought | | | 50 | 10 Debit | 40 |
| 2007 | Sold | 70 | 20 | | 10 Credit | Nil |
| | Bought | 75 | 20 | 55 | 11 Debit | 44 |

**7.22** On a part realisation the adjusted cost is calculated as follows:

Reduction in accounting value ÷ Previous accounting value

where:

Reduction in accounting value = the difference between the accounting value immediately before the part realisation compared with that immediately after the part realisation

Previous accounting value = the accounting value immediately before the part realisation

A company may wish to sell and reacquire the same asset. In which case this is treated as an independent disposal on which reinvestment relief is available. Deemed realisations are not recognised for reinvestment relief.

# GROUPS

## Meaning of a group

**7.23** Group for intangible assets purposes adopts the capital gains tax definition: see **10.20**.

A group member must be an effective 51% subsidiary of the principal company, but the principal company cannot be a 75% subsidiary of another group and a company cannot be a member of more than one group.

Four criteria are applied to determine to which group a company belongs in the following order: voting rights, profits available for distribution, assets on a winding-up and percentage of directly and indirectly owned ordinary shares (*FA 2002, Sch 29, para 50*).

The group remains intact until the principal company becomes a member of another group, in which case other companies join the group. The four criteria above must be applied to determine the group members.

## Intra-group asset transfers

**7.24** Intra-group transfers of assets have no tax effect except for tax-exempt friendly societies and dual resident investing companies. The transferee company adopts the asset as if it were its own.

Reinvestment relief is also available to group members but not in respect of intra-group asset transfers. Neither is it available to a dual resident investing company. Both companies involved are required to claim (*FA 2002, Sch 29, para 56*).

Purchase by a company of the controlling interest in a non-group company that subsequently becomes a member of the group is treated for reinvestment purposes as a purchase of the underlying assets on which relief is available. Expenditure incurred by a company on its new purchase is treated as the lesser of the tax written down value of the underlying assets immediately before acquisition and the consideration paid for the controlling interest. If the relief applies the tax value of the underlying intangible assets is reduced by the amount of the relief (*FA 2002, Sch 29, para 57*).

## Leaving a group

**7.25** When a company leaves a group, having acquired a chargeable intangible asset by intra-group transfer within the past six years, there is a de-grouping charge on the transferee based on market value at the date of transfer. A debit or credit adjustment is made in the accounting period in which the company leaves the group (*FA 2002, Sch 29, para 58*).

There is no de-grouping charge where two companies who have made intra-group transfers of assets within the time limits leave the group at the same time. There is no de-grouping charge if the entire group becomes a member of another group. If the transferee ceases to qualify as a member of the new group within six years of transfer, it is treated as having sold and reacquired the asset at the time of transfer. Any adjustment is included in the corporation tax computation for the period in which the company leaves the group. Group de-grouping charges can, by joint election between transferor and transferee company, be passed to the transferor company to form part of its income. It will be treated as a non-trading gain. The transferor company must be resident in the UK or be deemed to be carrying on a trade in the UK through a branch or agency. (The company must not be a friendly society or a dual resident holding company). Unpaid tax may be recovered from any group members or controlling directors of non-UK resident companies carrying on a trade in the UK, if not paid by the relevant company. Inter company roll-over and de-grouping charge payments are left out of account for corporation tax purposes provided they do not exceed the amount of relief (*FA 2002, Sch 29, para 71*). There is no de-grouping charge on a demerger carried out for bona fide commercial reasons.

## Reconstructions

**7.26** In general reconstructions avoid a tax charge. In order to ensure this effect a clearance procedure is available (*FA 2002, Sch 29, para 88*).

In a scheme of reconstruction where the whole or part of a business is transferred for shares or loan stock by a company, provided the company received no part of the consideration there is no tax charge. Although the consideration must be in shares apportionment is possible. The reconstruction must be made for bona fide commercial reasons and must not be part of a scheme of avoidance. (The company must not be friendly society or a dual resident holding company) (*FA 2002, Sch 29, para 84*).

There is no tax charge on transfers of UK trades and companies resident in EU states follow the same lines provided the consideration is in securities issued by the transferor to the transferee. The intangible asset is transferred to the transferee company complete with its tax history (*FA 2002, Sch 29, para 85*).

Where intangible assets are transferred from a UK company's overseas branch to a non-UK resident company the gain may be deferred, the trade must be transferred in exchange for securities. If the securities are later sold a taxable credit must be brought into account by the transferor equal to the deferred gain. Also, if at any time within six years after the transfer the transferee disposes of the relevant assets taxable credit must be brought into account by the transferor equal to the deferred gain (*FA 2002, Sch 29, para 86*). Relief for any foreign tax is available if there is no deferral of the gain (*FA 2002, Sch 29, para 87*(2)).

## Related parties

**7.27** Transfers of intangible assets between related parties take place at market value (*FA 2002, Sch 29, para 92*) subject to the transfer pricing provisions.

---

**Example 7.5**

Continued from **7.10**, Example 7.3.

Continuing with the same facts as Example7.2 in **7.4** and Example 7.3 in **7.10**, Bill had his goodwill upon incorporation professionally valued so there is no question of its value being adjusted.

However, if Bill had opted for a *TCGA 1992, s 165* hold-over claim (see Tottel's Capital Gains Tax) the amount held over will be deductible from the deemed market value of the goodwill for the purposes of calculating the annual write off (*FA 2002, Sch 29, para 92(4C)*).

Thus supposing Bill's hold-over relief amounted to £10,000, the annual write off will be £3,000 [10% × (40,000 – 10,000)].

---

**7.28** Part realisation roll-over relief is not available to a related party. Royalty payments to a related party not paid within 12 months of the accounting period in which they are accrued and not brought in as a credit by the recipient company are not allowed as a deduction for the payee.

A related party relationship exists where:

**Case 1**

A company has control or a major interest in another company

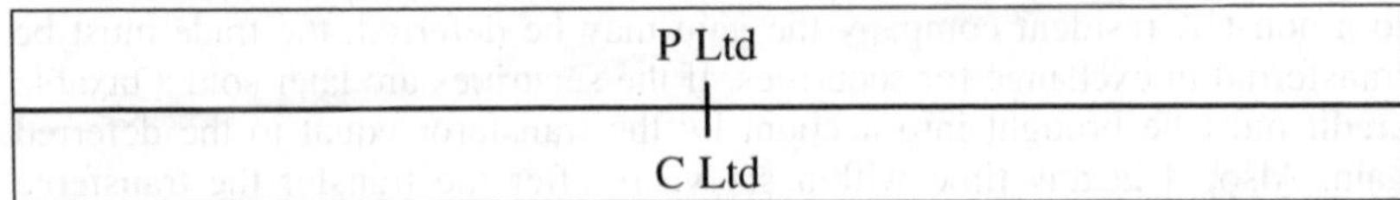


**Case 2**

Companies are under the control of the same person.

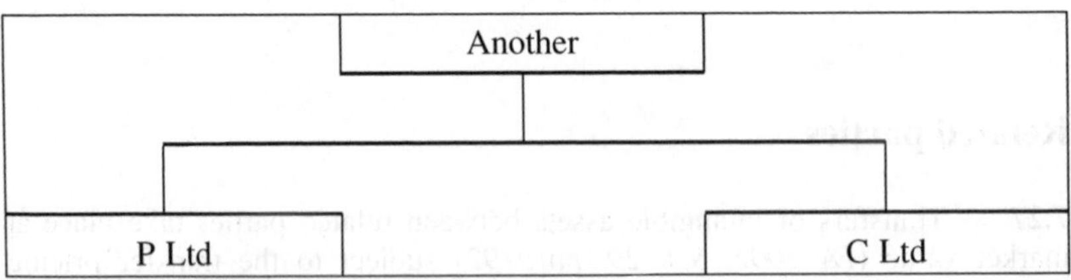


**Case 3**

C Ltd is a close company of which P is a participator or an associate of a participator (*ICTA 1988, s 417*; close company definitions apply: see **4.10**, **4.12**).

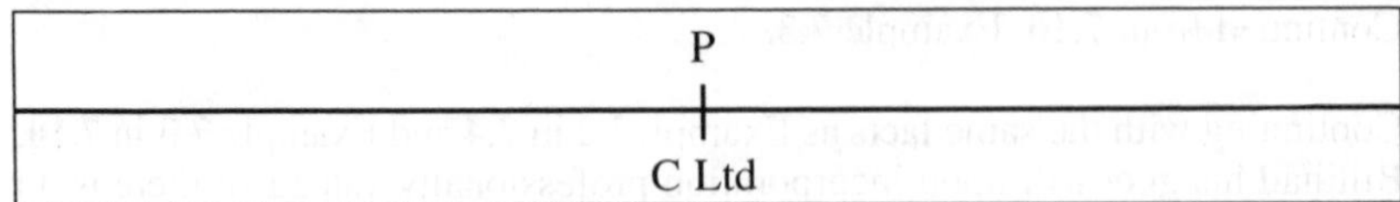


**Case 4**

P Ltd and C Ltd are companies in the same group.

| P Ltd | | C Ltd |
|---|---|---|

Control means that a person is able to secure that the company's affairs are conducted in accordance with their wishes either by shareholdings, voting power or by powers conferred by the Articles of Association. A major interest exists if two persons have control of a company and each of them has at least 40% of the total shareholding (*FA 2002, Sch 29, para 96*). Rights and powers owned singly and jointly are taken into account namely: rights and powers that he is entitled to acquire at a future date or will, at a future date, become entitled to acquire and others rights and powers that can be exercised on his behalf, under his direction or for his benefit. Rights and powers of a person connected with him are also taken into account, but not persons connected to a connected person (*FA 2002, Sch 29, para 97*). Loan security arrangements are not taken into account. Rights and powers of a person as a member of a partnership are only taken into account if the person has a major interest (40%) in the partnership (*FA 2002, Sch 29, para 99*).

## Connected persons

**7.29** Connected persons include spouses (and civil partners), relatives and relatives of their spouses. Relatives are siblings, grandparents and grandchildren. (Great-grandparents and great-grandchildren etc are also included). The trustee of a settlement is connected with the settlor, a person connected with the settlor and any company connected with the settlement. The company must be a close company (or only not a close company because it is non-UK resident) of which the trustees are participators (*FA 2002, Sch 29, para 101*). (Company has the same meaning (*ICTA 1988, s 832*) see **1.2**).

## Grants

**7.30** Regional development grants and certain Northern Ireland grants are not taxable credits for the purposes of computing corporation tax. All other grants received are taxable credits (*FA 2002, Sch 29, para 102*).

## Finance lessors

**7.31** Finance lessors are within the intangible assets regime for assets leased under finance leases to other companies. However, neither fixed rate depreciation nor reinvestment relief is available (*FA 2002, Sch 29, para 104* and the *Corporation Tax (Finance Leasing of Intangible Assets) Regulations 2002, SI 2002/1967*).

# INTERNATIONAL ASPECTS

## Company ceasing to be UK resident

**7.32** There is a deemed disposal of a chargeable intangible asset at market value when a company ceases to be UK resident (*FA 2002, Sch 29, para 108*). A UK holding company and a 75% subsidiary may jointly elect for the gain to be postponed on assets used for the purposes of the trade of the branch or agency where market value exceeds cost. The gain being the excess market value over cost is chargeable as a non-trading taxable credit on the UK holding company if the now non-resident subsidiary company disposes of the asset within six years of becoming non-resident. The gain is also chargeable on the holding company if it ceases to be UK resident or the non-resident company is no longer a subsidiary.

## Controlled foreign companies

**7.33** Gains relating to controlled foreign companies are brought into the assumed profits computation (see **13.25–13.40**) for *ICTA 1988, s 747* for apportionment purposes as taxable credits (*FA 2002, Sch 29, para 116*).

*Chapter 8*

# Research and Development

## INTRODUCTION

**8.1** Relief is available for capital research and development (R & D) through the capital allowance rules and for revenue R & D through the tax relief for expenditure on research and development.

## CAPITAL EXPENDITURE

### Capital allowances

**8.2** Capital allowances on research and development allowances may be claimed by any size of company but only if the company carries on a trade. If the company does not already carry on a trade it must set up and commence a trade connected with the R & D after incurring the expenditure (*CAA 2001, s 439(1)*). The company need not carry on the research itself; a third party may carry on the research on the company's behalf. The R & D must be related to the trade that is being carried on, known as 'the relevant trade'. R & D capital allowances can neither be claimed against investment income nor against professional and vocational income. Capital R & D expenditure qualifies for 100% initial allowance for capital allowance purposes. R & D is also available on oil and gas exploration. Thus the company is able to write off the full cost in the accounting period in which it is incurred (*CAA 2001, s 437*).

### Meaning of research and development

**8.3** For the purposes of claiming 100% capital allowances on R & D, the definition of R & D follows the accounting definition given in UK GAAP SSAP 13 (accounting for research and development) or IAS 38 (intangible assets) as appropriate (*ICTA 1988, s 837A*).

## The SSAP 13 definition

- Pure (or basic) research: experimental or theoretical work undertaken primarily to acquire new scientific or technical knowledge for its own sake rather than directed towards any specific aim or application.
- Applied research: original or critical investigation undertaken in order to gain new scientific or technical knowledge and directed towards a specific practical aim or objective.
- Development: use of scientific or technical knowledge in order to produce new or substantially improved materials, devices, products or services, to install new processes or systems prior to the commencement of commercial production or commercial applications, or to improving substantially those already produced or installed.

## The IAS 38 Definition

- Research is original and planned investigation undertaken with the prospect of gaining new scientific or technical knowledge and understanding.
- Development is the application of research findings or other knowledge to a plan or design for the production of new or substantially improved materials, devices, products, processes, systems or services before the start of commercial production or use.

**8.4** Allowances are given for pure and applied research in order to gain new or scientific knowledge. Oil and gas exploration is included. The trade related R & D may be of a sort that may lead to or facilitate an extension of the company's trade. It may also be of a medical nature, which has a special relation to the welfare of workers employed in that trade (*CAA 2001, s 439(5)*). If the research is carried on by a third party on the company's behalf, the company must retain responsibility for the research and the expenditure must be undertaken directly.

---

**Example 8.1**

S Ltd had a part share in a petroleum exploration licence. It arranged for G Ltd to provide the funds and the equipment to conduct operations. In return S Ltd gave G Ltd the rights to the ownership of all the petroleum won and saved to which it was entitled. G Ltd claimed that the expenditure incurred under that agreement qualified as R & D capital expenditure because it was incurred on scientific research directly undertaken on its behalf.

G Ltd is not entitled to the R & D capital allowance because the research was not directly undertaken by or on behalf of G Ltd. The facts are those of *Gaspet Ltd v Ellis* (1987) 60 TC 91, [1987] STC 362, [1987] 1 WLR 769.

---

**8.5** Medical research undertaken for the benefit of the community as a whole may qualify for R & D allowance if it may lead to or facilitate an extension of the trade. For example, medical research undertaken by a drug company for the purpose of its trade may qualify because it is related to its trade of manufacturing drugs (HMRC Capital Allowances Manual CA 60400).

With effect from 1 April 2000 R & D expenditure has been expanded to include payments made to clinical trial volunteers for taking part in such tests for companies that are not SMEs. The start date for SME companies has yet to be announced (*FA 2006, s 28* and *Sch 2*).

## Qualifying expenditure

**8.6** Relief may be claimed on providing facilities to carry out the research (*CAA 2001, s 438*). Land does not qualify for relief, nor does the cost of a dwelling that is more than 25% of the cost of the building (*CAA 2001, s 438(4)*). Expenditure on the acquisition of rights in research and development or rights arising out of research and development does not qualify for R & D (*CAA 2001, s 438(2)*).

---

**Example 8.2**

Novotech plc is engaged in a qualifying research project and incurs the following expenditure:

- A building for £2.5m excluding the cost of the land. The cost of the building is apportioned between research laboratories £2m and living accommodation £500,000.
- A car for each researcher who is required to travel about the country carrying out research activities.
- The patent rights to a patented invention that Novotech considers may be of assistance with the current project.

The building, including the living accommodation, will qualify for R & D. This is because the living accommodation is less than 25% of the cost of the whole building. The motor cars qualify as expenditure on research and development. The cost of acquiring the patent rights does not qualify for R & D because it is expenditure incurred in acquiring rights arising out of research and development.

---

## Allowances

**8.7** A 100% capital allowance may be claimed on the expenditure during the accounting period in which the expenditure is incurred. A reduced claim may be made (*CAA 2001, s 441(3)*) but there is no facility to claim further allowances (such as WDAs) in subsequent accounting periods.

If ownership of the asset changes hands or if it destroyed, a disposal value must be included within the company's corporation tax computation. On sale it will be the net proceeds of sale or market value in other cases. If the asset is demolished or destroyed any insurance or compensation monies received are taken as the disposal value. In the accounting period of disposal a balancing charge will be included being the smaller of the difference between the disposal value and the balance of unclaimed expenditure and the R & D allowance claimed (*CAA 2001, s 442*). There is no facility in the legislation for claiming a balancing allowance.

The balancing charge and R & D allowance are treated accordingly as receipts and expenses of the trade (*CAA 2001, s 450*).

---

**Example 8.3**

In the year of acquisition of a £2.5m research building, Novotech plc makes a claim for £1m R & D. Some years later it sells the building for £5m. The balancing charge is the smaller of:

- the difference between the disposal value and the balance of unclaimed expenditure:

  £5m – £(2.5m – 1m) = £3.5m

  and

- the R & D allowance claimed:

  £1m

The balancing charge is £1m, the R & D claim made.

---

**8.8** If the company ceases to use the asset for the R & D purpose this is not a disposal for R & D purposes. The R & D allowance is eventually recouped when the asset is sold. On a change of use the asset may qualify for plant and machinery allowances or industrial buildings allowance (see Chapter 6). The R & D allowance is not clawed back at this stage. It is only clawed back on the eventual sale of the asset.

## Disposal value

**8.9** If an R & D asset on which an R & D allowance has been claimed is demolished and the demolition costs exceed the disposal value, (which in many cases may be nil), the excess demolition costs may qualify for R & D allowance. They will only qualify if the asset has not begun to be used for any purpose other than research and development (*CAA 2001, s 445*). The excess is not to be treated as expenditure on any property that replaces the demolished asset.

Any additional VAT liability incurred on the R & D asset qualifies for R & D allowances provided that the company, which incurred the original expenditure on the asset, still owns it and the asset has not been demolished or destroyed. Any additional VAT rebate is treated as a disposal value provided that the company that incurred the original expenditure on the asset still owns it and the asset has not been demolished or destroyed. If there is no unclaimed R & D allowance, the VAT rebate is treated as a balancing charge. If there is unclaimed R & D allowance and the additional VAT rebate is less than the unclaimed R& D allowance, the additional VAT rebate is deducted from the unclaimed R & D allowance and the result treated as the unclaimed R & D allowance for future disposal events. If the additional VAT rebate is more than the unclaimed R & D allowance the difference is treated as a balancing charge (*CAA 2001, ss 448, 449*). (See also HMRC Capital Allowances Manual CA 60750.)

# REVENUE EXPENDITURE

## Revenue deductions

**8.10** The tax relief for expenditure on research and development provisions may be claimed by all companies. In general the small company rules are contained in *FA 2000, Sch 20* and the large company rules in *FA 2002, Sch 12*. The relief only applies to companies and for this purpose the company definition given in *TA 1988, s 832(1)* applies being 'any body corporate or unincorporated association but does not include a partnership, a local authority or a local authority association'. The company must also be within the charge to corporation tax (HMRC Corporate Intangibles Research and Development Manual CIRD 81200).

Companies qualify for an enhanced deduction if expenditure incurred is more than £10,000 in an accounting period. The enhanced deduction is included within the adjusted trading profits. Companies claim the enhanced relief by completing boxes 99 to 102 as appropriate. The following paragraphs provide a summary of the detailed rules.

## Meaning of research and development expenditure

**8.11** The same GAAP definitions are used as in **8.2**. In addition the research must be within the DTI guidelines. HMRC recommends that the DTI guideline tests be applied before the SSAP 13 and IAS 38 tests. Essentially a project will qualify as an R & D project if it is carried on in a field of science or technology and is undertaken with an aim to extend knowledge to which the relief applies (HMRC Corporate Intangibles Research and Development Manual CIRD 81300). The DTI Guidelines are reproduced in HMRC Corporate Intangibles Research and Development Manual CIRD 81900. Paragraph 19 of the DTI Guidelines defines the meaning of a project:

> 'A project consists of a number of activities conducted to a method or plans in order to achieve an advance in science or technology. It is important to get the boundaries of the project correct. It should encompass all the activities that collectively serve to resolve the scientific or technological uncertainty associated with achieving the advance, so it could include a number of different sub-projects. A project may itself be part of a larger commercial project, but that does not make the parts of the commercial project that do not address scientific or technological uncertainty into R & D.'

Therefore, in practice, every research activity should be broken down into its separate parts to ascertain whether or not it will qualify as R & D.

## Relevant research and development

**8.12** Relief can only be claimed on relevant research and development. Relevant research and development is defined in *FA 2000, Sch 20, para 4* (which essentially deals with small companies) to mean that it is research and development related to a trade carried on by the company, or from which it is intended that a trade to be carried on by the company will be derived. The same meaning is adopted in *FA 2002, Sch 12, para 4(4)* and *FA 2002, Sch 12, para 9(3)*, which deal with all company and SME research respectively.

The R & D expenditure may relate to a trade already carried on by the company or the expenditure may lead to or facilitate an extension of that trade and if medical research it has a special relation to the welfare of workers employed in that trade (*FA 2000, Sch 20, para 4*).

Staffing costs include salaries and wages for all employees actively engaged in the research, together with employer's NIC and employer's pension fund contributions relevant to them. Benefits are not included in staff costs with effect from 1 April 2004. Costs for employees only partly engaged in research are apportioned appropriately (*FA 2000, Sch 20, para 5*). (Employees in this context includes directors). Secretarial and administrative costs are excluded.

## Qualifying R & D expenditure

**8.13** Qualifying R & D expenditure for both the small and the large company schemes is similar but not identical. It can be summarised as follows:

The expenditure:

- must not be capital;
- is attributable to relevant R & D directly undertaken by the company or on its behalf;
- is incurred on staffing costs or on software or consumable items or on qualifying expenditure on externally provided workers or is qualifying expenditure on sub-contracted R & D, and from 1 April 2006 on clinical trials;
- is not incurred by the company in carrying on contracted-out activities;
- is not subsidised (SME scheme only);
- any intellectual property created as a result of the R & D will be vested in total or in part in the company (SME scheme only); and

if the expenditure is incurred in carrying on activities contracted out to the company, they are contracted out by:

- a large company, or
- a person otherwise than in the course of a trade, profession or vocation the profits of which are chargeable to tax under Case I or II of Schedule D.

(*FA 2000, Sch 20, para 3*; *FA 2002, Sch 12, para 4*).

## Intellectual property

**8.14** Intellectual property includes:

- any industrial information or technique likely to assist in:
  - the manufacture or processing of goods or materials, or

- the working of a mine, oil well or other source of mineral deposits or the winning of access thereto, or
- the carrying out of any agricultural, forestry or fishing operations;

- any patent, trademark, registered design, copyright, design right or plant breeder's right or overseas equivalent (*FA 2000, Sch 20, para 7*).

The intellectual property if vested should be vested at the time when the intellectual property is created.

## Subsidised expenditure

**8.15** Subsidised expenditure is any expenditure for which a grant or assistance is directly or indirectly received.

## Externally provided workers

**8.16** Externally provided workers are those engaged on the project who are not employed by the company but are under the company's supervision. The external workers' services must be supplied to the company through a staff provider. Self-employed consultants are not externally provided workers, although their costs may form part of subcontracted R & D (HMRC Corporate Intangibles Research and Development Manual CIRD 84100).

Where the staff provider and the company are not connected, 65% of the staff provision payment cost is treated as qualifying expenditure on externally provided workers.

If external workers are provided by a connected person, and the whole of the fee is included in the relevant provider's GAAP accounts for a period ending not more than 12 months after the end of the accounting period in which the company claiming the R & D allowance makes the payment, then the company may claim R & D tax credit on the lower of:

- the qualifying payment for staff that it makes to the staff provider, and
- the amount that the staff provider includes as relevant expenditure in its accounts (*FA 2000, Sch 20, para 8C*).

If the staff provided and the company are not connected they may jointly elect in writing, within two years of the end of the accounting period in which the contract arrangement is entered into, for the connected persons treatment to apply. This election must apply to all staff under the same arrangement (*FA 2000, Sch 20, paras 8A–8E* and *FA 2002, Sch 12, para 17(d)*).

## Subcontracted research & development

**8.17** An SME can claim relief on the payments that it makes to subcontractors. The treatment is similar to the externally provided workers treatment. If the parties are not connected, only 65% of the costs are deductible by the company.

If the contractor is a connected person, and the whole of the amount that is paid to the subcontractor is included in the subcontractor's GAAP accounts for a period ending not more than 12 months after the end of the accounting period in which the company claiming the R & D allowance makes the payment, then the company may claim R & D tax credit on the lower of:

- the payment that it makes to the subcontractor, and
- the amount that the subcontractor includes as relevant expenditure in his or her accounts.

If the subcontractor and the company are not connected they may jointly elect, in writing, within two years of the end of the accounting period in which the subcontract arrangement is entered into, for the connected persons treatment to apply (*FA 2000, Sch 20, paras 9–12*).

A large company's R & D expenditure that it subcontracts to other parties is generally not allowable (see HMRC Corporate Intangibles Research and Development Manual CIRD 84200) although it can have work subcontracted out to it (see **8.6**).

# DEFINITION OF AN SME

**8.18** An SME is defined in accordance with the European recommendation (*FA 2000, Sch 20, para 2*).

**Definition of a Micro, Small and Medium-sized company**

| | *Medium* | *Small* | *Micro* |
|---|---|---|---|
| If the company has fewer than | 250 employees | 50 employees | 10 employees |
| and | | | |
| **either** an annual turnover not exceeding | €50m | €10m | €2m |
| **or** | | | |
| a balance sheet total not exceeding | €43m | €10m | €2m |

(2003/361/EC)

The staff head count is based on the number of full-time person years attributable to people who have worked within or for the concern during the year in question. Part-time, seasonal and temporary workers are included on a pro-rata basis.

'Employees' includes actual employees, persons seconded to the enterprise, owner-managers and partners (other than sleeping partners). Apprentices or students engaged in vocational training with an apprenticeship or vocational training contract, or any periods of maternity or parental leave are excluded.

Turnover is taken per the accounts (net of VAT). The balance sheet total is the gross amount of assets shown in the accounts. Results are converted from sterling to euros to ascertain whether the tests are met.

The EC defines the enterprise as either autonomous, linked or partner. Autonomous means that there are no partner or linked enterprises. A linked enterprise is an enterprise whereby one company is able to exercise control directly or indirectly over the other. A partner enterprise exists where the enterprises are not linked but where one enterprise is able to exercise control either directly or indirectly over the affairs of the other. If a company has partner or linked enterprise relationships the results are aggregated. (See Flow Chart HMRC Corporate Intangibles Research and Development Manual CIRD 92850).

The conditions are relaxed for public investment corporations, and venture capital companies, 'business angels', provided the total investment of those business angels in the same enterprise is less than €1.25m, universities or non-profit research centres, institutional investors, including regional development funds and autonomous local authorities with an annual budget of less than €10m and fewer than 5,000 inhabitants.

A company may change its status from SME to large company. This will only take place if the conditions are satisfied for two consecutive years.

## SMALL OR MEDIUM-SIZED COMPANY

### Tax relief for expenditure on research and development

**8.19** A small or medium-sized company (SME) will qualify for an enhanced deduction from trading profits of 150% of its qualifying R & D expenditure if this expenditure amounts to £10,000 or more during a 12-month accounting period. The amount is reduced proportionately if the accounting period is less than 12 months (*FA 2000, Sch 20, para 1*). (The £10,000 limit was introduced for accounting periods ending on or after 27 September 2003. Previously the limit was £25,000). Qualifying expenditure is expenditure that would be allowable as a deduction in computing the taxable profits of a trade carried on by the company, or would have been allowable if the trade were being carried on at the time that the expenditure was incurred. Pre-trading expenditure is not treated as incurred on the first day of trading (*ICTA 1988, s 401*) but when it is actually incurred.

## Relief

**8.20** 150% relief can be obtained by the company if it is carrying on an R & D trade during that accounting period. An adjustment is included in the Schedule D Case I computation under the heading 'Deductible expenditure not included in the accounts' (*FA 2000, Sch 20, para 13*).

If the company has not yet started the trade it may elect to treat 150% of the expenditure as a trading loss of the accounting period in which the expenditure was incurred. The relief for pre-trading expenditure (*ICTA 1988, s 401*) is ignored. The election must be made in writing within two years of the accounting period to which the loss relates (*FA 2000, Sch 20, para 14*). However, this deemed trading loss may not be set off against profits of a preceding accounting period (where *ICTA 1988, s 393A(1)(b)* applies) where the company is also entitled to a deemed trading loss for that earlier period.

Alternatively, the company may surrender the loss for a cash payment of 16% of the loss for the chargeable period. The cash payment cannot exceed the total of the company's PAYE and NIC liabilities for the period. Employee child tax credits, working tax credit, statutory sick pay and statutory maternity pay are ignored in these calculations (*FA 2000, Sch 20, para 17*). The relief claimed is included in box 89 of the company tax return. Trading losses carried forward are restricted accordingly. The time limit for making the claim is two years from the end of the relevant accounting period.

The relief is only available to SMEs. If the SME is owned by a consortium no R &D relief may be surrendered to any group company that is not an SME (*FA 2000, Sch 20, para 22*).

# LARGE COMPANY

## Tax relief for expenditure on research and development

**8.21** A large company will qualify for an enhanced deduction from trading profits of 125% of its qualifying R & D expenditure if this expenditure amounts to £10,000 or more during a 12-month accounting period. The amount is reduced proportionately if the accounting period is less than 12 months (*FA 2002, Sch 12, para 1*). (The £10,000 limit was introduced for accounting periods beginning on or after 9 April 2003. Previously the limit was £25,000). Qualifying expenditure is expenditure that would be allowable as a deduction in computing the taxable profits of a trade carried on by the company, or it would have been allowable if the trade were being carried on at the time that the expenditure was incurred. Pre-trading expenditure is not treated as incurred on the first day of trading (*ICTA 1988, s 401*) but when it is actually incurred.

## Qualifying R & D expenditure

**8.22** Large company R & D not only includes direct research and development expenditure (as discussed in **8.8** onwards) but also subcontracted research and development and contributions to independent research and development (*FA 2002, Sch 12, para 3*).

## Subcontracted research and development

**8.23** Subcontracted R & D may qualify for relief if it is subcontracted to an individual, or a partnership made up of individuals. It may also qualify for relief if it is subcontracted to a qualifying body. A qualifying body is a charity, a higher education institution, a scientific research organisation or a health service body.

The research carried out must be relevant revenue research directly undertaken on the company's behalf. In addition if the work is subcontracted out to the company it must be subcontracted by a large company or by a person in the course of that person's trade (*FA 2002, Sch 12, para 5*).

## Contributions to independent research and development

**8.24** Contributions to independent relevant research and development qualify for relief if the expenditure known as 'funded R & D' is incurred in making payments to an individual, or a partnership made up of individuals or a qualifying body (as defined in **8.23**). The company must not be connected with an individual or any individual in the partnership when the payment is made. In addition the funded R & D must not be contracted out to the qualifying body, the individual or the partnership concerned by another person (*FA 2002, Sch 12, para 6*).

## Work subcontracted to small or medium-sized enterprise

**8.25** An SME can make a claim under *FA 2002* large company rules, for subcontract work that it carries out. The revenue expenditure concerned must consist of expenditure on staffing costs, software or consumable stores or externally provided workers.

It can also claim R & D on relevant research work that it subcontracts to others. The work must be contracted to an individual, a partnership made up of individuals or a qualifying body consisting of a charity, a higher education institution, a scientific research organisation or a health service body (*FA 2002, Sch 12, paras 9, 10*).

If the company claims under the large scheme rules the reliefs detailed above in **8.21** will be available.

## Location

**8.26** There is no statutory provision restricting the location of the R & D work carried out. In fact, the ECJ has ruled that article 49 EC precluded legislation of a member state, which restricted the benefit of a tax credit for research to research carried out in that member state (*Laboratoire Fournier SA v Direction des Verifications Nationales et Internationales* Case C-39/04 [2006] STC 538, [2005] ECRI-2057).

## Tax relief for expenditure on vaccine research

**8.27** Similar rules also allow for companies to deduct an additional 50% of research and development expenditure on vaccines and medicines, from taxable profits or to claim a 16% tax credit (*FA 2002, Sch 13*).

## Time limits for enhanced deduction

**8.28** For accounting periods ending before 31 March 2006, the time limit for making a claim for an enhanced deduction of 150% or 125% was six years from the end of the relevant accounting period. For accounting periods ended on or after 31 March 2006, the time limit is now two years from the end of the accounting period (*FA 2006, s 29* and *Sch 3*).

Transitional rules apply for accounting periods ended before 31 March 2006. Claims must be made by the earlier of six years after the end of the relevant accounting period, or 31 March 2008.

*Chapter 9*

# Single Company Trading Losses

## SCHEDULE D CASE I TRADING LOSSES

### Computation

**9.1** The vagaries of business life will mean that a company can make a loss on its trading ventures just as easily as it can make a profit. A 'trade loss' as it is termed in the legislation is computed in exactly the same way as a trading income, which is the profit of the trade (*ICTA 1988, ss 393(7)*, (*8*), *393A*(*9*)(*a*)). When a company incurs a trading loss it must prepare its corporation tax computation in the normal way to send to HMRC together with form CT600 and the statutory accounts. If a trading loss is incurred during the accounting period the chargeable profits are recorded as 'nil'. This is achieved by leaving box 3 (trading and professional profits) of the company tax return CT600 blank. The legislation allows the company to claim relief for the loss against its other income (**9.11–9.16**) or to carry forward the loss against future profits of the same trade (**9.2–9.10**).

## CARRY FORWARD OF TRADING LOSS AGAINST FUTURE TRADING PROFITS

### Loss claim

**9.2** Unless a trading loss is utilised in other ways it will automatically be carried forward to set against profits of the same trade in the next and subsequent accounting periods. The loss can only be used if there are available profits and once used it cannot be used again. There is no facility to disclaim the whole or even part of the loss, which must be matched consecutively year on year to available profits until depleted (*ICTA 1988, s 393*(*1*)). If a market gardening or farming business makes a loss for five consecutive years, the next year's loss can only be carried forward against future profits of the same trade (*ICTA 1988, s 397*).

The loss relief is only available if the trade continues to be carried on, when the loss is to be relieved (*ICTA 1988, ss 393(1), 393A(1)*). What is more, the trade has to be the same trade. Commercial dictum dictates that business shifts from unprofitable to profitable sources. As business life moves swiftly it is often difficult to determine whether a new activity is in fact an extension of the existing trade or a new trade. The former situation will permit the loss relief but the latter will deny it. Case law has determined the following.

## Case law

**9.3** Gordon & Blair Ltd traded as brewers. The company's activities consisted of brewing and selling beer to third parties. After a period of time Gordon & Blair Ltd stopped brewing beer and engaged another company to brew to its specification. Gordon & Blair Ltd continued to sell the beer. It was held that the brewing trade had ceased and a new trade of beer selling had commenced. The effect being that the brewing trade's losses could not be set against the beer sales profits (*Gordon & Blair Ltd v CIR* (1962) 40 TC 358).

Bolands Ltd, an Irish company, traded in Ireland as millers and bakers. The company owned two mills and it used about half of the flour it produced in its own bakeries. The company hit dire times. The company made losses and closed the mills. A year later it reopened one of the mills mainly to supply the bakeries. It was held that a single trade was carried on throughout. Therefore it was able to utilise its trading losses (*Bolands Ltd v Davis* (1925) I ITC 91, (1925) 4 ATC 532).

In contrast J G Ingram & Sons Ltd manufactured and sold surgical goods. At that time the company used rubber in its manufacturing process. The company suffered large losses. A receiver was appointed, the plant sold and the factory closed. The company continued to sell surgical goods under its own brand that were made by an associated company. A year later a change of ownership took place and the company recommenced manufacturing but used plastic rather than rubber in its production process. The sale of surgical goods continued. The company claimed that it carried on the continuing trade of the sale of surgical goods. The courts disagreed and deemed that a new trade commenced with the production of plastic surgical goods (*JG Ingram & Sons Ltd v Callaghan* (1968) 45 TC 151).

More recently in *Kawthar Consulting Ltd v HMRC*, the *JG Ingram* argument was used. Kawthar Ltd's trade was the provision of computers and monitors. Unfortunately the company's client went into liquidation and Kawthar Ltd suffered large losses. Two to three years later, the company won a lucrative contract for the supply of compliance software. The company regarded itself as an IT company and set the earlier trading losses against the current profits under *ICTA 1988, s 393(1)*. The Special Commissioners decided that the company's trade of dealing in computers had ceased and a new trade of providing IT consultancy services had begun. The result being that Kawthar Ltd was unable to utilise its brought forward trading losses against its current profits (*Kawthar Consulting Ltd v HMRC* [2005] SWTI 1237, [2005] STC (SCD) 524).

## Corporation tax self-assessment

**9.4** As *s 393(1)* loss relief is automatic, the legislation requires no formal claim. (A formal claim was required for accounting periods ended before 1 October 1993).

In order to satisfy the corporation tax self-assessment filing requirement the company, when completing form CT600, is required to state the amount of the loss to be relieved in box 4 of the return. Only the amount to actually be set against profits should be entered on the return. A separate loss calculation should be supplied with the company tax return to explain how the loss has been utilised. In particular, if more than one trade is being carried on, the computation should clearly show how the trading losses are utilised against each particular trade's income. As soon as the trade ceases it will no longer be possible to carry forward the loss.

The company in its corporation tax self-assessment submission must distinguish between an existing trade and a new or different trade when claiming loss relief.

This is where the practical difficulty lies.

From the earlier case law examples, it seems that, if a company changes its activities during the course of its existence, it must be able to demonstrate that these activities are sufficiently uninterrupted and interrelated to constitute a continuing trade.

## Losses and HMRC enquiries

**9.5** The fact that a company incurs a loss during the year rather than a profit has no effect on HMRC's powers of enquiry. They remain the same. (See Chapter 2). A brought forward trading loss shown on a corporation tax computation cannot be enquired into under *FA 1998, Sch 18, para 25* if the time limit of two years after the end of the accounting period in which the loss was incurred has expired. If HMRC wished to enquire into earlier losses it would have to open a discovery enquiry under *FA 1998, Sch 18, para 43*. A discovery enquiry can only be opened if HMRC suspects fraud or negligence on the part of the company, its representative or anyone who was in partnership with the company at the relevant time. Alternatively an enquiry may be opened into the use of a trading loss where there is a reconstruction (*ICTA 1988, s 343(3)*) or a change of ownership (*ICTA 1988, s 768*). *Section 343* permits losses to be transferred from one company to another company with substantially the same ownership, this is discussed in **15.6–15.19**. *Section 768* prevents loss utilisation where there is a change of ownership. (See **9.16**). HMRC have also stated that they will enquire into the use of a trading loss carried forward in a later accounting period where there is a dispute about whether a trade has continued or whether it has ceased and a new trade commenced (HMRC Company Taxation Manual CTM 04150).

### Within the charge to corporation tax

**9.6** In order to be granted loss relief, not only must the company be carrying on the same trade, but it must also be within the charge to corporation tax (*ICTA 1988, ss 393(10), 393A(9)(c)*). These clauses are most likely to affect companies who become resident in the UK after having been resident abroad.

When a company becomes UK resident it falls within the charge to corporation tax, if it has a source of income. If the company carries on the same trade when it becomes UK resident as it carried on before it became UK resident its loss relief capacity is restricted. The now resident, UK resident company will not be given relief for its trading losses incurred whilst non-UK resident against profits earned when it becomes UK resident. On the other hand a non-UK resident company that is carrying on a trade in the UK through a permanent establishment is within the charge to corporation tax (*ICTA 1988, s 11(1)*). A permanent establishment may consist of a branch or agency. Therefore the branch or agency will obtain relief for any UK losses it incurs against the UK income that it earns. If the accounts and records are kept in a foreign currency, the loss should be converted to sterling using the same exchange rate as used for the conversion of profits entered in box 3.

## CORPORATION TAX COMPUTATION

**9.7** The following example details the presentation of a corporation tax computation in circumstances where there are trading losses brought forward to set against future trading income from the same traded under *ICTA 1988, s 393(1)*.

**Example 9.1**

The Abracadabra Trading Company Ltd has the following results for the year ended 31 March 2007.

| | *£000* |
|---|---|
| Schedule D Case I profits | 200 |
| Schedule A | 1,600 |
| Schedule D Case III | 400 |
| Chargeable gains | 300 |
| Gift aid payment | 300 |
| Loss brought forward under *ICTA 1988, s 393(1)* | 5,000 |

The company calculates its profits chargeable to corporation tax and its trading loss carried forward as follows:

**Corporation tax computation for the year ended 31 March 2007**

| | *£000* |
|---|---|
| Schedule D Case I | 200 |
| Less: Loss brought forward under *ICTA 1988, s 393(1)* | (200) |
| | 0 |
| Schedule A income | 1,600 |
| Schedule D Case III income | 400 |
| Chargeable gains | 300 |
| Total profits | 2,300 |
| Less: Non-trade charge on income | (300) |
| Profits Chargeable to Corporation Tax | 2,000 |

**Loss utilisation**

| | *£000* |
|---|---|
| Loss brought forward | 5,000 |
| Used against trading income of the year | (200) |
| Loss carried forward *ICTA 1988, s 393(1)* | 4,800 |

## Charges on income

**9.8** *TA 1988, ss 393(9), 393A(8)* allow excess trade charges to be added to a trading loss caried forward. With the introduction of the intangible assets regime on 1 April 2002 very few items will qualify from this time as 'trade charges'. From 25 July 2002 the definition of charges is restricted to:

- annuities or other annual payments,
- qualifying donations to charity,
- amounts allowed as charges on income, namely gifts of shares etc to charity).

Any amount that is deductible in computing profits cannot be allowed as a charge on income (*ICTA 1988, s 338A* (2)).

If trade charges were to be added to a loss claim the following format would be adopted.

---

**Example 9.2**

A company has a trading loss brought forward for its accounting period ended 30 June 2002 of £5,000. In that year it has excess trade charges of £10,000. The company has no other income. The trading loss carried forward to the accounting period ended 30 June 2003 is therefore £15,000.

---

## Relief for trading losses against interest and dividends

**9.9** *TA 1988, s 393*(*8*) allows the inclusion of interest and dividends as trading income that would be included as trading income but for the fact that tax has been deducted at source. Dividends from UK companies are excluded. In practice this section will only be applied where investment forms part of the trade. The treatment was refused in *Bank Line Ltd v CIR* (1974) 49 TC 307, [1974] STC 342 and *Nuclear Electric plc v Bradley* (1996) 68 TC 670, [1996] STC 405 (HMRC Company Taxation Manual CTM 04250).

## Companies entering into partnership

**9.10** The business may determine that the company forms links with other companies in order to further its trading activities. Groups are discussed in Chapter 11. A company may be engaged in a certain trading activity and whilst carrying on this trade enters into partnership with another company or individual. Of concern to the company is whether and how it may utilise its trading losses. HMRC have confirmed that the company can relieve trading losses it incurred before it entered into partnership against profits earned whilst in partnership, provided the same trade is carried on. It can also relieve losses under *TA 1988, s 393(1)* against its share of the partnership trading income (HMRC Company Taxation Manual CTM 04200).

## Set the loss against other profits in the same accounting period and then accounting periods falling within the previous 12 months

**9.11** Rather than carry forward the trading loss to set against future trading profits the company may, by claim, offset the loss against its other profits.

---

**Example 9.3**

A Ltd's results for the year ending 31 March 2007 show:

| | £ | | £ |
|---|---|---|---|
| Trading loss | (10,000) | Chargeable gains | 7,200) |
| Schedule A | 3,000) | Trade charges | (2,000) |
| Schedule D Case III | 4,000) | Non-trade charges | (1,000) |

The loss may be relieved as follows.

| | £ |
|---|---|
| Schedule A | 3,000 |
| Schedule D Case III | 4,000 |
| Chargeable gains | 7,200 |
| | 14,200 |
| Deduct trading loss | (10,000) |
| | 4,200 |
| Deduct trade charges | (2,000) |
| Non-trade charges | (1,000) |
| Profits chargeable to CT | 1,200 |
| CT payable at 19% | 228 |

---

**9.12** The profits that are eligible are the total profits for the same accounting period as the loss followed by the total profits of the previous 12-month chargeable period, provided the trade was being carried on in that chargeable period, in the same accounting period and then accounting periods falling within the previous 12 months. The relief must be taken in that order and the relief for the same chargeable period must be taken in full up to the amount of the chargeable profits. It is not possible to make a partial claim. Only after this relief is taken can the balance of the loss be set against the total profits of the accounting period ended within the previous 12 months.

---

**Example 9.4**

A company made a trading loss of £35,000 in the accounting period 1 January 2007 to 31 December 2007. Other corporation tax profits of the period amounted to £20,000. The company continues to trade. The corporation tax profits of earlier accounting periods were as follows.

| | £ |
|---|---|
| 1 July 2006 to 31 December 2006 | 10,000 |
| 1 July 2005 to 30 June 2006 | 20,000 |

The trade in which the loss was incurred was carried on throughout the whole of the period from 1 July 2005 to 31 December 2007. The company claims relief under *TA 1988, s 393A(1)(b)* to extend the relief to the 'preceding period', the 12-month period, which ends on 31 December 2006.

Relief is given as follows:

| *Against profits of the accounting period* | £ |
|---|---|
| 1 January 2007 to 31 December 2007 | 20,000 |
| 1 July 2006 to 31 December 2006 | 10,000 |
| 1 July 2005 to 30 June 2006 | 5,000 |
| Total amount of profits relieved | 35,000 |

---

**Example 9.5**

The facts are the same as the previous example, except that the trading loss for the period from 1 January 2007 to 31 December 2007 was £45,000.

Relief is given as follows:

| *Against profits of the accounting period* | £ |
|---|---|
| 1 January 2007 to 31 December 2007 | 20,000 |
| 1 July 2006 to 31 December 2006 | 10,000 |
| 1 July 2005 to 30 June 2006 | 10,000 |
| Total amount of profits relieved | 40,000 |

The set-off for the accounting period ended 30 June 2006 is limited to the proportion (183/366 × £20,000 = £10,000) of the profits of the period that fall into the 12 months ending on 31 December 2006. The unused balance of the loss for accounting period ending 31 December 2007 (£5,000) is available for carry forward under *TA 1988, s 393(1)* (HMRC Company Taxation Manual CTM 04540 adapted)

Profits for the accounting period ended 30 June 2006 have been apportioned on a time basis. There is always the possibility to apportion the profits on an actual basis if this gives a more accurate result. For this see the discussion on *Marshall Hus & Partners Ltd v Bolton* (1980) 55 TC 539, [1981] STC 18 in **2.4**.

---

**9.13** It is not compulsory to take *s 393A(1)* relief. The relief can be ignored and the loss can be carried forward in an automatic *s 393(1)* set-off. If *s 393A(1)* is claimed current year relief must always be taken before prior year relief.

Where there are losses arising in consecutive accounting periods and relief is claimed under *TA 1988, s 393A(1)* for each accounting period the order of set-off is:

(i) loss of the first accounting period against total profits of the same accounting period;

(ii) loss of the first accounting period against the preceding 12 months' profits;

(iii) loss of the second accounting period against total profits of the same accounting period;

(iv) loss of the second accounting period against profits of the preceding 12 months, which in effect amounts to the 'first accounting period'.

This can often result in insufficient profits against which to make a carry back election for the second accounting period.

**Example 9.6**

A company commenced trading on 1 January 2006 and prepares six monthly accounts for its first two years of trading. It makes trading losses of £25,000 in its six-month accounting period ended 30 June 2007 and £40,000 in its six-month accounting period ended 31 December 2007. The corporation tax profits of the preceding periods were as follows.

| | £ |
|---|---|
| Accounting period 6 months to 31 December 2006 | 20,000 |
| Accounting period 6 months to 30 June 2006 | 10,000 |

Relief for the £25,000 loss for the period ended 30 June 2007 is given before relief for the £40,000 loss for the year ended 31 December 2007. Relief is given as follows:

**Loss for the period to 30 June 2007**

| | *Profit* £ | *Loss* £ | *Net* £ |
|---|---|---|---|
| Against profits of the accounting period: | | | |
| • 6 months to 31 December 2006 | 20,000 | 20,000 | — |
| • 6 months to 30 June 2006 | 10,000 | 5,000 | 5,000 |
| Total | 30,000 | 25,000 | 5,000 |

**Loss for the period to 31 December 2007**

The profits against which the loss can now be set against are reduced as follows after the 30 June 2007 loss relief.

| | *Profit* £ | *Loss* £ | *Net* £ |
|---|---|---|---|
| Against profits of the accounting period: | | | |
| • 6 months to 31 December 2007 | — | 40,000 | (40,000) |
| • 6 months to 30 June 2007 | — | 25,000 | (25,000) |
| Total | — | 65,000 | (65,000) |

This loss cannot be carried back. This is because all of the profits for accounting periods in the 12 months immediately preceding the accounting period ended 31 December 2007 (that is the 12 months to 30 June 2007) have already been covered by loss relief from the earlier period. The company would have preferred to claim relief for the period ended 31 December 2007 first. If it had been able to do this, relief for the period ended 31 December 2007 would have been given against the profits of the period ended 31 December 2006. The loss for the period ended 30 June 2007 could then have gone against the whole of the £10,000 profits for the period ended 30 June 2006. But the legislation does not allow this.

(HMRC Company Taxation Manual CTM 04550 adapted).

---

**9.14** The loss can only be set against the total profits of the accounting period ended in the previous 12 months if and only if the trade in question was carried on at some time in that accounting period on a commercial basis. It is not necessary for the trade to have been carried on for the whole of the preceding 12-month period. If the trade was carried on at some time during the previous 12 months the loss will still be relievable against total profits of that period (HMRC Company Taxation Manual CTM 04510).

Again the facts of each case must be reviewed carefully to ascertain whether or not a trade is being carried on, on a commercial basis. The loss up to the full amount of the total profits must be utilised or if less the full amount of the loss. The balance of any unused loss is available to carry forward under *ICTA 1988, s 393(1)*.

A claim must be made within two years of the end of the accounting period in which the loss is incurred. The claim can be made by completing box 122 of the company tax return and by giving full details of the loss and the trade to which it refers (*ICTA 1988, s 393A*).

## Charges on income

**9.15** Charges on income are now in the main restricted to donations and gifts to charities (*ICTA 1988, s 338A*) (see **9.8**). As such payments are not related to a company's trading activity they are termed as 'non-trade charges' (*ICTA 1988, s 393A*(*1*)(*b*)); loss carry back is given before non-trade charges for the year. Excess non-trade charges can only be relieved against current year profits.

---

**Example 9.7**

Wizard Ltd prepares accounts to 30 June each year. The company has recently changed its accounting date from 31 December.

Wizard Ltd's results both actual and forecast are as follows:

| | *Year ended 31 December 2005* | *Six months ended 30 June 2006* | *Year ended 30 June 2007* | *Year ended 30 June 2008* |
|---|---|---|---|---|
| | *£000* | *£000* | *£000* | *£000* |
| Schedule D Case I profit/(loss) | 35 | 20 | (120) | 90 |
| Schedule A | 5 | 3 | 6 | 4 |
| Chargeable gain | 10 | 0 | 8 | 0 |
| Gift aid payments | (3) | (2) | 0 | 0 |

*ICTA 1988, s 393A(1)(a)* claim for the year ended 30 June 2007

| | *Year ended 30 June 2007* |
|---|---|
| | *£000* |
| Schedule A | 6 |
| Chargeable gain | 8 |
| | 14 |
| Less: loss claim | (14) |
| Profits chargeable to corporation tax | 0 |

*ICTA 1988, s 393A(1)(b)* for the previous 12 months

| | *Year ended 31 December 2005* | *Six months ended 30 June 2006* |
|---|---|---|
| | *£000* | *£000* |
| Schedule D Case I profit | 35 | 20 |
| Schedule A | 5 | 3 |
| Chargeable gain | 10 | 0 |
| | 50 | 23 |
| Less: loss claim | (25) | (23) |
| | 25 | 0 |
| Non-trade charges | (3) | 0 |
| Profits chargeable to corporation tax | (3) | 0 |

The non-trade charges are lost for the six months ended 30 June 2006 as set-off is after loss relief.

*ICTA 1988, s 393(1)* loss carried forward against future trading profits

| | *Year ended 30 June 2008* |
|---|---|
| | *£000* |
| Schedule D Case I profit/(loss) | 90 |
| Less: loss claim | (58) |
| | 32 |
| Schedule A | 4 |
| Chargeable gain | 0 |
| Profits chargeable to corporation tax | 36 |

Loss utilisation

| | *£000* |
|---|---|
| Trading loss for the year ended 30 June 2007 | 120 |
| Less: *ICTA 1988, s 393A(1)(a)* claim for the current year | (14) |
| | 106 |
| Less: *ICTA 1988, s 393A(1)(b)* claim for the previous 12 months: | |
| • Six months to 30 June 2006 | (23) |
| • Six months to 31 December 2005 | (25) |
| Loss carried forward (*ICTA 1988, s 393(1)*) | 58 |
| 12 months to 30 June 2008 | (58) |
| Total | 0 |

**Example 9.8—Losses carried forward and back with trade charges**

B Ltd has carried on the same trade for many years. The results for the years ended 30 September 2004, 2005 and 2006 are shown below.

| *Year ended 30 September* | *2004* | *2005* | *2006* |
|---|---|---|---|
| | *£000* | *£000* | *£000* |
| Trading profit/(loss) | (20 ) | 20 | (17) |
| Schedule D Case III | 5 | 3 | 5 |
| Chargeable gains | 5.6 | 4.7 | 4 |
| Trade charges | (3 ) | (9 ) | (5) |
| Non-trade charges | — | (1 ) | — |

The losses may be relieved as follows.

| *Year ended 30 September* | *2004* | *2005* | *2006* |
|---|---|---|---|
| | *£000* | *£000* | *£000* |
| Schedule D Case I | | 20 | |
| Deduct loss brought forward | | (12.4) | |
| | | 7.6 | |
| Schedule D Case III | 5 | 3 | 5 |
| Chargeable gains | 5.6 | 4.7 | 4 |
| | 10.6 | 15.3 | 9 |
| Trading losses of same period | (10.6) | | (9) |
| Deduct trade charges | | (9 ) | |
| | | 6.3 | |
| Deduct trading loss carried back from year ended 30 September 2005 | | (6.3) | |
| Profits chargeable to CT | — | — | — |
| Non-trade charges unrelieved | | 1 | |

Loss memorandum

| *Year ended 30 September* | *2004* | *2005* | *2006* |
|---|---|---|---|
| | *£000* | *£000* | *£000* |
| Trading loss | 20 | | 17 |
| Trade charges | 3 | 9 | 5 |
| Non-trade charges | | 1 | |
| | 23 | 10 | 22 |
| Losses used in current year | (10.6) | | (9) |
| Charges used in current year | | (9) | |

| | | | |
|---|---|---|---|
| Carried back to year ended 30 September 2004 | | | (6.3) |
| | ___ | — | ___ |
| Losses/charges carried forward | 12.4 | — | 6.7 |
| Non-trade charges unrelieved | | 1 | |

# RELIEF FOR A TRADING LOSS AGAINST TOTAL PROFITS OF THE PRECEDING ACCOUNTING PERIODS WHEN A COMPANY CEASES TO TRADE

## Cessation of trade

**9.16** When a company ceases trading it is most likely to cease at or during its normal accounting period rather than on the last day of the accounting period. The legislation recognises this and allows the loss of the last 12 months of trading to be utilised in a carry back claim. The loss will most likely include the loss of the last trading period of less than 12 months and a proportionate part of a loss that falls into the preceding accounting period. In addition the loss carry back period of *ICTA 1988, s 393A(1)* is extended from a 12-month period to a three-year-period by *ICTA 1988 s 393A(2A)*, provided the trade was being carried on at that time. Losses are set off against profits of the preceding accounting period before earlier accounting periods.

**Example 9.9**

Hardwood ceased trading on 30 June 2007. It had the following results:

| *Accounting period ended* | *Months* | *Trade profit* £ | *Trade loss* £ |
|---|---|---|---|
| 30 June 2007 | 6 | | 30,000 |
| 31 December 2006 | 12 | | 40,000 |
| 31 December 2005 | 12 | | 3,000 |
| 31 December 2004 | 12 | 20,000 | |
| 31 December 2003 | 12 | 50,000 | |
| 31 December 2002 | 12 | 2,000 | |

*ICTA 1988, s 393A(2A)* and *(2B)* claims are made as follows:

| | £ |
|---|---|
| Loss arising in the accounting period falling wholly in the 12-month period prior to cessation – 6 months to 30 June 2007 | 30,000 |
| Proportion of the loss arising in the accounting period falling partly in the 12-month period prior to cessation – 6 months to 31 December 2006: (183/365) × 40,000 | 20,000 |
| Total | 50,000 |

The £20,000 loss for the period to 31 December 2006 is utilised before the £30,000 loss for the later period to 30 June 2007.

The losses are relieved as follows:

| *Accounting period ended* | *Months* | *Trade profit* | *Loss utilised* | *Profit assessed* | *ICTA 1988, s 393(2A), (2B)* | *ICTA 1988, s 393A(1)* |
|---|---|---|---|---|---|---|
| | | £ | £ | £ | £ | £ |
| 30 June 2007 | 6 | | | | (30,000) | |
| 31 December 2006 | 12 | | | | (20,000) | (20,000) |
| 31 December 2005 | 12 | | | | | (3,000) |
| 31 December 2004 | 12 | 20,000 | (3,000) | Nil | 17,000 | 3,000 |
| | | | (17,000) | | | |
| 31 December 2003 | 12 | 50,000 | (3,000) | 17,000 | 3,000 | |
| | | | (30,000) | | 30,000 | |
| 31 December 2002 | 12 | 2,000 | | 2,000 | | |
| Total | | 72,000 | (53,000) | 19,000 | Nil | (20,000) |

It is not possible to utilise the £20,000 loss remaining for the year ended 31 December 2006, as there are no profits in the year ended 31 December 2005 against which it can be set.

## LOSS RELIEF RESTRICTION

### Changes in situation

**9.17** Loss relief carry forward and carry back is denied where:

- in a three-year period there is both a change in the ownership of a company and a major change in the nature or conduct of the trade, or
- at any time after the scale of the company's activity becomes negligible and before any significant revival of the trade takes place there is a change in ownership of the company (*ICTA 1988, ss 768, 768A*).

### Change of ownership of a company

**9.18** A change of ownership of the company arises if a single person or a group of persons acquire more than half the ordinary share capital of the company. Holdings of 5% or less are ignored unless the acquisition is in respect of an existing holding (*ICTA 1988, s 769*). Any two points in a three-year period may be compared. Connected persons holdings are included. The *ICTA 1988, s 839* definition is used (see **4.25**), but unsolicited gifts of shares and legacies are not included. If the company is a 75% subsidiary, changes in ownership are ignored if it remains a 75% subsidiary of the same ultimate parent but a change in ownership of a holding company will extend to the subsidiary (*ICTA 1988, s 769*).

### Major change in the conduct or nature of trade

**9.19** What constitutes a major change in the nature or conduct of the trade is largely a question of fact but *ICTA 1988, s 768(4)* includes the following:

- a major change in the type of property dealt in, or services or facilities provided, in the trade; or
- a major change in customers, outlets or markets of the trade.

The effect of the change is to restrict the loss relief both before and after the change, with the activity before and the activity after the change being treated as two separate accounting periods. Balancing adjustments will be calculated for capital allowance purposes.

Examples of the Revenue's view of what would and would not constitute a major change in the conduct or nature of trade are given in SP 10/91.

These are:

**Examples where a major change would be regarded as occurring:**

(I) A company operating a dealership in cars switches to operating a dealership in tractors (a major change in the type of property dealt in).

(II) A company owning a public house switches to operating a discotheque in the same, but converted, premises (a major change in the services or facilities provided).

(III) A company fattening pigs for their owners switches to buying pigs for fattening and resale (a major change in the nature of the trade, being a change from providing a service to being a primary producer).

**Examples where a change would not in itself be regarded as a major change:**

(i) A company manufacturing kitchen fitments in three obsolescent factories moves production to one new factory (increasing efficiency).

(ii) A company manufacturing kitchen utensils replaces enamel by plastic, or a company manufacturing time pieces replaces mechanical by electrical components (keeping pace with developing technology).

(iii) A company operating a dealership in one make of car switches to operating a dealership in another make of car satisfying the same market (not a major change in the type of property dealt in).

(iv) A company manufacturing both filament and fluorescent lamps (of which filament lamps form the greater part of the output) concentrates solely on filament lamps (a rationalisation of product range without a major change in the type of property dealt in).

## Schedule D Case V

**9.20** Losses from an overseas business assessed under Schedule D Case V may only be carried forward and set off against profits from the same trade (*ICTA 1988, s 393*). They cannot be set against other profits of the accounting period of the loss or the previous 12 months (*ICTA 1988, s 393A*(*3*)). Profits arising from an overseas branch are included within the Schedule D Case I assessment.

## Government investment written off

**9.21** It has been part of the government's policy to invest in certain companies. Where the government writes off the debt, the company's losses that are carried forward are reduced accordingly. The losses affected are:

- *ICTA 1998, s 393(1)* – loss carried forward against future trading profits from the same trade;
- *ICTA 1988, s 75(3)* – excess management expenses or charges on income;
- *CAA 2001, s 260(1)*, (2) – special leasing allowances; and
- *TCGA 1992, s 8* – capital losses.

Where a claim is made to set the loss against current profits under *ICTA 1988, s 393A* (trading loss set against profits of the same or earlier accounting period), *CAA 2001, s 260(3)* (special leasing allowance to be set against current profits) or *ICTA 1988, s 402* (group relief), it will not be disturbed (*ICTA 1988, s 400*).

## SELF-ASSESSMENT

### Loss claims and elections

**9.22** If a company makes a loss claim it must quantify the amount of the loss at the time (*FA 1998, Sch 18, para 54*). Normally, this is included on the corporation tax computation and on the company tax return CT600 boxes 122–138. There is a general time limit of six years from the end of the accounting period to which the claim relates (*FA 1998, Sch 18, para 55*). This is overridden if the legislation gives a shorter time limit. In particular a loss claim under *ICTA 1988, s 393A(1)* must be made within two years of the end of the accounting period in which the loss arises. Normally, the loss is claimed on the company tax return CT600 and corporation tax computation for the year of the loss and this fulfils the claim requirement. If for any reason CT600 is delayed a separate quantified loss claim should be submitted to HMRC. Any errors in a claim or election can be corrected within the claim time limits (*FA 1998, Sch 18, para 56*).

The legislation differentiates between:

- claims affecting a single accounting period (*FA 1998, Sch 18, para 57*);
- claims or elections involving more than one accounting period (*FA 1998, Sch 18, para 58*);
- all other claims and elections (*FA 1998, Sch 18, para 59*).

### Claims affecting a single accounting period

**9.23** As stated above claims are usually included within the company tax return. If the company does not include the claim with the company tax return but submits it at another date, although still within the company tax return filing date period, the claim will be treated as an amendment to the return (*FA 1998, Sch 18, para 15*). The amendment should be made formally by letter; and more importantly the relief sought must be given a brief description and the amount of the claim must be quantified (HMRC Company Taxation Manual CTM 90625). If the 12-month period after the year end amendment period has expired, a claim can be made under *TMA 1970, Sch 1A*.

### Claims or elections involving more than one accounting period

**9.24** In this scenario a company makes a claim for an accounting period, which effects more than one accounting period. This will occur where a company claims to carry back a trading loss under *ICTA 1988, s 393A(1)* against its profits of the previous 12 months. The claim is made for the accounting period but it affects the previous accounting period. If the claim is made within the amendment period for the first accounting period, which contains the profits against which the losses are to be set, it will be treated as an amendment to the return. If the amendment period is past it is treated as an amendment under *TMA 1970, Sch 1A*. Depending on the circumstances the corporation tax repayment will either reduce the current year liability or be repaid direct to the company.

### All other claims and elections

**9.25** The corporation tax self-assessment enquiry period only runs to 12 months after the end of the filing date of the return. Some claims and elections may be submitted after this. This would mean that HMRC would be unable to enquire into the claim or election. Hence such elections fall under *TMA 1970, Sch 1A*. HMRC has similar powers of enquiry but they are extended to one year and the quarter day after the claim is filed (*TMA 1970, Sch 1A, para 5*). HMRC can amend obvious errors within 12 months of the claim being made (*TMA 1970, Sch 1A, para 3(a)*) and the company may amend the claim at any time within 12 months of the claim, provided that it is not under enquiry.

## HMRC AMENDMENTS TO TAX RETURNS AND CLAIMS AND ELECTIONS

**9.26** HMRC acknowledge that it has the following powers to amend returns:

- Amendment of a company tax return under *FA 1998, Sch 18, para 34*(2)(*a*).
- Discovery assessment made under *FA 1998, Sch 18, para 41*.
- An assessment to recover excess group relief under *FA 1998, Sch 18, para 76* (HMRC Company Taxation Manual CTM 90650)

In turn the company may make, revoke or vary certain claims (*FA 1998, Sch 18, para 61*) outside the normal time limit. The extended time limit is one year from the end of the accounting period in which the HMRC adjustment was made (*FA 1998, Sch 18, para 62*(*1*)).

Certain liabilities can be reduced by the claim. These are:

- the increased liability resulting from the amendment or assessment;
- any other tax liability for the accounting period to which the amendment or assessment relates; or
- any other tax liability for any subsequent accounting period, which ends not later than one year from the end of the relevant accounting period (*FA 1998, Sch 18, para 62*(*3*)).

However, the claim cannot reduce the eventual liability by more than the additional assessment (*FA 1998, Sch 18, para 64*).

Where the claim affects another person's tax liability, the company must obtain the other person's consent (*FA 1998, Sch 18, para 62*(*3*)).

In situations of fraud and neglect a company can make additional claims but only those that can be given effect in HMRC's assessment. The claims must be made before the assessment is raised (*FA 1998, Sch 18, para 65*(*1*), (*2*); HMRC Company Taxation Manual CTM 90665).

## Assessments under appeal

**9.27** If an HMRC amendment to a company tax return or an HMRC assessment is under appeal, claims cannot be made through the *FA 1998, Sch 18, para 54* etc claims procedures. Any claims that the company wishes to make must be made through an application to the Commissioners presiding over the appeal for a determination of the amount that is to be repaid, pending the final determination of the liability. The application is heard in the same way as an appeal (see **2.23–2.25**) (*TMA 1970, s 59DA*(*4*), (*5*)) (HMRC Company Taxation Manual CTM 92110).

# REPAYMENTS

## Repayment interest

**9.28** A loss carry back under *ICTA 1988, s 393A* (or a non-trading deficit under *FA 1996, s 83(2)(c)*) may bring about a corporation tax repayment for an earlier period. Repayment interest runs from the due date for the accounting period for which the loss is incurred (*ICTA 1988, s 826(7A), (7C)*).

The repayment interest will be calculated from the normal due date for the accounting period in which the loss or deficit is incurred (see **3.19**).

---

**Example 9.10**

Lettice Ltd made a Schedule D Case I trading loss in the accounting period ended 31 March 2007 of £100,000. It has no other income in the year and elects to carry the loss back against its total profits for the year ended 31 March 3006 of £90,000. Corporation tax of £17,100 was paid on 1 January 2007, the due date. The repayment interest is calculated from 1 January 2007.

If the loss is carried back further than 12 months repayment interest is calculated with reference to the period for which the loss was incurred.

---

*Chapter 10*

# Groups

## BUSINESS STRUCTURE

**10.1** As a business grows its affairs develop and the company may consider whether a simple single company structure remains appropriate for its activities or whether it should consider other forms of organisation.

From a taxation perspective the single company offers many advantages. The absence of associated companies means that the small companies rate is not unduly dissipated (see **4.7**). Capital gains and losses can be set against one another without the *TCGA 1992, s 179* restrictions (see **10.25**). Possibly more importantly all the company's activities fall within one company. The merged activities may form one trade, whereas if the trades are split amongst group members they become separate trades in themselves. Retaining activities in one company also avoids the practicalities of preparing group relief claims and company tax returns for each separate entity.

However, taxation does not rule a commercial world and separate business structures may be required. The company may consider buying or forming another company (see **15.1**). Ownership of another company's shares by a company may bring about a group situation. The rapid changes in projects and deals may mean that a business structure is only required for a short amount of time and an acquisition or a new formation may not be the best structure for a deal. Before entering into a group arrangement the company may well be advised to consider a partnership or a joint venture, which it may find simpler to operate.

Corporate partners' share of profits and losses are assessed to corporation tax on the basis of a separate trade being carried on by each partner (*ICTA 1988, s 114*). The company's share of the partnership losses are available to the company to set against its other income for the same or previous year, if the partnership and its trade existed at that time, or to carry forward against its share of future partnership trading income. The partnership can prepare accounts in any format they wish, although they must be in accordance with GAAP. If a corporate partner exercises a dominant influence the *CA 1985, s 258(2)(c)* and the FRS 2 (accounting for subsidiary undertakings) must be considered. Most notably each corporate partner will have joint and several liability. With this in mind the business partners may decide upon a limited liability partnership (LLP) as introduced by the *Limited Liability Partnership Act 2000* with effect from 6 April 2001.

A joint venture between the business partners may be a simpler structure. No special legal form is required and the business activities are included within the accounts of the venturer thus easing the loss utilisation.

Companies committed to growth may form or acquire new companies and create a group structure. Specific taxation provisions and compliance issues affect groups of companies.

## ACCOUNTING AND TAXATION REQUIREMENTS

### Accounting

**10.2** For company law, a group consists of parent and subsidiary undertakings (*CA 1985, s 262*). For these purposes an undertaking can be a body corporate, a partnership or an unincorporated association carrying on a business with a view to profit (*CA 1985, s 259*(*1*)). Groups of companies must prepare consolidated accounts unless they are exempted by the small and medium-sized group exemptions (*CA 1985, s 227*). Each company within the group must prepare its own individual company accounts (*CA 1985, s 226*).

### Taxation

**10.3** For corporation tax purposes each company within a group must submit its corporation tax computation, its company tax return and statutory accounts to HMRC (see **2.1**). Group accounts may be submitted as supporting information. Corporation tax is calculated in respect of each individual company's profits. Hence, there is no requirement to prepare a group company tax return. The group situation is brought into account when calculating the individual company's liability and when granting reliefs. Companies must prepare the supplementary form CT600C where group relief and eligible unused foreign tax is claimed or surrendered.

## RELIEFS AVAILABLE TO GROUPS

**10.4** The taxation legislation recognises that a group is one large trading or business entity made up of several components. Although each group company makes its own self-assessment return in its own name and is responsible for its own corporation tax liability (but see **3.23**), the taxation legislation permits a certain amount of loss sharing amongst group members. Groups have the opportunity to transfer losses to other group members to be relieved against that group member's profits and to transfer assets within the group without a charge to chargeable gain arising and to surrender eligible unused foreign tax (see Chapter 13). There are different definitions of a group applying to revenue losses, capital losses and consortium situations. These definitions are particular to the taxation legislation and will not always concur with the *Companies Act*.

## GROUP RELIEF

### Definition of a group

**10.5** Various conditions must be satisfied before losses can be transferred in this way between group members. The first condition is that a group actually exists.

A group exists if one company is a 75% subsidiary of the other company and both companies are 75% subsidiaries of a third company. Shares held by share dealing companies as stock in trade are ignored (*ICTA 1988, s 413*(*3*), (*5*)). A 75% subsidiary is a company whose ordinary share capital is owned directly or indirectly by another company. 'Own' in this context means possessing the beneficial ownership (*ICTA 1988, s 838*).

---

**Example 10.1**

A Ltd owns 100% of the ordinary share capital of B Ltd.

B Ltd owns 80% of the ordinary share capital of C Ltd.

A Ltd, B Ltd and C Ltd are a group.

A Ltd owns 100% of B Ltd and effectively 80% of C Ltd (100 × 80).

---

---

**Example 10.2**

A Ltd owns 75% of the ordinary share capital of B Ltd.

B Ltd owns 80% of the ordinary share capital of C Ltd.

A Ltd and B Ltd are a group as A Ltd owns 75% of B Ltd.

A Ltd and C Ltd are not a group because A Ltd only effectively owns 60% of C Ltd (75 × 80).

B Ltd and C Ltd are a separate group.

## Definition of a consortium

**10.6** A company is owned by a consortium if 75% or more of the ordinary share capital of the company is beneficially owned by companies of which none owns less than 5%. The consortium member's share is measured by the lowest of the members' percentage interests in shares, profits or assets. Where these have varied over the year the weighted average is taken (SP/C 6). A 90% trading company subsidiary of a company which is itself a 75% owned consortium company is also included (*ICTA 1988, s 413*(7)). With effect from 1 April 2000 overseas companies are included within the count of group companies (*FA 2000, Sch 27, para 4*). The UK branch of a non-resident subsidiary may also claim or surrender group relief.

**Example 10.3**

P Ltd has an issued share capital of 1,000 ordinary shares, which are within the following beneficial ownership:

| | |
|---|---|
| Q Ltd | 200 |
| R Ltd | 100 |
| S Ltd | 100 |
| T Ltd | 100 |
| U Ltd | 100 |
| V Ltd | 100 |
| X Ltd | 50 |
| Total | 750 |

The remaining shares are held by individual shareholders.

P Ltd is owned by a consortium because 75% of the ordinary share capital is beneficially owned by companies of which none owns less than 5%.

**Example 10.4**

Z Ltd has an issued share capital of 1000 ordinary shares, which are within the following beneficial ownership:

| | |
|---|---|
| Q Ltd | 200 |
| R Ltd | 100 |
| S Ltd | 100 |
| T Ltd | 100 |
| U Ltd | 100 |
| V Ltd | 50 |
| X Ltd | 50 |
| Total | 700 |

The remaining shares are held by individual shareholders.

Z Ltd is not owned by a consortium because 75% of the ordinary share capital is not beneficially owned by companies of which none owns less than 5%.

## Group relief

**10.7** Group relief is the surrender of and claim of group and consortium members' trading losses (*ICTA 1988, s 402*).

Surrenderable losses are those incurred for the current year and include:

- trading losses,
- excess capital allowances,
- non-trading loan relationship deficits,
- charges on income,
- Schedule A losses,
- management expenses, and
- a non-trading loss on intangible fixed assets (*ICTA 1988, s 403*).

Trading losses, excess capital allowances and non-trading loan relationship deficits may be set off against the claimant company's profits even though the surrendering company has other profits for the same accounting period against which they can be set.

Excess charges on income, Schedule A losses, excess management expenses and a non-trading loss on an intangible fixed asset are only available for surrender if in total they exceed the surrendering company's gross profits for that period. If a surrender is made, the order of set-off is deemed to be:

(i) charges on income,

(ii) Schedule A losses,

(iii) management expenses, and

(iv) a non-trading loss on an intangible fixed asset (ICTA 1988, s 403)

The surrendering company's gross profits are its profits for that period before deducting any trading losses, excess capital allowances, non-trade loan relationships deficits, charges, Schedule A losses or management expenses, without any deduction for losses etc from other accounting periods (*ICTA 1988, s 403ZE*).

All Schedule D Case I losses are available for group relief. Schedule D Case V losses may not be group relieved nor may losses from trades not carried out on a commercial basis. Farming and market gardening losses within the *ICTA 1988, s 397* restriction may not be group relieved. (There is a profit requirement every five years in order to be able to set these losses against the company's other income) (*ICTA 1988, s 403ZA*). Excess capital allowances are allowances that are required to be set in the first instance against a specified class of income, eg special leasing (*ICTA 1988, s 403ZB*). A non-trading loan relationship debit is discussed in **11.17**. Charges are the actual charges paid by the company during the period. A Schedule A loss must be a commercial loss and must not include any loss brought forward from a previous period. Management expenses means the annual amount deductible by the company for the accounting period, but does not include amounts brought forward from earlier periods. See **7.13** for a non-trading loss on an intangible fixed asset (*ICTA 1988, s 403ZD*).

A claimant company must use its own trading losses brought forward before it makes a group relief claim (*ICTA 1988, s 393*(*1*)).

---

**Example 10.5**

Omega Ltd owns 75% of the shares and voting rights of Epsilon Ltd and Zeta Ltd. All companies prepare accounts to 31 March each year. The results for the year ended 31 March 2007 are as follows:

| | *Omega Ltd* £ | *Epsilon Ltd* £ | *Zeta Ltd* £ |
|---|---|---|---|
| Schedule D Case I | 400,000 | 90,000 | -380,000 |
| Schedule A | 30,000 | 14,000 | 23,000 |
| Schedule D Case III | 6,000 | 1,000 | 2,000 |
| Chargeable gain | 40,000 | — | 10,000 |
| Gift aid payment | 1,000 | — | — |

Zeta Ltd is not expected to make a trading profit in the near future. Both Omega Ltd and Epsilon Ltd's future trading results are uncertain.

| | | *Small companies rate* |
|---|---|---|
| Upper limit | (1,500,000/3) | 500,000 |
| Lower limit | (300,000/3) | 100,000 |

The position for each company prior to group relief is as follows:

| | *Omega Ltd* £ | *Epsilon Ltd* £ | *Zeta Ltd* £ |
|---|---|---|---|
| Schedule D Case I | 400,000 | 90,000 | — |
| Schedule A | 30,000 | 14,000 | 23,000 |
| Schedule D Case III | 6,000 | 1,000 | 2,000 |
| Chargeable gain | 40,000 | — | 10,000 |
| Gift aid payment | (1,000) | — | — |
| PCTCT | 475,000 | 105,000 | 35,000 |
| Marginal rate | 32.75% | 32.75% | 19% |

Omega Ltd should receive the maximum relief, in order to bring profits down to the lower limits for the small companies rate.

| | *Omega Ltd* £ | *Epsilon Ltd* £ | *Zeta Ltd* £ |
|---|---|---|---|
| PCTCT | 475,000 | 105,000 | 35,000 |
| Less: *s 402* relief | 375,000 | 5,000 | |
| PCTCT | 100,000 | 100,000 | 35,000 |
| Corporation tax at 19% | 19,000 | 19,000 | 6,650 |

**Utilisation of loss**

| | | £ |
|---|---|---|
| Loss | | 380,000 |
| (i) | Omega Ltd | 375,000 |
| (ii) | Epsilon Ltd | 5,000 |
| (iii) | Zeta Ltd | 0 |
| | | 380,000 |

Zeta Ltd will have trading losses in the next accounting period, which it can carry back against this year's profits. Both Omega Ltd and Epsilon Ltd's future profits are uncertain.

---

**Example 10.6**

A Ltd (a group member) has the following results.

| | *Year ending 31 December 2005* | *Year ending 31 December 2006* |
|---|---|---|
| | £ | £ |
| Case I (loss) brought forward | (500) | — |
| Case I income/(loss) | 1,000 | (1,000) |
| Case III income | 500 | 500 |

For the accounting period ended 31 December 2005:

- The loss brought forward must be relieved in priority to group relief. The maximum amount of group relief claimable will be £1,000.
- If relief for this period is claimed for so much of the trading loss of the following period as cannot be relieved in that period, ie £500, such relief would be displaced by a group relief claim, and would then be available for carrying forward.

For the accounting period ending 31 December 2006:

No group relief is obtainable, whether or not the trading loss is carried back.

---

## AVAILABILITY OF GROUP RELIEF

### UK losses

**10.8** The next issue, assuming that losses as detailed in **10.7** have been incurred, is whether group relief is available.

A group relief loss claim for the items within the ambit of UK corporation tax may be made where:

- the surrendering company and the claimant company are both members of the same group,
- the surrendering company is resident in the UK or is not so resident but carries on a trade there through a permanent establishment, and
- the claimant company is resident in the UK or is not so resident but carries on a trade there through a permanent establishment (*ICTA 1988, s 402*(2); *FA 2006, Sch 1, para 1*).

UK group members and UK branches may inter alia claim and surrender losses, so may UK resident consortia.

## Overseas losses

**10.9** Following the decision in *Marks & Spencer v David Halsey* C-446/03 [2006] STC 237 with effect for accounting periods beginning on or after 1 April 2006, a 'qualifying overseas loss' may be surrendered for group relief (*ICTA 1988, s 403A, Sch 18A*).

For this to occur, the surrendering company must be chargeable to tax under the laws of any European Economic Area (EEA) territory and it must be:

- a 75% subsidiary of a UK resident claimant company, or
- both the surrendering company and the claimant company are 75% subsidiaries of a third company that is UK resident.

The company will be chargeable to tax in an EEA territory if it is resident in the territory or if it carries on a trade in any EEA territory through a permanent establishment (*ICTA 1988, s 402*(*2A*), (*2B*); *FA 2006, Sch 1, para 1*).

The following countries are members of the EEA:

| | | | | |
|---|---|---|---|---|
| Austria | Finland | Ireland | Malta | Slovenia |
| Belgium | France | Italy | Netherlands | Spain |
| Cyprus | Germany | Latvia | Norway | Sweden |
| Czech Republic | Greece | Liechtenstein | Poland | UK |
| Denmark | Hungary | Lithuania | Portugal | |
| Estonia | Iceland | Luxembourg | Slovakia | |

Comments in the *Marks & Spencer* case pointed to the fact that the UK was unfairly discriminating against overseas subsidiaries.

**Marks & Spencer ECJ ruling**

As Community law now stands, Articles 43 EC and 48 EC do not preclude provisions of a member state, which generally prevent a resident parent company from deducting from its taxable profits losses incurred in another member state by a subsidiary established in that member state although they allow it to deduct losses incurred by a resident subsidiary. However, it is contrary to Articles 43 EC and 48 EC to prevent the resident parent company from doing so where the non-resident subsidiary has exhausted the possibilities available in its state of residence of having the losses taken into account for the accounting period concerned by the claim for relief and also for previous accounting periods and where there are no possibilities for those losses to be taken into account in its state of residence for future periods either by the subsidiary itself or by a third party, in particular where the subsidiary has been sold to that third party.

## Relief in respect of overseas losses of non-resident companies

**10.10** An overseas loss of a non-resident company is available for surrender by way of group relief by a non-resident company if the 75% relationship is met.

The loss must meet the following conditions in relation to the EEA territory:

(a) The equivalence condition: The loss must be of a kind that would be available for relief by a UK company.

(b) The EEA tax loss condition:

For EEA resident companies:

- the loss is calculated under the laws of the EEA territory, and
- the loss is not attributed to a UK permanent establishment of the company.

For non-EEA resident companies:

- the company carries on a trade through a permanent establishment in the EEA territory,
- the loss is calculated under the laws of the EEA territory, and
- the activities are not exempt under a double tax treaty, as these would be ignored.

(c) The qualifying loss condition:

- The loss cannot be given qualifying relief for any period ('the current period') or any past or future period, and

- the loss has not been given any other qualifying relief under the law of any territory outside the United Kingdom (other than the EEA territory concerned).

(d) The precedence condition: The loss cannot be relieved in any other grouping (*ICTA 1988, s 403F*; *FA 2006, Sch 1, para 4(1)*).

The relevant accounting period concerned is the accounting period the company would have if it were UK resident (*ICTA 1988, Sch 18, para 1A*; *FA 2006, Sch 1, para 6(4)*). The loss will not qualify for relief if it arose from artificial arrangements (*ICTA 1988, s 403G*; *FA 2006, Sch 1, para 4*(2)).

## Application of UK rules to non-resident company

**10.11** The corporation tax computation must be recalculated using the applicable UK tax rules. The calculated loss cannot exceed the non-resident company actual loss and if the result is a profit, no relief is available (*ICTA 1988, Sch 18A, para 11*; *FA 2006, Sch 1, para 7*).

On preparing the computation it is necessary to assume that the company is UK resident and that its trade is carried on wholly or partly in the UK. Rental income and income from land is calculated on the assumption that the land is based in the UK and on Schedule A principles. The accounting period on which the computation is based is assumed to begin at the beginning of the loss period. If plant and machinery is purchased it is assumed that capital allowances are available (*ICTA 1988, Sch 18A, para 15*; *FA 2006, Sch 1, para 7*).

## Arrangement for transfer of a company to another group or consortium

**10.12** If a company has made arrangements that could result in it leaving the group, it will not be able to partake in the group relief claims by surrender of claim with other group companies (*ICTA 1988, s 410*). Its ineligibility for group relief will only last for the period in which the arrangements exist (*Shepherd v Law Land plc* (1990) 63 TC 692, [1990] STC 795).

Also all rights over shares are deemed to have been exercised at the earliest possible date. If rights differ over the ownership period the lowest common denominator is applied to the holdings to ascertain whether group relief is available (*ICTA 1988, Sch 18, para 5*).

## Group relief claim

**10.13** A group relief claim can be made for a corresponding accounting period. Often group member accounting periods are not co-terminous and the available profits and losses must be apportioned. The amount that may be surrendered is the smaller of:

- the unused part of the surrenderable amount for the overlapping period, and
- the unrelieved part of the claimant company's total profits for the overlapping period.

The overlapping period is the period common to both companies (*ICTA 1988, s 403A*).

---

**Example 10.7**

Mu Ltd owns 90% of the ordinary share capital of Nu Ltd.

Mu Ltd has prepared annual accounts to 30 June 2007.

Profits for the year amount to £48,000.

Nu Ltd has prepared annual accounts to 31 December 2007.

The trading loss for the year amounts to £56,000.

Although Mu Ltd and Nu Ltd are a group for group relief purposes, they can only claim and surrender losses pro rata to their common accounting periods.

**Nu Ltd's maximum loss surrender**

(1 January 2007 to 30 June 2007) ÷ (1 January 2007 to 31 December 2007) = 6/12

£56,000 × 6/12 = £28,000

The remaining £28,000 loss is available for relief against Nu Ltd's other income for the year.

**Mu Ltd's maximum profits against which loss may be surrendered**

(1 January 2007 to 30 June 2007) ÷ (1 January 2007 to 31 December 2007) = 6/12

£48,000 × 6/12 = £24,000

Only £24,000 of Nu Ltd's £56,000 trading loss can be group relieved against Mu Ltd's profits. The remaining £32,000 is available for relief against Nu Ltd's other income.

---

## Consortium relief claim

**10.14** Not only does the overlapping period restriction apply to consortium companies but also the claim is restricted to the members' interests in the consortium. The members' interest in the overlapping period for this purpose is the lower of the percentage of:

- ordinary share capital,
- profits available for distribution, and
- assets on a winding up.

If the percentages fluctuate over the period, the average is taken (*ICTA 1988, s 403C*).

---

**Example 10.8**

Delta Ltd is a consortium company, which is owned 60% by Alpha Ltd, 20% by Beta Ltd and 20% by Gamma Ltd. All companies prepare accounts to 31 December each year. In the accounting period ended 31 December 2006 Delta's trading loss amounts to £75,000. The maximum loss claim is as follows:

| | | £ |
|---|---|---|
| Total loss | | 75,000 |
| Alpha Ltd | 60% | 45,000 |
| Beta Ltd | 20% | 15,000 |
| Gamma Ltd | 20% | 15,000 |
| | | 75,000 |

Loss relief will be given provided each company has sufficient profits.

In the accounting period ended 31 December 2007, Delta Ltd makes a profit of £80,000. Alpha Ltd makes a loss of £120,000, Beta Ltd makes a loss of £30,000 and Gamma Ltd makes a profit of £60,000.

The maximum surrenderable losses are calculated as follows:

| | | £ | £ |
|---|---|---|---|
| Delta Ltd | Profit | | 80,000 |
| | Losses surrendered: | | |
| Alpha Ltd | Loss made | (120,000) | |
| | Maximum surrender is 60% of £80,000 | 48,000 | (48,000) |
| | Not available for surrender | (72,000) | |
| Beta Ltd | Loss made | (30,000) | |
| | Maximum surrender is 20% of £80,000 | 16,000 | (16,000) |
| | Not available for surrender | (14,000) | |
| Gamma Ltd | Not applicable | | |
| | PCTCT | | 16,000 |

**Example 10.9**

A Ltd owns 100% of the share capital of B Ltd.

B Ltd owns 40% of the share capital of D Ltd.

C Ltd owns 60% of the share capital of D Ltd.

D Ltd owns 100% of the share capital of E Ltd.

D Ltd owns 100% of the share capital of F Ltd.

This can be shown as follows.

| A | |
|---|---|
| 100% | |
| B | C |
| 40% | 60% |
| D | |
| 100% | 100% |
| E | F |

There are two groups:

- A and B, and
- D, E and F.

D are owned by a consortium of B and C. All companies have the same accounting periods. None of the companies has any losses brought forward.

The companies have the following results for the year ended 31 July 2007

| | | |
|---|---|---|
| A Ltd | £100,000 | profit |
| B Ltd | (£30,000) | loss |
| C Ltd | Nil | |
| D Ltd | (£20,000) | loss |
| E Ltd | £10,000 | profit |
| F Ltd | (£3,000) | loss |

E Ltd claims group relief (in priority to consortium relief) as follows.

| | £ | £ |
|---|---|---|
| Profit | | 10,000 |
| Deduct: | | |
| Group relief: loss surrendered by F Ltd | 3,000 | |
| Group relief: loss surrendered by D Ltd | 7,000 | |
| | | (10,000) |
| | | — |

A Ltd can claim group relief first and then consortium relief as follows.

| | £ | £ |
|---|---|---|
| Profit | | 100,000 |
| Deduct: | | |
| Group relief: loss surrendered by B Ltd | 30,000 | |
| Consortium relief: loss surrendered by D Ltd (£20,000 – £7,000) × 40% | 5,200 | |
| | | (35,200) |
| | | 64,800 |

## Group relief claimant company

**10.15** The claimant company sets the relief against its total profits for the year to reduce its overall corporation tax liability. The claimant company is not required to pay the surrendering company for utilisation of the loss. There is no tax effect if a payment is made (up to the amount of the loss) (*ICTA 1988, s 402(6)*). If a payment is not made this may be viewed as a depreciatory transaction (*TCGA 1992, s 176*). HMRC have stated that they will not seek an adjustment (IR letter, 3 February 1981).

## Company tax return

**10.16** Details of the group relief claim are included on Company Tax Return Form – Supplementary Pages Group and Consortium CT600C. Both the claimant and the surrendering company must each complete their respective CT600C forms, which formalise the claim. The claimant company includes the amount of group relief and consortium relief claimed in box 36 of the main Company Tax Return CT600. The claim must be made within the normal self-assessment time limits, ie two years after the end of the chargeable period for which the claim is made. A claim made out of time can be refused (*Farmer v Bankers Trust International Ltd* (1990) 64 TC 1, [1990] STC 564).

Alternatively, 'an authorised group company', normally the holding company, may request HMRC in writing to grant it the power to furnish group relief claims and surrender notices on behalf of the other group and consortium companies. The application should include:

- the name and the tax office reference of the authorised company,
- the names and the tax office references of the authorising companies,
- details relating to the authorised company and each of the authorising companies that are sufficient to demonstrate that the company concerned is a member of the group of companies or, as the case may be, a consortium company, and
- a statement by the authorised company and the authorising companies that they agree to be covered by the arrangements and to be bound by claims, surrenders and withdrawals made under the arrangements.

The application must be accompanied by:

- a specimen copy of group relief claim and surrender statement that the authorised company proposes to use for the purpose of making and withdrawing surrenders and claims on behalf of itself and the authorising companies; or
- in the case of a company that is a consortium company, an agreement, signed by each member of the consortium and the consortium company, consenting to the authorised company acting on their behalf in relation to the arrangements.

The application must be signed on behalf of each of the companies concerned by an officer of the company, normally the company secretary and be sent to the tax office dealing with the tax affairs of the authorised company (*FA 1998, Sch 18, para 77*; *SI 1999/2975*).

## Repayments of corporation tax

**10.17** Groups of companies with an *ICTA 1988, s 402* group relationship are able to jointly elect for repayment due to one company to be surrendered to another company in payment of its corporation tax liability. The facility is aimed at reducing the group's exposure to interest on overdue tax. The companies involved must have the same accounting period and must be members of the same group throughout the accounting period (*FA 1989, s 102*). Any intercompany tax payment up to the amount of the tax is ignored. There is no prescribed format for the election. A letter to HMRC will suffice with details of the company and tax district reference numbers. Each company should appoint an authorised person to sign the form on its behalf.

The joint notice is not given in the return form CT600, but must be made separately. The surrendering company should use the 'repayment' section of the return form to claim its refund and show how much is to be surrendered by completing boxes 145 to 148 accordingly. A copy of the joint notice should be enclosed with the return. (See HMRC Company Taxation Manual CTM 92440 for further details).

## Refunds of quarterly instalments

**10.18** The intra-group arrangement is also available for quarterly instalments (see **3.11**) (intra-group surrender: legislation *SI 1998/3175, reg 9*, as amended by *SI 1999/1929, reg 3*). A refund of tax that is paid under the instalment arrangements can be surrendered to fellow group members at the date of payment. Again the aim is to reduce the group's exposure to interest by netting off the debit and credit interest to eliminate the differential interest that it would otherwise suffer arising from underpaid and overpaid instalment tax.

The amended version only applies when a tax refund is due to be made to the surrendering company. The refund may be due either under *reg 6* or *TMA 1970, s 59D(2)*. HMRC explain the effects as follows: the result is that:

- payments made during the quarterly instalment payment period may retrospectively be allocated between group members to mitigate the interest position of the group, beyond that limited circumstance,

- *regulation 9* only applies in relation to CT paid on account of the surrendering company's own liability,
- a group is unable to make a global payment in the name of a dormant company or one that will have no CT liability, and then reallocate it between group members retrospectively.

Under *reg 9* the surrendering company must give notice to HMRC, at the time when the joint surrender notice is given, specifying the payment(s) out of which the refund is to be treated as made (*FA 1989, s 102* or *reg 9(5C)*). The surrendering company then has 30 days in which to bring its specification into line with the amount of the repayment due. If it fails to do so within that time, the repayment can be made as if no notice of surrender had been given (*FA 1989, s 102* and *reg 9(5D), (5E)*) (HMRC Company Taxation Manual CTM 92740).

**Example 10.10**

Red Ltd and Blue Ltd are within the same group and they both qualify under the special rules of *FA 1989, s 102*.

Both companies have 31 December year ends and each company makes the following quarterly payments:

| | *Red Ltd* | *Blue Ltd* |
|---|---|---|
| | £ | £ |
| 14 July 2007 | 500,000 | 500,000 |
| 14 October 2007 | 500,000 | 500,000 |
| 14 January 2008 | 250,000 | 500,000 |
| 14 April 2008 | 150,000 | 500,000 |
| Total paid | 1,400,000 | 2,000,000 |

The actual corporation tax liability for the year is as follows:

| | *Red Ltd* | *Blue Ltd* |
|---|---|---|
| | £ | £ |
| Corporation tax liability year ending 31 March 2007 | 10,000 | 3,500,000 |

Red Ltd makes a repayment claim for £1,390,000 under *reg 6* because it is now known that no instalment tax was due.

Blue Ltd should have paid quarterly instalments of £875,000.

So Blue Ltd's cumulative underpayment of instalments is:

| | *Instalments due* £ | *Instalments paid* £ | *Shortfall* £ |
|---|---|---|---|
| 14 July 2007 | 875,000 | 500,000 | 375,000 |
| 14 October 2007 | 875,000 | 500,000 | 375,000 |
| 14 January 2008 | 875.000 | 500,000 | 375,000 |
| 14 April 2008 | 875,000 | 500,000 | 375,000 |
| | 3,500,000 | 2,000,000 | 1,500,000 |

Red Ltd makes a repayment claim for the overpaid instalments.

Red Ltd and Blue Ltd give joint notice of surrender, so that the instalment tax paid by Red Ltd is treated as paid by Blue Ltd with Red Ltd's payment dates.

Red Ltd is treated as if the overpaid tax had been repaid to it on those dates.

The claim results in Red Ltd not making any quarterly payments. Its corporation tax of £10,000 is now due by 1 January 2008. Blue Ltd has to make a further instalment payment as soon as possible of £100,000, which is calculated as follows:

| | £ |
|---|---|
| Corporation tax due year ending 31 March 2007 | 3,500,000 |
| Quarterly instalments paid by Blue Ltd | (2,000,000) |
| Quarterly instalments paid by Red Ltd | (1,400,000) |
| Net amount due | 100,000 |

**10.19** *SI 1998/3175, reg 10* empowers HMRC, at any time after the filing date, to require a company to furnish such information as may reasonably be required about:

- the computation of any instalment payment,
- the reasons it omitted to make quarterly instalment payments, and
- a *reg 6* repayment claim.

The time allowed for providing the information must not be less than 30 days and must be shown on the notice.

*Regulation 11* empowers HMRC to require the company to produce 'books, documents and other records in its possession or power' for the purposes of reg 10. HMRC accept photostat copies as long as the originals are available for inspection. These powers are not part of the enquiry procedures.

## Group income

**10.20** A UK company is not required to deduct tax at source from intra-group interest and royalty payments where the other company is UK resident or if not UK resident operates from a permanent establishment (*FA 2001, s 85*; *FA 2002, s 96*).

# ASSET TRANSFER

## Group structure

**10.21** For chargeable gains purposes, a group consists of a company (known as the principal company) and all its 75% subsidiaries together with each subsidiary's 75% subsidiary company. Each subsidiary must be an effective 51% subsidiary of the principal company. A principal company must not be a 75% subsidiary of another company. The principal company can be UK or overseas resident and the inclusion of a non-resident subsidiary does not disturb the group relationship.

---

**Example 10.11**

A Ltd owns 75% of the ordinary share capital of B Ltd.

B Ltd owns 80% of the ordinary share capital of C Ltd.

A Ltd and B Ltd are a group, as A Ltd owns 75% of B Ltd.

A Ltd and C Ltd are a group because A Ltd effectively owns 60% of C Ltd (75 × 80).

---

**10.22** A company can only be a member of one group. Where the conditions qualify so that a company would be a member of two or more groups the group that it is deemed to be a member of is determined establishing its links to the principal company and if the group conditions are not met the links should be established with the next group (*TCGA 1992, s 170*).

---

**Example 10.12**

A Ltd owns 75% of the ordinary share capital of B Ltd.

B Ltd owns 80% of the ordinary share capital of C Ltd.

C Ltd owns 75% of the ordinary share capital of D Ltd.

D Ltd owns 75% of the ordinary share capital of E Ltd.

A Ltd and B Ltd are a group.

A Ltd and C Ltd are a group.

A Ltd and D Ltd are not a group because A Ltd effectively owns 45% of D Ltd (75 × 80 × 75).

D Ltd and E Ltd are a group.

---

## Relief

**10.23** For chargeable gains purposes intra-group transfers of assets are always deemed to be made at a price that results in neither gain nor loss for the transferee company (*TCGA 1992, s 171*) (*Innocent v Whaddon Estates Ltd* (1981) 55 TC 476, [1982] STC 115).

The relief is automatically applied and given without claim, but does not apply where a transfer arises in the satisfaction of a debt, a disposal of redeemable shares on redemption, a disposal by or to an investment trust, VCT or qualifying friendly society; or a disposal to a dual resident investing company. On a company reconstruction where *TCGA 1992, s 135* applies (see **15.8**), *s 135* takes preference so *s 171* does not apply.

Although a non UK company can be a member of the group, it cannot take part in the asset transfer unless it trades in the UK through a permanent branch or agency. The asset must be in the UK and be used for the branch or agency trade.

When a company eventually disposes of the asset to a third party the company selling adopts the original base cost of the asset to the group plus indexation for the capital gains computation.

## Election to treat a disposal as if made by another group member

**10.24** In order to fully utilise the group's capital losses, a group company may treat a disposal of an asset outside the group as though it were made by another group member. This will enable the asset to be placed in the company that has the capital losses. Both companies must make a joint election for the deemed transfer to apply, within two years of the end of the chargeable period in which the transfer takes place (*TCGA 1992, s 171A*).

## Transfers of assets to trading stock

**10.25** Where one group member acquires a capital asset, from another member, that it appropriates to trading stock, the intra-group asset transfer will be at no gain no loss, but as soon as the asset is transferred to stock a chargeable gain arises on the transferee. The transferee adopts the transferor's asset base cost and indexation. Alternatively, the transferee can elect under *TCGA 1992, s 161(3)* to treat the asset as acquired at market value less the capital gain arising. The gain will therefore be taken as part of the trading profit on the asset.

---

**Example 10.13**

O Ltd transfers a fixed asset to its holding company N Ltd. N Ltd appropriates the asset to its trading stock. The indexed cost of the asset was £12,500 to O Ltd and the market value on transfer is £20,000. N Ltd eventually sells the asset to a third party for £30,000.

Without a *TCGA 1992, s 161(3)* election the position is as follows:

| *N Ltd* | £ |
|---|---|
| Market value | 20,000 |
| Indexed cost | 12,500 |
| Capital gain | 7,500 |
| Sale proceeds | 30,000 |
| Deemed cost | 20,000 |
| Trading profit | 10,000 |

With a *TCGA 1992, s 161(3)* election the position is as follows:

| *N Ltd* | £ |
|---|---|
| Sales proceeds | 30,000 |
| Indexed cost | 12,500 |
| Trading profit | 17,500 |

**10.26** There is the potential here to turn a capital loss into a trading loss. The loss will only be allowed if there is a true trading intention (*Coates v Arndale Properties Ltd* (1984) 59 TC 516, [1984] STC 637, [1984] 1 WLR 1328, [1985] 1 All ER 15).

## Transfers of assets from trading stock

**10.27** Where a group company transfers an asset that it holds as trading stock to another group company that holds it as an asset it is deemed to be transferred at market value in the transferor's books giving rise to a trading profit. When the transferee company sells the asset outside the group it adopts the market value of the asset when it was transferred from the transferor company as base cost on which is based indexation allowance etc.

**Example 10.14**

N Ltd transfers a chargeable asset from its trading stock to its subsidiary company O Ltd. O Ltd will hold the asset as an investment. The cost of the asset was £10,000 and the market value on transfer is £30,000. O Ltd then sells the asset to a third party for £40,000. The indexation from the time of transfer is £500.

| *N Ltd* | £ | £ |
|---|---|---|
| Market value | | 30,000 |
| Cost | | 10,000 |
| Trading profit | | 20,000 |
| O Ltd | | |
| Sale proceeds | | 40,000 |
| Deemed cost | 30,000 | |
| Indexation | 500 | |

| | |
|---|---|
| | 30,500 |
| Capital gain | 9,500 |

## Replacement of business asset by members of a group.

**10.28** *TCGA 1992, s 152* roll-over relief is extended to group situations. For this purpose all group assets and trades are treated as one. The new assets must be purchased outside the group (*TCGA 1992, s 175*). See **6.51** et seq.

## Companies leaving the group

**10.29** If a company leaves a group within six years on an inter-group transfer a chargeable gain arises on assets acquired from other group members on a no gain/no loss basis within the previous six years that it still owns (*TCGA 1992, s 179*). The chargeable gain is calculated on the basis that the company leaving the group sold and repurchased the asset at market value on the day that it was acquired from the other group member (*TCGA 1992, s 179(3)*) but the gain is charged in the accounting period in which the company leaves the group.

The company and the other group member from whom the asset was acquired may jointly elect that the capital gain on leaving the group be treated as that of the other company (*TCGA 1992, s 179A*). If qualifying, the asset will be available for roll-over relief (*TCGA 1992, s 179B*).

**Example 10.15**

In 1988 N Ltd acquired a freehold property for £280,000. In 2001 when the market value was £500,000 and the indexation to date was £20,000 N Ltd transferred the freehold property to P Ltd a fellow group member. P Ltd leaves the group on 1 January 2007. Both companies prepare accounts to 30 June each year.

The *s 179* gain for the year ended 30 June 2007 is calculated as follows:

| *P Ltd* | *£* |
|---|---|
| Market value | 500,000 |
| Indexed cost | 300,000 |
| Capital gain | 200,000 |

If P Ltd purchases another qualifying asset P Ltd will be able to make a roll-over relief claim under *TCGA 1992, s 152*.

If N Ltd and P Ltd could jointly elect for the gain to fall in N Ltd only, N Ltd will be able to make a roll-over relief claim, which must be against its acquisition of a qualifying asset.

---

**10.30** HMRC have confirmed that a degrouping charge will not be imposed on assets transferred to the parent of a two-company group, which disposes of its single subsidiary (HMRC Capital Gains Tax Manual CG 45450).

## Losses attributable to depreciatory transactions

**10.31** If assets are transferred to group members at below market value this could fictitiously deflate the value of the company. If the shares were later sold, the market price would reflect the deflated price and hence a capital loss would arise. Such a loss will not be an allowable loss for capital gains tax purposes (*TCGA 1992, s 176*).

## Dividend stripping

**10.32** This legislation is aimed at situations where a company might hold 10% or more of the same class securities of another company in a non-dealing non-group situation. A distribution is then made, the effect of which reduces the value of the other company dramatically. If the shares are then sold the distribution is not taken into account when calculating the chargeable gain on disposal (*TCGA 1992, s 177*).

## Pre-entry losses and gains

**10.33** A pre-entry asset is any asset owned by a company before it joined a group. The asset may have ben transferred to other group members. An asset derived from a pre-entry asset is deemed to be part of the same asset, eg if the freehold reversion of a leasehold property is acquired (*TCGA 1992, Sch 7A, para 2(8)*).

If a company joins a group it is prevented from utilising its unrelieved losses arising prior to the time it joined the group against gains on the disposal of assets transferred (or deemed to be transferred) from another group member (*TCGA 1992, Sch 7AA*).

Similarly if a company joins a group and in the same accounting period realises a chargeable gain it is prevented from relieving the gain against the loss on sale of group assets transferred to the company during the same accounting period (*TCGA 1992, Sch 7AA*). See 18.16–18.23 for the situation with effect from 5 December 2005.

A realised pre-entry loss belonging to a company on joining a group can be set against a profit on disposal of any asset made before it joined the group or against the profit on disposal of any asset that the company owned when it joined the group and sells after joining. The losses can also be set against the gains on disposal of any assets that it acquired from outside the group and used for the purposes of the trade, which it has continued to carry on since it joined the group (*TCGA 1992, Sch 7A*(*1*)).

The pre-entry unrealised losses are apportioned accordingly to the time that the company joined the group (*TCGA 1992, Sch 7A*(*2*)).

## Other reliefs

**10.34** Gains on disposal of investments may be relieved by the substantial shareholdings exemption (see **12.28–12.32**). If an investment falls within the corporate venturing scheme capital loss relief may be available against trading income (see **12.33–12.43**).

*Chapter 11*

# Corporate Finance

## COMPANY FINANCE

### Equity v loan finance

**11.1** Companies raise finance by borrowing, issuing shares and exploiting their assets. A debt has a legal right to repayment whereas shares have no such rights. Various controls are exercised on a company's activities through the *Financial Services and Markets Act 2000*, the *Companies Act* and the Stock Exchange.

For taxation purposes the basic premise is that equity finance, which relates to the issue of shares, will have no direct effect on the company's corporation tax liability. UK distributions received are not taxable on a company. On eventual disposal the profit on sale to the vendor will be assessable as a capital gain.

Loan finance does have an effect on the company's corporation tax liability. Lenders are rewarded by an interest payment. Lenders look to some form of asset security or guarantee regarding the loan repayment. Interest payments are deductible against a company's corporation tax liability and interest receipts are taxable.

### The loan relationship provisions

**11.2** The provisions of *Finance Act 1996, ss 80–105* and *Schs 8–15* introduced the 'loan relationship' rules governing corporate debt, principally aimed at aligning the taxation treatment of loan finance with the accounting treatment. With the ever increasing sophistication of the financial markets the original rules have been amended by subsequent *Finance Acts*; notably *Finance Act 2002* (generally for accounting periods beginning on or after 1 October 2002), *Finance Act 2004*, *Finance* (*No* 2) *Act 2005* (generally for accounting periods beginning on or after 1 January 2005) and *Finance Act 2006* for accounting periods ended on or after 22 March 2006.

*Finance Act 2002* brought exchange gains and losses on loan relationships denominated in a foreign currency into the calculation of the overall profit or loss on the loan relationship. In general the *FA 1996* loan relationships legislation also applies to exchange gains and losses.

The loan relationship rules aim to treat capital and revenue receipts in a like manner and show no distinction between realised and unrealised amounts. Gains and losses are calculated according to the basis adopted in the accounts and are termed 'credits' and 'debits'. A different treatment is applied to trading and non-trading debits and credits. Trading debits and credits are included in the Schedule D Case I computation. Non-trading debits and credits are included within Schedule D Case III.

The loan relationship rules apply to both trading and non-trading companies, unincorporated associations subject to corporation tax, UK branches of overseas companies and controlled foreign companies. The rules apply to companies that are members of a partnership but not to individuals. Non-resident companies come within the loan relationship rules if they trade in the UK through a branch or agency, and the loan relationship is held for trading purposes by that branch or agency

## LOAN RELATIONSHIP

### Meaning

**11.3** The first issue that a company will want to address is whether the debt arrangement that it has entered into constitutes a loan relationship. In most situations this will be the case. A loan relationship exists where:

- the company stands in the position of a creditor or debtor as respects any money debt; and
- that debt is one arising from a transaction for the lending of money;

and references to a loan relationship and to a company's being a party to a loan relationship shall be construed accordingly (*FA 1996, s 81(1)*).

For a company to be within the loan relationship provisions it must have a money debt.

## MONEY DEBT

### Legislative definitions

**11.4** The legislation initially defined a money debt as a debt which falls to be settled by the payment of money or by the transfer of a right to settlement under a debt which is itself a money debt. When originally enacted it was understood that a money debt was one that was settled by the payment of money or the transfer of another money debt. *Finance Act 2006* amended the meaning of debt in response to anti-avoidance schemes that arranged to repay debt with a share issue on the basis that the transaction would fall out of the loan relationship provisions. In respect of loan relationships to which a company is party on 22 March 2006, *Finance Act 2006, Sch 6, para 10*(*2*) added that a money debt could be settled by the issue or transfer of shares in any company (*FA 1996, s 81*(*2*)). In circumstances that are divorced from loan relationships the disposal of a shareholding would bring about a chargeable gain or an allowable loss. Therefore, on 22 March 2006 the holding enters the loan relationship regime at fair value and a chargeable gain or an allowable loss is deemed to arise. The gain or loss is held over until the company ceases to be a party to the loan relationship. Therefore at this time there will not only be a loan relationship adjustment but also a chargeable gain or an allowable loss brought into charge (*FA 2006, Sch 6, para 10*(*6*)).

### Existence of a loan relationship

**11.5** A company has a loan relationship where the following two conditions are satisfied:

- it is a creditor or a debtor for a money debt, and
- that money debt has arisen from a transaction for the lending of money (*FA 1996, s 81*(*1*)).

A normal trade debt is not a loan relationship.

If an instrument has been created that represents the rights under the debt then this will be within the loan relationship rules (*FA 1996, s 81*(*3*)). The following types of debt have always been included within loan relationships: overdrafts, mortgages, advances, gilts, bank loans and deposits, building society shares and deposits, debentures, certificates of deposit, company securities and eurobonds, government stock, discounts, premiums, bills of exchange and promissory notes. For corporation tax a qualifying corporate bond is a loan relationship. A qualifying corporate bond is a security, which at all time has represented a normal commercial loan and which is only redeemable in sterling (*TCGA 1992, s 117*). A convertible loan note is not a qualifying corporate bond (*Weston v Garnett* [2005] EWCA Civ 742, [2005] STC 1134).

## Money debts included within the loan relationship rules

**11.6** A money debt is not necessarily a loan relationship. Certain money debts were brought within the loan relationship rules with effect from 1 October 2002. These include interest on late payment for goods and services, interest on judgment debts, late payment interest on completion and late payment of tax. Only the interest and exchange gains and losses are treated as loan relationships and included as debits or credits. Interest imputed under transfer pricing (see **14.20–14.21**) is also included within loan relationships (*FA 1996, s 100*). Whether the interest is trading or non-trading depends on whether it is receivable or payable for the purposes of the trade. Interest receivable from or payable to HMRC is always non-trading (*FA 1996, s 100(7)*).

Interest in excess of a reasonable commercial return, which is treated as a distribution by virtue of *ICTA 1988, s 209(2)(d)* (see **16.7**), is not a loan relationship (*FA 1996, Sch 9, para 1*). *FA 1996, Sch 9, para 1* ensures that interest that is characterised as a distribution under *ICTA 1988, s 209(2)(d)* or (*e*) cannot be a debit or credit.

With effect from 16 March 2005 discounts on money debts are also loan relationships, but discounts that are treated as distributions under *ICTA 1988, s 209(2)(e)* are not. With effect from 16 March 2005, shares are treated as loan relationships (see **11.7**).

## Shares treated as loan relationships

**11.7** From 16 March 2005 onwards certain shares are treated as loan relationships which include:

- **Shares subject to outstanding third party obligations**. The investing company holds a share in another company, the investee company that is subject to third party obligations and is an interest like investment. In other words another person must meet the calls on the shares and that its fair value increase represents a return at commercial rate of interest with no deviations. In that case the investing company must treat the share as a creditor loan relationship. The distributions received are neither treated as a dividend nor a repayment of capital. The investing company must bring the debits and credits into account on an accounting fair value basis (*FA 1996, s 91A*).
- **Non-qualifying shares**. A non-qualifying share is a share held by an investing company in another company, the investee company, which is

neither a holding in a unit trust or offshore fund (see *FA 2005, Sch 10, para 4*) nor a (*s 91A*) share subject to outstanding third party obligations. In addition the share is not a dealer share (*ICTA 1988, s 95*) but it satisfied one of three conditions:

1. Its fair value increase represents a return at a commercial rate of interest with no deviations.
2. The share is redeemable such that its return equates with a return on invested money, eg redeemable preference shares.
3. The share and one or more derivative contracts are together designed to produce a return based on a commercial rate of interest.

In that case the investing company must treat the share as a creditor loan relationship. The distributions received are neither treated as a dividend nor a repayment of capital. The investing company must bring the debits and credits into account on an accounting fair value basis.

Where condition 1 above applies no debits or transactions are to be brought into account which prevent the value of the share increasing at a rate of return representing a commercial rate of interest.

If condition 3 applies debits and credits are to be brought into account in respect of any associated transaction as if it were a derivative contract.

The (*ss 91A, 91B*) shares were deemed to be sold and reacquired when entering the loan relationship regime. The gain was subject to capital gains on 1 January 2005 (*FA 2004, Sch 10, para 9*).

## Non-loan relationships

**11.8** From the above it may be difficult to judge what arrangement can be considered not to be a loan relationship. However, the following are accepted as not being loan relationships (for the time being); namely trade debts arising from the purchase of goods and services are not within the loan relationship regime. Finance leases, HP agreements, court settlements and loan guarantees also fall outside the definition (HMRC Corporate Finance Manuals CFM 51150 and CFM 51160). A contingency cannot be a loan relationship as it does not derive from the lending of money (*FA 1996, s 81(1)*).

## Accounting treatment

**11.9** For accounting periods beginning on or after 1 January 2005 UK GAAP or IAS as appropriate, subject only to specific statutory override is the accepted accounting treatment. IAS 39 (financial instruments: recognition and measurement) and IAS 32 (financial instruments: presentation and disclosure) have direct significance in this context. Their counterparts in UK GAAP are FRS 25 (financial statement of authorised funds) and FRS 26 (financial instruments: measurement). Listed companies not applying IAS for single company accounts were required to adopt FRS 25 and FRS 26 for accounting periods beginning on or after 1 January 2005. For other companies, the presentation part of FRS 25 was mandatory for accounting periods ended on or after 1 January 2005, and for companies that use fair value accounting, adoption of the remainder of FRS 25 and of FRS 26 was mandatory for accounting periods beginning on or after 1 January 2006. There are proposals for all companies apart from those using the FRSSE (financial reporting standard for smaller entities) to use FRS 26 for accounting periods beginning on or after 1 January 2007.

Companies that apply the FRSSE continue to apply UK GAAP as it applied to accounting periods beginning on or after 1 January 2005. The FRSSE adopts certain elements of FRS 4 (capital instruments); namely the balance sheet recognition, the allocation of borrowing costs to the relevant periods at a constant rate of return on the carrying amount and the allocation of dividends on an accruals basis unless payment is remote.

The taxation legislation requires that GAAP be applied, specifying that, if a company does not use GAAP for this purpose, it will be treated as having done so (*FA 1996, s 85A*). Prior to this the two authorised methods of accounting applied; either the authorised accruals basis or the mark to market basis (*FA 1996, ss 85, 86*). More often the authorised accruals was used, which simply applied an accrual basis of accounting, ie transactions are allocated to the accounting period in which they accrue rather than the accounting period in which they fall due or are paid or received and operated a bad debt system. The mark to market basis brought amounts into account in each period at fair value; ie the amount the company would expect to receive or pay (according to the relationship) to an independent third party for the transfer of rights or the release of liabilities. With the introduction of IAS the authorised accruals basis and the mark to market basis have been rooted into IAS 39 as the amortised cost basis and the fair value basis respectively.

## CORPORATION TAX TREATMENT

### Trading and non-trading loan relationships

**11.10** It is necessary to distinguish between a trading and a non-trading loan relationship. Essentially, if a company owes funds or is due funds for the purposes of its trade, then it is within a trading loan relationship (*FA 1996,* *s 80*(2)). For lenders the test is tighter and they will only be within a trading loan relationship if it entered into the loan 'in the course of activities forming an integral part of its trade' (*FA 1996, s 103*(2)). In practice only companies within the financial sector such as insurance companies, banks and finance trades lend funds as an integral part of their trade.

Group finance companies may be an exception.

Money lending was not deemed to be the integral part of the trade of an electrical energy producer and supplier. It was not the normal activity of an energy producer or supplier. Hence, interest earned on money set aside by to meet future liabilities was deemed to relate to a non-trading loan relationship (*Nuclear Electric plc v Bradley* (1996) 68 TC 670).

## TRADING LOAN RELATIONSHIPS

### Schedule D Case I

**11.11** The appropriate accounting method will result in all credits and debits arising from profits, gains and losses, both capital and revenue, interest, charges and expenses together with exchange gains and losses relating to the company's loan relationships being brought into the corporation tax computation. Credits and debits resulting from a trading loan relationship are included as trading receipts or expenses within the Schedule D Case I computation (*FA 1996, s 82*). The loan relationship legislation overrides *ICTA 1988, s 74* (see **5.12**) (*FA 1996, s 82*(7)). Accounting matching procedures that result in the derecognition of matched income are ignored for corporation tax purposes (*FA 2006, Sch 6, para 6*). Any subsequent profits or losses arising are assessable or relievable accordingly under the rules of Schedule D Case I. This is not the case for non-trading loan relationships, which have special computational rules (See **11.16**, **11.17**).

---

**Example 11.1**

Aurora Ltd is a small trading company that requires additional finance for the purposes of its trade. The bank grants an additional £1m 6% fixed interest loan facility on 1 January 2007. The company is charged legal fees and other professional costs in relation to obtaining the loan of £5,000. The company applies the FRSSE. Accounts are prepared to 31 December each year.

The loan is a trading loan relationship as it has been taken out for trading purposes. As the company apples the FRSSE, the finance costs of borrowings are allocated to the accounting periods over the term of the borrowings at a constant rate on the carrying amount. The amounts charged will form the allowable debits and no adjustment to profits is required when preparing the corporation tax computation. The expenses will be allowable by reason of *FA 1996, s 84(3)*: see **11.15**.

---

**Example 11.2**

Q plc acquires shares in a new subsidiary for £10m. It pays the vendor company £8m in cash, and issues loan notes for the remaining £2m. Subsequently, Q plc finds out facts about the financial position of its new subsidiary that had not come to light in the due diligence process. Discussions with the vendor company follow, as a result of which it is agreed that the purchase price should be reduced by £1m. Accordingly, £1m of the loan notes issued by Q plc are cancelled. It accounts for the transaction as:

| | | |
|---|---|---|
| Cr | Cost of investment | £1 million |
| Dr | Creditors (loan notes) | £1 million |

For tax purposes, the loan notes are loan relationships since, although there has been no lending of money, an instrument has been issued representing security for the creditor's rights under the £2m money debt. The cancellation of £1m of the notes does not, however, give rise to a tax charge under the loan relationships rules. Although a credit appears in the company's books, there is no amount that has been recognised in determining the company's profit or loss for the period. Nothing therefore falls within *FA 1996, s 85A(1)* (HMRC Corporate Finance Manual CFM 5203a).

---

## UNALLOWABLE PURPOSE

### Non-business or non-commercial

**11.12** Relief is denied for debits arising from an unallowable purpose.

An unallowable purpose is any non-business or non business or commercial or any purpose that consists of securing a tax advantage (*FA 1996, Sch 9, para 13*(2)).

---

**Example 11.3**

The CASH Bank plc grants the Village Tennis Club a loan to finance the construction of a new club house.

For corporation tax purposes the allowable and non-allowable interest expense is apportioned pro rata to the club's taxable income from non-members and non-taxable income from members.

---

**Example 11.4**

Chekov is the UK branch of Zagrev, a non-UK resident Russian holding company. The company uses British banks to fund its global activities. A £12m loan is raised from the CASH Bank plc to fund Zagrev's activities in Guatemala. Chekov has no involvement in these activities but agrees to pay the interest.

The interest charged is deemed to be 'an unallowable purpose' for Chekov, and hence is disallowable (*FA 1996, Sch 9, para 13*(*3*)) (HMRC Corporate Finance Manual CFM 6214).

---

## A tax avoidance purpose

**11.13** A tax avoidance purpose is any purpose that consists in securing a tax advantage either for the company or for any other person (*FA 1996, Sch 9, para 13*(*5*)). A tax avoidance purpose becomes an unallowable purpose when it is the main purpose or one of the main reasons that the company became a party to the relationship or entered into a related transaction. The usage of funds to secure or finance a tax avoidance scheme will amount to an unallowable purpose (*FA 1996, Sch 9, para 13*(*5*)).

Whether a tax avoidance purpose is the main, or one of the main, purposes is a question of fact, which depends on all the circumstances of the particular case.

---

**Example 11.5**

A company borrows £50m from a finance company at arm's length. The company becomes insolvent and disposes of all its assets. This leaves it with an outstanding debt of £40m. The company is not liquidated and interest continues to accrue on the debt. The finance company either omits to accrue the interest receivable or it accrues the interest and then writes it off as a bad debt. The company accrues the interest and makes a deficit on which group relief claims are made. The company has no activity which is within the charge to corporation tax (*FA 1996, Sch 9, para 13*(*3*)). The purpose of the loan relationship is therefore specifically excluded from being a business or commercial purpose and it is an unallowable purpose. In addition, although the loan relationship was originally bona fide, its continued existence is not commercial. The relating debits to the loan relationship are disallowed.

The only purpose of the loan relationship in the current accounting period is to generate group relief thereby securing a tax advantage for another group company (*FA 1996, Sch 9, para 13*(*5*)) (HMRC Corporate Finance Manual CFM 6215a).

---

## Write off of loans for an unallowable purpose

**11.14** Write off of loans for an unallowable purpose will also not qualify for relief. For example, an interest-free loan made by a company, whose business consists of manufacturing kitchen tables, which had lent the money to a yacht club supported by one of the directors of the company for the purpose of providing financial support to the yacht club. If the company borrowed to make the loan to the yacht club, the interest will also be disallowed.

If the purpose of the loan included a commercial or other business purpose such as advertising, then this would be taken into account in arriving at the amount attributable to the unallowable purpose on a just and reasonable basis (*FA 1996, Sch 9, para 13*(*1*)) (HMRC Corporate Finance Manual CFM 6224).

## HMRC advice

**11.15** If taxpayers or their advisers seek advice from HMRC as to whether a proposed course of action would be deemed to be an unallowable purpose under *FA 1996, Sch 9, para 13* they will be referred by HMRC to the Economic Secretary's Finance Bill 1996 Report Stage comments at HMRC Corporate Finance Manual CFM 6216a, particularly the penultimate paragraph.

The comments are as follows:

> 'The Government are aware of concerns that have been raised by my hon. Friends and by others regarding the particular anti-avoidance provisions in paragraph 13. This paragraph was amended significantly in Standing Committee but, because of the concerns that my hon. Friends and others have raised, I take the opportunity to allay some of the fears that have been expressed about the anti-avoidance rules. Paragraph 13 of the schedule disallows tax deductions to the extent that tax avoidance is the main motive behind a loan relation-

ship. We have been told of concerns that this could be interpreted as preventing companies from getting tax relief for legitimate financing arrangements. I am happy to offer a reassurance that this is not the intention of the legislation. The paragraph denies tax deductions on loans that are for the purpose of activities outside the charge to corporation tax. Among other things, this will ensure that United Kingdom branches of overseas companies do not get tax relief for borrowings that are for overseas activities outside the United Kingdom tax net. We have been asked whether financing – which, for example, is to acquire shares in companies, whether in the United Kingdom or overseas, or is to pay dividends – would be affected by the paragraph. In general terms, the answer is no, but the paragraph might bite if the financing were structured in an artificial way. It has been suggested that structuring a company's legitimate activities to attract a tax relief could bring financing within this paragraph – some have gone so far as to suggest that the paragraph might deny any tax deduction for borrowing costs. These suggestions are clearly a nonsense. A large part of what the new rules are about is ensuring that companies get tax relief for the cost of their borrowing. One specific point has been put to me by my hon. Friend the Member for Gloucester – that is, borrowing by a finance leasing company to acquire assets where this is more tax efficient than the lessee investing in the asset direct. Again, I am happy to offer a reassurance. Where a company is choosing between different ways of arranging its commercial affairs, it is acceptable for it to choose the course that gives a favourable tax outcome. Where paragraph 13 will come into play is where tax avoidance is the object, or one of the main objects, of the exercise. Companies that enter into schemes with the primary aim of avoiding tax will inevitably be aware of that. The transactions we are aiming at are not ones which companies stumble into inadvertently. As one top tax adviser said recently, companies will know when they are into serious tax avoidance; apart from anything else, they are likely to be paying fat fees for clever tax advice and there will commonly be wads of documentation. The last thing I want to do, however, is set out a list of so-called acceptable or unacceptable activities. Borrowing for commercial purposes can be structured in a highly artificial way in order to avoid tax. If we said that borrowing for certain types of activity would always be okay, tax advisers would quickly take advantage and devise artificial financial arrangements simply to avoid tax. Provided that companies are funding commercial activities or investments in a commercial way, they should have nothing to fear. If they opt for artificial, tax-driven arrangements, they may find themselves caught. It is clear that a balance must be struck between meeting the concerns that have been raised and weakening the provision in those instances where it needs to apply, but I can assure my hon. Friends that we shall keep the matter under review.' (Hansard, 28 March 1996, Finance Bill Report Stage, Columns 1192–1193.)

The Economic Secretary's comments are the extent of the guidance HMRC are able to give in accordance with Code of Practice 10 (information and advice) and regard the application of Para 13 as a matter of careful judgment (HMRC Corporate Finance Manual CFM 6228).

## NON-TRADING LOAN RELATIONSHIPS

### Schedule D Case III

**11.16** A company is party to a non-trading loan relationship, if it is party to the relationship not for the purposes of the trade. For many companies their only non-trading income will be bank interest received from an investment of surplus funds. Schedule A business or an overseas property business is not a trade for these purposes. Interest paid by banks and building societies is paid gross, as is interest on loans for fixed periods of less than a year. Income tax is deducted at source from other interest at the lower rate of 20%, unless (from 1 April 2001) the recipient is a company chargeable to corporation tax in respect of the income. Before 1 April 2001, groups could elect to make intra-group payments gross.

Non-trading loan relationship debits and credits are aggregated to result in a Schedule D Case III surplus or deficit. A surplus will be assessable as Schedule D Case III income.

---

**Example 11.6**

On 1 January 2007 Aurora Ltd bought £20,000 nominal gilt-edged stock at £95 per £100 nominal stock. The investment was not for the purposes of trade. The securities are redeemable on 31 December 2011 at par. Interest at 3% is payable annually on 31 December.

As the investment has no relationship to the trade this amounts to a non-trading loan relationship and the interest and the discount is assessable under Schedule D Case III.

Again the accounting treatment will be adopted and the assessable amounts are as follows:

| *Year ended* | *31 December 2007* | *31 December 2008* | *31 December 2009* | *31 December 2010* | *31 December 2011* |
|---|---|---|---|---|---|
| | £ | £ | £ | £ | £ |
| Interest received | 600 | 600 | 600 | 600 | 600 |
| Discount | 100 | 100 | 100 | 100 | 100 |
| Schedule D Case III | 700 | 700 | 700 | 700 | 700 |

## RELIEF FOR NON-TRADING DEFICITS

### Manner of non-trading deficit relief

**11.17** Relief is given as follows for all or part of the deficit to be;

(a) by claim in a group relief claim (*ICTA 1988, s 403*); or

(b) by claim:

   (i) set against any profits of the company for the deficit period (*FA 1996, s 83*(2)(*a*)), or

   (ii) carried back and set against profits of the accounting periods for the previous 12 months that are chargeable under Schedule D Case III as profits or gains from loan relationships (*FA 1996, s 83*(2)(*c*)); or

(c) any remaining amount will be carried forward and set against non-trading profits in succeeding accounting periods (*FA 1996, s 83*(2), *Sch 8, para 3*).

A claim under *ICTA 1988, s 403* can be made at any time up to the first anniversary of the filing date of the return (*FA 1998, Sch 18, para 74*). A claim under *FA 1996, s 83*(*3A*) must be made within two years of the end of the accounting period in which the deficit arose (*FA 1996, s 83*(*6*)).

**Example 11.7—Single company—No deficits in previous years**

Aurora Ltd's results in years to come are shown below. Aurora Ltd has a non-trading deficit for the year ended 31 December 2010 of £10,000. There are no group companies.

| *Year ended* | *31 December 2007* | *31 December 2008* | *31 December 2009* | *31 December 2010* | *31 December 2011* |
|---|---|---|---|---|---|
| | £ | £ | £ | £ | £ |
| Schedule D Case I | 10,000 | 20,000 | 30,000 | 500 | 900 |
| Schedule D Case III | 1,000 | 1,000 | 5,000 | 200 | 300 |
| PCTCT | 11,000 | 21,000 | 35,000 | 700 | 1,200 |

Relief is obtained as follows:

| | £ | £ |
|---|---|---|
| Total loss | | 10,000 |
| Set against any profits of the company for the deficit period | 700 | |
| Carried back and set against profits of the accounting periods for the previous 12 months that are chargeable under Schedule D Case III as profits or gains from loan relationships | 5,000 | |
| Carried forward and set against non-trading profits in succeeding accounting periods (*FA 1996, s 83*(2)) | 300 | |
| Loss utilised | | 6,000 |
| Balance available to carry forward | | 4,000 |

**Example 11.8—Group company—No deficit in previous years**

Horatio Ltd has the following results for the years ended 30 June 2005, 2006 and 2007.

| *Year ended* | *30 June 2005* | *30 June 2006* | *30 June 2007* |
|---|---|---|---|
| | £ | £ | £ |
| Schedule D Case I | 5,000 | 15,000 | 40,000 |
| Schedule D Case III surplus | 10,000 | 10,000 | |
| Schedule D Case III deficit | | | (5,000) |

Horatio Ltd has the option of utilising the £5,000 deficit in:

(i) a group relief claim (*ICTA 1988, s 403*), or

(ii) against profits for the year ending 30 June 2007 (*FA 1996, s 83*(2)), or

(iii) against the Schedule D Case III surplus for the year ending 30 June 2006, or

(iv) carry forward against non-trading profits in succeeding periods (*FA 1996, s 83*(*3A*)).

---

**Example 11.9—Single company partial loss claim for current year**

Nelson Ltd has the following results for the year ended 31 December 2006 and makes a partial claim to set its non-trading deficit against profits of the same period.

| | £ |
|---|---|
| Schedule D Case I | 78,000 |
| Schedule D Case V (foreign tax paid £9,000) | 40,000 |
| Non-trading deficit | 152,000 |

Nelson Ltd's partial loss claim is as follows:

| | *Schedule D Case I* | *Schedule D Case V* | *Total* | *Schedule D Case III deficit utilisation memorandum* |
|---|---|---|---|---|
| | £ | £ | £ | £ |
| Income | 78,000 | 40,000 | 118,000 | (152,000) |
| Partial deficit claim (*FA 1996, s 83*(*2*)(*a*)). | (78,000) | (10,000) | (88,000) | 88,000 |
| PCTCT | 0 | 30,000 | 30,000 | |
| Corporation tax @ 30% | | | 9,000 | |
| Tax credit relief | | | 9,000 | |
| Corporation tax payable | | | nil | |
| Deficit available to:<br>(i) carry back under *FA 1996, s 83*(*2*)(*c*) or<br>(iii) carry forward *FA 1996, s 83*(*3A*). | | | | 64,000 |

## Current year order of non-trading deficit relief set-off

**11.18** If the deficit is set against profits of the period the order of set-off is as follows:

(i) after relief for trading losses carried forward, but

before relief for

(ii) Sch A losses set against profits for the same period (*ICTA 1988, s 392A(1)*),

(iii) trading losses set against profits for the same period, or carried back from a later period (*ICTA 1988, s 393A(1)*),

(iv) a non-trading deficit carried back from a later period (*FA 1996, s 83(2)(c)*) (*FA 1996, Sch 8, para 1*).

## Carry back previous year order of non-trading deficit relief set-off

**11.19** If the deficit is carried back to the previous 12-month accounting period the order of set-off is as follows:

after any amounts claimed that relate to:

(i) losses or deficits from any period before the deficit period – or treated as coming from an earlier period,

(ii) charges for trade purposes under *ICTA 1988, s 338* before 24 July 2002,

(iii) trading losses set against profits of the same or preceding year under *ICTA 1988, s 393A*,

(iv) deficits of the claim period.

If the company is a company with investment business (or an investment company for accounting periods beginning before 31 March 2004), the following are given prior relief:

- capital allowances,
- management expenses under *ICTA 1988, s 75*,
- business charges under *ICTA 1988, s 338*, paid before 16 March 2005 (*FA 1996, Sch 8, para 3*).

**Example 11.10—Group company with deficit in previous year**

If Horatio Ltd's results for the years ended 30 June 2005, 2006 and 2007 (see Example 11.8) had been as follows:

| *Year ended* | *30 June 2005* | *30 June 2006* | *30 June 2007* |
|---|---|---|---|
| | £ | £ | £ |
| Schedule D Case I | — | 15,000 | 40,000 |
| Schedule D Case III surplus | | 10,000 | |
| Schedule D Case III deficit | (8,000) | | (5,000) |

Horatio Ltd can still use the £5,000 deficit for the year ended 30 June 2007 in a group relief claim or against other profits but can only relieve £2,000 of the deficit in 2006 as the brought forward deficit has priority.

**Example 11.11—Single company with deficit in previous years**

Kiora Ltd is a single company, prepares accounts to 31 March each year and has the following actual and forecast results:

| *Year ended* | *31 March 2006* | *31 March 2007* | *31 March 2008* |
|---|---|---|---|
| | *£000* | *£000* | *£000* |
| Schedule D Case I loss brought forward | (90) | | |
| Schedule D Case I | 400 | 200 | 500 |
| Schedule A | 50 | 50 | 20 |
| Chargeable gain | 100 | 100 | 2 |
| Schedule D Case III: | | | |
| Interest accrued (credits) | (10) | (8) | (20) |
| Interest accrued (debits) | | 400 | 400 |
| Net debits | | 392 | 380 |

Schedule D Case III debits can be relieved as follows:

| *Year ended* | *31 March 2006* | *31 March 2007* | *31 March 2008* |
|---|---|---|---|
| | *£000* | *£000* | *£000* |
| Schedule D Case I | 400 | 200 | 500 |
| Loss: *ICTA 1988, s 393(1)* brought forward | (90) | | |
| Schedule D Case I (post loss relief) | 310 | 200 | 500 |
| Schedule D Case III | 10 | — | — |
| Schedule A | 50 | 50 | 20 |
| Chargeable gain | 100 | 100 | 2 |
| Total non-trading profits | 160 | 150 | 22 |
| Total profits | 470 | 350 | 522 |
| Set-off against current profits of whatever description (*FA 1996, s 83(2)(a)*) | | (350) | (380) |
| Set-off against Schedule D Case III income of the previous 12 months (*FA 1996, s 83(2)(a)*) | (10) | | |
| Carry forward to set against future non-trading profits (*FA 1996, s 83(3A)*) | | | (22) |
| Total relief | (10) | (350) | (402) |
| PCTCT | 460 | 0 | 120 |
| Non-trading deficit memorandum | | | |
| Net deficit | | 392 | 380 |
| Current year relief | | (350) | (380) |
| Prior year relief | | (10) | |
| Future year relief | | (22) | |
| Balance carried | | 10 | 0 |

## Carry forward of non-trading deficit relief

**11.20** If no other claim is made the deficit will be carried forward by default under *FA 1996, s 83(3A)*. The deficit may be set against the company's non-trading profits for the following years, which will include Schedule D Case V income, chargeable gains, Schedule A income and Schedule D Case III income.

## Disclaimer of carry forward non-trading deficit relief

**11.21** Within two years of the end of the accounting period in which the brought-forward non-trading deficit would otherwise be utilised the company may claim that a specified amount of this deficit is not to be set against the non-trading profits of the following period. This would, for example, facilitate a double taxation relief claim against Schedule D Case V income. Any unused relief is carried forward to the following period and set against the non-trading profits of that period or disclaimed accordingly (*FA 1996, Sch 8, para 4(3)*).

---

**Example 11.12—Single company partial claim for deficit brought forward**

Josephine Ltd only carries on overseas activities for which the company receives an overseas dividend of £90,000 for the year ended 30 September 2007. The overseas tax credit is £18,000. Many years ago Josephine Ltd incurred a Schedule D Case III deficit. The balance brought forward under *FA 1996, s 83(3A)* at 30 September 2006 is £100,000.

Josephine Ltd claims under *FA 1996, Sch 8, para 4(3)* that only part of the deficit be set against the current year's income with the following result:

| | *Year ending 30 June 2007* £ |
|---|---|
| Schedule D Case V | 90,000 |
| Schedule D Case III part deficit | (30,000) |
| PCTCT | 60,000 |
| Corporation tax @ 30% | 18,000 |
| Tax credit | 18,000 |

The balance of deficit available to carry forward is £70,000.

---

## Pre-trading expenditure

**11.22** Any interest that a company incurs before trading commences is classified as a non-trading debit (*FA 1996, s 84(4)*). The company may elect within two years of the end of the accounting period in which the debit arose under the provisions of *ICTA 1988, s 401(1AB)* that it is not to be brought in as a non-trading debit. A trading company may wish to do this as non-trading deficits carried forward can only be set against future non-trading income, which may not accrue to the company. If the company commences to trade within seven years of that period and the debit would have been allowable if incurred in a period since trading commenced, then the company may treat the debit as a trading expense of that later year.

## TRADING AND NON-TRADING LOAN RELATIONSHIPS

### Costs of obtaining loan finance

**11.23** HMRC consider that the following expenses directly incurred in the following activities are an allowable debit for both trading and non-trading loan relationships under *FA 1996, s 84(3)*.

| | *Expense* | *Examples* |
|---|---|---|
| *FA 1996, s 84(3)* | | |
| (a) | Bringing a loan relationship into existence | Arrangement fees with banks.<br>Fee or commission for a loan guarantee.<br>DTI fees for investing surplus cash in a liquidation. |
| (b) | Entering into, or giving effect to, a related transaction | Broker's fees on purchase or sale of existing securities.<br>Legal fees on the transfer of a security |
| (c) | Making a payment under a loan relationship or related transaction | Cost of making interest payments.<br>Early redemption penalties. |
| (d) | Pursuing payments due under a loan relationship or related transaction | Solicitor's fees incurred in pursuing a debt defaulter. |
| *FA 1996, s 84(4)* | Attempting to bring a loan relationship into existence | This covers abortive expenditure. As long as the expense would have been allowable had the company raised the loan, it is still allowable even if the loan never exists. |

Key person insurance premiums, other insurance policies or general investment advice, are not considered to be directly incurred (HMRC Corporate Finance Manual CFM 5210).

## Costs of finance included in the accounts as required by GAAP

**11.24** Under GAAP, when accounting for the incidental costs of purchase of shares in a subsidiary the costs of the loan finance to buy the shares are normally spread over more than one accounting period. Where this takes place relief will be granted in each respective accounting period. However, where the shares are held as a fixed asset and it is within GAAP to capitalise the costs, relief will be given by adjusting the corporation tax computation (*FA 1996, Sch 9, para 14*) (HMRC Corporate Finance Manual CFM 5230b).

Interest and loan expenses on fixed capital assets, which have been capitalised according to GAAP, should be relieved against profits chargeable to tax by adjusting the corporation tax computation. This treatment is mandatory. Where capitalised interest on loans of this type is not included in the tax computation, the company must amend its self-assessment. HMRC will keep a record of the relief given, to check that the company makes an adjustment when amortisation of the asset is taken to profit and loss account, or when the asset is sold, and the interest then appears in the profit and loss account (*FA 1996, Sch 9, para 14*) (HMRC Corporate Finance Manual CFM 5230). This treatment does not apply where interest is charged to work-in-progress. This is because interest has been charged in the profit and loss account albeit there has been a rise in the value of work-in-progress (HMRC Corporate Finance Manual CFM 5230a).

# CONNECTED PERSONS

## Meaning of connection

**11.25** Special rules apply for connected parties. A connection exists in the following circumstances:

### Circumstances for a connection

'… there is a connection between the company and:

(a) in the case of a debtor relationship of the company, a person standing in the position of a creditor as respects the debt in question; or

(b) in the case of a creditor relationship of the company, a person standing in the position of debtor as regards that debt.' (*FA 1996, s 87(1)*)

The person standing in the position of a creditor is the lender.

The person standing in the position of the debtor is the borrower.

Connection in these circumstances means:

> '… there is a connection between a company and another person for an accounting period if …
>
> (a) the other person is a company and there is a time in that period when one of the companies has had control of the other; or
>
> (b) the other person is a company and there is a time in that period when both companies have been under the control of the same person' (*FA 1996, s 87(3)*)

Although an individual or a partnership cannot be a party to a loan relationship, in a loan relationship series he or she may be considered to indirectly stand in the position of debtor or creditor and so bring about a loan relationship (*FA 1996, s 87(5)*).

## Control prior to 1 October 2002

**11.26** For accounting periods ending prior to 1 October 2002 the definition of control was that given by *ICTA 1988, s 416(2)–(6)*. (See **4.4**). In essence, companies were connected if a person (through his or her associates) has control over the company's affairs and possessed or was entitled to acquire the greater part of the share capital, voting, dividend or assets on winding up, within the two previous accounting periods. A two-year time limit was given for the conditions to apply ending at the beginning of the accounting period in question.

## Control post 1 October 2002

**11.27** The definition was amended to the other meaning of control akin to *ICTA 1988, s 840* and the two-year time limit was withdrawn.

### Meaning of control

Control in relation to a company means the power of a person to secure:

(a) by means of the holding of shares or the possession of voting power in or relation to the company or any other company; or

(b) by virtue of any powers conferred by the articles of association or other document regulating the company or any other company,

that the affairs of the company are conducted in accordance with his wishes (*FA 1996, s 87A(1)*).

Shares held as trading stock are not included (*FA 1996, s 87A*(2)) and in general creditor relationships that result from activities forming an integral part of the trade carried on by that company during the accounting period are exempted.

# CONSEQUENCES OF CONNECTION

## Amortised cost basis of accounting

**11.28** Where a loan relationship debtor and creditor are connected certain rules are applied to the accounting treatment.

Regardless of the accounting method used in the company's accounts, the debits and credits brought into account must be determined according to the amortised cost basis of accounting (*FA 1996, s 87*(2)).

The amortised cost of a financial asset or a financial liability is the amount at which the asset or liability is measured at initial recognition (usually its cost) less any repayments of principal, less any reduction for impairment or uncollectibility, and in addition or less the cumulative amortisation of the difference between that initial amount and the maturity amount (*FA 1996, s 103(1)*).

HMRC comment that the amortised cost basis of accounting is broadly equivalent to the authorised accruals basis that applied in periods of account beginning before 1 January 2005. If a company does not adopt IAS 39 or FRS 26 – for example, where a small company continues to use the FRSSE – and the company previously accounted for loan relationships on an authorised accruals basis, the *FA 2004* changes to the loan relationships legislation should not bring about any change in the basis on which its debt assets and liabilities are taxed (HMRC Corporate Finance Manuals CFM 5151, CFM16025).

The amortisation is calculated using the effective interest rate. The effective interest rate is the internal rate of return (IRR), ie the rate at which the net present value of the instrument is nil.

---

**Example 11.13**

A £200,000 bond will pay £210,000 on maturity in a year's time.

The IRR is £200,000 × $(1 + r)^1$ = £210,000

r = [(210,000 – 200,000) ÷ 200,000]

= 0.05

= 5%

The future value of £200,000 @ 5% = £200,000 × $(1 + 0.05)^1$ = £210,000

The present value of £210,000 = £210,000 × $\{1 \div (1 + 0.5)^1\}$ = £200,000

The present value £200,000 less the initial investment £200,000 equals the net present value which is Nil.

Therefore the effective rate of return is 5%.

---

**11.29** More complex calculations may be made by using the financial IRR (internal rate of return) function in Microsoft Excel (HMRC Corporate Finance Manual CFM 16025a).

Any resultant deficit or surplus in carrying value resulting from the change to amortised cost basis of accounting must be accounted for accordingly as a debit or credit (*FA 1996, s 87(2A), (2B)* and *(2C)*).

If the creditor company is connected to the debtor in exempt circumstances, ie in the course of its trade, it is not required to apply the amortised cost basis of accounting (or, for periods beginning before 1 January 2005, the accruals basis of accounting) or to follow the other provisions that apply to connected persons. The debtor company must apply the connected persons rules (*FA 1996, s 88(5)*).

---

**Example 11.14**

The CASH Bank plc issues listed security bonds worth £10m, which it places with its security trader subsidiary company Rowbowthams plc. Rowbothams plc is to place the bonds with unconnected investors.

The market is slow and Rowbothams plc holds the bonds for three months whilst it finds buyers. The bonds are part of its trading stock. It applies GAAP when preparing its accounts. The parties are connected under *FA 1996, s 87*. Without the *FA 1996, s 88* exemption Rowbothams plc would have to account for the bonds using the amortised cost basis of accounting. However, this is an ordinary commercial arrangement, with Rowbothams plc buying and selling the bonds as part of its trade. By applying *FA 1996, s 88*, Rowbothams plc can continue to account for the debt as trading stock. The CASH Bank plc is not exempted by *s 88* and will therefore use the amortised cost basis when accounting for the securities (HMRC Corporate Finance Manual CFM 5421c).

---

## Unpaid interest

**11.30** There is no debit for accrued unpaid interest for the debtor relationship company, unless the creditor relationship company has a corresponding credit. If the accrued unpaid interest is not paid within 12 months of the end of the accounting period, relief will only be given when that interest is eventually paid (*FA 1996, Sch 9, para 2*).

## Discounted securities

**11.31** Where the parties have a connection, relief on securities issued at a discount is deferred until redemption rather than being allowed as a debit over the life of the loan (*FA 1996, Sch 9, paras 17, 18*).

## Creditor relationships and benefit derived by connected persons

**11.32** Benefit directly or indirectly received by a company that is connected with a company that has a third party creditor loan relationship as a result of the loan relationship is treated as a credit using fair value accounting of the creditor company if the actual return that the creditor company receives is below a commercial rate of interest. This applies to loan relationships to which the companies are parties to on or after 22 March 2006 (*FA 2006, Sch 6, para 16*).

## Bad debt relief and impairment losses generally

**11.33** The loan relationship rules in general grant relief for bad debts. For accounting periods commencing on or after 1 January 2005 impairment losses are accounted for using the IAS 39 or FRS 26 principles. The exception is a change in the rules relating to the acquisition of impaired debt (see **11.34**). The standards prescribe rules for identifying and measuring impairment losses at the year end. If the company correctly applies the relevant standard, to arrive at a debit for impairment losses (or a credit for reversal of impairment losses), the debit will be allowable (or the credit taxable) in accordance with the normal computational provisions of *FA 1996, s 85B*.

In periods of account beginning before 1 January 2005, the authorised accruals basis of accounting required the company to assume that every amount under a creditor loan relationship was payable in full, unless a departure from that assumption was specifically permitted. Departure from the assumption ('bad debt relief') was allowed only where a debt was bad or doubtful. Bad debt relief was granted by *FA 1996, Sch 9, para 5* to companies applying the authorised accruals accounting method. Bad debt relief was automatically given to companies applying the mark to market basis of accounting.

## Connected parties and bad debt relief and impairment losses

**11.34** Special rules apply to bad debt relief and impairment losses for connected parties. The general rule is that bad debt or impairment loss relief is denied if the companies to the loan relationship are connected (*FA 1996, Sch 9, para 6*).

For accounting periods commencing before 1 January 2005 connected companies had to use the accruals basis of accounting but were denied bad debt relief. For accounting periods commencing on or after 1 January 2005 connected companies are prevented from receiving debits for impairment losses.

For accounting periods only commencing before 1 January 2005 bad debt relief was not denied if the bad debt relief was given before the companies were connected or if the creditor acquired impaired debt in certain circumstances. Normally this was at an arm's-length price and there was no connection during the period four years before and 12 months after it acquired the debt (*FA 1996, Sch 9, para 6B*(*1*)–(*7*)).

Impairment loss relief is not denied if the connection only arises because the debt is exchanged for equity, provided that the companies were not connected when the creditor company acquired possession of or entitlement to the shares (*FA 1996, Sch 9, para 6*(*4*)). Neither is it denied if the creditor company goes into insolvent liquidation (*FA 1996, Sch 9, para 6A*).

The corresponding creditor company is not required to include a credit for the loss or bad debt relief reversal (*FA 1996, Sch 9, para 6*(*3A*)), whether or not the companies are still connected when the reversal takes place.

If any rights or liabilities (known as related transactions) are acquired at a non-arms length price they are accounted for as though they were a transaction between independent persons (*FA 1996, Sch 9, para 11*).

## GROUPS AND CONSORTIA

**11.35** Group companies are connected under the loan relationship rules. Loan relationship intra-group transfers are tax neutral (*FA 2006, Sch 9, para 12*).

Consortia companies may not be connected under *FA 1996, s 87*, but consortium members are in a position to obtain not only consortium relief but also bad debt or impairment relief. Therefore there are restrictions on the available amount of bad debt relief where there has been a claim to group relief and vice versa.

The effect of the restriction is to reduce the impairment relief by the amount of the group relief claimed, with the result that overall impairment and group relief claimed will not exceed the greater of the bad debts claimed or the group relief (*FA 1996, Sch 9, para 5A*).

The rules apply to each consortium member and all group loans are taken into account.

---

**Example 11.15**

Winston Ltd is a consortium company with £1,000 issued ordinary shares.

Its ownership is as follows:

| | *No of shares* |
|---|---|
| A Ltd | 400 |
| B Ltd | 400 |
| C Ltd | 200 |

All companies prepare accounts to 31 December.

Winston Ltd incurs a loss of £40,000 for the year ended 31 December 2007, which is used in a group relief claim by the consortium members.

On 1 January 2007 C Ltd made a £50,000 loan to Winston Ltd. At 31 December 2007 it seems unlikely that Winston Ltd will be able to repay C Ltd's loan. C Ltd writes off £25,000 as bad. *FA 1996, Sch 9, para 5A(5)* will restrict C Ltd's impairment loss by the amount of the group relief claim, ie £16,000. Therefore only £9,000 (25,000 – 16,000) may be claimed. The group relief claim remains intact and the £16,000 restricted amount is carried forward, to be considered for future group and impairment loss claims.

The group's total group relief for the year ended 31 December 2008 is £20,000 and the group's impairment loss for the year ended 31 December 2009 is £50,000.

The position may be summarised as follows:

**Cumulative position**

| *Year ending* | *Brought forward* | *Impairment loss* | *Group relief* | *Impairment loss* | *Group relief claim allowed* | *Total relief* |
|---|---|---|---|---|---|---|
| | £ | £ | £ | £ | £ | £ |
| 31 December 2006 | | 25,000 | 16,000 | 9,000 | | 25,000 |
| 31 December 2007 | 9,000 | | 20,000 | | 11,000 | 11,000 |
| 31 December 2008 | 11,000 | 50,000 | | 39,000 | | 39,000 |
| Total | | 75,000 | 36,000 | | | 75,000 |

Therefore the total relief is the greater of the bad debt or the group relief claim, ie £75,000.

## LOAN RELATIONSHIPS, DERIVATIVES AND FOREIGN EXCHANGE GAINS AND LOSSES (FOREX)

**11.36** *FA 2002* brought derivatives and FOREX within the same loan relationship treatment regime. (*FA 2002, s 79, Sch 23*; *FA 2002, s 83, Schs 26, 27, 28*).

Therefore 'credits' and 'debits' are brought into the corporation tax computation following the accepted accounting principles. All relevant capital and revenue profits, gains and losses must be included together with charges and expenses. Trading and non-trading surpluses are included within the respective Schedule D Case I or Schedule D Case III computations. Non-trading deficits are aggregated with other non-trade debits and credits and included within the Case III profit or non-trade deficit for the year (*FA 1996, s 84A*).

A company may match its foreign currency non-monetary assets with its foreign currency borrowings to provide a commercial hedge. The tax treatment will follow the accounts treatment and the gain or loss on foreign currency liabilities or on currency contracts will be deferred until accounted for or until a disposal (*FA 2002, Sch 26, para 16*).

*Loan Relationships and Derivative Contracts (Disregard and Bringing into Account of Profits and Losses) (Amendment) Regulations, SI 2005/2012* came into force on 11 August 2005. Changes in fair value of some derivative contracts are to be disregarded for tax purposes when they are recognised in the accounts and in some cases to be brought back on maturity or disposal. An election from the old to the proposed new rules should be made by 31 December 2005. FRS 26 was brought into line with IAS 39 with effect from 1 January 2006.

*Finance (No 2) Act 2005, s 40* brought loan relationships within the transfer pricing regime with effect from 4 March 2005. (See Chapter 14).

## COMPANY TAX RETURN

**11.37** Companies provided details of their non-trade deficits on loan relationships in boxes 20 and 28 of the company tax return. All other details are supplied by means of the corporation tax computation and the accounts.

*Chapter 12*

# Investment Business

## INTRODUCTION

**12.1** Prior to 1 April 2004, a company with purely investment business was classed as an investment company and thus obtained relief for management expenses. Post 1 April 2004, all companies are able to claim management expenses in respect of their investment business.

Close investment holding companies retain their separate status. A company is a 'close investment holding company' (CIHC), unless it exists wholly or mainly as a trading company, an investment company letting land and property other than to connected persons or a trading group member. A CIHC's profits will be subject to the main rate of corporation tax (30%), irrespective of income levels (see **4.23–4.26**).

## CORPORATION TAX COMPUTATION

**12.2** A company's investment income will typically include Schedule A and income from non-trading loan relationships. As stated in **12.1** all companies may now claim a deduction for management expenses if they have investment business.

---

**Example 12.1**

XYZ Ltd draws up accounts to 31 March each year. Results for the year ended 31 March 2007 show the following:

| | *£000* |
|---|---|
| Rents receivable | 197 |
| Interest receivable accrued (gross) | 5 |
| Chargeable gains | 48 |

| | |
|---|---|
| Management expenses | |
| attributable to property | 25 |
| attributable to management | 40 |
| Capital allowances | |
| attributable to property | 5 |
| attributable to management | 1 |
| Charitable charges on income | 10 |

The company has unrelieved management expenses brought forward from previous accounting periods of £42,000.

XYZ Ltd corporation tax computations for the year ending 31 March 2007

| | *£000* | *£000* |
|---|---|---|
| Schedule A | | 197 |
| Less | | |
| Capital allowances | 5 | |
| Management expenses | 25 | |
| | | 30 |
| | | 167 |
| Schedule D Case III | | 5 |
| Chargeable gains | | 48 |
| | | 220 |
| Less | | |
| Management expenses unrelieved brought forward for year | | |
| Unrelieved brought forward | 42 | |
| For year | 40 | |
| Capital allowances | 1 | |
| | | 83 |
| | | 137 |
| Less charges | | 10 |
| PCTCT | | 127 |

# MANAGEMENT EXPENSES

## Definitions

**12.3** The definition of an investment company is:

> 'an investment company means any company whose business consists wholly or mainly of making investments and the principal part of whose income is derived from those investments ......... but includes any savings bank or other bank for savings except ......... a trustee savings bank' (*ICTA 1988, s 130*).

With effect from 1 April 2004, the definition regarding investment activities was extended to include a company with investment business:

> 'A company with investment business means any company whose business consists wholly or partly in the making of investments' (*ICTA 1988, s 130*).

The importance of the criteria being the relief for management expenses (*ICTA 1988, s 130*). As each type of income is assessed to corporation tax according to its source rules it may occur that an investment company could be put at a disadvantage if say it only had bank interest or dividend income (see HMRC Company Taxation Manuals CTM 08040 and CTM 08050 for a discussion of investment business).

## Management expenses

**12.4** A deduction for management expenses for an accounting period is allowed against the total profits of the accounting period (*ICTA 1988, s 75*(*1*)). Management expenses include all those expenses that are not otherwise deductible in computing profits, but do not include capital expenditure (*ICTA 1988, s 75*(2)). Capital allowances may be claimed on capital expenditure (*ICTA 1988, s 75*(*7*)).

The type of expense that can be included in 'management expenses' is as the name describes being:

> 'the expenses are in respect of so much of the company's business as consists in the making of investments and the investments concerned are not held by the company for an unallowable purpose during the accounting period' (*ICTA 1988, s 75*(*4*)(*a*)).

The description is specific and unlike the *ICTA 1988, s 74* 'wholly and exclusively' trading company criteria. Expenses of management cannot just amount to general administration costs.

Running costs in connection with managing the company's investment business, including reasonable directors' remuneration, staff salaries and pension contributions are chargeable as management expenses (*LG Berry Investments Ltd v Attwooll* (1964) 41 TC 547). The same timing rules for remuneration payments apply as for Schedule D Case I (see **5.14**) (*FA 1989, s 44*). Company secretarial costs such as maintaining the share register, printing annual accounts and holding an AGM are regarded as expenses of management. Entertaining expenditure and expenditure involving crime is specifically prohibited (*ICTA 1988, ss 577, 577A*). No relief is given if the expenses are incurred for an unallowable purpose. An unallowable purpose occurs when the company holds investments neither for a business nor a commercial purpose or the company is not within the charge to corporation tax. (See **12.7** below).

Management expenses are deductible from investment income of both UK resident companies and non-resident companies with a permanent establishment in the UK from where the income is derived (*ICTA 1988, s 75(6)*).

Management expenses are charged on an accruals basis provided the accounts follow GAAP (*ICTA 1988, s 75A*). Prior to 1 April 2004, the management expenses had to be 'disbursed', ie paid but not necessarily within the accounting period for which they were properly charged. This rule no longer applies. Credits for management expenses first reduce the management expenses for the year and are then brought into charge as Schedule D Case VI income (*ICTA 1988, s 75B*). In practice, company expenditure may relate to a number of activities in which case it should be allocated between them on a just and reasonable basis.

## Management activities

**12.5** Management expenses cannot be claimed unless the company is chargeable to corporation tax. This would, for example, exclude a mutual trading company, as its profits are not chargeable to corporation tax (see **5.47**). In order for a company to be chargeable to corporation tax it must have an activity, otherwise it would be totally dormant. On the assumption that the company had no other business, activities that would bring a company with investment business within the charge to corporation tax would be the holding of shares in another non-dormant company (*ICTA 1988, s 12(4)*) or the disposal of an asset resulting in a chargeable gain or allowable loss (*TCGA 1992, s 8(3)*). The management expenses claim for the year is made by completing box 24. A claim for management expenses carried forward is included in box 136, with the maximum available for group relief surrender in box 137.

## Group companies

**12.6** Group companies often recharge expenses to other group members such as administration charges. Provided the allocation is done on a reasonable basis this will result in each group member deducting its share of administration costs from its relevant trade or activity. See **5.16**. (HMRC Business Income Manual BIM 42140).

## Unallowable purpose

**12.7** Expenses in connection with investments held for a non-business or non-commercial purpose or in connection with activities not within the charge to corporation tax are not chargeable as management expenses. Such activities will include:

- investments held by a company for social or recreational purposes;
- provision of services and facilities by a members' club to its members;
- UK branch expenses of a non-resident company in respect of activities not connected with the UK branch;
- mutual trading activities (these fall outside the scope of Schedule D Case I).

However, a company that merely receives dividends from UK companies within *ICTA 1988, s 208* will still be classed as an investment company or a company with investment business. As will any company whose capital gains are covered by the substantial shareholding exemption or collective investment scheme gains exempt under *TCGA 1992, s 100(1)* (HMRC Company Taxation Manual CTM 08230).

## Capital expenditure

**12.8** From 1 April 2004 capital expenditure is specifically excluded as a deduction for management expenses purposes (*ICTA 1988, s 75(3)*). HMRC's view is that expenditure incurred on appraising the purchase or sale of an investment up to the decision point is revenue and expenditure following the decision to acquire or dispose of an investment is capital (HMRC Company

Taxation Manual CTM 08260). Success fees that are only payable when the deal goes through must by their very nature be capital and therefore excluded from management expenses. It is necessary to examine the facts of each case and to apply *the same criteria to abortive expenditure*. The costs associated with purchase and sale are not regarded as management expenses. Brokerage and stamp duties were not allowed as management expenses (*Capital and National Trust Ltd v Golder* (1949) 31 TC 265, [1949] 2 All ER 956 and *Sun Life Assurance Society v Davidson* (1957) 37 TC 330).

Cost of asset valuations for accounts purposes (*CA 1985, Sch 7, para 1*) are considered to be management expenses but valuations related to the acquisition and disposal of assets are not (HMRC Company Taxation Manual CTM 08420).

Capital expenditure on assets used for the purpose of management qualifies for capital allowances. The capital allowances are a management expense. Balancing charges are income of the investment business. See **12.4**. (*CAA 2001, ss 18, 253*).

## Insurance premiums

**12.9** Premiums paid on assets used in the management of the company are considered to be management expenses but not premiums paid on the insurance of the investments. This is because the view is taken that the expenses incurred must relate to management and not to general administration (HMRC Company Taxation Manual CTM 08320). Depending on the circumstances such premiums may be classed as capital expenditure.

## Companies ceasing to trade

**12.10** Practical considerations may arise when a company ceased to trade. The holding of a static bank account when trading ceased classifies a company as 'dormant' (*Jowett v O'Neill & Brennan Construction Ltd* (1998) 70 TC 566). In such circumstances it would be necessary for the company to show that it intends to continue with an investment activity if it wishes to claim management expenses for that period. The same criteria will apply to a company that is in liquidation. It will be necessary to show that it is 'making investments'.

Pensions paid to former employees by a company that ceases to trade and becomes an investment company or a company with investment business are not expenses of management if the former employees at no time were employees of the company after it ceased to trade. This is because the pension payments relate to the former trade and not to the investment activity (HMRC Company Taxation Manual CTM 08350).

## Self-assessment

**12.11** The corporation tax computation for a company with investment business would normally show income and gains from the investment activity in full, rather than adjusted profits. Appeals may be heard by the General Commissioners. Appeals in respect of expenditure incurred prior to 1 April 2004 could only he heard by the Special Commissioners.

## Management expenses set-off

**12.12** Management expenses are deducted from the company's profits chargeable to corporation tax before charges and before loss relief claimed under *ICTA 1988, s 393A* (ICTA 1988, s 75(1)). Excess management expenses are carried forward to be used in the subsequent accounting period as management expenses of that period (*ICTA 1988, s 75(9)*). A company may group relieve management expenses for the chargeable period against group income.

A company may only surrender management expenses that exceed the gross profits for the accounting period (*ICTA 1988, ss 402, 403(1)*). The order of set-off being charges on income, Schedule A losses and management expenses or a non-trading loss on intangible fixed assets in that order. (See **10.7**).

---

**Example 12.2**

Kappa Ltd owns 90% of the ordinary share capital of Lamda Ltd. Kappa Ltd is the group investment holding company.

Both companies prepare accounts to 31 December each year.

Results for the year ended 31 December 2006 are as follows:

| | *Kappa Ltd* | *Lamda Ltd* |
|---|---|---|
| | *£000* | *£000* |
| Schedule D Case I | | 50 |
| Schedule A | 10 | 20 |
| Schedule D Case III | 40 | 30 |
| Charges | | 2 |

Kappa Ltd's corporation tax liability after management expenses and management expenses for group relief are as follows:

| | £000 |
|---|---|
| **Management expenses** | |
| (*ICTA 1988, s 75*(*1*)) for the year | 100 |
| (*ICTA 1988, s 75*(*3*)) brought forward | 5 |
| | 105 |
| **Excess management expenses for group relief** | |
| Management expenses | |
| (*ICTA 1988, s 75*(*1*)) for the year | 100 |
| Schedule A | 10 |
| Schedule D Case III | 40 |
| | 50 |
| Excess management expenses | 50 |
| Group relief | 50 |
| | 0 |
| Excess management expenses brought forward and carry forward | 5 |

Lamda Ltd corporation tax computation after group relief is as follows:

| | £000 |
|---|---|
| Schedule D Case I | 50 |
| Schedule A | 20 |
| Schedule D Case III | 30 |
| | 100 |
| Charges | 2 |
| Total profits | 98 |
| Group relief (management expenses) | 50 |
| PCTCT | 48 |

## Restriction on management expenses

**12.13** Management expenses are restricted where there is a change of ownership and after the change there is a significant increase in the company's capital. Alternatively, within a period of six years beginning three years before the change, there is a major change in the nature or conduct of the business, or the change in ownership occurs after the scale of activities has become small or negligible and before any considerable revival of the business (*ICTA 1988, s 768B*).

A change of ownership occurs where:

(i) a single person acquires more than half the ordinary share capital of the company or

(ii) two or more persons each acquire a holding of 5% or more of the ordinary share capital of the company, and those holdings together amount to more than half the ordinary share capital of the company or

(iii) two or more persons each acquire a holding of the ordinary share capital of a company, and those holdings together amount to more than half the ordinary share capital of the company. Holdings of less than 5% are disregarded unless it is in addition to an existing holding and the two holdings together amount to 5% or more of the ordinary share capital (*ICTA 1988, s 769*).

The 5% threshold means there is no need to examine small shareholdings, particularly those of public companies.

Note, it is possible for more than half of a company's shares to change hands and yet not trigger a change of ownership if the shares are purchased by a number of unconnected persons, each of whom acquires a holding of less than 5%.

A major change in the nature or conduct of the business includes a major change in the nature of the investments held, even if that change was the result of a gradual process which began before the period of six years within which the change has to take place (*ICTA 1988, s 768B(3)*).

## INVESTMENT IN PROPERTY

**12.14** If a company invests in property it will show the property as a fixed asset on the balance sheet and will record letting income as Schedule A income. Property disposals will attract a capital gain. Letting income will be assessable under Schedule A rules.

A company could be a property dealer or developer in which case the property cost is shown in trading stock on the balance sheet. The company earns its income from the sale of properties and the business is assessed as a trade under Schedule D Case I.

Transactions between property dealing companies and their non-dealing associates are brought into charge on the associate as either Schedule D Case I income or Schedule D Case VI income (*ICTA 1988, s 774*).

# SCHEDULE A INCOME

## Income from UK land and buildings

**12.15** Companies are charged to corporation tax on income arising from the letting of UK land and property. The income is treated as a single 'Schedule A business' (*ICTA 1988, s 15*(*1*)).

The types of income assessable include receipts from:

- payments for a licence to occupy, use or exercise a right over land;
- rent charges, ground annuals, feu duties and other annual payments in respect of land;
- income from furnished lettings, including furnished holiday lettings; and
- income from caravans or houseboats where their use is confined to one location in the UK.

Schedule A income is included in box 11 of form CT600.

## Computation of profit

**12.16** Schedule A business profits are computed in accordance with GAAP. Capital allowances are available on plant used in the letting business, eg a motor vehicle used in connection with site visits, and are deductible as a Schedule A business expense.

Capital allowances are not available for plant let for use in a dwelling house (*CAA 2001, s 35*). Relief is given for furnished lettings by allowing 10% of rental income (net of the landlord's outlay on council tax and water rates if any) as a wear and tear deduction. Alternatively, relief can be claimed on a renewals basis for capital items replaced in a let property. Interest is excluded from a Schedule A computation and dealt with as a non-trading 'debit' under the loan relationship rules.

## Lease premiums

**12.17** Where a lease is granted for a duration of 50 years or less (a 'short' lease) any premium paid is treated partly as a disposal for capital gains and partly as income. The income portion is treated as rental income in the year in which the lease is granted. The income portion is calculated as the amount of the premium less 2% for each complete year of the lease except the first (*ICTA 1988, s 34*). Where the company is the tenant and pays a lease premium, the income portion is an allowable Schedule D Case I deduction, spread over the life of the lease (*ICTA 1988, s 87*).

---

**Example 12.3**

Horatio Ltd granted a 21-year lease to Eustace Ltd on 1 January 2007 with a £50,000 premium and £60,000 annual rent. Horatio Ltd prepares accounts to 31 December each year. The rental business receipts for the year ended 31 December 2007 are as follows:

| *Schedule A* | *£000* |
|---|---|
| Premium receivable | 50 |
| Less: (2% of £50,000) × 20 years | 20 |
| | 30 |
| Plus: rent for the year ended 31 December 2007 | 60 |
| Schedule A rental business | 90 |

Eustace Ltd leases the property for business purposes and claims the following Schedule D Case I deduction in its accounting period ending 31 December 2007:

| | *£000* |
|---|---|
| Rental costs | 60 |
| Amount of premium treated as additional rent: £30,000 ÷ 21 = £1,428 | 1 |
| Total Schedule D Case I deduction for rent | 61 |

(*ICTA 1988, s 70(2)*).

---

## Reverse premiums

**12.18** Where a landlord pays a sum to induce a tenant to take a lease (a reverse premium) then (unless it reduces expenditure qualifying for capital allowances) it is generally treated as Schedule D Case I income of the tenant corresponding with the treatment of the rental payments. However, certain benefits (eg the grant of a rent-free period) are not taxable under these rules (*FA 1999, s 54, Sch 6*).

## Repair expenditure

**12.19** Property repair expenditure is an allowable deduction. If the repair takes the asset beyond its condition prior to the repair this will be deemed a capital expense and hence disallowable. Repair expenditure of the subsidiary parts of an asset is classed as revenue expenditure (HMRC Property Income Manual PIM 2020).

## Legal fees

**12.20** Legal fees of a revenue nature wholly and exclusively in connection with the rental business are deductible.

The expenses incurred in connection with the first letting or subletting of a property for more than one year are capital expenditure and therefore not allowable. The expenses may include, legal expenses, lease preparation costs, agent's and surveyor's fees and commission. If the lease is for less than one year the expenses are deductible.

Legal and professional costs incurred in respect of the renewal of a lease for less than 50 years are allowable. Legal costs in relation to the payment of a premium on the renewal of a lease are not deductible.

Legal expenses in connection with letting arrangements that closely follows the terms of previous arrangements are considered to be a revenue expense and will not be disallowable except for the legal or other costs that relate to the payment of a premium on the renewal of a lease.

Legal costs in connection with a change of use of the premises in between lets will be treated as a capital expense and hence disallowable.

HMRC have identified the following legal and professional costs as allowable:

- costs of obtaining a valuation for insurance purposes,
- the normal accountancy expenses incurred in preparing rental business,
- subscriptions to associations representing the interests of landlords,
- the cost of arbitration to determine the rent of a holding,

- the cost of evicting an unsatisfactory tenant in order to relet the property.

The following costs are disallowable:

- legal costs incurred in acquiring, or adding to, a property,
- costs in connection with negotiations under the *Town and Country Planning Acts*,
- fees pursuing debts of a capital nature, for example, the proceeds due on the sale of the property.

Normal accountancy costs are deductible, including, by concession, agreeing the taxation liabilities. However, legal costs in connection with acquisition of a property or costs in connection with negotiations under the *Town and Country Planning Acts* are not deductible. Legal fees on drawing up a new lease are allowable if the lease is for less than one year. If more than one year, it is not allowable because the expense is capital (HMRC Property Income Manual PIM 2205).

## Treatment as Schedule D Case I

**12.21** Where rent is received from the letting of surplus accommodation on a short-term basis, this by concession is taxable under Schedule D Case I, and no adjustment is required in the computations (HMRC Tax Bulletin, Issue 10).

Moderate rental income from the temporary letting of part of the trader's business premises may be treated as Schedule D Case I income. This treatment only applies to the letting of accommodation and not to the letting of land.

The letting income from properties held as trading stock is Schedule A rental income. Expenses must be apportioned on a reasonable basis.

Rents and premiums received from tied premises are Schedule D Case I income and not Schedule A income. The same applies to the taxable amount of any premium received. Any expenditure on the tied premises will be deducted in the computation of the trading profits and should similarly be excluded from the rental business (*ICTA 1988, s 98*). If other services are provided that go beyond those normally provided by a landlord they may constitute a separate trade and not a rental business. Expenses normally provided by a landlord are:

- the cleaning of stairs and passages in multi-unit premises,
- the provision of hot water and heating,
- supervision involving rent collection and arranging new tenancies,

- arranging for repairs to the property.

The facts of each case must be examined on their merits to see if a separate trade is being carried out (HMRC Property Income Manual PIM 4300).

Travelling expenses to and between properties when incurred wholly and exclusively for the rental business are deductible (HMRC Property Income Manual PIM 2210).

## SCHEDULE A LOSSES

**12.22** Losses incurred in an accounting period in a Schedule A business which is carried on commercially is set against the company's total profits for the same accounting period. If there are insufficient profits, against which to set the loss, it is carried forward to the next accounting period and treated as a loss of that period to be set against total profits. Excess losses are carried forward in this way until the Schedule A business ceases. When the Schedule A business ceases the remaining loss will be carried forward and treated as management expenses under *ICTA 1988, s 75* (*ICTA 1988, s 392A*).

Where there is a change of company ownership, as described in **12.13**, the losses arising before the change of ownership cannot be carried forward to be set against profits arising after the change of ownership. If the change of ownership occurs during an accounting period losses pre and post the change are apportioned according to the length of the accounting bases or if this is unjust, on a just and reasonable basis (*ICTA 1988, s 768D*).

Schedule A losses are included in CT600 boxes 127 and 128.

## CHARGEABLE GAINS

**12.23** Companies are not liable to capital gains tax, but instead pay corporation tax on chargeable gains, at the same rate as trading profits and other income. The capital gains are broadly computed in accordance with normal capital gains tax principles but there is no taper relief or annual exemption.

### Indexation

**12.24** A company's chargeable gains are adjusted for post-March 1982 indexation allowances. The reform of capital gains tax for individuals, trustees and personal representatives, which froze indexation relief at April 1998 and introduced taper relief provisions, does not extend to the capital gains of companies.

Indexation allowance cannot be used to increase a loss, or turn an unindexed gain into a loss, although in appropriate circumstances it may reduce a gain to nil. (See **5.39**).

## Capital losses

**12.25** The company's chargeable gains for the accounting period are reduced by allowable losses of the same period, and any unrelieved allowable capital losses brought forward from previous accounting periods.

Unused capital losses are carried forward for offset against capital gains of subsequent accounting periods. There are no provisions allowing for the carry back of capital losses, the surrender of capital losses between group companies, or the offset of capital losses against trading or other income (except for losses of investment companies on shares in qualifying unquoted trading companies, or losses of trading companies on shares within the Corporate Venturing Scheme: see **12.33–12.43**).

# INVESTMENT IN OTHER LIMITED COMPANIES

**12.26** An investment in another limited company will bring about share ownership for the company. The subsequent disposal of the shares will bring about a capital gain. Income will take the form of dividend receipts. UK dividends have in effect already borne corporation tax (see **1.1**). Overseas dividends may bring an entitlement to a tax credit (see **13.16–13.24**). There are important reliefs for share disposals:

- losses on shares in unquoted trading companies,
- substantial shareholding exemption,
- corporate venturing scheme relief.

## Capital losses

**12.27** An investment company may claim relief against income for capital losses arising on the disposal of shares in unquoted qualifying trading companies, which had been subscribed for by the investment company. The loss incurred, which is calculated under normal CGT rules, may be set off against income (before management expenses and charges) of the same and (if not wholly relieved) preceding accounting periods (*ICTA 1988, s 573*). A loss claim may also be made where an asset has proven to be of negligible value (*TCGA 1992, s 24*). A computation must be prepared by taking the negligible value of the asset as its sale proceeds.

Loss relief for allowable capital losses is available to an investment company (irrespective of whether it is a close investment-holding company), which has subscribed for shares in a qualifying trading company (*ICTA 1988, s 573*). The relief must be claimed, in writing, within two years after the end of the accounting period in which the loss was incurred.

The investment company obtains relief for its capital loss by set-off against its income chargeable to corporation tax. The loss relief is set against income of the accounting period in which the loss is incurred and income of previous accounting periods ending within the 12 months immediately preceding the accounting period in which the loss was incurred. Where an accounting period falls partly within and partly outside the 12-month period, only a proportion of its income can be relieved.

The loss relief against income is given before deduction of charges on income and expenses of management. Where loss relief is given under these provisions, the loss is ignored for the purpose of corporation tax on chargeable gains.

The main conditions to be satisfied in order to qualify for this relief against income are as follows:

- The company subscribing for shares and incurring the capital loss must, generally, have been an investment company for the whole of the previous six years.

- The shares subscribed for must be share capital of a qualifying trading company as defined in *ICTA 1988, s 576(4)*.

- The investment company must not control the trading company, the two companies must not be under common control, and the two companies cannot be members of the same group.

For this purpose the distinction between an investment company and a trading company is maintained. An investment company has the same meaning as *ICTA 1988, s 130* (see **12.3**) but does not include the holding company of a trading group. A trading company is defined as a company whose business consists wholly or mainly of the carrying on of a trade or trades (*ICTA 1988, s 576*).

## Substantial shareholdings exemption

### The relief

**12.28** Provided all relevant conditions are met, the gain on the disposal of shares or an interest in shares held by a company in another company will not be a chargeable gain. However, if a loss were to arise on the disposal of the shares, this loss will not be an allowable loss and hence not available for set-off against other gains. The company has the benefit of no tax payable on the gain but all loss relief is 'lost'.

The exemption does not apply where disposal is deemed to be a no gain/no loss transfer for capital gains under *TCGA 1992, s 171* (see **10.23**).

### Substantial shareholding

**12.29** Essentially the investing company must hold at least 10% of the investee company's share capital and be entitled to at least 10% of the profits and assets available for distribution to equity holders by the investee company. The investing company must have held the shares for a continuous period of at least 12 months ending not more than one year before the disposal (*TCGA 1992, Sch 7AC*).

Group member holdings can be aggregated in order to calculate whether the 10% holding criteria is met (*TCGA 1992, Sch 7AC, para 26*). The capital gains tax group definition is used (see **10.21**) using a 51% relationship rather than a 75% relationship.

Even if shares are vested in a liquidator the company continues to be treated as the beneficial owner of the assets (*TCGA 1992, Sch 7AC, para 16*). The shares must have been held for at least 12 months ending not more than one year before disposal. If some of the shares have been sold during the 12-month period the remainder of the holding will continue to qualify (*TCGA 1992, Sch 7AC, para 7*). The period of ownership also looks back through the no gain/no loss transfers and share reorganisations so that this time of ownership is also brought into consideration (*TCGA 1992, Sch 7AC, paras 10, 14*). However, for deemed sales and reacquisitions, the time of ownership commences with the reacquisition of the holding (*TCGA 1992, Sch 7AC, para 11*). Repurchase agreement arrangements treat the time of ownership as that commencing with the original owner (*TCGA 1992, Sch 7AC, para 12*). Similarly, stock lending arrangements have no effect on the original ownership time span (*TCGA 1992, Sch 7AC, para 13*). A demerger that has a reorganisation treatment (*TCGA 1992, s 192*) is also looked through when calculating the period of ownership (*TCGA 1992, Sch 7AC, para 15*). In addition, if the

10% shareholding exemption applies as described above, the exemption will also be extended to an option or conversion right connected with the shares (*TCGA 1992, Sch 7AC, para 2*).

## Conditions affecting the investing company

**12.30** The investing company must have been a sole trading company or a member of a trading group throughout the 12-month period and immediately after the disposal (*TCGA 1992, Sch 7AC, para 18*). The relief also applies in a group situation where the company holding the shares does not qualify, but assuming an intra-group transfer under *TCGA 1992, s 171* another company would qualify. Where there is a deferral of the completion date on disposal the investing company must qualify at the time of completion (*TCGA 1992, Sch 7AC, para 18*).

## Conditions affecting the investee company

**12.31** The investee company must have been a trading company or the holding company or a trading group during the 12-month period and also be a trading company immediately after the disposal of the shares (*TCGA 1992, Sch 7AC, para 19*). The responsibility for determining whether a company, in which shares (or interests in shares or assets related to shares) were held and since disposed of, was a qualifying company, lies with the investor company concerned (Tax Bulletin 84, August 2006).

As for the investor, where there is a contract for sale with delayed completion the investee company must quantify at the time of sale (*TCGA 1992, Sch 7AC, para 19*).

## Trading activities

**12.32** Trading activities for these purposes will include activities carried on by a company:

- in the course of, or for the purposes of, a trade it is carrying on;
- for the purposes of a trade it is preparing to carry on;
- with a view to it acquiring or starting to carry on a trade;
- with a view to it acquiring a significant interest in the share capital of a trading company, or the holding company of a trading group or sub-group (subject to the restrictions outlined below).

The company's view to acquire or start a trade or its view to acquire a shareholding must materialise as soon as is reasonably practical in the circumstances. 'Significant' for these purposes only refers to ordinary share capital and the company to be acquired must not already be a member of the same group (*TCGA 1992, Sch 7AC, para 20*). Any non-trading activities should be insubstantial. This is normally understood to be 20% of all the activities or less (*TCGA 1992, Sch 7, para 20*).

Trading activities also include a qualifying interest in a joint venture company (*TCGA 1992, Sch 7AC, para 20*).

---

**Example 12.4**

Atlantic Ltd is a trading company, with two wholly-owned subsidiary companies, India Ltd and China Ltd.

On 1 July 2006, Atlantic Ltd acquired 25% of the ordinary share capital of Pacific Ltd.

On 1 September 2006 Pacific Ltd is taken over by Adriatic Ltd.

Atlantic Ltd received an exchange of shares under the no gain/no loss treatment (*TCGA 1992, s 135* applied *TCGA 1992, s 127*). As a result Atlantic Ltd now owns 20% of Adriatic Ltd.

On 1 March 2007 Atlantic Ltd transfers its holding in Adriatic Ltd on a no gain/no loss basis so that *TCGA 1992, s 171* applies to its 100% subsidiary India Ltd.

On 1 July 2007 India Ltd sells the holding to a third party.

The holding was bought on 1 July 2006 and sold on 1 July 2007. It is necessary to look back through the period of ownership to ascertain whether the substantial shareholdings exemption applies (*TCGA 1992, Sch 7AC, para 10*). The holding throughout has remained within the group. India Ltd is treated as owning the shares for 12 months prior to disposal and so the substantial shareholding example applies.

---

## Corporate venturing scheme

**12.33** The corporate venturing scheme rules are contained in *FA 2000, Sch 15*.

The rules offer companies relief for investment in qualifying shares in other companies during the period from 1 April 2000 until 1 April 2010. The companies involved can be of any size, but more usually between a larger company and a smaller one in the same line of business; thus providing the smaller company with another form of finance.

The larger company may invest in the smaller company. The connection provides an alternative or supplementary source of finance for the investee firm and a useful business outlet for the investor company. The investor company may take an interest in the investee by offering its skills and financial advice but must not have a major interest in the company.

## Tax reliefs

**12.34** There are three types of relief available:

- **Investment relief**. Relief against corporation tax of up 20% of the amount subscribed for the full-risk ordinary shares held for three years.
- **Deferral relief**. Any gain on the sale of shares can be rolled into the cost of new shares acquired under the scheme.
- **Loss relief**. Any loss on the sale of the shares can be relieved against income or chargeable gains.

## The investing company

**12.35** The investing company's interest in the investee company must not be more than 30% and it must not be in a position to control the company (*FA 2000, Sch 15, paras 5–8*). Connected company interests are taken into account together with directors' and the directors' relatives' interests. A relative is taken to mean a spouse, civil partner, parent and grandparent, child and grandchild etc. No reciprocal arrangements must exist regarding the investment (*FA 2000, Sch 15, para 6*). The investing company must be a trading company or the holding company of a trading group and financial activities are precluded. If the investment does not qualify for some reason the relief will be withdrawn.

## The issuing company

**12.36** The issuing company must be an unquoted trading company or the holding company of a trading group, when the shares are issued (AIM and

OFEX shares are unquoted for this purpose). The company can be preparing to carry on a trade. It must not have made any arrangements to become a quoted company.

The company must have gross assets of no more than £7 million immediately before, and £8 million immediately after the issue (if the issuing company is the parent company of a group, this test is applied to the group as a whole). For shares issued before 6 April 2006, the limits are £15 million before and £16 million after.

Throughout the qualification period the issuing company must not be a member of a group of companies, unless it is the parent company of the group, and must not be under the control of another company.

At least 20% of the issuing company's ordinary share capital must be held by individuals other than directors or employees (or their relatives) of an investing company, or any company connected with it (*FA 2000, Sch 15, para 18*).

## The investment

**12.37** The investment must be in cash and the shares must be fully paid-up at the time they are issued. There can be no arrangement in force to protect investors from normal commercial investment risk.

The investing company must use at least 80% of the funds it receives from issuing the shares for the purposes of a qualifying trade, or for research and development intended to lead to or benefit a qualifying trade. The funds must be used no later than the end of the period of 12 months starting with the issue of the share or the 12 months following the commencement of the trade if later. The remaining 20% of the funds must be used within the following 12 months (*FA 2000, Sch 15, para 36*).

## Obtaining clearance

**12.38** The investee company can obtain clearance before the shares are issued (*FA 2000, Sch 15, para 89*). If the issue goes ahead the issuing company should complete form CVS 1 confirming it has met all the necessary conditions with which it must comply. The company must submit the form to HMRC and if satisfied HMRC will authorise the issuing company to provide the investing company with a compliance certificate to enable it to claim investment relief (and, where applicable, deferral relief). The compliance certificate can only be issued after the issuing company has been carrying on the trade (or, where appropriate, research and development) for which the funds were raised for at least four months.

## Obtaining relief

**12.39** The investing company claims investment relief against its corporation tax liability by completing the corporate venturing scheme CT600G supplementary pages and including the relief claimed in box 71 of the main return. Loss relief is included in CT600 box 22.

The necessary conditions must be complied with for three years or else the relief is withdrawn. The relief is only available during the accounting period for which the investment is made. The relief is given against corporation tax after marginal relief but before any double taxation relief.

---

**Example 12.5**

If during an accounting period, an investing company subscribes £30,000 for 3,000 shares in company A and £90,000 for 6,000 shares in company B, then the maximum investment relief available is £24,000 (20% of £30,000 + £90,000).

If the investing company's corporation tax liability for the accounting period is £18,000 before taking account of any investment relief, then only three-quarters of the available investment relief can be used.

So, the amount attributable to the shares in A is:

£30,000 × £18,000/£120,000 = £4,500

The amount attributable to the shares in B is:

£90,000 × £18,000/£120,000 = £13,500

It would also be possible for the investing company to claim investment relief only in respect of the shares in company B, so all the investment relief would be attributable to those shares. But, this would prevent shares in company A from qualifying for CVS loss relief and deferral relief, because there would be no investment relief attributable to the shares in company A immediately before any future disposal.

---

**12.40** If value, other than insignificant value, is received from the investee company, relief is withdrawn accordingly, being 20% of the value received. Receiving value could amount to acquiring an asset at undervalue, money lending etc. The provision of goods and services at market rates during the course of trade is not understood to be receipt of value (*FA 2000, Sch 15, para 47*).

An insignificant amount is £1,000 or if more, the amount is insignificant in relation to the amount subscribed for the shares (*FA 2000, Sch 15, para 47*(*7*)) (HMRC Venture Capital Manual VCM 50630).

## Deferral relief

**12.41** The reinvesting company may claim deferral relief on its disposal of qualifying shares, if investment relief was attributable to the shares immediately before the disposal and, if the investing company holds the shares continuously from the time they were issued until the disposal. The new company in which the investee company invests must comply with the investment relief conditions. The gain must be reinvested in the other qualifying company at any time beginning four years before the deferred gain arose.

The gain is deferred until the shares in the other company are disposed of, or an event occurs (such as, a receipt of value or certain share reorganisations), which causes any of the investment relief attributable to the shares to be withdrawn.

The investing company claims deferral relief on the corporate venturing scheme supplementary pages. It may do so after it has received the second investment's compliance certificate. The amount of the deferral must be shown on the claim.

If the investment relief is withdrawn for any reason, this does not affect the deferral relief.

## Relief for losses

**12.42** A loss on disposal can be set against a chargeable gain, or carried forward to set against future chargeable gains, in the normal way. Alternatively, the investing company may claim that the loss be set against its income for the accounting period in which the disposal was made, with any excess carried back to periods ending in the 12 months before that period.

The loss must have arisen from an arm's-length disposal and not arise from a scheme or arrangement. The shares must have been held continuously by the company since issue. The amount of the loss is reduced by the amount of any investment relief retained (*FA 2000, Sch 15, paras 67–71*).

---

**Example 12.6**

An investing company subscribes £100,000 for 100,000 shares (obtaining investment relief of £20,000).

It retains the shares for four years before disposing of them all for £55,000.

The allowable loss is calculated as follows:

Disposal proceeds £55,000 – £80,000 (consideration given for shares less investment relief given and not withdrawn).

So the allowable loss is £25,000.

Any unutilised loss cannot be carried forward as a trading loss but may be carried forward as a capital loss.

---

## Other reliefs

**12.43** The investing company will hold the shares in the investee company as an investment. This should not have any effect on the taper relief expectations for the individual shareholders of the investing company except where the company's total investment activities are more than 20% of the trade of business.

Corporate venture scheme holdings will not qualify for group relief but if all necessary conditions apply they may qualify for consortium relief (see **10.14**). For further information see HMRC Guidance, The Corporate Venturing Scheme: www.hmrc.gov.uk/guidance/cvs.

## INVESTMENT IN COMPANY OR GOVERNMENT LOAN STOCK

**12.44** Loan stock investments are within the loan relationships regime (see Chapter 11).

# Chapter 13

# Overseas Matters

## INTRODUCTION

**13.1** Companies may be resident in the UK with overseas income or vice versa. Alternatively, they may invest abroad, in which case they will be able to receive tax relief on their income or their investment may fall within the controlled foreign companies regime.

## COMPANY RESIDENCE

**13.2** A company is resident in the UK if it is incorporated in the UK (*FA 1988, s 66*).

If a company is not incorporated in the UK if will be resident in the UK if it is centrally managed and controlled in the UK. The case of *De Beers Consolidated Mines Ltd v Howe* (1906) 5 TC 198, [1906] AC 455 involved a company that was registered in South Africa where it worked diamond mines. The company's head office and shareholders' general meetings were held in South Africa, but the directors' meetings took place in both South Africa and the UK. The majority of directors lived in the UK. The company claimed that it was not resident in the UK. It was held that the company was resident in the UK because the majority of the directors who had the overall control were situated in London.

The place where the management and control is exercised from then on has been interpreted as the place where the effective management decisions are taken and not necessarily where it was constitutionally managed. In *Wood v Holden* (*Inspector of Taxes*) [2006] EWCA Civ 26, [2006] 2 BCLC 210 although a company's board meetings took place in London, the authority given by those board meetings was usurped by the overseas parent and the company was held to be non-UK resident.

If a double tax treaty is in place between the UK and the overseas territory it should be consulted in order to verify the company's deemed place of residence.

A company may be 'treaty non-resident'; in other words, solely resident in the other country. A discussion is given in HMRC International Manual INTM 120070.

If residence is or could be awarded to the treaty partner, the company becomes treaty non-resident. A treaty non-resident company is not resident for UK tax purposes (*FA 1994, s 249*).

## UK RESIDENT COMPANY WITH OVERSEAS INCOME

**13.3** A company resident in the UK is chargeable to corporation tax on all its profits wherever the income arises and wherever the assets on which the gain on whose disposal the gain was calculated were situated and whether or not received or transmitted to the UK. Trading income of a UK trade earned abroad will be assessed within the Schedule D Case I computation.

## NON UK RESIDENT COMPANY CARRYING ON A TRADE IN THE UK

### Circumstances in which chargeable to UK corporation tax

**13.4** A non-resident company is chargeable to corporation tax, if, and only if, it carries on a trade in the UK through a permanent establishment in which case the following becomes chargeable:

- any trading income arising directly or indirectly through or from the permanent establishment;
- any income from property or rights used by, or held by or for, the permanent establishment;
- chargeable gains accruing on the disposal of assets situated in the UK used for the purposes of the trade of the use of the permanent establishment (*ICTA 1988, s 11*; *TCGA 1992, s 10*).

### Meaning of 'permanent establishment'

**13.5** Non-resident companies are assessed to UK corporation tax (subject to treaty override: see **13.2**), if they have a permanent establishment in the UK. Prior to 1 January 2003 non-resident companies were assessed to UK corporation tax if they had a branch or agency in the UK. A permanent establishment may of course be a branch or agency, but the precise change of wording was introduced to bring the UK legislation in line with various internationally recognised characteristics commonly used in the UK's double tax agreements.

*FA 2003, s 148* states that a company has a permanent establishment in a territory if, and only if, it has a fixed place of business there through which the business of the company is wholly or partly carried on, or an agent acting on behalf of the company has and habitually exercises there authority to do business on behalf of the company.

## A fixed place of business

**13.6** A fixed place of business can be a place of management, a branch, an office, a factory, a workshop, an installation or structure for the exploration of natural resources, a mine, an oil or gas well, a quarry or any other place of extraction of natural resources or a building site or construction or installation project (*FA 2003, s 148*(*1*), (*2*)).

## Circumstances in which there is no permanent establishment

**13.7** A company is not regarded as having a permanent establishment if it carries on business there through an independent agent acting in the ordinary course of the agency business. A company is regarded as having a permanent establishment if it maintains a fixed place of business for the purpose of carrying on activities that have not yet commenced. Neither will the company be regarded as having a permanent establishment if an agent carries on preparatory or auxiliary activities in relation to the business of the company as a whole.

The legislation provides examples of preparatory or auxiliary activities, of a company as a whole, which will not be considered sufficient business activities to constitute the existence of a permanent establishment. The list is not exhaustive but includes:

- the use of facilities for the purpose of storage, display or delivery of goods or merchandise belonging to the company;
- the maintenance of a stock of goods or merchandise belonging to the company for the purpose of storage, display or delivery;
- the maintenance of a stock of goods or merchandise belonging to the company for the purpose of processing by another person (*FA 2003, s 148*(*4*), (*5*)).

# NON-RESIDENT COMPANY BECOMING LIABLE TO UK CORPORATION TAX

## Assessment, collection and recovery of corporation tax

**13.8** When an overseas company commences trading in the UK it should notify HMRC that it is within the charge to corporation tax. This will be the commencement of an accounting period (*ICTA 1988, s 337*). When it becomes chargeable to UK corporation tax, it is chargeable to corporation tax, subject to any exceptions provided for by the *Corporation Tax Acts*, on all profits, wherever arising, that are attributable to its permanent establishment in the UK (*ICTA 1988, s 11AA*).

UK permanent establishments compute their taxable profits on the same principles as UK resident companies. Only where the UK has a tax treaty with the permanent establishment's home country and there is a conflict between the treaty and the UK corporation tax domestic law the effect of the treaty will be to modify or prevent the application of UK corporation tax principles (*FA 2003, s 149*). *ICTA 1988, s 788*(*3*) specifies that relevant treaty provisions take precedence over domestic legislation.

*ICTA 1988, s 11AA*(2) adopts the wording of Article 7(2) of the OECD model tax convention and states that the permanent establishment's taxable profits are the profits that it would have made if it were a distinct and separate enterprise, engaged in the same or similar activities under the same or similar conditions, dealing wholly independently with the rest of the non-resident company of which it is a part.

When calculating the profits it is assumed that the permanent establishment has the same credit rating as the non-resident company of which it is a part and has such equity capital and loan capital as it could reasonably be expected to have in regard to its circumstance (*ICTA 1988, s 11AA*(2), (*3*)).

A deduction is given for expenses, wherever they are incurred, if they are incurred for the purposes of the permanent establishment and if they would be deductible if incurred by a company resident in the UK (*ICTA 1988, s 11AA*(*4*)).

A non-resident company pays corporation tax at the full rate. No claim can be made for the small companies rate (*ICTA 1988, s 13*(*1*)).

## Responsibility for UK corporation tax

**13.9** The UK representative of the overseas company is responsible for the permanent establishment's corporaton tax affairs (*FA 2003, s 150*). The company in turn is bound by the acts or omissions of the UK representative. However, a non-resident company is not bound by mistakes in information provided by its UK representative in pursuance of an obligation imposed on the representative by this section, unless the mistake is the result of an act or omission of the company itself, or to which the company consented or in which it connived. Therefore, the UK representative of a non-resident company can only be prosecuted for a criminal offence if it committed the offence itself, or consented to or connived in its commission (*FA 2003, s 150*).

# NON-UK RESIDENT COMPANY NOT CARRYING ON A TRADE IN THE UK BUT WITH OTHER UK INCOME

## Liability to income tax

**13.10** A non-resident company not carrying on a trade in the UK through a branch or agency is chargeable to income tax at the basic rate on any other UK income. Therefore a UK property investment business operated by a non-resident company will be subject to income tax at the basic rate on its profits. The profits are computed according to income tax rules (see Tottel's Income Tax).

Where tax is deducted at source from such income the tax payable is limited to the tax deducted at source. This includes savings and dividend income (*FA 2003, s 151*).

# UK COMPANY BECOMING NON-UK RESIDENT

## HMRC notification and outstanding liabilities

**13.11** When a company ceases to be chargeable to corporation tax, for example, by becoming non-UK resident it must comply with *FA 1988, s 130* requirements. It must notify HMRC of the date that it intends to become non-resident, provide a statement of all amounts owing and provide details of the arrangements it will make for payment. The Revenue will require a payment guarantor to be provided and the arrangements must be approved by HMRC or otherwise they are void. (Treasury consent is not required for companies ceasing to be UK resident from 15 March 1988 onwards). If a company becomes non-resident without HMRC approval, it and its directors together with controlling company directors may be liable to a penalty based on its outstanding liabilities (*ICTA 1988, s 131*). Outstanding amounts of tax may be recovered from the company directors or directors of other companies in the group (*ICTA 1988, s 132*).

The company's UK departure will be the cessation of an accounting period (ICTA 1988, s 337). Therefore balancing adjustments must be calculated for capital allowance purposes.

It is unlawful without Treasury consent for a UK resident company to cause or permit a non-UK resident company over which it has control to create or issue any shares or debentures. It is also unlawful without Treasury consent for a resident company to dispose of any shares or debentures in a non-resident company that it controls (*ICTA 1988, s 765*). These are criminal offences. A £10,000 fine can be levied and those involved may be sentenced to two years imprisonment (*ICTA 1988, s 766*).

## Deemed disposal of chargeable assets

**13.12** Also the company will be deemed to have disposed of all its chargeable assets at market value thus creating a chargeable gain under *TCGA 1992, s 185*. A charge under *TCGA 1992, s 185* will also arise where a company becomes treaty non-resident. Roll-over relief is not available. If the chargeable assets are assets used in a trade that the company carries on, say through a branch or agency in the UK, there is no chargeable gain and therefore roll-over relief would be available.

## Postponement of exit charge

**13.13** Postponement of the exit charge may occur if:

- the assets are situated outside the UK and are used in or for the purposes of a trade carried on outside the UK ('foreign assets'),
- the company is a 75% subsidiary (by ordinary shares) of a UK resident company (the 'principal company') and
- both companies make an election within two years of the company becoming non-resident.

The postponed gain becomes a chargeable gain of the principal company in whole or in part if:

- the asset is disposed of within six years of the company becoming non-resident; and
- the company ceases to be a 75% subsidiary:
    - by disposal of ordinary shares,
    - for any other reason, or

- by the principal company ceasing to be UK resident.

HMRC do not consider that the issue of new shares by the principal company to a third party will bring the gain into charge (*TCGA 1992, s 187*).

The capital gains charge under *TCGA 1992, s 185* also applies to companies who become treaty non-resident.

## DUAL RESIDENT COMPANY

### Restrictions

**13.14** The transfer of the central management and control of a non-UK resident company to the UK will result in the company being UK resident. In practical terms the foreign jurisdiction may determine that the company remains resident abroad because of incorporation or because of trading activities. Hence, the company becomes a dual resident company. In such situations the relevant double tax treaty, if any, should be examined.

A dual resident investment company (ie a non-trading company) cannot claim or surrender group relief for the chargeable period (*ICTA 1988, s 404*). Neither can it make intra-group asset transfers on a no gain/no loss basis (*TCGA 1992, s 171*). Group roll-over relief is unavailable (*TCGA 1992, s 175*(2)).

The carry forward of trading losses on a succession to a trade without a change of ownership is also prohibited, together with the transfer of assets at written-down value for capital allowance purposes (*ICTA 1988, s 343*(2)).

### Double tax relief

**13.15** The double tax treaty between the UK and the country concerned may exempt the income in question from corporation tax. It should be examined in every case. (Double tax agreements can be viewed in HMRC Double Taxation Relief Manual DT 2140 onwards).

Credit relief for overseas corporate taxes paid is available against UK corporation tax payable. A claim should be made according to the terms of the double taxation agreement (*ICTA 1988, s 793A*).

Where there is no entitlement to relief under a double taxation agreement, unilateral relief (*ICTA 1988, ss 790, 793*) together with relief for withholding tax may be claimed. The general rule is that income is calculated according to

UK principles (*George Wimpey International Ltd v Rolfe* [1989] STC 609) and the credit cannot exceed the calculated UK corporation tax.

## OVERSEAS DIVIDENDS

### Underlying tax

**13.16** The only credit available for overseas dividends is withholding tax unless the UK company owns more than 10% of the overseas company's equity, in which case relief for underlying tax is available (*ICTA 1988, s 790*). Underlying tax is the tax on profits out of which the dividend is paid whereas withholding tax is tax deducted at source from the dividend payment.

---

**Example 13.1**

England Ltd, a UK resident company, receives a dividend of £9,000 net of 10% withholding tax, from Overseas Ltd, a foreign company in respect of the accounting period ended 31 December 2006.

Extracts from Overseas Ltd's profit and loss account (converted to sterling) show the following:

| | £ |
|---|---|
| Profit before tax | 450,000 |
| Provision for corporation tax | 90,000 |
| Distributable profits | 360,000 |

Corporation tax paid £140,000.

**Computation of underlying tax**

| | £ |
|---|---|
| Distributable profits | 360,000 |
| Foreign tax paid | 140,000 |
| | 500,000 |

The effective rate of underlying tax is 28%.

Relief for underlying tax on a dividend received from outside the UK is restricted where the reclaim only emanates from an avoidance scheme (*ICTA 1988, s 801A*).

---

## Credit relief

### Limit

**13.17** The credit relief given is limited to the lower of the overseas tax paid or the UK corporation tax. The following formula is used:

(D + U) × M%

where

D = the dividend,

U = the amount of underlying tax paid overseas, and

M = the UK Corporation tax rate when the dividend was paid (*ICTA 1988, s 799(1A)*).

The formula looks back through the paying company to the source of the dividends.

---

**Example 13.2**

England Ltd receives two dividends from Overseas Ltd of £9,000 each arising in its accounting period ended 31 March 2007. The dividends are paid out of the foreign company's profits for the years ended 31 December 2006 and 31 December 2007 with respective underlying rates of tax of 28% and 50%. Each net dividend plus withholding tax amounts to £10,000.

Schedule D Case V income

| | £ | £ |
|---|---|---|
| Dividend 1: £10,000 + £2,800 underlying tax | 12,800 | |
| Dividend 2: £10,000 + £5,000 underlying tax | 15,000 | |
| | 27,800 | |
| UK corporation tax: £27,800 at 30% | | 8,340 |
| Less credit | | |
| Dividend 1 | 2,800 | |
| Dividend 2 (restricted to £15,000 at 30%) | 4,500 | |
| | | 7,300 |
| Corporation tax payable | | 1,040 |

---

## Unrelieved tax credits

### Carry back and carry forward

**13.18** Unrelieved tax credits on Schedule D Case V dividends known as eligible unrelieved foreign tax (EUFT) may be eligible for relief by:

- carry back to the three previous accounting periods,
- carry forward to the next accounting period, or
- through the mixer cap (*ICTA 1988, s 806D*).

Eligible unrelieved tax credits are those that have not been restricted, eg by *ICTA 1988, s 801A* (see **13.16**), and is the difference between the credits allowed and the foreign tax suffered up to a maximum of 45%. The EUFT that may be relieved is calculated by the following formula:

(D + U) × M%

where

D = the dividend,

U = the amount of underlying tax paid overseas, and

M = the UK Corporation tax rate when the dividend was paid (*ICTA 1988, s 799(1A)*).

---

**Example 13.3**

England Ltd's EUFT on its second dividend receipt amounts to:

| | £ |
|---|---|
| (D + U ) × 45% = (10,000 + 5,000) × 45% | 6,750 |
| Less foreign tax relievable | 4,500 |
| Eligible EUFT | 2,250 |

---

**13.19** EUFT may be relieved by carry back to accounting periods beginning no more than three years before the current period. The later years are relieved before the earlier years but after relief for the current period (*ICTA 1988,* *s 806E*). Alternatively EUFT can be carried forward to the next accounting period (*ICTA 1988, s 806D*). Credit relief is given for underlying tax before withholding tax in all cases (*ICTA 1988, s 806F*).

The EUFT may be carried forward to the next accounting period or back to previous accounting periods.

The order of carry back is:

1 the accounting periods beginning not more than three years before the accounting period in which the relievable tax arises;

2 later accounting periods are relieved in priority to earlier accounting periods, but

3 after current tax is offset in the following order:

   (i) aggregated foreign tax in respect of the single dividend for that period (so far as it does not consist of relievable tax arising in another accounting period), and

   (ii) relievable tax arising in any accounting period before that in which this relievable tax arises.

However the amount of credit given must not exceed the corporation tax liability on that single dividend, ie it cannot produce EUFT (*ICTA 1988, s 806E*).

Credit is given for underlying tax before withholding tax. Current year set-off is given priority to other years (*ICTA 1988, s 806F*).

Claims must be made within six years from the end of the chargeable period for which the income is chargeable to corporation tax (*ICTA 1988, s 806*). Claims are made in writing or by completion of boxes 73, 74 and 75 of the company tax return.

## Credit relief and eligible unrelieved foreign tax: the 'mixer cap'

**13.20** In calculating credit relief it is necessary to look back to the source of the dividends. In the case of a group this will mean looking back to dividends paid by the subsidiary companies.

**Example 13.4**

There are four companies:

| | |
|---|---|
| UK Ltd | UK resident company |
| Foreign Land BV | foreign company (non-UK resident) |
| Faraway SA | foreign company (non-UK resident) |
| Furtheraway SA | foreign company (non-UK resident) |

Faraway SA pays corporate taxes of £25,000 and a £75,000 dividend to Foreign Land BV.

Furtheraway SA pays corporate taxes of £45,000 and a £65,000 dividend to Foreign Land BV.

Foreign Land BV pays a £140,000 dividend to UK Ltd.

The mixer cap formula with a 30% corporation tax rate and an upper EUFT rate of 45% is applied to each dividend paid which in effect contributes to the final dividend payable to the UK company.

| *Dividend* | *Tax* *£000* | *(D + U) × 30%* | *Credit* *£000* |
|---|---|---|---|
| Faraway SA | 25 | (75 + 25) × 30% = 30 | 25 |
| Furtheraway S | 35 | (65 + 35) × 30% = 30 | 30 |
| Foreign Land BV | 60 | (140 + 60) × 30% = 60 | 60 |

The UK foreign tax credit is restricted to £55 (25 + 30).

**13.21** Similarly, the eligible unrelieved foreign tax is calculated at each level but dividend and tax relating to lower levels are excluded (*ICTA 1988, s 806B*). Negative results are treated as zero.

**Example 13.5**

| *Dividend* | *Tax* *£000* | | *EUFT* *£000* |
|---|---|---|---|
| Faraway SA | 25 | (75 + 25) × 45% = 45 | |
| Furtheraway S | 35 | (65 + 35) × 45% = 45 | |
| Foreign Land BV | 60 | [(140 – 75 – 65) + (60 -25 – 30)] × 45% = 2.25 | 2.25 |

The total EUFT is £2,250.

## Onshore pooling

**13.22** For credit relief purposes all Schedule D Case V qualifying foreign dividends (QFDs) may be pooled. The pooling does not apply where the dividends are treated as trading income or to dividends from controlled foreign companies following an acceptable distribution policy (ADP) or where an eligible unrelieved foreign tax credit arises.

The credit is calculated by subtotalling the following:

- Qualifying dividends paid by a related company.
- Qualifying dividends paid by an unrelated company.
- Underlying tax on related qualifying foreign dividends.
- Other taxes on both related and unrelated qualifying foreign dividends.

A related company is a subsidiary or one in which the holding is greater than 10%.

Credit relief is given as if each total were the only single dividend and single amount of tax paid respectively. A related company exists where the UK company owns 10% of the voting power.

---

**Example 13.6**

UK company receives the following dividends from overseas companies, all of whom are in different countries:

| *Company* | *Holding* | *Dividend* | *Underlying tax* | *Withholding tax* | *Qualifying foreign dividend* | *Comment* |
|---|---|---|---|---|---|---|
| P | 100% | 55 | 45 | Nil | No: | EUFT will arise |
| Q | 100% | 80 | 20 | 8 | Yes | Related QFD |
| R | 90% | 90 | 10 | | Yes | Related QFD |
| S | 100% | CFC: ADP dividend 95, underlying tax 5 | 5 | | No | No: ADP dividend |

| | | | | | | |
|---|---|---|---|---|---|---|
| T | 1% | 200 | n/a | 30 | Yes | Unre-lated QFD |
| U | 1% | 50 | n/a | 10 | Yes | Unre-lated QFD |

These are subtotalled as follows:

| | *Underlying tax* | *Withholding tax* |
|---|---|---|
| Qualifying dividends paid by a related company | | |
| Q | 20 | 8 |
| R | 10 | |
| Qualifying dividends paid by an unrelated company | | |
| T | | 30 |
| U | — | 10 |
| Total | 30 | 48 |

The £30 underlying tax is treated as though it arose from a single dividend and full credit relief is given for the £48 withholding tax.

## Dividends received from controlled foreign companies (CFCs)

**13.23** CFCs are overseas companies controlled by UK persons. A CFC follows an acceptable dividend policy (ADP) if it distributes 90% of its net chargeable profits as a dividend. Acceptable distribution policy dividends are not 'mixed' with dividends from other companies but are treated as being received direct by the UK holding company, with the result that the foreign tax set-off is restricted to the tax actually paid.

The rule does not apply to a dividend paid by a non-resident company that is exempt from the CFC rules because it passes the exempt activity or motive tests.

## Groups

**13.24** Group companies may surrender their EUFT to other group companies (but not consortium companies) (*ICTA 1988, s 806H*; *SI 2001/1163*). The definition of a group is as used for group relief: see **10.5**.

The companies must be members of the same group throughout the surrendering company's accounting period in which the surrenderable EUFT arises.

A company can only surrender current year surplus EUFT following its own current and previous year actual and available utilisation.

A company can claim all or part of the amount of any available EUFT from the surrendering company, which will then be treated as the claimant company's own EUFT for all purposes.

Where there are non coterminous accounting periods the surrendering company's accounting period is followed. The dividend to which the EUFT belongs is treated as arising in the claimant company's accounting periods in which the last day of the surrendering company's accounting period falls.

The time limit for claim and surrender is the same as for all claims to utilise EUFT. The normal time limits relating to the amending of a company's tax return do not apply to making or withdrawing a claim for EUFT (*SI 2001/1163, reg 9*).

Supplementary pages CT600C of the company tax return provides a section to surrender and claim EUFT within a group.

## CONTROLLED FOREIGN COMPANIES

### Meaning

**13.25** A company resident outside the UK, that is controlled by UK residents and which pays less than three quarters of the tax in its country of residence, which it would have paid on its income had it been resident in the UK is known as a controlled foreign company (*ICTA 1988, s 747(1)*). This being the case, the CFC's income may be apportioned to the UK resident owners.

### Residence

**13.26** For these purposes the company is resident in the country where its place of management is situated. A company may be resident in two countries. In order to decide the country of residence it is taken to be the country which has the greatest amount of assets at the accounting year end. The assets are valued at market value (*ICTA 1988, s 749*).

A company may make an irrevocable election for a CFC to be treated as resident in a certain territory. The election must be made within 12 months of the end of the first accounting period to which it is to apply (*ICTA 1988, s 749A*).

If HMRC deems a country of residence it must give notice to all persons with an interest in the CFC. A person has an interest in a company if he can secure that the assets or income can be applied directly or indirectly for his benefit or if either alone or with others he has control of the company.

A UK company that becomes treaty non-resident after 1 April 2002 (see **13.2**) remains UK resident for controlled foreign company purposes (*ICTA 1988, s 747*). (This does not apply to companies that migrated before 1 April 2002.)

## Self-assessment requirements

**13.27** Under self-assessment companies are required to make their own assessment of any liability. Form CT600B is used. The information that is required is:

- a calculation of the profits chargeable to tax on a UK corporation tax basis (exclusive of capital gains);
- an apportionment of the profits among those with an interest in the company; and
- corporation tax self-assessment where 25% or more of the profits are allocated.

Associates are included when considering the 25% threshold but are not included in the calculation of corporation tax due.

For accounting periods commencing before 16 March 2005, the self-assessment the accounts are prepared in accordance with the accountancy rules of the country concerned. If no accounts are required they are drawn up along *Companies Act* principles (*ICTA 1988, s 747A*). Profits computed in a foreign currency are converted to sterling at the rate for the last day of the accounting period (*ICTA 1988, s 748(4), (5)*). For accounting periods commencing on or after 16 March 2005, the accounts are drawn up in accordance with GAAP (*FA 2005, s 24*).

## Apportionment

**13.28** Apportionment can be made to the following persons who have an interest in the company (*ICTA 1988, s 752*):

- members of the company who are entitled to acquire voting rights and to participate in distributions,
- loan creditors entitled to a premium on redemption,
- persons who are able to secure that income or assets are applied directly or indirectly for their benefit,
- those who alone or with others control the company (*ICTA 1988, s 749B*).

## Distributions

**13.29** Distributions follow the meaning of *ICTA 1988, s 209*: see **16.2–16.8**, with the exception of close company distributions (*ICTA 1988, s 749*).

## Calculation of the profits chargeable

**13.30** Each year the company should calculate its chargeable profit irrespective of HMRC direction or whether an apportionment is required (*ICTA 1988, Sch 24, para 1*).

The profits chargeable to corporation tax are calculated in the normal way with the following added criteria:

- The company is assumed to be UK resident from the beginning of the first accounting period for which a direction is given. The company then continues to be notionally UK resident for subsequent accounting periods until it ceases to be controlled by UK residents (*ICTA 1988, Sch 24, para 2*).
- The company is assumed to be an open company (ie not a close company) (*ICTA 1988, Sch 24, para 3*).
- The company assumed to make full use of any claims or reliefs against corporation tax (*ICTA 1988, Sch 24, para 4*).
- Group relief is denied. If the company is a member of a group and relief has already been given, it is added back to the chargeable profits (*ICTA 1988, Sch 24, para 5*).
- If a CFC transfers a trade to a UK company the *ICTA 1988, s 343* succession treatment for losses carried forward from the CFC predecessor company to the UK successor company will apply (see **15.11–15.21**). The same does not apply to a transfer of trade from another company to a CFC company (*ICTA 1988, Sch 24, para 8*).

- Losses incurred within six years before the first year in which a direction or apportionment is made on a non-UK resident CFC may be treated as incurred within the first year. A claim must be made within 20 months of the CFC's first accounting period (*ICTA 1988, Sch 24, para 9*).
- Notional capital allowances are given in calculating the tax due (*ICTA 1988, Sch 24, para 10*).
- Unremittable income is ignored in the calculation until it is remitted to the UK (*ICTA 1988, Sch 24, para 12*).

## Control

**13.31** Two or more persons taken together may control the company. A UK resident and a non-UK resident may control a company together if the UK person has interests, rights and powers representing at least 40% of the holdings, rights and powers by which the company is controlled and the non-UK person has interests, rights and powers representing at least 40% but not more than 55% of such holdings, rights and powers. Attribution of connected persons' rights and powers applies (*ICTA 1988, s 755D*).

## Exclusion from profit apportionment

**13.32** No apportionment of profits is required for an accounting period in which:

- the CFC pursues an acceptable distribution policy or
- the CFC is engaged in exempt activities throughout the period or
- the CFC has a public quotation or
- the chargeable profits are £50,000 or less or
- the CFC is situated in one of the exempt territories (*ICTA 1988, s 748*).

## Acceptable distribution policy

**13.33** An acceptable distribution policy is in place if the company pays a dividend equal to or greater than 90% of its net chargeable profits within 18 months of the end of its accounting period to UK resident persons (*ICTA 1988, Sch 25, paras 1–4A*).

## Exempt activities test

**13.34** The exempt activities test is met if the company satisfies the following requirements throughout the accounting period:

- it has a 'business establishment' in its territory of residence;
- its business affairs are 'effectively managed' in its territory of residence; and
- its main business at no time consists of certain defined activities; namely investment business, import and exports and trading with connected or associated persons (*ICTA 1988, Sch 25, paras 5–12A*).

## Public quotation condition

**13.35** The public quotation condition is met if the public holds at least 35% of the company's voting rights and the shares are dealt with on a recognised stock exchange. The condition is not met if at any time the principal members own more than 85% of the voting power. A principal member is a member holding 5% or more of the voting power (*ICTA 1988, Sch 25, paras 13–15*).

## De minimis exclusion

**13.36** The de minimis test excludes a company's chargeable profits of £50,000 or less in a 12-month accounting period from the apportionment requirements (*SI 1998/3081, reg 5*).

## Motive test

**13.37** Transactions that result in a minimal reduction in UK tax and for which the main purpose was not to achieve a reduction in tax by diversifying profits away from the UK will satisfy the motive test and will not be included in the apportionment calculation (*ICTA 1988, Sch 25, paras 16–19*)

## Territorial exclusion from exemption

**13.38** No apportionment is required if the company is situated in one of the excluded countries. See *Part I* or *II* of the *Excluded Countries Regulations 1998, SI 1998/3081, regs 4, 5*.

## Creditable tax and reliefs

**13.39** A company can claim set-off of:

- trading losses,
- charges on income,
- non-trading deficits on loan relationships,
- management expenses,
- certain capital allowances, and
- group relief (*ICTA 1988, Sch 26, para 1*).

Tax suffered but unrelieved in any other way may be offset in the capital gains computation if the shares are later sold (*ICTA 1988, Sch 26, para 1*(5)).

## Dividends from controlled foreign companies

**13.40** Dividends paid by CFCs to UK companies are assessable as Schedule D Case V income. If the dividend is paid out of apportioned profits the apportioned tax paid is treated as underlying tax in respect of the dividend received (*ICTA 1988, Sch 26, para 4*).

# Chapter 14

# Transfer Pricing

## INTRODUCTION

**14.1** The transfer pricing modus operandi dictates that transactions between connected parties should be treated for tax purposes as if the same transactions had taken place between unconnected parties. The 'arm's-length principle' should apply. Modern business these days is transacted globally with many business partners and associates. Groups are able to pick the country or regime that best suits their business in order to minimize their corporation tax liabilities. To prevent any unfairness taxation legislation requires that the 'arm's-length principle' be applied to all relevant transactions. The UK transfer pricing rules are included in *ICTA 1988, s 770A, Sch 28AA*. It is more than likely that other countries will have their own comparable domestic legislation. For countries that have a double taxation treaty it is included in the OECD Model Tax Convention on Income and on Capital (OECD Model Treaty), art 9.

For periods beginning 1 April 2004 inter-company UK trading is brought within the ambit of transfer pricing.

## THE UK TRANSFER PRICING RULES

**14.2** The rules apply for accounting periods ending on or after 1 July 1999. The transfer pricing rules cover:

- the purchase and sale of goods,
- the provision of management and other services,
- rents and hire charges,
- transfers of intangible property, such as trademarks, patents and know-how,
- sharing of expertise, business contacts, supply systems, etc,
- provision of finance, and other financial arrangements, and

- interest.

The legislation aims to mitigate the loss of tax arising from non-arm's-length pricing; irrespective of a tax motive.

## Application of transfer pricing

**14.3** Transfer pricing rules apply for accounting periods ending on or after 1 July 1999 if there is a provision by means of a transaction or a series of transactions between any two companies under common control where:

- one of the affected persons was directly or indirectly participating in the management, control or capital of the other, or
- the same person or persons was or were directly or indirectly participating in the management, control or capital of each of the affected persons.

The controlling person may be an individual.

The provision made is different to an arm's-length provision that would be made between independent parties and gives one of the two affected parties a UK taxation benefit (*ICTA 1988, Sch 28AA, para 1*). An adjustment must be made to the taxable profits of the person or persons enjoying the tax advantage.

These rules also apply to securities issued by one company to another for accounting periods beginning after 31 March 2004 (*ICTA 1988, Sch 28AA, paras 1A, 1B*).

## Control

**14.4** Control is defined by *ICTA 1988, s 840* as the power to secure that the company's affairs are conducted in accordance with a person's wishes. The powers so recognized are voting power, power given by the Articles of Association and the actual ability of a person to direct the affairs of the company in the absence of the visible signs of such rights.

Indirect participation examines the following issues.

A person participates indirectly in another entity if:

- he would be participating directly had certain rights and powers been attributed to him, or

- he is one of the major participants in the other entity.

The rights and powers that can be attributed are those:

- which the potential participant is entitled to acquire at a future date,
- exercisable by other persons on behalf of the potential participant or under his direction or for his benefit and
- of connected persons.

A person is a major participant in a company or partnership if the participant and another person together have a 40% interest therein thus creating a joint venture (*ICTA 1988, Sch 28AA, para 4(7)*).

Transfer pricing only applies to transactions between at least one of the joint venture parties and the joint venture itself and not between the two joint venturers unless they are under common control.

## Corporation tax self-assessment

**14.5** Transfer pricing is within the self-assessment regime. It closely follows the OECD Model Treaty, art 9. From 1 April 2004 transactions between UK entities are included within the transfer pricing rules (previously only transactions between foreign entities and UK entities were included). Also from 1 April 2004 small and medium-sized enterprises and dormant companies are excluded from the legislation.

Companies are required to include the adjustment to profits within their own self-assessment.

## The transaction

**14.6** The basic pricing rule follows the OECD Model Tax Convention (*ICTA 1988, Sch 28AA, para 2*). The meaning of transactions is extremely wide and includes binding and unbinding arrangements, understandings and mutual practices. A series of transactions is considered to be a sequence in any order that is in connection with a single arrangement (*ICTA 1988, Sch 28AA, para 3*). In comparing the actual provision with the arm's-length provision it is necessary to look at all of the terms and conditions of the transactions in question and to adjust them to arm's-length terms if necessary.

A third party can be involved in a series of transactions. Interest payments to third parties under finance arrangements guaranteed by related companies.

A potential advantage arises from a non-arm's-length price, if, as a result, taxable profits are reduced, or losses together with expenses of management or group relief are increased. The transfer pricing adjustment may only increase profits or reduce losses (*ICTA 1988, Sch 28AA, para 5*).

## SMALL AND MEDIUM-SIZED ENTERPRISES

### Exemption

**14.7** In this context SMEs are defined according to the European Recommendation 2003/361/EC. They are exempt from the basic transfer pricing except in the following circumstances:

- where the company irrevocably elects to disapply the provision in relation to a chargeable period or
- where the company enters into transactions with a company resident in a territory with which the UK does not have a tax treaty containing a suitable non-discrimination clause (*ICTA 1988, Sch 28AA, para 5B*).
- Alternatively, HMRC may issue the company with a transfer pricing notice for that chargeable period (*ICTA 1988, Sch 28AA, para 5C(1)*).

If an SME carries on activities with overseas associates it must indicate on the front of the return if it qualifies for an SME exemption. This will not be possible if the company transacts business in a country with which the UK does not have a tax treaty with a suitable non discrimination clause. See **14.12**.

### Definition

**14.8** The SME definition follows that given by the European Recommendation (2003/361/EC). The definition and the User Guide can be viewed on europa.eu.int/comm/enterprise/enterprise_policy/sme_definition/index_en.htm

The definition not only applies to companies but to any entity engaged in an economic activity, irrespective of its legal form and includes entities subject to income tax as well as corporation tax.

An entity qualifies as either small or medium if it meets the staff headcount ceiling for that class and either one or both of the following financial limits.

| | *Maximum number of staff* | *And less than one of the following limits:* | |
|---|---|---|---|
| | | *Annual turnover* | *Balance sheet total* |
| Small enterprise | 50 | €10 million | €10 million |
| Medium enterprise | 250 | €50 million | €43 million |

This test is made and determined solely by reference to the period for which a return is being made.

Staff includes employees, persons seconded to work for a business, owner managers and partners; proportioned accordingly to the amount of time that they work.

Turnover and balance sheet totals are net of VAT and otherwise have their ordinary meaning for accounting purposes. Balance sheet total means total gross assets without any deduction for liabilities.

Conversion to sterling should be made at the average exchange rate for the period of account whose profit is being computed or the exchange rate on the date the account was drawn up if this produces a fairer result.

As with any of the thresholds, companies close to the limit should not rely on changes to the exchange rate but should plan in advance to meet the requirements (if any) which changing designation requires.

If the entity is a member or a group or has an associated entity the limits are applied to the whole group. For this purpose the company is said to have linked or partnership enterprises (HMRC International Manual INTM 432112).

## Linked enterprises

**14.9** A linked enterprise is an enterprise which has the right either directly or indirectly to control the affairs of another enterprise. Control can be by shareholding, voting rights or contractual rights.

In order to ascertain which is the dominant linked company the following is taken into consideration:

- majority of the shareholders or members' voting rights in another enterprise;
- the right to appoint or remove a majority of the members of the administrative, management or supervisory body of another enterprise;

- the right to exercise a dominant influence over another enterprise pursuant to a contract entered into with that enterprise or to a provision in its memorandum or articles of association.

The data for all linked companies and partnership companies must be aggregated to ascertain whether the SME limits have been exceeded.

## Partnership enterprises

**14.10** A partnership enterprise is one that holds 25% or more of the capital or voting rights of another company but is not a linked company. Where linked enterprises jointly hold rights these must be aggregated to see if the 25% threshold has been passed.

## Excluded holdings

**14.11** Holdings and investments by the following are ignored for the purposes of aggregation: public investment corporations, venture capital companies, individuals or groups of individuals with a regular venture capital investment activity who invest equity capital in unquoted businesses ('business angels'), provided the total investment of those business angels in the same enterprise is less than €1,250,000; universities or non-profit research centres; institutional investors, including regional development funds; autonomous local authorities with an annual budget of less than €10 million and fewer than 5,000 inhabitants.

The rights of a person in office as a liquidator or administrator are not to be taken into account when considering partnership or linked enterprises (HMRC International Manual INTM 432112). Dormant companies are excluded (*ICTA 1988, Sch 28AA, para 5A*) but there is the possibility that the party to the transaction may remain within transfer pricing (HMRC International Manual INTM 432114).

## Appropriate non-discrimination clause

**14.12** With effect from 1 April 2004, small and medium-sized companies may be exempted from the transfer pricing rules. The exemption does not apply where a business has transactions with or provisions that include a related business in a territory with which the UK does not have a double tax treaty with an appropriate non-discrimination article. Such transactions remain subject to the transfer pricing rules.

An appropriate non-discrimination article is one that ensures that the nationals of a contracting state may not be less favourably treated in the other contracting state than nationals of that latter state in the same circumstances (in particular with respect to residence).

HMRC regards the following double taxation treaties as containing an appropriate non-discrimination article as at 1 April 2004 (except where stated otherwise).

Argentina
Australia
Austria
Azerbaijan
Bangladesh
Barbados
Belarus
Belgium
Bolivia
Bosnia-Herzegovina
Botswana
Bulgaria
Canada
Chile (wef 21/12/2004)
China
Croatia
Cyprus
Czech Republic
Denmark
Egypt
Estonia
Falkland Islands
Fiji
Finland
France
Gambia
Georgia
Germany
Ghana
Greece
Guyana
Hungary
Iceland
Luxembourg
Macedonia
Malaysia
Malta
Mauritius
Mexico
Mongolia
Morocco
Myanmar
Namibia
Netherlands
New Zealand
Nigeria
Norway
Oman
Pakistan
Papua New Guinea
Philippines
Poland
Portugal
Reunion
Romania
Russian Federation
Serbia and Montenegro
Singapore
Slovak Republic
Slovenia
South Africa
Spain
Sri Lanka
Sudan
Swaziland
Sweden

| | |
|---|---|
| Argentina | Luxembourg |
| India | Switzerland |
| Indonesia | Taiwan |
| Ireland | Tajikistan |
| Israel | Thailand |
| Italy | Trinidad & Tobago |
| Ivory Coast | Tunisia |
| Jamaica | Turkey |
| Japan | Turkmenistan |
| Jordan | Uganda |
| Kazakhstan | Ukraine |
| Kenya | USA |
| Korea | Uzbekistan |
| Kuwait | Venezuela |
| Latvia | Vietnam |
| Lesotho | Zambia |
| Lithuania | Zimbabwe |

The Treasury has the power to make regulations adding to the list of territories that qualify even if the double taxation treaty in question does not contain an appropriate non-discrimination article, or to exclude territories even if the treaty in question does contain such an article (HMRC International Manual INTM 432112).

## Election to remain subject to transfer pricing rules

**14.13** There may be occasions where a business wishes to apply transfer pricing rules even though it would qualify for exemption. A business can elect that the exemption will not apply. An election can be made for a specified chargeable period and will cover all transactions or provisions made in that period. It will be irrevocable.

## A pre-existing dormant company

**14.14** A dormant company that was dormant for an accounting period ending on 31 March 2004, or for the whole of the three months prior to 1 April 2004, is exempt from transfer pricing for accounting periods commencing on or after 1 April 2004 as long as it remains dormant. If it engages in any business activity it will lose its exemption (*ICTA 1988, Sch 28AA, para 5A*).

## Compensating relief

**14.15** Where transactions take place between two UK taxpayers and a transfer pricing adjustment is made to the corporation tax return of one taxpayer, the other party may claim compensating relief in its corporation tax return in order to prevent profits being taxed twice (*ICTA 1988, Sch 28AA, para 6*). The claimant company is required to indicate on the front of CT600 if a compensating adjustment has been claimed.

This may bring about other adjustments if the effects are worked through, for example, to the double tax credit if double taxation is involved (*ICTA 1988, Sch 28AA, para 7*).

## Balancing payments

**14.16** If the claimant company makes a payment to the tax advantage company up to the amount of the compensating relief this is without any tax effect (*ICTA 1988, Sch 28AA, para 7A*).

Transfer pricing does not apply to FOREX or to financial instrument legislation.

Other provisions deal with transactions not at arm's length in these cases (*ICTA 1988, Sch 28AA, para 8*) but transfer pricing rules apply to sales of oil and gas produced by a company in which the buyer and linked companies have an interest of 20% or more (*ICTA 1988, Sch 28AA, para 9*).

## Appeal hearings

**14.17** Appeal hearings are heard by the Special Commissioners (*ICTA 1988, Sch 28AA, para 12*).

## Capital allowances and chargeable gains

**14.18** The transfer pricing rules do not apply to capital allowances (including balancing charges), chargeable gains or allowable capital losses (*ICTA 1988, Sch 28AA, para 13*).

## Matching loans and derivatives

**14.19** A corporate group structure may assist with the external borrowing facilities for the individual group members. Further advantage may be taken of the group structure by one group member taking out a foreign currency loan to match a non-monetary asset acquired by another group member. The loan may then be further lent to the asset acquiring company interest-free. In addition, the company may enter into a forward exchange contract to cover the forward exchange risk. From 1 April 2004 no transfer pricing adjustment is required for foreign exchange gains and losses on 'matching' loans (*ICTA 1988, Sch 28AA, para 8*). However, from 22 March 2006 artificial losses created by contrived arrangements were disallowed (*Loan Relationships and Derivative Contracts* (*Disregard and Bringing into Account of Profits and Losses*) *Regulations 2006, SI 2006/843, reg 5* and *Loan Relationships and Derivative Contracts* (*Disregard and Bringing into Account of Profits and Losses*) (*Amendment*) *Regulations 2006, SI 2006/936, reg 5*).

## Interest-free loans

**14.20** Under the transfer pricing regulations an interest-free loan between related parties will attract a tax charge on the lender (*ICTA 1988, Sch 28AA, para 1*) and a compensating adjustment for the ultimate borrower (*ICTA 1988, Sch 28AA, para 6*). The foreign exchange element of these adjustments is ignored for transfer pricing purposes (*ICTA 1988, Sch 28AA, para 8*).

Where asset backed matching loans are involved, the company with the debtor loan relationship would normally follow SSAP 20 and take the foreign exchange gains and losses on both the asset and the matching loan to reserves. The company with the creditor loan relationship will record foreign exchange gains and losses on the loan to the group company and the loan from a third party (external to the group) in its loans in its profit and loss account.

Foreign exchange gains and losses of the debtor loan relationship company are excluded from taxable income for corporation tax purposes, where they can be matched against gains and losses from an asset (*FA 1996, s 84A*(*3*)(*b*)). *Loan Relationships and Derivative Contracts* (*Disregard and Bringing into Account of Profits and Losses*) *Regulations 2004, SI 2004/3256, reg 3*, from 1 January 2005 to 22 March 2006, will apply to disregard such exchange differences. Where an arm's length adjustment is required, only the arm's-length element will become chargeable. If the company would not have been able to borrow at all in an arm's-length situation no amount of the foreign exchange gain or loss will be taxable.

Foreign exchange gains and losses of the creditor loan relationship are brought to account immediately through the profit and loss account (*FA 1996, s 84A*(*1*)).

## Loans on which interest is charged

**14.21** If interest is charged on an intra-group loan the tax treatment for the company with the debtor loan relationship is exactly the same. This is because the effect of the matching rules is to disregard the foreign exchange gain or loss arising.

The company with a non-arm's-length creditor loan relationship that receives a less than arm's-length amount of interest is in the same position as if no interest had been charged on the loan.

If the amount of interest receivable on the loan is more than an arm's-length amount the non-arm's-length amount of the foreign exchange gain or loss is disregarded. If a group company acts as guarantor it can make a compensating adjustment claim (*ICTA 1988, Sch 28AA, para 6D*).

Otherwise the result is that the creditor does not have a symmetrical position as far as its foreign exchange gains and losses on its lending and borrowing are concerned.

## Currency contracts

**14.22** In general the foreign exchange gains and losses on 'matching' currency contracts are also disregarded for transfer pricing purposes (*ICTA 1988, Sch 28AA, para 8*).

However, transfer pricing rules will apply to premium receipts and to non-arm's-length interest payments. Arrangements to assign, terminate or vary a currency contract may also fall within the transfer pricing conditions. *FA 2002, Sch 26, para 27* applies to tax the amount of the gain that would have been taxed had an arm's-length rate applied.

# SELF-ASSESSMENT

**14.23** There are no supplementary pages to a tax return, which relate to transfer pricing; businesses make computational adjustments in their returns in cases where transactions as recorded in their accounts are not at arm's length. A business (as in **14.13**) wishing to make an election to remain subject to transfer pricing rules should do so as part of its computation of taxable income in its return.

Companies are required to make tax returns in accordance with the arm's-length principle. If a company submits a fraudulent or negligent return (see

**2.27**) a tax-related penalty may be charged (*ICTA 1988, Sch 18, para 20*). The maximum penalty is the tax lost. A Revenue officer authorised by HMRC has the power to determine a penalty at any amount he considers appropriate (*TMA 1970, s 100*(*1*)).

Such a penalty can ensue if a company fails to comply with the transfer pricing requirements. This is the case if the company had been negligent.

Negligence must be judged on its own facts and merits, with the guiding principle being that a company will not have been negligent if it has done what 'a reasonable person would do'. Where a company can show that it has made an honest and reasonable attempt to comply with the legislation, there will be no penalty even if there is an adjustment. Indeed, the onus will be on the Revenue in this area, as it is more generally, to show that there has been fraudulent or negligent conduct by the taxpayer before any penalty can be charged.

There is therefore an obligation on taxpayers to do what a reasonable person would to ensure that their returns are made in accordance with the arm's-length principle. This would involve, but not be limited to:

- using their commercial knowledge and judgment to make arrangements and set prices, which conform to the arm's-length standard (or to make computational adjustments in their returns where they do not);
- being able to show (for example, by means of good quality documentation) that they made an honest and reasonable attempt to comply with the arm's-length standard and with the legislation; and
- seeking professional help where they know they need it.

Taxpayers should document what they do to the extent necessary to enable them to sustain the arm's-length nature of their arrangements and prices in any discussions with the Revenue. The documentation will include the following:

- the relevant commercial or financial relations falling within the scope of the new legislation;
- the nature and terms (including prices) of relevant transactions (including transactions which form a series, and any relevant offsetting transactions). Transactions which are clearly in one family (eg regular purchases made by a distributor throughout a return period of the same or similar products for resale) may be aggregated, provided any significant changes during the period in the nature or terms of the transactions are recorded;
- the method or methods by which the nature and terms of relevant transactions were arrived at, including any study of comparables and any functional analysis undertaken;

- how that method has resulted in arm's-length terms etc or, where it has not, what computational adjustment is required and how it has been calculated. This will usually include an analysis of market data or other information on third party comparables;
- the terms of relevant commercial arrangements with both third party and affiliated customers. These will include commercial agreements (eg service or distribution contracts, loan agreements), and any budgets, forecasts or other papers containing information relied on in arriving at arm's-length terms etc or in calculating any adjustment made in order to satisfy the requirements of the new transfer pricing legislation.

In order to be adequate the documentation must show that the company had good grounds for believing their arrangements and prices were in accordance with the arm's-length principle.

HMRC have provided the following examples for illustration purposes.

---

**Example 14.1**

A company, whose business is to provide services to other group members, charges out its services at cost plus 5%. 5% accords with a policy in place throughout the group, and is documented in correspondence involving members of the main Board, the Finance Directorate, and the Tax Department; and in a group agreement. It is established in discussion with the Revenue that the arm's-length range for the services in question is 10%–15%. The company cannot show from its records that it even considered whether its own 5% rate complied with the arm's-length principle. The Revenue would view any tax lost as a result of the undercharge as having been lost through negligence, and would wish to consider a penalty.

---

**Example 14.2**

As Example 14.1, except that in the correspondence it is asserted several times that the group's policy is to comply with the arm's-length standard, and that 5% is an arm's-length price. However, the company is unable to bring forward any convincing evidence in support of its assertions, while the Revenue is able to show that an arm's-length price would be in the 10%–15% range. The Revenue would wish to consider a penalty.

---

**Example 14.3**

As Example 14.1, except that the company charges out at cost plus 8%, and can show that at the time the rate was set it had run a check of available industry data, and had found what it considered to be a comparable uncontrolled price supporting the 8% rate. In discussion with the Revenue, the company agrees that the comparable it used was flawed, and that the weight of evidence points towards a price in the 10%–15% range. The Revenue accepts that the company had made an honest and reasonable attempt to comply with the arm's-length principle. There is an adjustment but no penalty.

---

**Example 14.4**

A company, whose business is to provide services to other group members, charges at cost plus 5%. As in Example 14.1, 5% accords with a policy in place throughout the group, and is documented in correspondence and a group agreement. The company includes an adjustment in its computation, bringing the effective rate of charge-out up to 8%. It did so after searching available industry data for possible comparable uncontrolled prices, this search being made at the time the tax computation was being prepared. As with Example 14.3, the company sees this information as supporting its opinion that 8% accorded with the arm's-length principle, but it later agrees that the price should have fallen in the 10%–15% range. Once again, the Revenue accepts that the company had made an honest and reasonable attempt to comply with the arm's-length principle, and there is an adjustment but no penalty.

---

**14.24** The factors which the Board takes into account when considering abatement are described in leaflet IR 160 (see **2.19**). These will apply to penalties arising from transfer pricing adjustments.

When considering the abatement in relation to the size and gravity of the failure the Revenue will take into account the absolute size of the adjustment; the size of the adjustment relative to the turnover and profitability of the business against which the adjustment is being made; and where this is possible, the size of the adjustment in relation to the volume and value of the related party transactions giving rise to the adjustment (Tax Bulletins, Issues 37 October 1998 and 38 December 1998).

## Record keeping

**14.25** The record keeping in **14.22** above was suggested in 1998. Under self-assessment, the requirement is for companies to keep records to support its transfer pricing policy, its arm's-length justification policy and the adjustments made to the corporation tax return. The records kept will vary to each country and to each particular company's circumstances. General guidance is given in Chapter V of the OECD Transfer Pricing Guidelines.

The self-assessment penalties will ensue upon the company if the company were unable to supply supporting records. As a transitional measure, businesses were relieved from penalty exposure for failure to provide 'arm's-length' evidence for the two years ended 31 March 2006.

As regards evidence to support an arm's-length policy HMRC have now suggested the following:

- Associated businesses should be identified and the form of association.
- Description of business activity in which transactions took place.
- Details of contractual relationship and understanding between the parties involved.
- Description and justification for method used to establish the arm's length result.
- Evidence need not be provided where companies do not fall within the UK transfer pricing rules.
- Useful to provide supporting information regarding the company's general strategy.
- English translations of documentation should also be given.

The European Commission has adopted a proposal for a Code of Conduct to standardise the documentation that multinationals must provide to tax authorities on their pricing of cross-border intra-group transactions. The documentation would consist of two main parts; namely a 'blueprint' master file of the transfer pricing system together with business information and standardised documents for intra-group transactions.

It is expected that member states would implement the Code by legislating for it in national law or through administrative guidelines. Until then companies must comply with the national documentation requirement IP/05/1403 and MEMO/05/414.

## Enquiries

**14.26** An enquiry would follow normal HMRC enquiry procedures. In particular HMRC would seek evidence to support the arm's-length policy.

## Thin capitalisation

**14.27** Where a UK group member company borrows more from an internal or external lender than it would do if it were not part of a group, it is said to be thinly capitalized. Interest payments are deductible from taxable profits but dividend payments are not so deductible. Companies who structure their investments in subsidiaries by means of inordinate large loans may also fall within the thin capitalisation rules.

The result is that the admissible interest deduction from assessable profits is restricted to an arm's-length amount. All parts of the borrowing arrangement will be examined to ascertain if thin capitalisation is involved including guarantees and the like.

Thin capitalisation falls within the transfer pricing regime (*ICTA 1988, Sch 28AA*). Until 1 April 2004 it was dealt with by treating the amount as a dividend (*ICTA 1988, s 209*(2)(*da*)). *ICTA 1988, s 209*(2)(*da*) only applied where there was a 75% overseas relationship (together with effective 51% subsidiaries) between borrower and lender, whereas transfer pricing applies to all UK and overseas relationships with no 75% demarcation.

## Payments of interest abroad

**14.28** Subject to any existing double taxation agreement, payments of annual interest to an overseas lender are made net of withholding tax. The rate of withholding tax is linked to the basic rate of income tax (HMRC International Manual INTM 542010) (*ICTA 1988, s 349*(2)). Assessments can be raised to recover any outstanding withholding tax together with any accrued interest (*ICTA 1988, Sch 16*; *TMA 1970, s 87*).

## Advance pricing agreement (APA)

**14.29** A company with more complex affairs can enter into an APA with HMRC (*FA 1999, s 85*). APAs are written agreements between a taxpayer and HMRC, which determine a method for resolving intricate transfer pricing issues in advance of a return being made. If the terms of the arrangement are complied with, the company can be assured that HMRC will accept those transfer issues covered by the agreement.

The matters that can be covered include the determination of:

- the arm's-length provision for the purposes of *ICTA 1988, Sch 28AA, s 770A*;
- the profits attributable to a branch or agency through which a trade is carried on in the UK; and
- the amount of any income arising outside the UK and attributable to the overseas branch of a UK company.

HMRC recommend bilateral agreements rather than unilateral agreements. The APA will be operative for a specified number of years from the date of entry into force as set out in the agreement. The term is normally for a minimum of three, and a maximum of five, years. The formal submission of an APA request should normally be made no later than six months before the start of the first chargeable period to be covered by the APA. The APA process will typically comprise four stages: expression of interest, formal submission of application for clarification, evaluation, and agreement. In essence, when agreed if prices are set in accordance with the APA they will satisfy the transfer pricing regulations. SP 3/99 gives further details.

*Chapter 15*

# Reconstructions and Amalgamations

## BUYING AND SELLING A COMPANY

### Buying a company

**15.1** Purchase of another company's share capital requires careful consideration. Depending upon the percentage acquired the new acquisition will be a subsidiary or an investment for the acquiree. All taxation aspects of the transaction must be considered, not only corporation tax but also VAT and stamp duty land tax (for VAT: see *Tottel's Tax Annual VAT 2006/07*).

### Asset purchase

**15.2** Alternatively the company may wish to consider an asset purchase. In this case the acquired company is absorbed into the existing company rather than being maintained as a separate corporate unit. Apart from the normal funding and synergy issues the acquiring company will need to consider a variety of issues affecting the taxation impact of the transaction.

The purchased tangible and intangible assets will be included within the company's fixed assets as shown on the balance sheet. In particular the excess of the purchase price of the assets acquired over the price paid: namely the goodwill will also be shown on the balance sheet. This in turn will form an intangible asset for which an annual tax-deductible write down is available (see **7.10**).

The company will also be able to utilise the newly acquired asset in a roll-over relief claim for fixed assets (see **6.51**) and intangible assets (see **7.21**). The assets are also established at a high base cost for capital gains tax purposes, because the gain to date is assessed on the predecessor company.

The acquisition of stock will be a deduction from trading profits. Importantly the purchaser avoids taking over any of the vendor's liabilities.

For capital allowances purposes the assets in question are disposed of by the vendor; balancing charges and allowances arising and acquired by the successor. If the companies are connected within the definition given by *ICTA 1988, s 839* then *ICTA 1988, s 343* may apply as described later in this chapter. If *s 343* does not apply both companies may elect for the assets to be transferred at tax written-down value. If this occurs during an accounting period the allowances are proportioned pro-rata (*CAA 2001, ss 266, 569*).

Whether or not connected, the purchaser and the vendor may wish to make use of the provisions of *CAA 2001, s 198*, which allows the parties to jointly elect that sale proceeds relating to a building inclusive of fixtures be allocated agreed by the parties. The value must not be more than cost (*CAA 2001, s 198*).

### Acquisition finance costs

**15.3** Regardless of a share or asset purchase, the company will invariably require the use of borrowed funds to finance the acquisition. Any interest or finance costs charged in acquiring a company are non-trading debits within the loan relationship regime. They are not costs in connection with the trade (see **11.25** for the utilisation of non-trading debits).

### Selling a company

**15.4** The 'reversed' considerations to acquiring a company must be considered when selling a company. If the assets are to be sold a chargeable gain may arise within the company. The company may be cash-rich, which then presents a problem for cash extraction. If the company is owned by individual investors they will need to consider their own capital gains position if the company is to be wound up or sold (see *Tottel's Capital Gains Tax 2006/07*). In practical terms the sale may be negotiated to make use of the *s 343* relief as described in **15.11** onwards.

If shares are to be sold and another company owns the company it may be able to make use of the substantial shareholdings exemption, see **12.28–12.32**.

## COMPANY RECONSTRUCTIONS AND AMALGAMATIONS

### Introduction

**15.5** The development of a limited company's trading activity may mean that it has to change its structure. Shares in a corporate structure can be bought or sold or created or cancelled. Shares may be owned by individuals or large corporations alike. A change in a company's capital structure may be a necessity to enable it to carry on its future activities. Such changes will have taxation consequences. This may involve the formation of a new company and the transfer of the predecessor's assets to the new company. The result being that the ownership of the business remains in the same hands, but is earned through a different corporate structure. The shareholders receive a share for share exchange.

## Companies Act 1985

**15.6** The *Companies Act 1985* permits reconstructions and amalgamations subject to certain conditions. The requirements are detailed in *Companies Act 1985, ss 425–427A* and in *Insolvency Act 1986, s 110.*

The court will authorise an arrangement with the members (or creditors) of the company provided this is voted on with 75% agreeing to the scheme at the company meeting (*CA 1985, s 425*). *Companies Act 1985, s 427* gives the courts the power to order a scheme. *Insolvency Act 1986, s 110* permits a liquidator to transfer the company's business or property to another company. The liquidator will receive shares for the distribution. Any dissenting member may require the liquidator to purchase his shares.

# CAPITAL GAINS TAX

## Reorganisation of share capital

**15.7** In effect the action that the company takes is to transfer the company's assets to another company in exchange for shares. A reorganisation of share capital whereby the shareholder receives new shares in exactly the same proportion as the old shares is tax neutral. No charge to CGT arises. The new shares are deemed to have been acquired at exactly the same time as the old shares (*TCGA 1992, ss 126–131*).

Any cash received is treated either as a capital distribution or as a part disposal (*TCGA 1992, ss 122, 128*). Consideration given for the new holding is treated as being given for the original holding but is indexed from the time that it is given rather than from the time that the original shareholding was acquired.

## Company reconstructions

**15.8** The no gain/no loss treatment contained in *TCGA 1992, ss 127–131*, will also apply to a company reconstruction in the following situation. The situation is such that a company issues shares or debentures to a person in exchange for shares or debentures that person owns in another company and:

- as a result of the exchange, the successor company holds or will hold more than 25% of the ordinary share capital of the original company, or
- the successor company issues shares or debentures as a result of a general offer made conditional upon the successor company acquiring control over the original company to the members of the successor company or any class of them, or
- the successor company holds or will hold as a result of the exchange the greater part of the voting power of the original company (*TCGA 1992, s 135*).

Further rules apply if the shares in the successor company are cancelled. The shareholders will benefit from the *TCGA 1992, ss 127–131* treatment provided the following conditions are satisfied. Conditions one and two must be met together with either condition three or condition four.

**Condition 1**. The successor must only issue ordinary shares to the original company's ordinary shareholders (*TCGA 1992, Sch 5AA, para 2*) and not to any other party.

**Condition 2**. The original shareholders all obtain the same proportional entitlement to shares in the new company. There is no requirement that all the shareholders of the old company become shareholders in the new company but the shares must be issued to the same persons (*TCGA 1992, Sch 5AA, para 3*).

**Condition 3**. There must be continuity of the business. The whole of the business must be carried on by one successor company or by two or more successor companies of which the original company may be one (*TGCA 1992, Sch 5AA, para 4*).

**Condition 4**. The scheme is carried out in pursuance of a compromise arrangement under *CA 1985, s 425* or foreign equivalent and no part of the business is transferred to any other person (*TCGA 1992, Sch 5AA, para 5*).

## Bona fide commercial arrangements

**15.9** The conditions only apply if the scheme is made for bona fide commercial arrangements where the main purpose is not the avoidance of capital gains tax. This restriction does not apply to holders of less than 5% of the shares. If the conditions are not met or there is found to be an anti-avoidance purpose, HMRC can collect the tax from any of the shareholders concerned (*TCGA 1992, s 137*). A tax avoidance purpose was found in *Snell v*

*HMRC Comrs* SpC 532, [2006] STC (SCD) 296. On advice received from an adviser, a taxpayer became non-resident to avoid a capital gains tax liability. The Special Commissioners decided that as the taxpayer had full knowledge and understanding of the proposed course of action it arose from a tax avoidance purpose.

The company may apply for a clearance to HMRC that the proposed reconstruction or reorganisation is for bona fide commercial purposes. The full facts of the transaction should be given to HMRC who have 30 days to reply. If HMRC does not issue a clearance notice to the company, the company may refer its case to the Special Commissioners (*TCGA 1992, s 138*). See **18.4** for further details regarding clearance procedures.

## Reconstruction involving transfer of business

**15.10** Where the whole or part of a business is transferred to another company for no consideration apart from taking over the liabilities, the asset transfer apart from the trading stock is deemed to take place for such consideration that provides neither gain nor loss (*TCGA 1992, s 139*). More often than not the consideration in such circumstances is a share exchange for the shareholders concerned.

Again for this section to apply the transfer must be made for bona fide commercial purposes. Similar provisions relate to intangible assets (*FA 2002, Sch 29, para 84*). A clearance procedure is also available (*FA 2002, Sch 29, para 88*).

This situation whereby some or all of a company's assets or liabilities are transferred from one company to a successor company is commonly known as 'a hive down'. The successor company is often newly formed. Such a transaction is used to facilitate a company sale; so that only the chosen activities and assets and liabilities are taken over. The transaction may also facilitate a division in a group's activities.

If the reconstruction involves a group relationship (see **10.21** for a definition of a group), company assets can be transferred between group members without a charge to capital gains arising (*TCGA 1992, s 171*). However, if the company subsequently leaves the group a capital gains tax charge will crystallise. The capital gain is based on the market value of the asset at the date of transfer. The gain is deemed to arise at the end of the accounting period in which the company leaves the group (*TCGA 1992, s 179*).

This provision does not apply to inter-group asset transfers between associated companies who cease to be group members at the same time (*TCGA 1992, s 179*(*2*)). The companies must remain associated after they leave the group. For this purpose 'associated companies' are defined as companies that would themselves form a group (*TCGA 1992, s 179*(*10*)).

## TRADING LOSSES

### Company reconstruction without a change of ownership

**15.11** The utilisation of trading losses is restricted where a trade ceases and where there is a change of ownership of the company (*ICTA 1988, ss 768, 768A*) as discussed in **9.17–9.19**. Where there is a company reconstruction without a change of ownership and a continuing trade, the losses incurred by the previous company will be available to set against profits earned by the new company provided the same ownership and charging conditions apply pre and post transfer (*ICTA 1988, s 343*). Loss relief is given automatically without claim. It is necessary for the same trade to continue.

There is also a restriction on management expenses and Schedule A losses. See **12.13**, **12.22**. The restrictions placed on an intangible assets unused non-trading loss are similar to trading losses (*ICTA 1988, s 768C*).

### Ownership

**15.12** Ownership of the trade is the beneficial ownership obtained by ownership of the share capital. The ownership condition is met if, at any time within two years after the transfer of trade, the beneficial ownership was held by the same person or persons as at any time within the 12 months prior to the transfer of trade (*ICTA 1988, s 343*(*1*)(*a*)). No minimum period of ownership is required, but in practice HMRC may query short periods of ownership.

### Charge to corporation tax

**15.13** The charging condition is met if the trade has been carried on by companies within the charge to corporation tax within the prescribed period of ownership (*ICTA 1988, s 343*(*1*)(*b*)). The situation not only applies to UK resident companies but also to non-resident companies chargeable to corporation tax in respect of a trade carried on by a UK branch or agent. The relief applies to a 'trade' and will also apply if part of a trade is transferred (*ICTA 1988, s 343*(*8*)).

## Relief

**15.14** Normally, when a company ceases to trade, its corporation tax liability is computed as though this was a discontinuance (*ICTA 1988, s 337*). This is not the case under *s 343*.

Essentially the trade is not treated as discontinued and a new one commenced. Capital allowances continue uninterrupted with balancing charges falling on the successor company (*ICTA 1988, s 343*(2)). The loss carried forward by the successor is reduced by any excess of liabilities taken over (*ICTA 1988, s 343*(*4*)).

It should be noted that the relief only applies to trading losses. Schedule A losses; the remaining Schedule D losses, management expenses, non-trading loan relationship deficits etc are not included.

## Beneficial ownership

**15.15** Ownership of the ordinary share capital for these purposes is the beneficial ownership. Ordinary share capital is defined in *ICTA 1988, s 832* and means all the issued share capital of the company, by whatever name it is called, other than capital whose holders have only a right to a dividend at a fixed rate, but have no other right to share in the profits.

A beneficial owner is not necessarily the person in whose name the ordinary shares are registered. A person who holds shares as a nominee is not a beneficial owner (*ICTA 1988, s 344*(*3*)(*a*)). Beneficial ownership is established by looking through to the ultimate owners.

**15.16** The ownership of a trade is established whenever the *s 343* and *s 344* trade ownership tests are met. Ownership can fall to the holders of the ordinary share capital of the company carrying it on under *ICTA 1988, s 344*(2)(*a*), or to the parent of the company carrying on the trade under *ICTA 1988, s 344*(2)(*b*). Ultimately the holders of the ordinary share capital of the parent under *ICTA 1988, s 344*(2)(*b*) may be the beneficial owners of the company. Finally, as will apply in most owner-manager controlled companies, the person or persons who by voting power, or by powers given in the Articles of Association or other document regulating the company, can direct or control the affairs of a company, which directly or indirectly owns the ordinary share capital of the company carrying on the trade (*ICTA 1988, s 344*(2)). HMRC will look to the person who can control the company 'by other means', which seems to imply that they may accept an arrangement not formalised by a written document (HMRC Company Taxation Manual CTM 06020).

A 75% parent and subsidiary ownership relationship is required for *ICTA 1988, s 344*(2)(*b*) above, under *ICTA 1988, s 344*(3)(*b*). Relatives are treated as a single person and include spouses, civil partners (with effect from 5 December 2005), siblings, children and grandchildren etc, and parents and grandparents etc.

---

**Example 15.1**

Matthew, Mark and Luke each own 33.33% outright of the ordinary share capital of the publishing company W Ltd. H Ltd takes over the publishing trade from W Ltd. Matthew, Mark, Luke and John each own 25% of H Ltd.

Common ownership of the trade is achieved because the same group of persons owns not less than 75% of both companies.

---

---

**Example 15.2**

Sleekstyles Ltd manufactured hairdressing products but is now dormant. On 1 January 2007 Sleekstyles Ltd trade was taken over by Crazystyles Ltd. The percentage ownership of the ordinary shares of both companies is as follows:

| | *Sleekstyles Ltd* % | *Crazystyles Ltd* % |
|---|---|---|
| William | 60 | 40 |
| Nathan | 20 | 40 |
| Roger | 10 | 8 |
| Susan | 5 | 7 |
| Clementine | 3 | 3 |
| Nadia | 2 | 2 |
| Total | 100 | 100 |

William and Nathan formalised their relationship by entering into civil partnership on 5 December 2005. Roger and Susan became engaged to be married on 1 January 2006. Clementine and Nadia are senior employees. William and Nathan's shares are aggregated. Common ownership of the trade is achieved because the same group of persons owns not less than 75% of both companies.

---

**15.17** For the relief to be given beneficial ownership of the shares must be in place.

In *Wood Preservation Ltd v Prior* (1969) 45 TC 112, [1969] 1 All ER 364, the carry forward of loss relief was denied because Wood Preservation Ltd's trade was transferred after its parent company lost beneficial ownership of Wood's shares. HMRC explain that beneficial ownership passes from vendor to purchaser where an unconditional sale document is signed. If the contract is subject to a condition the beneficial ownership does not pass until the condition is satisfied. Equally a legal owner of shares can lose the beneficial ownership if that person entered into an unconditional contract to sell the shares in advance of signing a contract. An oral agreement can be an unconditional contract (HMRC Company Taxation Manual CTM 06030). Therefore a potential vendor should be particularly vigilant with respect to the point in time at which beneficial ownership is transferred.

## Transfer of trade

**15.18** HMRC has identified the following four practical situations where either a trade or part of a trade is transferred between companies. Firstly, a succession to an entire trade, arising under *ICTA 1988, s 343*(*1*), where a company ceases to carry on a trade and another company begins to carry it on. Secondly, a transfer of the activities of a trade under *ICTA 1988, s 343*(*8*), where a company ceases to carry on a trade and another begins to carry on the activities of that trade as part of its trade. Thirdly, a transfer of the activities of part of a trade, where a company ceases to carry on part of a trade and another company begins to carry on the activities of that part as its trade, again under *ICTA 1988, s 343*(*8*). Finally, also under *ICTA 1988, s 343*(*8*), where a company ceases to carry on part of a trade and another company begins to carry on the activities of that part as part of its trade (HMRC Company Taxation Manual CTM 06060).

## Succession

**15.19** In practical terms sufficient of the predecessor's trading activities must be transferred to the new company. For example, if, as in the case of Example 15.2, Sleekstyles Ltd transferred its factory, its manufacturing operations and its employees to Crazystyles Ltd without its book debts or its sales distribution unit, this may be a sufficient trading activity transfer to qualify as a succession. In *Malayam Plantations Ltd v Clark* (1935) 19 TC 314 the acquisition of a rubber plantation and its employees without the book debts or the selling organisation was considered to be a 'succession'. The fact that one company actually succeeds to the trade of another company within the same ownership will bring about the relief as in *Wadsworth Morton Ltd v Jenkinson* (1966) 43 TC 479, [1967] 1 WLR 79, [1966] 3 All ER 702.

## Activities of a trade

**15.20** The relief is also given if the predecessor's trade is added to the successor's trade in an identifiable form. For example, two shoe-manufacturing companies supplied shoes wholesale to their parent company for retail sale. The parent company wound up the subsidiaries. It took over the factories and the staff and manufactured the shoes itself. The parent company was denied use of the subsidiaries' losses because although the manufacturing activities continued the wholesale activities failed to continue. The trade was not carried on in the same identifiable form as before the transfer (*Laycock v Freeman Hardy and Willis Ltd* (1938) 22 TC 288, [1939] 2 KB 1, [1938] 4 All ER 609). In *Rolls Royce Motors Ltd v Bamford* (1976) 51 TC 319, [1976] STC 152, it was held that the successor trade was different to that of the predecessor and *s 343* loss relief was denied.

A jeans and casual clothing company made trading losses. A company with which it was associated marketed its merchandise. The marketing company bought the manufacturing company and carried on its trade. The trading losses were available for relief after transfer because the trade continued, although the profits were not earned separately (*Falmer Jeans Ltd v Rodin* (1990) 63 TC 55, [1990] STC 270).

The identifiable form test was also met in *Briton Ferry Steel Co Ltd v Barry* (1939) 23 TC 414, [1940] 1 KB 463, [1939] 4 All ER 541.

## Activities of part of a trade

**15.21** There is no definition of part of a trade within the legislation. HMRC regard part of a trade as being a free-standing apparatus and making profits or losses in its own right. A part of a trade does not have to amount to anything as distinctive as a branch or a division (HMRC Company Taxation Manual CTM 06060).

# LATER EVENTS

**15.22** When a trade is transferred between two companies but the full ownership test is never met, although within two years there is a transfer to a company that does meet the ownership test then *s 343* still applies and it is still possible to transfer losses to the third company (*ICTA 1988, s 343*(*7*)).

## PRACTICAL EFFECTS OF *S 343* RELIEF

### Trading losses carried forward

**15.23** If all conditions apply the successor is able to utilise the remaining predecessor's loss in an *ICTA 1988, s 393(1)* claim against future income from the same trade (*ICTA 1988, s 343(4)*). The remaining loss is the loss that the predecessor has not utilised less the relevant liabilities restriction. The relevant liabilities restriction is the difference between the retained relevant liabilities, the retained relevant assets and the consideration (*ICTA 1988, s 343(5), (6)*).

The relevant liabilities are taken at their actual value immediately before the predecessor ceased to trade. Relevant liabilities exclude share capital, share premium, reserves or relevant loan stock and any liabilities transferred to the successor. Inter-group debts are included in relevant liabilities (*ICTA 1988, s 344(6)*). Relevant loan stock can be secured or unsecured but not that arising from a person carrying on the trade of moneylending (*ICTA 1988, s 344(11), (12)*).

Relevant assets are the assets that the company owned immediately before it ceased to trade (*ICTA 1988, s 344(5)(a)*) and are valued at market value (*ICTA 1988, s 344(7)*).

The consideration is the amount given by the predecessor to the successor of the trade. Liabilities assumed by the successor are not included within the consideration (*ICTA 1988, s 344(5)(b)*). However, if a liability is transferred to the successor and the creditor agrees to accept less than the full amount due in settlement of the outstanding debt, the shortfall is treated as a liability for the purposes of the restriction.

If losses exceed the net relevant liabilities there is no restriction. Any losses disallowed are not available to the predecessor company (*ICTA 1988, s 343(4)*). Where part of a trade is transferred, a just apportionment of receipts, expenses, assets or liabilities is to be made for this purpose (*ICTA 1988, s 343(9)*). The restriction only applies to trading losses and not to capital allowances and balancing charges.

The release of a trading debt will be a taxable receipt of the trade (*ICTA 1988, s 94*).

---

**Example 15.3**

Alfonso Ltd took over the trade and assets of Bertino Ltd on 1 January 2007. *Section 343* relief applies. Bertino Ltd's unutilised trading losses amount to £150,000. Neither cash nor trade creditors are included in the sale. The balance sheet at 31 December 2006 directly before transfer is shown below. The business is assumed to be sold by Alfonso Ltd to Bertino Ltd for:

(i) £10,000, and

(ii) £100,000.

**Bertino Ltd: Balance sheet at 31 December 2006**

| | *£000* | *£000* |
|---|---|---|
| Fixed assets | | |
| Plant and machinery | | 60 |
| Current assets | | |
| Stock | 20 | |
| Debtors | 10 | |
| Cash | 5 | |
| | 35 | |
| Current liabilities | | |
| Trade creditors | 30 | |
| | | 5 |
| | | 65 |
| Shareholders' funds | | |
| Share capital | | 50 |
| Profit and loss account | | 15 |
| | | 65 |

The restriction is calculated as follows:

(i) Sale proceeds: £10,000

| | *£000* |
|---|---|
| Trade creditors | 30 |
| Less cash | (5) |
| | 25 |
| Less sale consideration | (10) |
| Loss relief restriction | 15 |

The losses that are available for relief are £150,000 – 15,000 = £145,000

(ii) Sale proceeds: £100,000

| | *£000* |
|---|---|
| Trade creditors | 30 |
| Less cash | (5) |
| | 25 |
| Less sale consideration | (100) |
| Loss relief restriction | (75) |

As the sale consideration exceeds the value of the liabilities and assets not taken over there is no loss restriction.

If only £50,000 of the plant were taken over the restriction would be calculated as follows:

| *Sale proceeds* | *£10,000* | *£100,000* |
|---|---|---|
| | *£000* | *£000* |
| Trade creditors | 30 | 30 |
| Less plant retained | (10) | (10) |
| Less cash | (5) | (5) |
| | 15 | 15 |
| Less sale consideration | (10) | (100) |
| Loss relief restriction | 5 | (75) |

If the company is sold for £10,000 the losses that are available for relief are £150,000 – £10,000 = £140,000

If the company is sold for £100,000 there is no loss restriction as the sale consideration continues to exceed the value of the liabilities and assets not taken over.

## Capital allowances

**15.24** For capital allowances purposes where a company is sold to a successor such that the original company's trade ceases (*ICTA 1988, s 337*(*1*)) the assets are deemed to be sold to the new company at market value. Therefore balancing charges and allowances will ensue for the predecessor (*CAA 2001, s 559*).

If the conditions of *s 343* apply the assets are transferred from predecessor to successor at tax written-down value. If the transfer is made during the accounting period the writing-down allowances are reduced proportionately. When the assets are eventually sold any balancing charge or allowances will fall upon the party carrying on the trade at the time, ie the successor as if he had always owned the assets (*ICTA 1988, s 343*(2)).

*Chapter 16*

# Distributions

## INTRODUCTION

**16.1** A dividend is a shareholder's expected reward for an investment in a limited company. Under company law, a company may declare and distribute a dividend out of its realised profits. The dividend is then payable to the shareholders pro rata to their shareholdings.

For corporation tax purposes, the distribution rules apply whenever cash or assets are passed to the members of the company. For taxation purposes, a dividend is a distribution of profits falling within *ICTA 1988, s 209*(2)(*a*). If the payment relates to the member's services to the company it is not a distribution but a payment for services performed for the company. The payment will be chargeable upon the member as employment income under the rules of *ITEPA 2003* and any payments so made should be relievable by the company for corporation tax purposes.

However, a distribution can take a variety of forms and includes capital (other than a repayment of capital) or assets. For a company shareholder a distribution constitutes franked investment income (if non group) and dividend income for an individual assessable under *ITTOIA 2005, s 384* (see *Tottel's Income Tax 2006/07*).

## MEANING

**16.2** Distribution for corporation tax purposes does not have the same meaning as the company law meaning of distribution of share capital in a winding up. The former deals with allocating profits and the latter with apportioning a company's assets (*ICTA 1988, s 209*(*1*)).

## PAYMENTS CLASSED AS A DISTRIBUTION

**16.3** Particular payments are classed as distributions. These include not only dividends but also bonus securities or redeemable shares, transfers of assets and of liabilities between a company and its members, payments of interest or other distributions to the extent that they exceed a commercial rate, payments of interest or other distributions on certain securities, a bonus issue on or following a repayment of share capital and any other distributions out of assets of the company in respect of shares in the company.

## Dividend

**16.4** In general a dividend paid by a company including a capital dividend is a distribution (*ICTA 1988, s 209*(2)(*a*)). Exceptions are stock dividends and dividends paid by building societies and industrial provident societies. If a company transfers an asset to a member the amount of the distribution is the market value of the asset less the market value of any new consideration given by the member (*ICTA 1988, s 209*(*4*)–(*6*)).

A distribution of shares by a close company to its members when they are worth more is not a distribution but can be a transfer of value between members (*IHTA 1984, s 94*). A dividend waiver may constitute a settlement if there is an element of bounty in the arrangement (*ITTOIA 2005, ss 619–648*).

## Distribution of assets

**16.5** If a distribution of a company's asset is made to members at an undervalue the difference between that and the market value of the asset is treated as a distribution (*ICTA 1988, s 209*(*4*)). If the person to whom the asset is passed is also a director then it is a matter of fact whether he or she receives the asset as shareholder or as employee. If received as an employee the amount will be assessed as employment income (*ICTA 1988, s 209*(2)(*b*), (*4*)). There is no distribution if the payer and the recipient are both UK companies and one is a subsidiary of the other or both are subsidiaries of a third company (*ICTA 1988, s 209*(*5*)). Again there is no distribution between two independent companies, neither of which is a 51% subsidiary of a non-resident company where the companies are not under common control. The *ICTA 1988, s 416* definition of control is used here (*ICTA 1988, s 209*(*6*)). If an asset is transferred from one company to another, any material difference between the market value and the consideration given should be treated as a distribution within *ICTA 1988, s 209*(*4*) or *ICTA 1988, s 209*(2)(*b*) as appropriate unless *ICTA 1988, s 209*(*5*) or *ICTA 1988, s 209*(*6*) applies.

Unless the payments are intra company for *ICTA 1988, s 209*(*5*), (*6*) purposes other payments or asset transfers may be classed as distributions (*ICTA 1988, s 209*(2)(*b*)).

A repayment of share capital is not a distribution.

## Bonus issue subsequent to a repayment

**16.6** A bonus issue subsequent to a repayment of share capital (other than fully paid preference shares) is deemed to be a distribution of the nominal value of the shares so issued and is added to the purchase price of the shares (*ICTA 1988, s 210*). This does not apply to a bonus issue of non-redeemable share capital by a non-close listed company, which takes place more than ten years after the repayment of capital (*ICTA 1988, s 211*).

The distribution is calculated as follows:

the nominal amount of the bonus issue up to the amount of the capital repaid,

*minus*

the new consideration received,

*minus*

any amounts in respect of the same repayment of capital, already treated as distributions under *ICTA 1988, s 210(1)*.

---

**Example 16.1**

A Ltd repays £200,000 of its share capital.

It then issues:

- 100,000 fully paid £1 ordinary shares at 30p per share, and later
- 500,000 fully paid £1 preference shares for no new consideration.

The issue of ordinary shares results in a distribution of:

100,000 × (£1 – £0.30) = £70,000.

The second (bonus) issue is of shares with par value of £500,000 (500,000 × £1).

This distribution is restricted to a maximum of the repayment of share capital less the earlier distribution. The amount of this distribution is, therefore:

£200,000 – £70,000 = £130,000.

---

## Interest and other situations

**16.7** Interest payments in excess of a normal commercial rate of return may be treated as a dividend.

Distributions in a winding up are not income distributions and are subject to capital gains tax. A distribution has an extended meaning for close companies *s 418* (see **4.13**).

There is a general anti-avoidance provision where two companies enter into reciprocal arrangements. Each company makes payments to the other company's members. In this instance the payments are classed as distributions (*ICTA 1988, s 254(8)*).

# NON-QUALIFYING DISTRIBUTION

**16.8** Non-qualifying distributions are bonus issues of redeemable shares or securities. They can be issued directly or issued from bonus redeemable shares or securities received from another company (*ICTA 1988, s 209(2)(c)*).

The amount of the non-qualifying distribution for the purposes of *ICTA 1988, s 209(2)(c)* for redeemable share capital is the excess of the nominal amount of the share capital together with any premium payable on redemption, in a winding up or in any other circumstances over any new consideration received.

Individual shareholders receive a 10% credit and may be charged at the 32.5% upper rate. The company must notify HMRC on form CT2 within 14 days after the end of the quarter in which the non-qualifying distribution is made (*ICTA 1988, s 234(5)*).

# SMALL COMPANY DIVIDEND PAYMENTS

**16.9** Small private company owner managers generally take their reward from their companies in the form of dividends and or remuneration. Remuneration is deductible for corporation tax purposes. Dividend payments are not tax deductible.

If there are no special clauses regarding dividend payments in the Articles of Association Table A *1985 Regulations* will preside. Table A draws a distinction between interim and final dividends.

Final dividends may be declared by the company in general meeting but no dividend shall exceed the amount recommended by the directors (*Article 102*

*Table A 1985 Regulations*). Interim dividends may be paid by directors from time to time (*Article 103 Table A 1985 Regulations*). Directors may only pay interim dividends if it appears to them that they are justified by the profits of the company available for distribution.

The timing of the dividend payment may have a marked impact on the directors' personal taxation situation. A dividend is not paid until the shareholder receives the funds direct or the dividend amount is unreservedly put at his or her disposal, for example by a credit to a loan account from which the shareholder has the power to draw.

Final dividends are normally due and payable on the date of the resolution unless a future date is set for payment. Interim dividends are not an enforceable debt and can be varied or rescinded prior to payment. Interim dividends are due when paid or when the funds are placed at the disposal of the director/shareholders as part of their current accounts with the company. HMRC state that 'payment is not made until such a right to draw on the dividend exists (presumably) when the appropriate entries are made in the company's books. If, as may happen with a small company, such entries are not made until the annual audit, and this takes place after the end of the accounting period in which the directors resolved that an interim dividend be paid, then the "due and payable" date is in the later rather than the earlier accounting period' (HMRC Company Taxation Manual CTM 20095).

For taxation purposes an 'illegal dividend' will be treated in the same way as a legal dividend. However, there is the possibility that if the directors were to pay an interim dividend during an accounting period and it is not possible to demonstrate that the interim dividend payment was paid out of available profits (or alternatively as a repayment of loans due from the company) that HMRC could attack that nature of the payment classing it as remuneration and assess the company for PAYE and NIC. If a shareholder knew or was in a position to know that a dividend was illegal at the time of payment it is refundable to the company. See **4.18**. Companies must therefore be meticulous in their statutory record keeping as regards interim dividend payments.

A final dividend can only be waived before payment. An interim dividend must be waived before entitlement to payment because payment and entitlement take place at the same time. If waiver takes place afterwards it is not an effective waiver but merely a transfer of income.

## SURPLUS ACT

**16.10** Post 6 April 1999 there is no liability to corporation tax if a company makes a distribution payment. Prior to 6 April 1999 if a company made a dividend payment it had to account for advance corporation tax (ACT). ACT was calculated as ¼ of the dividend paid. The ACT paid was, as its name describes, an advance payment of corporation tax. The advance payment could be set against the mainstream liability up to a 20% limit. Any surplus was carried forward for relief in the next year. The problem for companies post 6 April 1999 is to obtain relief for its pre-6 April 1999 surplus ACT against its post-6 April 1999 mainstream corporation tax. It can only do this if it takes account of its 'shadow' or notional ACT.

The company is required to follow this procedure:

1 Calculate the ACT that it would have paid on its distributions.

2 Calculate the maximum ACT set-off.

3 Calculate the remaining offset capacity after the notional ACT has been used.

This can be used to set off the surplus ACT.

---

**Example 16.2**

Lotus Ltd's profits chargeable to corporation tax for the year ended 31 March 2007 amount to £300,000. The company paid a dividend of £35,000 during the year. Surplus ACT brought forward at 1 April 2006 amounts to £90,000. The position is as follows:

| | £ |
|---|---|
| Maximum ACT set-off £300,000 × 20% | 60,000 |
| Less shadow ACT £35,000 × 20/80 | 8,750 |
| Surplus ACT set-off | 51,250 |
| Surplus ACT brought forward | 90,000 |
| Less set-off accounting period ended 31 March 2007 | 51,250 |
| Surplus ACT carried forward | 38,750 |
| The final corporation tax liability is: | |
| Corporation tax | 57,000 |
| Less surplus ACT set-off | 51,250 |
| Final tax liability | 5,750 |

---

**16.11** If a company wishes to make large payments to shareholders it may choose to do so in the form of share capital rather than as a distribution.

However, from 6 April 1999 non-qualifying distributions are included with qualifying distributions for the purposes of calculating shadow ACT (*FA 1998, s 32*; *Corporation Tax* (*Treatment of Unrelieved Surplus Advance Corporation Tax*) *Regulations 1999, SI 1999/358*).

## EXEMPTIONS FROM THE DISTRIBUTION RULES

**16.12** Certain transactions are relieved or exempted from the overall distribution rules. These include:

- Demergers by *ICTA 1988, s 213* and *TCGA 1992, s 192*.
- Purchase by a company of its own shares (*ICTA 1988, s 219*).
- Distributions in a winding up by ESC 16.

## DEMERGERS

**16.13** It may be seen as beneficial for a subsidiary company to leave a group. For this to happen the ownership of the subsidiary's shares passes out of the control of the ultimate holding company to another company or group. This transfer of capital will not be treated as a distribution provided certain conditions apply. Both the distributing and the subsidiary company, whose share are transferred, must be trading companies or holding companies of a trading group at the time of the distribution (*ICTA 1988, s 213*). Both companies must be resident in the UK at the time of the distribution.

**16.14** *ICTA 1988, s 213* facilitates three types of transaction where subject to additional conditions such a transaction is treated as an exempt distribution. SP 13/80 provides additional interpretation and guidance. Exempt distributions may consist of:

(i) A distribution by a company of its shares in one or more 75% subsidiaries.

(ii) A transfer of a company's trade to one or more companies in consideration for the issue of shares in the transferor company.

(iii) A distribution of shares in a 75% subsidiary or subsidiaries to one or more companies which issue their shares to the members of the distributing company.

---

**Example 16.3—(i) A distribution by a company of its shares in one or more 75% subsidiaries (*ICTA 1988, s 213*(3)(*a*))**

This results in a direct demerger.

In this situation B Ltd, a group company, leaves the group, but its ultimate ownership remains with A and B.

Before the demerger:

- A and B owned A Ltd, and
- A Ltd owned B Ltd and C Ltd.

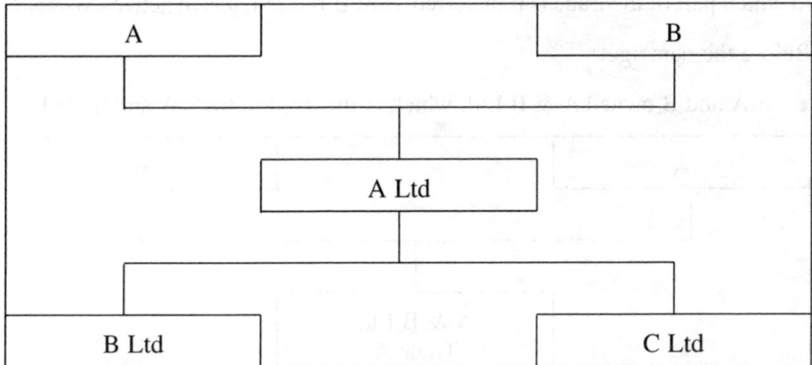

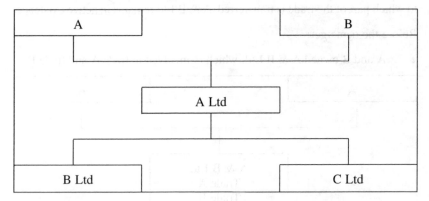

After the demerger:

- A and B own A Ltd and B Ltd, and
- A Ltd owns C Ltd.

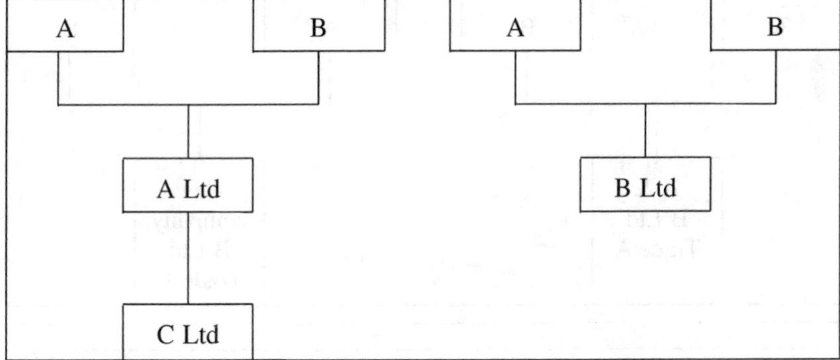


In particular, in this situation, the B Ltd shares that are distributed by A Ltd to A and B, must be non-redeemable and must be the whole or substantially the whole of the ordinary shares and voting rights that A Ltd holds in B Ltd (*ICTA 1988, s 213*(*6*)(*a*)). 'Whole' is interpreted as around 90% or more (SP 13/80).

**Example 16.4—(ii) A distribution of a company's trade or shares in one or more 75% subsidiary companies in consideration for the issue of shares in the transferor company (*ICTA 1988, s 213*(*3*)(*b*))**

This is known as an indirect demerger.

A & B Ltd carries on a trade or trades and the desired effect is for another company to carry on some of its activities. A new company, B Ltd, is formed to which part of the trade is transferred. A & B Ltd remains in active existence.

Before the demerger:

- A and B owned A & B Ltd, which is involved in trade A and trade B.

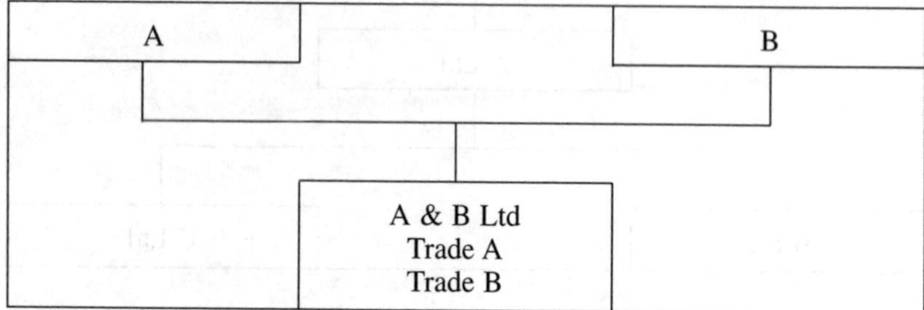


After the demerger:

- A and B own A & B Ltd, which is involved in trade A, and
- A and B own B Ltd, which is involved in trade B.

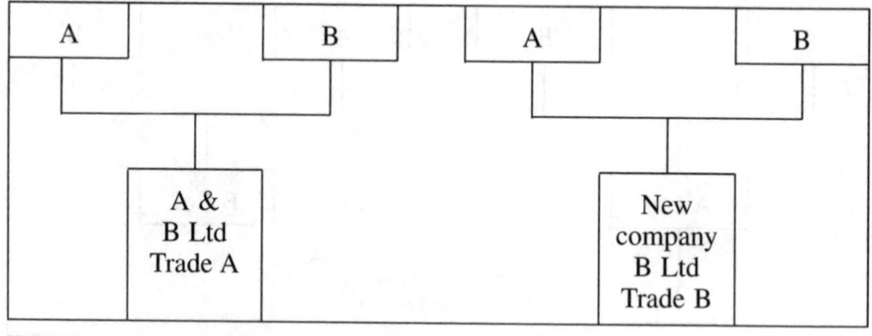


**Example 16.5—(iii) A distribution of shares in a 75% subsidiary or subsidiaries to one or more companies, which issue their shares to the members of the distributing company**

B Ltd, a subsidiary company, leaves the group to be within the ownership of a newly formed company but remains within A and B's ultimate ownership.

Before the demerger:

- A and B owned A Ltd, and
- A Ltd owned B Ltd and C Ltd.

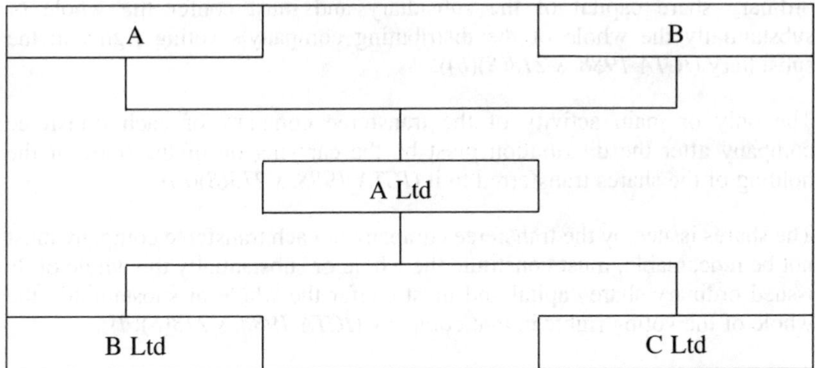


After the demerger:

- A and B own A Ltd and the new company D Ltd,
- A Ltd owns B Ltd, and
- D Ltd owns C Ltd.

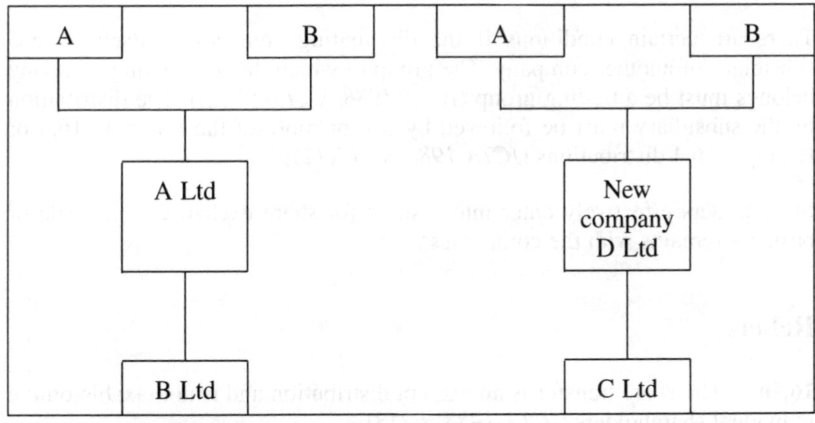


---

**16.15** In the cases above, the transferor, ie A & B Ltd in Example 16.4 and A Ltd in Example 16.5, must not retain any material interest in the transferred trade (*ICTA 1988, s 213(8)(a)*). HMRC give a wide meaning. If the transferor company retained control of the trade or assets or had a material influence on the profit destination this would amount to retaining an interest in the trade. Otherwise a minor interest would amount to around 10% (SP 13/80).

If shares in a subsidiary are transferred those shares must constitute the whole or substantially the whole of the distributing company's holding of the ordinary share capital of the subsidiary and must confer the whole or substantially the whole of the distributing company's voting rights in the subsidiary (*ICTA 1988, s 213*(*8*)(*b*)).

The only or main activity of the transferee company or each transferee company after the distribution must be the carrying on of the trade or the holding of the shares transferred to it (*ICTA 1988, s 213*(*8*)(*c*)).

The shares issued by the transferee company or each transferee company must not be redeemable, must constitute the whole or substantially the whole of its issued ordinary share capital and must confer the whole or substantially the whole of the voting rights in that company (*ICTA 1988, s 213*(*8*)(*d*)).

After (but not 'for ever after' SP13/80) the distribution the distributing company must be either a trading company or the holding company of a trading group unless the transfer relates to two or more subsidiaries and the transferor is dissolved and has no other assets available for distribution or it is itself a 75% subsidiary (*ICTA 1988, s 213*(*6*)(*b*), (*8*)(*d*)). ESC C11 permits the company to retain funds to meet the costs of liquidation and to repay a negligible amount of share capital remaining. Negligible is interpreted as meaning £5,000 or less.

There are certain conditions if the distributing company is itself a 75% subsidiary of another company. The group to which the distributing company belongs must be a trading group (*ICTA 1988, s 213*(*12*)(*a*)). The distribution by the subsidiary must be followed by one or more of the Example 16.3 or Example 16.4 distributions (*ICTA 1988, s 213*(*12*)).

Shareholders effectively enter into a share for share exchange. The trade or business remains with the companies.

## Reliefs

**16.16** The share transfer is an exempt distribution and is not taxable on the individual shareholders (*ICTA 1988, s 213*).

The direct demerger is not treated as a capital distribution under *TCGA 1992, s 122* but instead is treated as a paper for paper reconstruction under *TCGA 1992, ss 126–130*. Thus the capital gains base cost is apportioned to the shares in the transferee company and in the distributing company in proportion to their values at the time of the distribution. There is no charge if the company leaves the group provided the company has not made a chargeable payment within five years of making the exempt distribution. A chargeable payment is a payment that is neither for money's worth nor for commercial purposes but will possibly be part of a tax avoidance scheme (*ICTA 1988, s 214*; *TCGA 1992, s 192*). In the case of an indirect demerger, capital gains relief is obtained in practice under *TCGA 1992, s 136* because the demerger is often a reconstruction (see HMRC Capital Gains Tax Manuals CG 52720/1 and CG 33920A for HMRC's comments).

## General conditions

**16.17** All companies involved in the transactions must be UK resident at the time of the distribution (*ICTA 1988, s 213(4)*). The distributing company and any company whose shares are distributed must be a trading company or a member of a trading group (*ICTA 1988, s 213(5)*). The distribution must be made wholly or mainly for the benefit of some or all of the trading activities formerly carried on by a single company or group and after the distribution carried on by two or more companies or groups (*ICTA 1988, s 213(10)*). The distribution must not form part of a scheme or arrangement for:

- the avoidance of tax;
- the making of a chargeable payment;
- the transfer of control of a relevant company to persons other than members of the distributing company;
- the cessation of a trade or its sale after the distribution (*ICTA 1988, s 213(11)*).

## Clearance procedure

**16.18** A clearance procedure is available under *ICTA 1988, s 215* for the distributing company and also for any person considering making a chargeable payment within five years of an exempt distribution. A chargeable payment is any payment not made for money's worth. This will be treated as a company distribution if made during the five-year period of an exempt distribution. Individuals receiving a chargeable payment will be charged to income tax in full. Companies receiving a chargeable payment will be charged to corporation tax under Schedule D Case VI on the full amount of the receipt (*ICTA 1988, s 214(1A), (1B)*). A return of exempt distributions must be provided to HMRC within 30 days of making the distribution (*ICTA 1988, s 216*).

# PURCHASE OF OWN SHARES

## Effects of the legislation

**16.19** *Companies Act 1985* permits a company to purchase and redeem their own share capital. In absence of any relieving legislation a distribution will arise under *ICTA 1988*, s 209(2)(b) on the difference between the subscribed capital and the purchase or redemption proceeds.

Relief is given under *ICTA 1988, s 219* for payments made by an unquoted trading company or the unquoted holding company of a trading group on the purchase or redemption of their own shares. A quoted company is 'a company whose shares are listed in the official list of the Stock Exchange' (*ICTA 1988, s 229(1)*). Shares dealt in by the unlisted securities market or the alternative investment market are unquoted for these purposes (HMRC Corporation Tax Manual CTM 17507).

Payments on purchase and redemption to quoted companies remain within the distribution legislation. The excess of the payment above the refund of share capital is treated as a distribution. If certain conditions are complied with there is no distribution treatment. Instead the disposal receives the capital gains treatment in the hands of the vendor shareholder.

## Conditions—purpose

**16.20** The purpose of the transaction must be to benefit the company's trade or any of its 75% subsidiary's trade. It must not form part of a scheme or arrangement to enable a shareholder to participate in company profits without receiving a dividend, or any other form of tax avoidance (*ICTA 1988, s 219(1)(a)*). HMRC will review the circumstances of each case. The case of *Allum v Marsh* SpC 446, [2005] STC (SCD) 191 was subject to such a review. The facts are as follows: Mr and Mrs A owned 99% and their son 1% of the ordinary shares in A Ltd an unquoted trading company. Mr and Mrs A and their son were all directors. The company owned a property from which the business was carried out and there was a large loan due to the directors. The company approved a contract for the sale of the property and when the sale had been completed it voted to purchase Mr and Mrs A's shares in A Ltd. Mr and Mrs A resigned as company directors. A new company secretary was appointed and the board voted to make voluntary payments to Mr and Mrs A in appreciation for their services to the company. Their shareholdings were duly purchased by the company. The next year the company's activities became small and negligible and the company could not find suitable premises from which to carry out its activities. Mr and Mrs A were assessed to a distribution on the basis that the exemption under *ICTA 1988, s 219(1)(a)* did not apply because the purchase of the shares was not made wholly or mainly for benefiting the company's trade. The voluntary payments were assessed as emoluments. Therefore it is necessary to demonstrate that the purchase takes place for the benefit of the trade.

Alternatively, the whole of the payment (apart from any sum applied in paying capital gains tax charged on the redemption, repayment or purchase) may be applied by the recipient in discharging a liability of his for inheritance tax charged on a death and is so applied within the period of two years after the death (*ICTA 1988, s 219*).

## Conditions—shareholder residence

**16.21** The vendor shareholder must be resident and ordinarily resident in the United Kingdom in the year of assessment in which the purchase is made. If the shares are held through a nominee, the nominee must also be so resident and ordinarily resident (*ICTA 1988, s 220(1)*).

The shares must have been owned by the vendor throughout the period of five years ending with the date of the purchase (*ICTA 1988, s 220(5)*). For an individual a spouse's period of ownership is also taken into consideration (*ICTA 1988, s 220(6)*).

## Shareholder's interest in the company

**16.22** Immediately after purchase the shareholder's interest or the combined interests with associates must be substantially reduced (*ICTA 1988, s 221(1)*, (2)). By this it is meant first that the total nominal value of the shares owned by him immediately after the purchase, expressed as a fraction of the issued share capital of the company at that time, does not exceed 75% of the corresponding fraction immediately before the purchase (*ICTA 1988, s 221(4)*). Second, if the share of profits available for distribution immediately after purchase exceeds 75% of the corresponding fraction immediately before the purchase, the shareholding will not be treated as substantially reduced (*ICTA 1988, s 221(5)*).

In a group situation other group members' and associates' interests are also taken into account (*ICTA 1988, s 222(4)*). Group for these purposes is a 51% relationship (*ICTA 1988, s 222(7)*).

After the purchase the ex-shareholders must not be connected with the company making the purchase or with any company that is a member of the same group as that company (*ICTA 1988, s 223(1)*).

## Clearance procedure

**16.23** An advance clearance procedure is available under *ICTA 1988, s 225*. The full procedure is set out in SP 2/82. 60 days after making the payments the company must make a return to HMRC giving details of the payment and the circumstances (*ICTA 1988, s 226*).

## Associated persons

**16.24** Associated persons include spouses who are living together and children under the age of 18 together with their respective associates. With effect from 5 December 2005, civil partners are also associated persons. Two or more companies are connected if they are both under the same control. Trustees are connected with the settlor, the beneficiaries and the respective associates.

A personal representative is associated with the beneficiaries. A person connected with a company is an associate of the company and of any company controlled by it, and the company and any company controlled by it are his associates. Trustees are associated with the settlor or an associate of his or the beneficiaries if any one of the beneficiaries has an interest of more than 5%. Personal representatives are associated with beneficiaries if the beneficiary has an interest of more than 5% in the estate.

Also, if one person is accustomed to act on the directions of another in relation to the affairs of a company, then in relation to that company the two persons are associates of one another. Exempt approved pension schemes and employee trusts are not included in these arrangements (*ICTA 1988, s 227(8)*).

## Connected persons

**16.25** A person is connected with a company if he directly or indirectly possesses or is entitled to acquire more than 30% of the issued ordinary share capital, 30% of the combined loan capital and issued share capital, 30% of the voting power or 30% of the assets available for distribution on a winding up.

An interest in loan capital, acquired during the normal course of a moneylending business, is disregarded, if the person takes no part in the management or conduct of the company.

# DISTRIBUTIONS IN A WINDING UP BY ESC 16

## Striking off a defunct company

**16.26** If the registrar of companies believes that a company is not carrying on a business he may strike it off. The procedure involves the registrar writing to the company. If a reply is not received within a month a second letter is sent, this time by registered post. If no reply is received within one month, the registrar may send a notice to the company stating that within three months from the date of the notice the company will be struck off the registrar and dissolved (*CA 1985, s 652*).

## Request for striking off by a private company

**16.27** A private company may voluntarily request that the registrar strike it off. In practice the company completes a Companies House form 652a, which it sends to the registrar of companies, together with a cheque for £10. The form must be signed by all or a majority of the directors. The directors must confirm that in the previous three months it has not carried on any business, or changed its name, disposed of any of its assets or engaged in any other activities apart from making the application, settling its affairs or meeting a statutory requirement. The company must of course not be involved in any other insolvency proceedings (*CA 1985, s 652A*).

## ESC 16

**16.28** As this method of striking off is not a formal winding up, HMRC regards any distribution of assets as an income distribution within *s 209*. By concession HMRC will treat the distribution as a capital distribution provided certain criteria are complied with. HMRC will require written signed statements from the company and its shareholders.

The company must provide assurances that it:

- does not intend to trade or carry on business in future;
- intends to collect its debts, pay off its creditors and distribute any balance of its assets to its shareholders (or has already done so); and
- intends to seek or accept striking off and dissolution.

The company and its shareholders agree that:

- they will supply such information as is necessary to determine and will pay any corporation tax liability on income or capital gains; and

- the shareholders will pay any capital gains tax liability (or corporation tax in the case of a corporate shareholder) in respect of any amount distributed to them in cash or otherwise as if the distributions had been made during a winding up (ESC 16).

This method of winding up is widely used by small private companies. Assuming all other conditions apply, the capital gains tax treatment enables the shareholders to take advantage of business asset taper relief. As the capital gains tax treatment is only a concession, HMRC could refuse to apply it if they perceived a tax avoidance motive.

The company is well advised to settle all debts and close all bank accounts before the company is formally struck off. If not, all remaining assets become *bona vacantia* and property of the Crown. The company should request well in advance and whilst the company is still in existence for any corporation tax repayments to be made to the shareholders or directors. Otherwise with a closed bank account the company will not be able to receive the repayment and with a company no longer in existence it will not be possible to give alternative payment instructions to HMRC with the result that the corporation tax repayment will also be *bona vacantia.*

*Chapter 17*

# Accounting and Taxation

## GENERALLY ACCEPTED ACCOUNTING STANDARDS

**17.1** For accounting periods beginning from 1 January 2005 either UK GAAP or international accounting standards (IAS) as set out in EC Regulation 1606/2002 may be used (*FA 2004, s 50*). UK GAAP will be applied in cases of inter-group transactions where one group member to the transaction obtains a tax advantage by the use of UK GAAP whilst the other group member to the transaction uses IAS (*FA 2004, s 51*).

Those companies whose securities are traded on an EU regulated market are required to prepare their consolidated accounts in accordance with IAS for accounting periods ended on or after 1 January 2005.

A change in accounting practice following UK accounting principles from 1 January 2005, a change from UK GAAP to IAS, may bring about a prior period adjustment. Positive adjustments are taxed as receipts and negative adjustments are allowed as expenses. For accounting periods beginning on or after 1 January 2005, these prior period adjustments are treated as arising on the first day of the first period of account for which the new basis is adopted. For accounting periods beginning before 1 January 2005, the prior period adjustment was treated as taking place on the last day of the first period of account for which the new basis was adopted (*FA 2005, s 81*; *FA 2002, s 64, Sch 22*).

Companies qualifying as small under the *Companies Act 1985* definition (see **3.8**) may opt to apply the financial reporting standard for smaller entities (FRSSE). The FRSSE replaces all other accounting standards and UITF abstracts. A smaller companies IAS has been proposed.

## ACCOUNTING POLICIES

**17.2** A company's accounts prepared in accordance with GAAP form the basis for the company's corporation tax computation (see **1.9–1.10**). This rule applies to trading profits, a letting business, an overseas property business, loan relationships, derivatives, intangible property, management expenses and leases.

Taxation law has no authority to impose compliance with the *Companies Act* or to impose any requirements as to audit disclosure upon the company (*FA 1998, s 42*(2)). Accounts prepared according to GAAP and in accordance with the *Companies Act* form the basis of the corporation tax computation. The profits are then normally adjusted further because the laws of taxation take precedence over accounting principles (see **Chapter 5**).

As regards the accounts basis, HMRC employ revenue accountants with wide auditing and accounting experience to whom they refer all their accountancy queries (see Tax Bulletin, Issue 58, April 2002). If HMRC open an enquiry into a company's corporation tax return, the Revenue accountants may also enquire into the accounting policies which the company has adopted (see 'TAXline', February 2003 and Working Together, Issue 13, June 2003).

**17.3** A synopsis of the current UK and international standards is given on the accompanying pages, together with notes on the interaction of accounting and taxation principles where appropriate. The UK accounting standards are published by the Accounting Standards Board (ASB) and are based on overriding principles rather than detailed prescription.

**17.4** The urgent issues task force (UITF) assists the ASB where unsatisfactory or conflicting interpretations have developed (or seem likely to develop) about a requirement of an accounting standard or the *Companies Act*. The UITF seeks to arrive at a consensus on the accounting treatment within the ASB framework that should be adopted. UITF consensuses are published in the form of UITF Abstracts. Compliance with UITF Abstracts is necessary (other than in exceptional circumstances) in accounts that claim to give a true and fair view. International accounting standards are published by the International Accounting Standards Board. Overall there is a general convergence between UK GAAP and IAS.

## UK GAAP

**17.5**

| | *Financial reporting standards* | *Commentary* |
|---|---|---|
| FRS 29 | (IFRS 7) Financial instruments: disclosures** | |
| FRS 28 | Corresponding amounts* | |

| | *Financial reporting standards* | *Commentary* |
|---|---|---|
| FRSSE (2005) | Financial reporting standard for smaller entities* | **17.8** |
| FRS 27 | Life assurance+ | |
| FRS 26 | (IAS 39) Financial instruments: measurement* | **17.9** |
| FRS 25 | (IAS 32) Financial instruments: disclosure and presentation* | |
| FRS 24 | (IAS 29) Financial reporting in hyperinflationary economies* | |
| FRS 23 | (IAS 21) The effects of changes in foreign exchange rates* | **17.10** |
| FRS 22 | (IAS 33) Earnings per share* | |
| FRS 21 | (IAS 10) Events after the balance sheet date* | **17.11** |
| FRS 20 | (IFRS 2) Share-based payment* | |
| *FRSSE (2002)* | *Financial reporting standard for smaller entities* (FRSSE 2005) | |
| FRS 19 | Deferred tax | **17.30** |
| FRS 18 | Accounting policies | **17.12** |
| FRS 17 | Retirement benefits | **17.21** |
| FRS 16 | Current tax | **17.28** |
| FRS 15 | Tangible fixed assets | **17.13, 17.14** |
| *FRS 14* | *Earnings per share* (FRS 22) | |
| FRS 13 | Derivatives and other financial instruments: disclosures | |
| FRS 12 | Provisions, contingent liabilities and contingent assets | **17.15, 17.16** |
| FRS 11 | Impairment of fixed assets and goodwill | |
| FRS 10 | Goodwill and intangible assets | **17.17** |
| FRS 9 | Associates and joint ventures | |
| FRS 8 | Related party disclosures | |
| FRS 7 | Fair values in acquisition accounting | |
| FRS 6 | Acquisitions and mergers | |
| FRS 5 | Reporting the substance of transactions | **17.18** |
| FRS 4 | Capital instruments | |
| FRS 3 | Reporting financial performance | **17.19, 17.20** |
| FRS 2 | Accounting for subsidiary undertakings | |
| FRS 1 | Cash flow statements | |

| | *Financial reporting standards* | *Commentary* |
|---|---|---|
| | *Statements of standard accounting practice* | |
| SSAP 25 | Segmental reporting | |
| SSAP 24 | Accounting for pension costs | **17.21** |
| SSAP 21 | Accounting for lease and hire purchase contracts | **17.22** |
| *SSAP 20* | *Foreign currency translation* (FRS 23) | |
| SSAP 19 | Accounting for investment properties | **17.23** |
| *SSAP 17* | *Accounting for post balance sheet events* (FRS 21) | **17.11** |
| SSAP 13 | Accounting for research and development | **17.17** |
| SSAP 9 | Stocks and long-term contracts | **17.24** |
| SSAP 4 | Accounting for government grants | **17.25** |
| SSAP 5 | Accounting for value added tax | |

**Notes**

Bracketed references show the identical IFRS.

* Effective for accounting periods beginning on or after 1 January 2005 – see standard for extent of application.

** Effective for accounting periods beginning on or after 1 January 2007 – see standard for extent of application.

\+ Effective for accounting periods ending on or after 23 December 2005 – see standard for extent of application.

Superseded standards are italicised. Replacement standard is shown in brackets.

## INTERNATIONAL GAAP

**17.6**

| | *International financial reporting standards* | *Commentary* |
|---|---|---|
| IFRS 1 | First-time adoption of international financial reporting standards | **17.26** |

| | *International financial reporting standards* | *Commentary* |
|---|---|---|
| IFRS 2 | Share-based payments | |
| IFRS 3 | Business combinations | |
| IFRS 4 | Insurance contracts | |
| IFRS 5 | Non-current assets held for sale and discontinued operations | |
| IFRS 6 | Exploration for and evaluation of mineral assets | |
| IFRS 7 | Financial instruments disclosures | |
| | *International accounting standards* | |
| IAS 1 | Presentation of financial statements | **17.19** |
| IAS 2 | Inventories | **17.24** |
| IAS 7 | Cash flow statements | |
| IAS 8 | Accounting policies, changes in accounting estimates and errors | **17.20** |
| IAS 10 | Events after the balance sheet date | **17.11** |
| IAS 11 | Construction contracts | **17.24** |
| IAS 12 | Income taxes | **17.29, 17.39** |
| IAS 14 | Segment reporting | |
| IAS 16 | Property, plant and equipment | **17.13** |
| IAS 17 | Leases | **17.22** |
| IAS 18 | Revenue | |
| IAS19 | Employee benefits | **17.21** |
| IAS 20 | Accounting for government grants and disclosure of government assistance | |
| IAS 21 | The effects of changes in foreign exchange rates | **17.10** |
| IAS 23 | Borrowing costs | **17.14** |
| IAS 24 | Related party disclosure | |
| IAS 26 | Accounting and reporting by retirement benefit plans | |
| IAS 27 | Consolidated and separate financial statements | |
| IAS 28 | Investments in associates | |
| IAS 29 | Financial reporting in hyperinflationary economies | |
| IAS 31 | Interests in joint ventures | |
| IAS 32 | Financial instruments: presentation | |
| IAS 33 | Earnings per share | |
| IAS 34 | Interim financial reporting | |
| IAS 36 | Impairment of assets | **17.17** |
| IAS 37 | Provisions, contingent liabilities and contingent assets | **17.15** |

| | *International financial reporting standards* | *Commentary* |
|---|---|---|
| IAS 38 | Intangible assets | **17.17** |
| IAS 39 | Financial instruments: recognition and measurement | **17.9** |
| IAS 40 | Investment property | **17.23** |
| IAS 41 | Agriculture | |

# INTERACTION OF ACCOUNTING AND TAXATION PRINCIPLES

**17.7** Accounting standards deal with accounting treatments. Certain aspects of the accounting treatment may have a direct impact for taxation purposes.

# FRSSE

**17.8** The FRSSE consolidates and modifies the relevant accounting requirements and disclosures from the other accounting standards and UITF Abstracts for smaller entities and was originally introduced in November 1997. Companies who qualify as 'small' under the *Companies Act* may apply the standard (see **3.8**). The FRSSE is under review as regards changes in company law and accounting standards. A company complying with the FRSSE complies with GAAP.

## FRS 26 Financial instruments: measurement and IAS 39 Financial instruments: recognition and measurement

**17.9** IAS 39 and FRS 26 require assets and liabilities to be measured at fair value (see **11.9**).

## FRS 23 The effects of changes in foreign exchange rates and IAS 21 Currency accounting

**17.10** Under IAS 21 and FRS 23 income and expenditure of foreign operations (including branches) are translated at actual or average rates (not at closing or average rates).

*FA 1993, s 92D* requires that foreign currency be converted at the average exchange rate for the current accounting period of the appropriate spot rate of exchange for the transaction in question.

For accounting periods beginning on or after 1 January 2005, accounts for taxation purposes must be prepared in sterling (*FA 1993, s 92*). If a UK resident company prepares accounts in a currency other than sterling, for corporation tax purposes the accounts must be computed for GAAP in sterling (*FA 1993, s 92A*). If a UK resident company prepares accounts in a currency other than sterling, but then uses another non-sterling currency as its functional currency, that functional currency is used for preparing accounts according to GAAP. The resulting profits or loss are then converted to sterling (*FA 1993, s 92B*). Similar rules apply if a UK resident company prepares accounts in a currency other than sterling and neither *s 92A* nor *s 92B* applies, or if a non-resident company prepares its accounts in a non-sterling currency. The accounts currency is used for preparing accounts according to GAAP. The resulting profits or loss are then converted to sterling (*FA 1993, s 92C*).

## FRS 21 (IAS 10) Events after the balance sheet date and SSAP 17 Accounting for post balance sheet events

**17.11** FRS 21 specifies the accounting treatment to be adopted (including the disclosures to be provided) by entities for events occurring between the balance sheet date and the date when the financial statements are authorised for issue. It replaces SSAP 17 Accounting for post balance sheet events.

FRS 21 sets out the recognition and measurement requirements for two types of event after the balance sheet date:

- **Adjusting events**. Those events that provide evidence of conditions that existed at the balance sheet date for which the entity shall adjust the amounts recognised in its financial statements or recognise items that were not previously recognised (adjusting events). For example, the settlement of a court case that confirms the entity had a present obligation at the balance sheet date.

- **Non adjusting events**. Those events that are indicative of conditions that arose after the balance sheet date for which the entity does not adjust the amounts recognised in its financial statements. For example, a decline in market value of investments between the balance sheet date and the date when the financial statements are authorised for issue.

Dividends declared after the balance sheet date should no longer be reported as liabilities. The FRS removes the requirement to report dividends proposed after the balance sheet date in the profit and loss account and instead requires disclosures in the notes to the financial statements.

The FRS sets out other disclosure requirements. These include:

- the disclosure of the date when the financial statements were authorised for issue;
- the disclosure of information received about conditions that existed at the balance sheet date; and
- if non-adjusting events after the balance sheet date are material and non-disclosure could influence the economic decisions of users, the entity should disclose the nature of the event and an estimate of its financial effect, or a statement that such an estimate cannot be made.

The FRS also requires that an entity shall not prepare its financial statements on a going concern basis if management determines after the balance sheet date that it intends to liquidate the entity or to cease trading or that it has no realistic alternative but to do so (see Chapter 19).

When SSAP 17 (Accounting for post balance sheet events) applied HMRC found that companies paid insufficient or no attention to adjusting post balance sheet events as regards stock obsolescence provisions, impairment provisions (where the debts are recovered in full) and provisions for claims against an entity that were settled for less in the post balance sheet period (Working Together, Issue 11, June 2003).

## FRS 18 Accounting policies

**17.12** HMRC have commented that in some cases work completed before the year end has been invoiced after the year end but not correctly accounted for (FRS 18, para 26; Working Together, Issue 11, June 2003).

## FRS 15 Tangible fixed assets and IAS 16 Property, plant and equipment

**17.13** For taxation purposes the distinction between capital and revenue expenditure is maintained. Revenue deductions will follow the timing of recognition in the accounts. FRS15 provides principles for measurement, valuation and depreciation of fixed assets that are not recognised for taxation purposes (HMRC Business Income Manual BIM 31060).

FRS 15 permits renewals accounting (FRS 15, para 97) on infrastructure assets only in specified circumstances; that is, where the infrastructure is treated as a single system, is maintained by continuing replacement of parts according to a projected asset management plan (AMP) calculated by a qualified and independent person. The system or network has to be in a mature or steady state. Under renewals accounting, the estimated level of expenditure required to maintain the operating capacity (over the AMP period) is treated as depreciation and is charged to the profit and loss account. Actual maintenance expenditure is capitalised. There is no direct link between the actual expenditure in any one year and the amount charged to the profit and loss account. Renewals accounting provides a mechanism to smooth the profile of maintenance expenditure (HMRC Business Income Manual BIM 31065).

FRS 15 renewals accounting is not specifically permitted under IAS 16. If a company adopts IAS16 there may be a change of accounting policy adjustment (*FA 2002, s 64*; HMRC International Accounting Standards – the UK Tax Implications, July 2006).

## FRS 15 Tangible fixed assets and IAS 23 Borrowing costs

**17.14** IAS 23 and FRS 15 permit the capitalisation of borrowing costs. UK tax law departs from FRS 15 by allowing relief for capitalised borrowing costs as if they were a profit and loss account item but only where they relate to a fixed asset or project (*FA 1996, Sch 9, para 14*). The same approach will continue where IAS 23 is followed (HMRC International Accounting Standards – the UK Tax Implications, July 2006).

## FRS 12 Provisions, contingent liabilities and contingent assets and IAS 37 Provisions, contingent liabilities and contingent assets

**17.15** There is no significant difference between IAS 37 and FRS 12, which is followed for tax purposes (subject to adjustment where the expenditure is capital for tax purposes or otherwise disallowable).

Under FRS 12 provisions must satisfy the definition of liabilities: 'obligations of an entity to transfer economic benefits as a result of past transactions or events'. Mere anticipation of future expenditure, however probable and no matter how detailed the estimates, is not enough, in the absence of an obligation at the balance sheet date. Provisions are defined by FRS 12 as 'liabilities of uncertain timing or amount' (HMRC Business Income Manual BIM 46515).

Under FRS 12 a provision should be recognised when:

- an entity has a present obligation (legal or constructive) as a result of a past event;
- it is probable that a transfer of economic benefits will be required to settle the obligation; and
- a reliable estimate can be made of the amount of the obligation.

If these conditions are not met, no provision should be recognised.

FRS 12 does not apply to trade creditors, accruals, adjustments to the carrying value of assets, insurance company provisions arising from contracts with policy holders, provisions that are specifically addressed by other accounting standards, such as losses on long-term contracts (SSAP 9), provisions relating to leases (SSAP 21) other than operating leases that have become onerous and pension costs (SSAP 24).

Trade creditors are understood to be liabilities to pay for formally invoiced received goods or services. Accruals are understood to be liabilities to pay for received goods or services, not yet formally invoiced.

HMRC have commented that because of the changes brought about by FRS 12 (effective for accounting periods ending on or after 23 March 1999), the following provisions are no longer allowable for tax purposes:

- provisions for 'future operating losses' that is, losses that will or may arise from obligations entered into subsequent to the balance sheet date;
- restructuring provisions until the business has a 'detailed formal plan' for restructuring and has created a 'valid expectation' in those affected that it will carry it out;
- provisions where the only event that might require them is an unpublished decision of the directors;
- provisions for future expenditure required by legislation where the business could avoid the obligation by changing its method of operation, for example, by stopping doing whatever is affected by the legislation;
- provisions for future repairs of plant and machinery owned by the business (HMRC Business Income Manual BIM 46535).

HMRC have commented that the following provisions will be allowable:

- in the period of sale for the cost of work under a warranty which a trader gives on the sale of merchandise (or under consumer protection legislation);
- for commission refundable by an insurance intermediary on the lapse of a policy where the commission is recognised as income at the inception of the policy;

- by builders for rectification work, including retentions up to the level that these have been recognised as income within accounts (HMRC Business Income Manual BIM 46545).

## FRS 12 Provisions, contingent liabilities and contingent assets

**17.16** If HMRC wish to challenge a provision they will firstly ascertain whether it accords with GAAP and then possibly look into the accuracy of the provision. HMRC comment that when enquiring into company accounting matters they have found problems with companies applying this standard.

In particular where provisions are incorrectly made for recurring periodic expenditure on assets owned by the entity (FRS 12, para 19 and example 11). Sometimes excessive provisions have been made for onerous leases, in circumstances where no account is taken of expected rental income or surrender or sale of the lease (FRS 12, para 73). Also, provisions have been made where the facts show that there is no real likelihood of having to pay, for example, where the creditor company has already been wound up and the liquidator has decided not to pursue the debt (FRS 12, para 23). Finally, provisions have been made to 'smooth profits' rather than to comply with FRS 12, para 14 (Working Together, Issue 13, June 2003).

## FRS 10 Goodwill and intangibles; SSAP 13 Accounting for research and development; IAS 38 Intangible assets and IAS 36 Impairment

**17.17** IAS 38 does not permit goodwill amortisation. Under IFRS 1 a company has the option of keeping goodwill at the amortised cost at the date of the opening comparative balance sheet in a company's first IAS accounts, and only impairing from that basis figure. *FA 2002, Sch 29, paras 116A, 116B* ensure that any write up on the transition from UK GAAP to IAS will be a taxable credit for *Sch 29*, and *para 116F* ensures that any such credit is limited to the net amount of relief already given. Any impairment from written up cost will be deductible.

IAS 38 requires the capitalisation of development expenditure in R&D. *FA 2004, s 53* nevertheless permits a revenue deduction.

IAS 38 requires website costs, when capitalised, to be treated as an intangible asset.

Where website costs have been the subject of capital allowance claims, but are reclassified as intangible fixed assets under IAS 38, *FA 2002, Sch 29, para 73A* disapplies the intangibles rules so that capital allowances may continue. If intangible asset costs have been written off to the profit and loss account and are then brought into the balance sheet under IAS 38 as an asset there will be an intangibles credit and possibly an adjustment under *FA 2002, s 64*. Rules for the transition from UK GAAP to IAS are within *FA 2002, Sch 29, paras 116A–116H*.

## FRS 5 Reporting the substance of transactions

**17.18** In general, the reporting of revenue in accounts is followed for tax purposes. There is no general standard for revenue recognition in UK GAAP, but the recently added Application Note G to FRS 5 goes some way to dealing with certain aspects of IAS 18. In March 2005 the UITF of the ASB issued UITF Abstract 40 (Revenue recognition and service contracts) to provide further guidance on Note G. *FA 2005, Sch 15* permits a spreading adjustment (see **5.35**).

## FRS 3 Reporting financial performance and IAS 1 Presentation of financial statements

**17.19** UK tax law uses the balance on a profit and loss account as the starting point for Case I basis computations (including Schedule A, overseas property, Case V trades; *FA 1998, s 42* non-trading income from loan relationships, derivative contracts and intangibles). Amounts are recognised when they are included in the profit and loss account or in the statement of recognised gains and losses or the IAS equivalent statement of changes in equity or other statement used for calculating the company's profit (*FA 1996, s 85B*; HMRC International Accounting Standards – the UK Tax Implications, July 2006).

## FRS 3 Reporting financial performance and IAS 8 Accounting policies, changes in accounting estimates and errors

**17.20** Prior period accounting adjustments are brought into the Schedule D Case I computation, in the year of change (*FA 2002, s 64, Sch 22*). A change in valuation from a realisation basis to a market to market basis (possibly occurring in a financial trade) may be spread over six years (*FA 2002, Sch 22, paras 8, 9*). Where amounts have been allowed as a deduction on an old basis they will not be allowed again on a new basis (*FA 2002, Sch 22, para 6*).

*FA 2002, s 64* does not apply to fundamental errors. In such cases prior periods must be restated. This is effected by an amendment to the corporation tax return (see **2.9**).

## SSAP 24 Accounting for pension costs; FRS 17 Retirement benefits; and IAS 19 Employee benefits

**17.21** The accounts figures for contributions to and changes in value of pension schemes are irrelevant for tax purposes. Relief is given on a paid (and sometimes deferred basis). For pension scheme contributions with effect from 6 April 2006: see **5.27**. See **5.28** for non-pension employee benefits (HMRC International Accounting Standards – the UK Tax Implications, July 2006).

## SSAP 21 Accounting for lease and hire puchase contracts and IAS 17 Leases

**17.22** UK tax law is not entirely consistent with SSAP 21 (see **6.35**). IAS 17 is drawn up along similar lines to SSAP 21.

## SSAP 19 Accounting for investment properties and IAS 40 Investment property

**17.23** The accounts treatment of investment properties is generally irrelevant for tax, as the capital gains rules apply. There may be cases where a property developer uses land for investment purposes before sale, and in such cases IAS 40 may apply. If the company adopts the fair value basis, a transitional adjustment may arise falling within *FA 2002, s 64*.

Where a company elects to treat an interest in a property held, which it holds as a lessee under an operating lease, as an investment property it is required to account for it as a finance lease. Where this happens the tax rules applying to finance leases will apply (HMRC International Accounting Standards – the UK Tax Implications, July 2006).

## SSAP 9 Stocks and long-term contracts; IAS 2 Inventories; and IAS 11 Construction contracts

**17.24** SSAP 9 is followed for tax purposes. If a trade ceases, the stock is valued at market value. If the stock is transferred to an unconnected party for the purposes of their trade, stock is valued at the consideration given. If stock is sold to a connected party, it is valued at an arm's-length value (*ICTA 1988, s 100*). If stock is taken for a participator's own use, it is valued at selling price (*Sharkey v Wernher* (1955) 36 TC 275, [1956] AC 58, [1955] 3 All ER 493).

HMRC comment that they have found problems with aspects of SSAP 9.

In particular they have found that where companies have made stock provisions they have not been supported by the facts of the case. Long-term contracts are not always identified and accounted for as such (SSAP 9, para 22). Companies have sometimes valued stock and work in progress at net realisable value on the theoretical basis that it would have to be sold as an emergency sale in its current condition, rather than being sold in the normal course of business (SSAP 9, Appendix 1, paras 19, 20; Working Together, Issue 11, June 2003).

HMRC comment that they see no difference between SSAP 9, IAS 2 and IAS 11 except that they do not recognise the IAS 2 LIFO (last in first out) stock valuation method (HMRC International Accounting Standards – the UK Tax Implications, July 2006).

## SSAP 4 Accounting for government grants and IAS 20 Government grants

**17.25** For both taxation and accounting purposes grants are treated as income (HMRC International Accounting Standards – the UK Tax Implications, July 2006).

## IFRS 1 First time adoption of international financial reporting standards

**17.26** Differences between the previous GAAP and the current IFRS treatment are recognised in the opening comparative balance sheet thus enabling any adjustments to be made under *FA 2002, s 64*.

# ACCOUNTING FOR TAX

**17.27** Tax is represented in the accounts in both the profit and loss account and the balance sheet. The two types of tax to be shown are current year tax and deferred tax.

## FRS 16 Current tax

**17.28** Current tax is the estimated tax charge payable based on the taxable profits for the company for the year. Current tax is measured using the tax rates and laws applicable at the balance sheet date.

Dividends received from UK companies are reported as the net amount received. Dividends received from other countries are reported gross only to the extent that they have suffered a withholding tax. Interest received or receivable is shown gross of withholding tax.

Current tax for the period must be recognised in the profit and loss account except to the extent that it relates to gains or losses that have been recognised directly in the statement of total recognised gains and losses. Such tax should also be recognised in the statement of total recognised gains and losses (STRGL).

The profits per the accounts are usually different to the profits chargeable to corporation tax. This is because the nature of the accounts is to attain a profit that incorporates all the expenses and income that have been charged and received as true business expenses and income and incurred during the accounting period, irrelevant of whether payment has actually been made or not. Taxable profits on the other hand have disallowable expenses and income, which must be added back or removed from the profit. In instances where there are timing differences between the accounting profits and the taxable profits an adjustment is made for deferred tax (see **17.31**).

For accounts purposes, the current year's tax provision is disclosed as a current liability, together with a disclosure note. The format of the note is as follows:

**Illustration of profit and loss account disclosure**

| | *£000* | *£000* |
|---|---|---|
| **UK Corporation tax** | | |
| Current tax on income for the period | a | |
| Adjustments in respect of prior periods | b | |
| | C | |
| Double taxation relief | (d) | |
| | | E |
| **Foreign tax** | | |
| Current tax on income for the period | f | |
| Adjustments in respect of prior periods | g | |
| | | H |
| Tax on profit in ordinary activities | | I |

If an item of tax relates to an item in the statement of total recognised gains and losses, where the tax is also recognised there, then it should not be recognised in the profit and loss account per FRS 16. This includes gains on disposals of fixed assets previously revalued and differences on foreign currencies. The format for the STRGL as per FRS 3 is set out below:

**Statement of total recognised gains and losses for the year**

| | *£000* |
|---|---|
| Profit for the financial year (per the profit and loss account) | x |
| Items taken directly to reserves: | |
| Unrealised surplus on revaluation of fixed assets | x |
| Surplus/deficit on revaluation of investment principles | x |
| Foreign currency exchange differences | x |
| Total recognised gains and losses for the year | x |
| Prior period adjustments | (x) |
| Total gains and losses recognised since last annual report | x |

## IAS 12 Income taxes

**17.29** IAS 12 is drawn up along similar lines with the following notable differences. IAS 12 requires current tax to be shown separately on the face of the balance sheet. FRS 16 has no such requirement. IAS 12 also requires items to be charged to equity if they relate to equity. FRS 16 does not have this requirement. IAS 12 also requires disclosure of the tax expense relating to discontinued operations. FRS 16 does not require this. IAS12 has no requirement as to the presentation of outgoing or incoming dividends.

## FRS 19 Deferred tax

### FRS 19's objective

**17.30** Deferred tax is sometimes considered more of an accounting issue as opposed to a tax issue. This is largely due to the nature of deferred tax and what it intends to cover. Income and expenditure are often recognised in the accounts at different times to when they are necessarily taxable or relievable. FRS 19 prescribes timing different accounts adjustments to enable the accounts to show a true and fair view.

The overall objective of FRS 19 is to require 'full provision to be made for deferred tax assets and liabilities arising from timing differences between the recognition of gains and losses in the financial statements and their recognition in a tax computation' (FRS 19 Summary).

Deferred tax should be recognised as a liability or asset if the transactions or events that give the entity an obligation to pay more tax in future or a right to pay less tax in future have occurred by the balance sheet date.

Deferred tax should be recognised on most types of timing difference, including those attributable to:

- accelerated capital allowances;
- accruals for pension costs and other post retirement benefits that will be deductible for tax purposes only when paid;
- elimination of unrealised intra-group profits on consolidation;
- unrelieved tax losses;
- other sources of short-term timing differences.

FRS 19 prohibits the recognition of deferred tax on timing differences arising when:

- a fixed asset is revalued without there being any commitment to sell the asset;
- the gain on sale of an asset is rolled over into replacement assets;
- the remittance of a subsidiary, associate or joint venture's earnings would cause tax to be payable, but no commitment has been made to the remittance of the earnings.

As an exception to the general requirement not to recognise deferred tax on revaluation gains and losses, the FRS requires deferred tax to be recognised when assets are continuously revalued to fair value, with changes in fair value being recognised in the profit and loss account.

There is also the requirement that deferred tax assets are to be recognised to the extent that they are regarded as more likely than not that they will be recovered.

## Calculation of deferred tax

### Fixed assets

**17.31** FRS 19 deals with the depreciation, disposal and revaluation aspects of fixed assets.

The depreciation charge within the accounts is likely to differ to the capital allowances granted for tax purposes. The difference is usually removed when the asset is sold, however, whilst the asset is still owned by the company, the difference in depreciation of the asset can result in timing differences and thus the asset will have a differing value to that of the accounts and as recognised in the accounts. Thus an adjustment will be made to reflect the timing differences within the accounts. When the asset is sold, an adjustment will be made in the tax computation reversing the excess capital allowances previously given.

The timing differences for accelerated capital allowances for an asset bought in 2005 for £5,000 with a depreciation charge of 25% straight line and sold at the end of 2007 can be shown thus:

| *Year* | *2005*<br>*£* | *2006*<br>*£* | *2007*<br>*£* |
|---|---|---|---|
| Depreciation charge | 1,250 | 1,250 | 1,250 |
| Capital allowances | 2,000 | 750 | 563 |
| Timing differences | 750 | (750) | (687) |

The cumulative timing difference at 31 December 2007 is (£687). The cumulative timing difference at 31 December 2006 is nil being £750 at 31 December 2005 and £(750) at 31 December 2006.

Deferred tax should not be recognised on timing differences arising where fixed assets are revalued or sold unless by the balance sheet date the reporting entity has entered into a binding agreement to sell the revalued asset and has recognised the gains and losses expected to arise on sale. There is an exception to this rule, however, in that if the asset is to be replaced and roll-over relief is obtained or expected to be obtained then no deferred tax should be recognised. Even if the gain from the sale of the asset is to be rolled over for use in replacement assets, as long as no roll-over relief is obtained or expected to be obtained then an adjustment for deferred tax should be made.

## Pension costs

**17.32** Another element of deferred tax where an adjustment may need to be made is with pension liabilities. The FRS describes the use of deferred tax here as when the liabilities are 'accrued in the financial statements but are allowed for tax purposes only when paid or contributed at a later date'. Pension costs are only allowable in a tax computation for the period in which they are paid. Thus, where they have not been paid in the accounts, but are shown in the profit and loss account in the accounts, then an adjustment for the deferred tax will be made as it relates to a timing difference between expenses in an accounting period and in a tax period.

## Tax losses

**17.33** Timing differences may occur with unrelieved tax losses leading to a tax reduction or refund. If, however, they are used against future profits a deferred tax asset may arise as per FRS 19 a timing difference can arise if a tax loss is not relieved against past or present taxable profits but can be carried forward to reduce future taxable profits.

## Unremitted earnings of subsidiaries, associates and joint ventures

**17.34** As regards the unremitted earnings of subsidiaries, associates and joint ventures FRS 19 states that tax that could be payable (taking account of any double taxation relief) on any future remittance of the past earnings of a subsidiary, associate or joint venture should be provided for in certain circumstances. These are only to the extent that, at the balance sheet date, dividends have been accrued as receivable or a binding agreement to distribute the past earnings in the future has been entered into by the subsidiary, associate or joint venture. This again refers to timing differences between the accounting and tax periods, as all earnings by the parent or related company are either accrued or past profits.

## Full provision liability method

**17.35** FRS 19 adopts the full provision liability method as opposed to the partial provision deferral method. Full provision rationale records the tax effect of all gains and losses in the accounts in full. Partial provision provides for tax liabilities that are expected to arise.

The deferral method provides for deferred tax at the rate of taxation in use when the differences occur. No adjustment is made if the rates subsequently change. If the timing differences reverse, the tax is calculated again at the rate in force when the differences first arose. The liability method provides for deferred tax at the rate that is expected to apply when the timing differences reverse. This method is considered to more accurately reflect the amount of tax that is expected to be paid.

## Discounting

**17.36** FRS 19 permits but does not require a company to discount its deferred tax assets and liabilities to reflect the time value of money. The discount period being the number of years between the balance sheet dates and the date on which it is estimated that the underlying timing differences will reverse (FRS 19, para 47). The discount rates prescribed are the post-tax yields to maturity that could be obtained at the balance sheet date on government bonds with maturity dates and in currencies similar to those of the deferred tax assets or liabilities (FRS 19, para 52).

## Recognition of deferred tax assets

**17.37** Deferred tax assets should be recognised to the extent that they are regarded as recoverable. This judgment should be made from all available evidence (FRS 19, para 23). Deferred tax should only be recognised if it is likely that the company has sufficient taxable profit to cover any future reversal of the underlying timing differences. In making this assessment the company should also consider its tax planning opportunities.

## Accounts presentation

**17.38** FRS 19 requires that deferred tax be recognised in the profit and loss account for the period, except to the extent that it is attributable to a gain or loss that is or has been recognised directly in the statement of total recognised gains and losses.

Within the profit and loss account the charge for the period should be included under the heading *Tax on profit or loss on ordinary activities*. The deferred tax balance will be shown separately in the balance sheet within either *Provisions for liabilities and charges* if the balance is a net deferred tax liability or within *Debtor*s should the balance be a net deferred tax asset.

The deferred tax debit and credit balance should only be offset within the debtor and creditors if they relate to taxes levied by the same tax authority and arise in the same taxable entry or in a group of taxable entries where the tax losses of one entity can reduce the taxable profits of another meaning that the liabilities have to match in time period and transaction and so be offset without confusion in the accounts.

The accounts must also show within the balance sheet the total deferred tax balance showing the amount recognised for each significant type of timing difference separately showing the impact of discounting on, and the discounted amount of, the deferred tax balance and the movement between the opening and closing net deferred tax balance analysing separately:

- the amount charged or credited in the profit and loss account for the period;
- the amount charged or credited directly in the statement of total recognised gains and losses for the period; and

- movements arising from the acquisition or disposal of businesses.

The deferred tax will also need to be shown in a disclosure note showing the different elements as per the example below.

---

**Example 17.1**

**Taxation on profit on ordinary activities**

**(a) Analysis of charge in the period**

| | *£000* | *£000* |
|---|---|---|
| Current tax | | |
| UK corporation tax on profits of the period | 40 | |
| Adjustments in respect of previous periods | 10 | |
| Total current tax | | 50 |
| Deferred tax | | |
| Origination and reversal of timing differences | 27 | |
| Adjustments in respect of previous periods | | |
| Total deferred tax | | 27 |
| Total tax charge | | 77 |

**(b) Factors affecting the tax charge for the period**

The difference between the tax charge based on applying the UK corporation tax rates to the reported profit before taxation to the actual current tax charge is reconciled below.

| | *£000* |
|---|---|
| Profit on ordinary activities before taxation | 500 |
| Profit on ordinary activities before taxation multiplied by the standard rate of corporation tax in the UK of 30% | 150 |
| Effects of: | |
| Expenses not deductible for tax purposes | 30 |
| Capital allowances (more than) less than depreciation | (60) |
| Utilisation of tax losses | (80) |
| Current tax charge for the period | 40 |

**(c) Factors that may affect future tax charges**

Based on current capital investment plans, the company expects to be able to continue to claim capital allowances in excess of depreciation in future years but at a slightly lower level than in the current year. The company has tax losses that have not been recognised due to the uncertainty over their availability. If they become available they will reduce the future tax charge.

**Provisions for deferred tax**

**(a) Deferred tax liability/(asset) provided in the accounts comprises:**

| | *£000* |
|---|---|
| Accelerated capital allowances | 140 |
| Tax losses | (60) |
| Other short-term timing differences | (1) |
| | (79) |

**(b) Deferred tax liability/(asset) not provided in the accounts comprises:**

| | *£000* |
|---|---|
| Chargeable gains subject to roll-over relief | 70 |
| Tax losses | (20) |
| Other short-term timing differences | (1) |
| | 49 |

The potential deferred tax asset has not been recognised in the accounts because it is unlikely that the losses will be utilised in the foreseeable future.

**(c) Analysis of movement in the period**

| | *£000* |
|---|---|
| Deferred tax asset at 1 January 2007 | (106) |
| Deferred tax charge in the profit and loss account | 27 |
| Deferred tax asset at 31 December 2007 | (79) |

Deferred tax has been calculated at 30% (2006 – 30%) being the prevailing rate of UK corporation tax rate at 31 December 2007 and 2006.

As can be seen FRS 19 provides in-depth analysis to assist account users in comprehending the effects of the overall tax charge. There are significant differences between FRS 19 and IAS 12 that are summarised below.

## IAS 12 Income tax

**17.39** IAS 12 (Income tax) deals with deferred taxation. It is drawn up on similar lines except that provisions are required in the following circumstances:

- on a revaluation of a non-monetary asset whether or not it is intended that the asset will be sold and whether or not roll-over relief could be claimed;
- on a sale of assets where the gain has been or might be rolled over into replacement assets;
- where adjustments recognise assets and liabilities at their fair values on the acquisition of a business;
- on the unremitted earnings of subsidiaries, associates and joint ventures;
- on exchange differences on consolidation of non-monetary assets;
- on unrealised intra-group profits eliminated on consolidation, provision is required on the temporary difference rather than on the timing difference of the profit that has been taxed but not recognised in the consolidated financial statements.

# *Chapter 18*

# Avoidance

## INTRODUCTION

### Tax mitigation, tax avoidance and tax evasion

**18.1** Tax mitigation, tax avoidance and tax evasion are often referred to in common parlance. Their understanding over the years has been developed by case law principles. Tax mitigation is understood to mean making full use of the tax relieving provisions as intended by the legislation. Tax avoidance is understood to mean legally utilising the tax regime to one's own advantage, but not necessarily with the intention with which it was drafted, in order to minimise the amount of tax payable. Tax evasion in contrast is the deceit to purposefully evade the payment of taxes by misrepresentation or other dishonest means. Tax evasion is a crime punishable by penalties and fines and or imprisonment for the taxpayer and adviser.

### Case law

**18.2** The UK has a developed economy and a sophisticated taxation system. The law is constantly updated to meet the changing times and the nation's needs. Legal drafting of taxation statutes over the years unknowingly created situations whereby taxpayers used legislation to their advantage rather than the purpose for which the legislation was introduced in the first place. Taxpayers were able to make use of the form of the legislation rather than its substance. This was confirmed in *Duke of Westminster v CIR* (1935) 19 TC 490 where Lord Tomlin commented 'every man is entitled if he can to order his affairs so that the tax attaching under the appropriate Acts is less than it otherwise be'. Such a comment shows no distinction between tax avoidance and tax mitigation and overall the courts from that time seemed to have shown a neutral approach.

However, times moved on. Tax legislation and economies became more complex and the courts showed hostility to contrived tax avoidance schemes. In 1981 the case of *WT Ramsay Ltd v CIR* (1981) TC 101, [1981] STC 174 reached the House of Lords. The case involved a series of transactions whose purpose was to avoid tax. The judgment went against the taxpayer and was based on reviewing all the transactions as a whole. Looking behind these transactions it was found that there was no commercial justification for them whatsoever. This approach was upheld in *Furniss v Dawson* (1984) 55 TC 324, [1984] STC 153 and *Craven v White* (1988) 62 TC 1, [1988] STC 476.

In the meantime the case of *New Zealand Commr of Inland Revenue v Challenge Corpn Ltd* [1986] STC 548 recognised the distinction between tax avoidance and tax mitigation. Lord Templeman stated that tax mitigation occurs 'where the taxpayer obtains a tax advantage by reducing his income or incurring expenditure in circumstances in which the taxing statute affords a reduction in tax liability'. Tax avoidance occurs 'when the taxpayer reduces his liability to tax without involving him in the loss or expenditure which entitles him to that reduction. The taxpayer engaged in tax avoidance does not reduce his income or suffer a loss or incur expenditure but nevertheless obtains a reduction in his liability to tax as if he had'.

The view was supported by Lord Nolan in *CIR v Willoughby* (1997) 70 TC 57, [1997] STC 995. Lord Nolan described tax mitigation as 'the acceptance of an offer of freedom of tax which Parliament had deliberately made' and tax avoidance as 'a course of action designed to conflict with or defeat the evident intention of Parliament'.

The tax avoidance motive was challenged in *Ensign Tankers (Leasing) Ltd v Stokes* (1992) 64 TC 617, [1992] STC 226 and in *Pigott v Staines Investments Ltd* (1995) 68 TC 342, [1995] STC 114. Both cases were decided in favour of the taxpayer. The first because, although a taxpayer invested in a project for its tax saving advantages, the project's activities involved a true trading motive. The second failed because the courts looking into the facts considered that a normal commercial transaction could not be treated as an abnormal transaction.

The Ramsay approach continues to be applied by the courts. In *Mason v Barclays Mercantile Business Finance Ltd* [2004] UKHL 51, (2004) 76 TC 446, [2005] STC 1, [2005] 1 All ER 97 the company entered into a normal trading transaction, this was associated with an abnormal transaction but the facts turned in favour of the taxpayer. In *Inland Revenue Commissioners v Scottish Provident Institution* [2004] UKHL 52, (2004) 76 TC 538, [2005] STC 15, when a complicated set of transactions was treated as a composite transaction with no commercial purpose, the taxpayer lost. The taxpayer lost again in *EDI Services Ltd v HMRC* (SpC 515) when paying employee bonuses in gold coins to avoid Class 1 NIC showed a tax avoidance intention.

Tax evasion remains a crime. HMRC is seeking to extend its criminal investigatory powers and published a Modernising Powers, Deterrents and Safeguards consultative document in August 2006.

As HMRC is responsible for investigating suspected criminal activity across the whole range of its responsibilities throughout the UK, including investigating tax fraud and tax credit fraud involving organised crime, it is seeking the appropriate powers to enable it to carry out its work.

In order to investigate tax crime, HMRC currently has powers to apply for production orders for search warrants and to make arrests. HMRC has inherited differing powers from the old HM Customs and Excise to the Board of Inland Revenue. HMRC is seeking to extend these powers to include the power to take fingerprints, to charge or bail suspects and to search persons as well as premises. HMRC also has more specialised powers used to protect frontiers, powers under the *Proceeds of Crime Act 2002* and various surveillance powers, which it wishes to retain and review at a later date.

## UK ANTI-AVOIDANCE LEGISLATION

### UK approach to anti-avoidance

**18.3** Once known, a 'tax avoidance' scheme or method is swiftly removed by legislation. This of course begs the question that if a type of transaction has been entered into previously by other parties and not removed by legislation, is that transaction being indirectly approved as genuine mitigation?

The UK has no general anti-avoidance rule (GAAR). Instead, there are anti-avoidance clauses within the legislation and since 18 March 2004 there has been formal disclosure of tax avoidance schemes.

## EXISTING CORPORATION TAX AVOIDANCE LEGISLATION

### Taxes Act 1988

**18.4** The main corporation tax avoidance legislation is contained in *ICTA 1988, Pt XVII*. *Chapter I* refers to tax advantages from certain transactions in securities. It will be invoked if the transaction in securities was entered into to gain a tax advantage and not as a bona fide commercial transaction. This could result in a Schedule D Case VI assessment. *Chapters II* and *III* deal with income tax. *Chapter IV* deals with controlled foreign companies, which is discussed in this book (see **13.25–13.40**). *Chapter V* applies to collective investment schemes.

*Chapter VI* deals with miscellaneous matters. The sections applicable to corporation tax and where they are discussed in this book are detailed as follows:

| *ICTA 1988* | *Section* | *Commentary* |
|---|---|---|
| ss 765–767 | Migration of companies | **13.11** |
| ss 767A–769 | Change in ownership | **15.11** |
| ss 770A–774 | Transactions between associated persons | **14.1–14.29**, **12.14** |

**18.5** There are many other anti-avoidance clauses written into statute. The danger is always that a bona fide commercial transaction may fall into the realms of anti-avoidance. To counteract this clearance with HMRC may be obtained in a 'One Stop Shop' as set out in Working Together Bulletin, Issue 11, November 2002 for the following:

Where clearance is required under any one or more of the following provisions:

- *ICTA 1988, s 215* (demergers);
- *ICTA 1988, s 225* (purchase of own shares);
- *ICTA 1988, s 707* (transactions in securities);
- *TCGA 1992, s 138(1)* (share exchanges);
- *TCGA 1992, s 139* (reconstructions involving the transfer of a business);
- *TCGA 1992, s 140B* (transfer of a UK trade between EU member states);
- *TCGA 1992, s 140D* (transfer of non-UK trade between EU member states); and
- *FA 2002, Sch 29, para 88* (intangible fixed assets),

A single letter to the Business Tax Clearance Team at the London addresses given below, no extra copy is required as the same person will deal with each of the clearances asked for. A single response will be given covering all of the clearances asked for.

Clearances required should be marked clearly on the letter. Only the section number as shown above is required.

The application should be sent to:

- Non market sensitive:
  Mohini Sawhney
  Fifth Floor
  22 Kingsway
  London
  WC2B 6NR

- Market sensitive:
  Ray McCann
  Fifth Floor
  22 Kingsway
  London
  WC2B 6NR

**Email applications**: send to: reconstructions@gtnet.gov.uk.

**Fax applications**: send to 020 7438 4409.

## DISCLOSURE OF TAX AVOIDANCE SCHEMES

### HMRC strategy

**18.6** *FA 2004, ss 307–319* introduced procedures for the disclosure of tax avoidance schemes with effect from 18 March 2004. HMRC are determined to crack down on those who use the system to their advantage. Their strategy in this matter is as follows:

- To discourage taxpayers from using schemes. This includes a critical appraisal of all new legislation to reduce the potential for tax avoidance as well as publicising successes in closing down avoidance schemes.
- To identify as early as possible schemes that are being used.
- To challenge avoidance schemes by contesting returns and, where necessary, pursuing the matter through the courts.
- To produce legislative changes that will close down avoidance schemes where litigation is not appropriate or where the amount of tax at stake is particularly large.

On tax avoidance schemes Dawn Primarolo has commented:

> 'HMRC has not prosecuted any accountancy firm for selling aggressive tax avoidance schemes; selling an avoidance scheme would not normally involve activity that amounts to a criminal offence' (*House of Lords Hansard col 1428W 28 June 2005*).

However, with the proposed introduction of extended criminal investigatory powers (see **18.2**) practitioners and taxpayers must remain ever vigilant.

When first introduced in 2004, the disclosure rules only applied to employment and financial products. This has resulted in a number of tax avoidance methods being legislated against in *FA 2006, s 76, Sch 6*.

From 1 August 2006 the disclosure rules have been widened to include corporation tax together with income tax, capital gains tax and stamp duty land tax. The *Tax Avoidance Schemes (Prescribed Descriptions of Arrangements) Regulations 2006, SI 2006/1543* came into force on 1 August 2006 to replace the *Tax Avoidance Schemes (Prescribed Descriptions of Arrangements) Regulations 2004, SI 2004/1863* regarding notification to HMRC of any tax avoidance scheme (*FA 2004, ss 306–319*). The *Tax Avoidance Schemes (Information) Regulations 2004, SI 2004/1864* (as amended by *SI 2004/2613, SI 2005/1869* and *SI 2006/1544*) and the *Tax Avoidance Schemes (Promoters and Prescribed Circumstances) Regulations 2004, SI 2004/1865* (as amended by *SI 2004/2613*) are still currently in force.

## NOTIFICATION

**18.7** A notifiable arrangement is any which obtains a tax advantage. Persons who are responsible for the design of such arrangements or who make the arrangement notifiable for implementation by other persons could be promoters.

A promoter is required to notify HMRC of the scheme within five days of it becoming available. Form AAG 1 (notification of scheme by promoter) is used for this purpose. The user may be required to notify HMRC if the promoter is based outside the UK, an adviser has legal privilege or there is no promoter. Form AAG 2 (notification of scheme by user where the promoter is offshore) is available for use. HMRC will then issue the promoter with an eight digit reference number which the promoter is required to give to each client using the scheme. A person who designs and implements a hallmarked scheme (own scheme) must disclose the scheme within 30 days of implementation. Form AAG 3 (notification of scheme by user in other circumstances) (eg where legal privilege applies or the scheme is devised for use 'in-house') is used for these purposes. Form AAG 5 (continuation sheets) are also available. (See HMRC Disclosure of Tax Avoidance Schemes, June 2006 for further guidance.)

## DISCLOSEABLE ARRANGEMENTS

### Pre 1 August 2006

**18.8** Prior to 1 August 2006 disclosure of anti-avoidance measures was determined according to a series of filters. These included the premium test, the confidentiality test and the off-market test. If the promoter charged a fee for his advice aligned to the tax savings advantage from the scheme, disclosure was required. If the promoter's advice was provided on a confidential basis, so that the promoter could obtain it to maintain the premium fee potential, disclosure was required. If the 'off-market' test involved the promoter charging a small fee for the arrangement but a much larger fee for the financial product that he sold as part of the tax avoidance arrangement, disclosure was required.

## From 1 August 2006

**18.9** From 1 August 2006 a scheme is discloseable if it meets any one of a series of hallmark tests. 'Discloseable' is defined by HMRC as 'the requirement to provide prescribed information to HMRC'. Hallmarks is defined as the descriptions prescribed, for the purpose of *FA 2004, s 306(1)(a)*, (b), and the *Tax Avoidance Schemes (Prescribed Descriptions of Arrangements) Regulations 2006*.

## Hallmarked tests

**18.10** HMRC have devised a series of tests to determine whether a hallmarked scheme exists, which when applied to corporation tax are as follows:

| *Test* | *Question* | *Consequence for a positive answer Positive* | *Consequence for a negative answer Negative* |
|---|---|---|---|
| 1 | Are there arrangements (including any scheme, transaction or series of transactions), or proposals for arrangements, that enable, or might be expected to enable, any person to obtain an advantage in relation to income tax, corporation tax or capital gains tax? | Yes: apply test 2 | No: not a hallmarked scheme |
| 2 | Are those arrangements or proposals such that the main benefit, or one of the main benefits that might be expected to arise from them, is the obtaining of that advantage? | Yes: apply test 3 | No: not a hallmarked scheme |

| *Test* | *Question* | *Consequence for a positive answer* | *Consequence for a negative answer* |
|---|---|---|---|
| 3 | Is there a promoter of the arrangements or are they devised for use 'in-house'? | Yes, a promoter: apply test 4. Yes, in-house: apply test 5 | |
| 4 | Do any of the hallmarks for arrangements where there is a promoter apply? | Yes: a hallmarked scheme | No: not a hallmarked scheme |
| 5 | Is the tax advantage intended to be obtained by a business that is not a small or medium enterprise? | Yes: apply test 6 | No: not a hallmarked scheme |
| 6 | Do any of the in-house hallmarks apply? | Yes: a hallmarked scheme | No: not a hallmarked scheme |

## Hallmarks

**18.11** The hallmarks for arrangements where there is a promoter are as follows:

1 Confidentiality from other promoters.

2 Confidentiality from HMRC.

3 Premium fee.

4 Off-market terms.

5 Standardised tax products.

6 Loss schemes.

7 Leasing arrangements.

The hallmarks for in-house arrangements are:

2 Confidentiality from HMRC.

3 Premium fee.

7 Leasing arrangements.

The small business definition is the same as is used for research and development (see **8.18**).

The confidentiality, premium fee and off-market terms hallmarks follow through from the pre 1 August 2006 filters mentioned in **18.10**. The confidentiality from HMRC hallmark has been added and applies to a promoter who would wish to keep matters confidential from HMRC, for example, to secure future fee income.

A standardised tax product hallmark exists where there is a promoter of a mass-marketed product that needs little or no alteration to suit a client's situation. Enterprise investment schemes (EIS), venture capital trust schemes (VCTs) and corporate venturing schemes (CVS) arrangements are specifically excluded; as are approved employee share schemes and regulated pension schemes. The hallmark for a loss scheme is the existence of a promoter and is intended to capture various loss creation schemes used by wealthy individuals. The leasing arrangement applies to promoted and in-house arrangements. In-house arrangements do not apply if the party intended to benefit from the arrangement is an SME. The hallmark applies to certain high value sale and leaseback arrangements which involve a party outside the charge to corporation tax and a removal of risk from the lessor.

## Clearances

**18.12** There are special rules to avoid the duplication of information where the arrangement includes transactions for which a statutory clearance exists (*SI 2004/1864, para 5*).

They apply for the purposes of:

- Purchase of own shares by an unquoted company (ICTA 1988, s 215) (see **16.19–16.25**);
- Company demergers (*ICTA 1988, s 225*) (see **16.13–16.18**);
- Transfer of business (*ICTA 1988, s 444*);
- Transactions in securities (*ICTA 1988, s 707*);
- Reconstruction of company or trade (TCGA 1992*, ss 138, 139, 140B* or *140D*) (see **15.7–15.10**).

Where statutory clearance is available then the promoter or user may apply for clearance at the same time as making the disclosure. If there is no clearance request the promoter must make the disclosure no later than five working days following the day on which reasonable intention to make a clearance application ceased or the normal 'relevant date' if this is later.

Where a transaction occurs prior to the submission of a clearance application then the disclosure must be made within five working days of any transaction that is part of the scheme occurring.

HMRC have confirmed that clearance applications will be considered in the usual way and clearance will not be refused merely on the grounds that some part of the proposed transaction involves a disclosable scheme.

Disclosures made in this way should be sent with the clearance application.

## CORPORATION TAX SELF-ASSESSMENT

### CT600 completion

**18.13** Companies who use a tax avoidance scheme are required to put an 'X' in the box so named on the first page of CT600 and to complete the disclosure of tax avoidance schemes supplementary pages form CT600J. The scheme number is required in box J and the accounting periods that benefit in JA.

### Penalties

**18.14** Failure to notify incurs the following penalties:

| | | |
|---|---|---|
| Taxpayer failing to disclose a scheme | Initial penalty maximum<br>Daily penalty | £5,000<br>£600 per day |
| Promoters failing to give registration number to client | Initial penalty maximum | £5,000 |
| Taxpayer failing to disclose scheme registration numbers on returns | Initial penalty<br>Second failure penalty<br>Third and subsequent failure penalty | £100<br>£500<br>£1,000 |

Subject to right of appeal, the Special Commissioners will determine the initial penalties for both the promoters and the taxpayers.

## INTERNATIONAL TAX AVOIDANCE

### International agreements

**18.15** The UK is also extending its network of international tax avoidance intelligence (*ICTA 1988, s 815C*). In May 2005, exchange of information agreements were entered into between Jersey, Guernsey and the Isle of Man (*SI 2005/1261*; *SI 2005/1262*; *SI 2005/1263*). In June 2005, exchange of information agreements were entered into between the Virgin Islands, Aruba, Montserrat and Netherlands Antilles (*SI 2005/1457*; *SI 2005/1458*; *SI 2005/1459*; *SI 2005/1460*).

The EU entered into a co-operation agreement with Switzerland on 14 February 2006 (*SI 2006/307*).

## CAPITAL LOSSES

**18.16** With effect from 5 December 2005 three targeted anti-avoidance rules (TAARs) were introduced. The legislation is aimed at the buying of capital losses and gains (*TCGA 1992, ss 184A and 184B*) and the conversion of an income stream into a capital gain or a capital gain matched by an income stream thus covering the gain with an allowable loss (*TCGA 1992, s 184G*) and the artificial generation of capital losses (*TCGA 1992, s 184H*).

The company's allowable losses exclude losses generated as part of a company tax avoidance scheme (*FA 2006, s 69*; *TCGA 1992, s 8*(2), (2A)). A loss will not now be an allowable loss if it accrues in disqualifying circumstances. A loss accrues in disqualifying circumstances if it accrues directly or indirectly in consequence or in connection with any arrangements of which the main purpose is to secure a tax advantage (*FA 2006, s 69*; *TCGA 1992, s 8*(*2A*)).

Measures to counter bed and breakfast arrangements existed up to 5 December 2005 (*TCGA 1992, s 106*). This prevented companies selling and buying shareholdings within a short space of time in order to utilise a capital loss. The current anti-avoidance rule supersedes the bed and breakfast rule.

### Restrictions on buying losses: tax avoidance schemes (TCGA 1992, s 184A)

**18.17** The restriction of pre-entry loss rules within *TCGA 1992, Sch 7A* remains (see **10.33**) but *TCGA 1992, s 184A* has precedence (*TCGA 1992, s 184F*(*3*)). The pre-entry gains legislation of *TCGA 1992, Sch 7AA* ceases to have effect (*TCGA 1992, s 184F*(*4*)). The *TCGA 1992, Sch 7A* rules are aimed at a group acquiring another company with latent losses. *TCGA 1992, s 184A* focuses on a company with latent losses changing its ownership. The rule only applies where there is an arrangement to avoid tax.

## Situations where the restriction is applied

**18.18** A group company is able to set its capital loss against the capital gain of another group company. However, this will be denied in the following circumstances:

- where there is a direct or indirect change of ownership of a company,
- where a loss accrues to the company or any other company on the disposal of an asset acquired prior to the change in ownership (a pre-change asset),
- where the main purpose of the change of ownership is to secure a tax advantage, and
- where the advantage involves the deduction of a qualifying loss from any chargeable gains, whether or not any other transactions or events are involved.

The resulting loss is not deductible from gains arising on assets belonging to the new owners.

Arrangements include any agreement, understanding, scheme, transaction or series of transactions whether or not they are legally enforceable. It is irrelevant as to whether the loss accrues before or after the change of ownership. It is irrelevant whether there are any chargeable gains at the time against which it can be utilised or whether the tax advantage accrues to the company to whom the loss has accrued or to any other company.

A qualifying change of ownership occurs at any time that:

- a company joins a group of companies,
- the company ceases to be a member of a group of companies,
- the company becomes subject to different control (*TCGA 1992, s 184C*).

A group is determined by *TCGA 1992, s 170* (see **10.21–10.22**) (*TCGA 1992, s 184C*).

A tax advantage means relief or increased relief from corporation tax or repayment or increased repayment of corporation tax. It also means the avoidance or reduction of a charge to corporation tax or an assessment to corporation tax or the avoidance or a possible assessment to corporation tax (*TCGA 1992, s 184D*).

---

**Example 18.1**

Sam Arkwright and Bill Weatherspoon each own 50% of Solo Ltd a single company with substantial capital losses. Solo Ltd owns Nevercourt, a property that it is in negotiations to sell. Solo Ltd issues ordinary shares that amount to 30% of the nominal value of the ordinary share capital to Alfonso Roderigo (an unconnected third party). Mr Roderigo's shares only have dividend rights. Sam Arkwright and Bill Weatherspoon then sell the original shares in Solo Ltd to the Multi Group plc. Although in economic terms Solo Ltd has joined the Multi Group plc it has not joined the Multi Group plc's capital gains group because Multi Group plc owns less that 75% of the issued share capital. Multi Group plc intends to transfer all of its assets that have not yet risen in value, but that it expects to rise in value to Solo Ltd in the expectation that any resulting chargeable gains could be covered by the purchased losses. The issue of shares in Solo Ltd to Alfonso Roderigo is clearly intended to prevent Solo Ltd joining the Multi Group plc when the original shareholders sell their shares. This prevents *TCGA 1992, Sch 7A* applying.

Solo Ltd has neither left nor joined a chargeable gains group but it has become subject to a different control. There has therefore been a qualifying change of ownership as defined by *TCGA 1992, s 184C*. Solo Ltd has accrued losses on pre-change assets. The change of ownership has occurred in connection with arrangements, the main purpose of which is to secure a tax advantage for the Multi Group plc. *TCGA 1992, s 184A* applies and Solo Ltd's losses are qualifying losses and are not to be deducted from any gains arising to the company, except those accruing to Solo Ltd on a disposal of pre-change assets. If Nevercourt, the property owned by Solo Ltd at the time of the change of ownership is then sold giving rise to a chargeable gain, this gain can be covered by the losses.

---

## Restrictions on buying gains: tax avoidance schemes (TCGA 1992, s 184B)

**18.19** The same criteria apply to a change of company ownership and the realisation of a chargeable gain to be relieved by capital losses, which accrued prior to the change in ownership.

## Disposal of pre-change assets

**18.20** If a company has disposed of a pre-change asset but still retains an interest in the asset that interest will remain as a pre-change asset.

The capital gain on the following disposals may be deferred:

- Reconstructions involving transfers of business (*TCGA 1992, s 139*).

- Postponement of charge on transfer of assets to non-resident companies (*TCGA 1992, s 140*).
- Transfer of a UK trade (*TCGA 1992, s 140A*).
- Merger leaving assets within UK tax charge (*TCGA 1992, s 140E*).
- Replacement of business assets (*TCGA 1992, ss 152, 153*).
- Postponement of charge on deemed disposal under *s 187* (*TCGA 1992, s 185*).

Any gain or loss accruing as a result of any subsequent event will be treated as accruing on a pre-change asset (*TCGA 1992, s 184E*).

Pre-change securities are pooled. Any disposal is matched first for these purposes; pre-change securities are pooled separately from post-change securities. A disposal of securities after the change is to be matched first against the post-change pool, then against the pre-change pool and then in accordance with the usual share identification rules (*TCGA 1992, s 184F*).

## Avoidance involving losses: schemes converting income to capital (TCGA 1992, s 184G)

**18.21** This situation arises where a company receives a receipt directly or indirectly on the disposal of an asset in connection with any arrangements. A chargeable gain accrues to the company on the asset disposal but capital losses accrue on other assets before or after the first asset's disposal as part of the arrangements. The arrangements enable a capital receipt to be accounted for instead of an income receipt, which would indeed have happened had the arrangements not been in place. The main purpose of the arrangement is to obtain a capital loss deduction from the capital gain irrespective of any other purpose.

## Avoidance involving losses: schemes securing a deduction (TCGA 1992, s 184H)

**18.22** This situation arises where a chargeable gain accrues to a company directly or indirectly in consequence of or in connection with any arrangements and losses accrued on any disposal of any asset before or after the first asset's disposal as part of the arrangements. Also as part of the arrangements the company or a connected company incurs expenditure which is allowable as a deduction in computing total profits but is not allowable in computing its chargeable gains. The main purpose of the arrangement is to obtain a deduction for the expenditure in computing profits and a capital loss deduction from the relevant gain irrespective of any other purpose.

Arm's-length arrangements, arrangements in respect of land, unconnected party arrangements and certain sale and leaseback arrangements are excluded.

## HMRC notice

**18.23** If HMRC consider that the purpose of these arrangements is to secure a tax advantage they may give the company a notice under *TCGA 1992, s 184G* or *184H*. If all conditions are satisfied no loss accruing to the relevant company may be deducted from the relevant gain.

If a company submits its tax return within a 90-day period after the receipt of the notice it may disregard the notice in preparing the return and within the 90-day period amend the return in order to comply with the notice.

If the company has already submitted its company tax return, HMRC can only give the company a notice in respect of these anti-avoidance schemes if a notice of enquiry has also been given to the company in respect of the return for the same period.

HMRC may give the company a notice after any enquiries into the return have been completed if two conditions are satisfied. First, that at the time the enquiries into the return were completed HMRC could not have been reasonably expected on the basis of information made available to them before or at that time or to an officer of theirs before that time to have been aware that the circumstances necessitated the issue of a notice. The second condition is that the company or any other person was requested to produce or provide information during an enquiry into the return for that period and if the request had been duly complied with HMRC could have been reasonably expected to give a notice in relation to that period.

# HUSBAND AND WIFE COMPANIES

**18.24** Spouses or civil partners, who jointly own and manage a private company, each have a personal allowance and the various tax brackets to apply to any income withdrawn from the company. In some circumstances HMRC regard all the income to fall to the income-producing spouse by means of a settlement where the other spouse is seen as taking no part in the function of the business and possessing a holding that only reflects an income right. This situation is currently being tested in the case of *Jones v Garnett* (*Inspector of Taxes*) [2005] EWCA 1553 and will reach the High Court in due course. See *Tottel's Income Tax 2006/07*.

*Chapter 19*

# Liquidations

## INSOLVENCY

### Insolvent company

**19.1** If a company becomes insolvent the only option may be to 'wind up' or liquidate the company. A solvent company may also be put into liquidation.

If a company becomes insolvent there are various courses or mixtures of courses of action that it can take. Firstly, the company can enter into a 'voluntary arrangement' with its creditors. Secondly, a secured creditor, with either a fixed or floating charge, such as the bank, may appoint a receiver who then assumes control of the company's business, who then becomes an administrative receiver. Thirdly, the court may make an administration order. An administrator will then take control of the company. An administrator has similar powers to a receiver. Finally, a compulsory liquidation may take place with the company being wound up by a court order under the *Insolvency Act 1986, s 73* or a voluntary liquidation may take place following a resolution passed at a general meeting of the company.

### Solvent company

**19.2** A solvent company may be put into liquidation when there is no further use for the company, say in a group reconstruction or when the shareholders or directors of a family company want to extract their capital. When such a course is contemplated the company directors, or a majority of them, must make a statutory declaration of solvency to the Registrar of Companies to the effect that the company will be able to pay or provide for all of its debts (including interest) within 12 months. Within five weeks of that declaration the directors must pass a resolution to wind up the company. A members' voluntary winding up starts on the day the resolution to wind up the company is passed.

# ADMINISTRATION PROCEEDINGS

## Administration order

**19.3** An administration order is a court order placing a company that is, or is likely to become, insolvent under the control of an administrator following an application by the company, its directors or a creditor. The purpose of the order is to preserve the company's business, allow a reorganisation or ensure the most advantageous realisation of its assets whilst protecting it from action of its creditors.

## Receivers and administrators

**19.4** A receiver takes his appointment from a secured creditor. Sometimes this is through a court order on behalf of the creditor. The receiver is assigned to take control of the secured assets on behalf of the creditor and to sell them if need be to pay off the creditors. If the receiver succeeds in this work, the directors continue with their responsibilities. If the receiver is unable to discharge the secured debt it normally follows that the company is put into liquidation. Prior to 15 September 2003, a receiver normally assumed control of the company's business as an administrative receiver with statutory powers. An administrative receiver is an insolvency practitioner. Administrative receivership was abolished for floating charges created on and after 15 September 2003 with certain exceptions (such as financial market transactions and public private partnerships). Under the *Enterprise Act 2002* lenders appoint administrators in situations that would previously have been dealt with by administrative receivership. From 15 September 2003 an administrative receiver in post must vacate office on the appointment of an administrator (HMRC Insolvency Manual INS 1203).

The administrator may be appointed by the court, the creditors or the directors to manage the affairs, business and property of company. Essentially, the administrator seeks to rescue the company and if possible seek better results for the creditors. Eventually he may realise property in order to make a distribution.

## Effect of appointment

**19.5** The appointment does not affect the corporate existence of the company. The directors and officers retain their respective positions and are not relieved of their duties and liabilities although the administrator has effective control of the company.

## Corporation tax in administration

**19.6** For companies entering administration on or after 15 September 2003, a new accounting period begins where the company enters into administration (*ICTA 1988, s 12(7ZA)*) and an accounting period ends where it ceases to be in administration (*ICTA 1988, s 12(3)(da)*). Within this time the accounting period may run to the next 12 months or to the original accounting date if so required. If the company is to be dissolved at the end of the administration period, the corporation tax will be charged on the company's profits for the final year based on current rates available at the time (*ICTA 1988, s 342A*). If the company receives any interest on overdue tax in the final accounting period, provided that it does not exceed £2,000, it will not be subject to corporation tax.

When a company enters into administration it does not cease to be the beneficial owner of its assets. Therefore the reconstruction procedure described in **15.5–15.24** will still apply.

Whether the company may claim group relief is a debatable point. As the administrator or receiver is effectively controlling the company, the company's shareholders cannot secure that the affairs of the company are conducted in accordance with their wishes (*ICTA 1988, s 840*). Therefore it could cease to be grouped with parent and subsidiaries for group relief (*ICTA 1988, s 410(1)(b)(ii)*). If the company arranges to dispose of a subsidiary it may lose entitlement to group relief (*ICTA 1988, s 410*).

## Effect of cessation of trade

**19.7** A company may continue to trade during its administration or liquidation period. However, such an event is unlikely. The date of cessation of trade marks the end of an accounting period (*ICTA 1988, s 12(3)*).

A cessation of trade has various corporation tax implications. Trading stock, if sold to an unconnected UK trade, is valued at sales price. In other circumstances, such as a sale to a connected party or an overseas trader it is valued at market value. The company should provide for all known bad debts and impairment losses. If trading ceases and a debt proves to be irrecoverable it can only be relieved against post-cessation receipts. Similarly all known expenses should be provided for.

The permanent cessation will give rise to a balancing charge or balancing allowance in the final period (*CAA 2001, s 65*). Disposal proceeds will be the sale price if sold to an unconnected third party or market value in any other case. Trading losses in the final period accounting period can be utilised in a group relief claim (see **10.7**) or carried back in a terminal loss claim (see **9.16**).

When a company ceases to trade its unrelieved trading losses are not available to shelter other income received in the period. It may still offset its non-trading deficits against its non-trading credits.

Unrelieved trading losses may be set against post cessation receipt income (*ICTA 1988, s 105*). In addition any balancing charge arising from the disposal of a building that is temporarily out of use may be relieved by the unutilised losses (*CAA 2001, s 354*).

## LIQUIDATION PROCEEDINGS

### Winding up

**19.8** The winding up of a company may take place voluntarily by company resolution or by order of the court (*IA 1986, s 73*). Following the winding-up order or resolution a liquidator is appointed to 'wind up' the affairs of the company; namely to realise the assets and settle outstanding liabilities. The liquidator will then apply to have the company dissolved and removed from the Register at Companies House. The company will then cease to exist. In a member's voluntary winding up the company is dissolved three months after the date on which the Registrar of Companies is advised that the winding up is complete.

### Liquidator

**19.9** A liquidator can be appointed by the creditors, the members or the court, depending on the type of liquidation. The liquidator is assigned to realise all company assets within his control and to apply the proceeds in payment of the company's debts in order of priority. If any surplus funds remain, the liquidator will repay the members the amounts paid up on their shares. If any further surplus remains he will distribute the surplus amongst the members according to their entitlement.

### Commencement

**19.10** A winding up commences on the date that the resolution is passed for a voluntary members' or creditors' winding up or the date of the winding-up petition in any other case (HMRC Insolvency Manual INS 1520). On hearing a petition the court will make an order for the winding up of the company if all necessary conditions have been followed and the court is satisfied that the company is unable to pay its debts. If the winding up follows a company administration the date the company went into administration is the date of the liquidation (HMRC Insolvency Manual INS 1612).

## Corporation tax

**19.11** The date of the winding-up order marks the end of one accounting period and the beginning of the next. Thereafter the accounting periods run to the 12-month anniversary of the winding up (*ICTA 1988, s 12*(*7*)). The profits during the winding up remain chargeable to corporation tax on the company and not on the liquidator (*ICTA 1988, s 344*(*2*)). If the company receives any interest on overdue tax in the final accounting period, provided that it does not exceed £2,000 it will not be subject to corporation tax (*ICTA 1988, s 342*(*3A*)).

The liquidator will provide HMRC with a provisional date for completion of the winding up. The corporation tax will be charged on the company's profits for the final year based on current rates available at the time (*ICTA 1988, s 342*(*2*)(*a*)).

If it transpires that the provisional date is incorrect an accounting period is deemed to end on that date and a new one commences (*ICTA 1988, s 342*(*6*)).

## Effect of winding-up order

**19.12** When a company has entered into liquidation it loses the beneficial interest in its assets (*Ayerst v C & K* (*Construction*) *Ltd* (1975) 50 TC 651, [1975] STC 345, [1976] AC 167, [1975] 2 All ER 537). Hence group relief both for groups and consortiums is no longer available (*ICTA 1988, s 410*(*1*)(*b*)(*ii*)) and reconstruction hive down utilising *ICTA 1988, s 343* (see **15.5–15.24**) is also prohibited. The company remains a group member for capital gains purposes (*TCGA 1992, s 170*(*11*)); therefore the liquidator may transfer assets to group members with *TCGA 1992, s 171* continuing to apply (see **10.21**).

No distributions of profits may be made to shareholders in respect of their share capital (*ICTA 1988, s 209*(*1*)). The close company distribution rules of *ICTA 1988, s 418* continue to apply. However, distributions of assets may still be made (*ICTA 1988, s 209*(*4*), (*5*), (*6*)) (see **16.5**).

## Loans to participators

**19.13** Loans to participators may either be called in, in order to pay out the shareholders or alternatively they will be written off. The normal procedures will follow as described in **4.6–4.22**.

## ESC 16

**19.14** Where a company has ceased business it may ask the Registrar of Companies to strike it off under *CA 1985, s 652A* or wait for the Registrar of Companies to strike off the company (see **16.26–16.28** and HMRC Company Taxation Manual CTM 36220).

## Taxation liabilities of office holders

**19.15** Although a receiver deals with all preferential claims, the corporation tax arising during receivership remains the responsibility of the company and will be dealt with by any subsequent liquidator either as an unsecured claim or to the extent that the income and gains arose after the commencement of winding up as a liquidation expense.

When appointed a liquidator or an administrator becomes the proper officer of the company dealing with its corporation tax affairs (*TMA 1970, s 108*(*3*)).

Corporation tax arising prior to appointment is an unsecured claim; post appointment it is an administration or liquidation expense and strictly must be paid ahead of the liquidator's remuneration (*Re Mesco Properties Ltd* (1979) 54 TC 238, [1979] STC 788, [1980] 1 WLR 96, [1980] 1 All ER 117).

## Subsidiary company in liquidation

**19.16** The substantial shareholding exemption (*TCGA 1992, Sch 7AC*(*3*)) prevents a capital gain and a capital loss accruing where more than 10% of the shares of a trading company are owned by another UK company (see **12.28–12.32**) if the shares are held throughout a 12-month period beginning not more than two years before the date of disposal. In other circumstances the holding company may be able to make a negligible asset claim under *TCGA 1992, s 24*.

During the liquidation period it is unlikely that the company will be carrying on a trade. Therefore the liquidator's costs will not be relievable. They may form part of the incidental costs of disposal of certain assets, but apart from that no relief will be given.

A close company in liquidation may be treated as a close investment holding company (CIC) (see **4.23–4.26**). Where a close company commences liquidation, *ICTA 1988, s 13A(4)* provides that it is not to be treated as a CIC in the accounting period immediately following the commencement of winding-up if it was not a CIC in the accounting period immediately before liquidation commenced. In any subsequent accounting period a close company in liquidation will be excluded from being a CIC only if it then meets the usual conditions of *ICTA 1988, s 13A(2)* (see **4.24**). HMRC have commented that it may happen that there is a very short gap between the end of a period in which the company was not a CIC and the commencement of winding up, so that strictly the company will not have the benefit of *s 13A(4)*. This may cause difficulties in some cases and an undertaking has been given to review the position where a company has not been able to avoid a short gap and would suffer significantly if not given the protection of *s 13(4)* (HMRC Company Taxation Manual CTM 60780).

From a practical perspective HMRC should be contacted to ascertain whether any enquiries are to be made. Any distributions to shareholders during the liquidation period are capital distributions and do not fall within *ICTA 1988, s 209(1)*.

*Chapter 20*

# The Year End

## CORPORATION TAX COMPUTATION

**20.1** Shortly after the year end the company will prepare its annual accounts, whereupon it will be able to prepare its corporation tax computation and self-assessment return. Sample returns have been reproduced in the following pages by kind permission of HMRC.

## Adjusted profits

**20.2** A master corporation tax computation and capital allowances computation is shown on the following pages that may be adapted to suit individual company needs. The company will commence by adjusting its trading profits in the following manner.

**Adjustment of profits under Schedule D Case I**

**Pro forma**

| | | £ | £ |
|---|---|---|---|
| Profit before tax per accounts | | | |
| Add: | Expenditure charged in the accounts, but not allowable as a deduction for Schedule D Case I purposes | | |
| | Income which has not been credited in the accounts but which is taxable under Schedule D Case I | _______ | |
| | | | _______ |

| | | £ | £ |
|---|---|---|---|
| Less: | Income credited in the accounts, but not taxable under Schedule D Case I | | |
| | Expenditure not charged in the accounts, but allowable as a deduction under Schedule D Case I | | |
| Schedule D Case I | | | |

The corporation tax payable will then be calculated. See Chapter 2 for rates and marginal relief computations.

## Corporation tax computation

**20.3** The company will then bring all its income into charge under the various schedule headings to calculation it PCTCT (profits chargeable to corporation tax).

**Corporation tax computation for the accounting period of ... months ended on .........**

| | | £ |
|---|---|---|
| Schedule D Case I | | |
| Schedule A | | |
| Schedule D Case III | | |
| Schedule D Case V | | |
| Other income | | |
| Schedule VI | | |
| Chargeable gains | | |
| Less: | Expenses of management | |
| | Charges on income | |
| Profits chargeable to corporation tax (PCTCT) | | |

## Capital allowance computation

**20.4** The company will also prepare its capital allowances claim. The following is a master pro-forma computation that may be used for this purpose.

**Capital allowances—plant and machinery computation for the ... months ended on .........**

| | | *Main pool* | *Long-life pool* | *Expensive car* | *Short-life asset* | *Allowance given* |
|---|---|---|---|---|---|---|
| | £ | £ | £ | £ | £ | £ |
| Allowable qualifying expenditure b/f | | | | | | |
| Additions not qualifying for FYA | | | | | | |
| Disposal proceeds | | | | | | |
| Balancing allowance/ balancing charge | | | | | | |
| WDA (25%) | | | | | | |
| WDA (6%) (restricted) | | | | | | |
| Additions qualifying for FYA | | | | | | |
| Less: FYA | | | | | | |
| Allowable qualifying expenditure c/f | | | | | | |
| Total allowances for year | | | | | | |

## Capital gains

**20.5** A company's chargeable gains incurred during an accounting period are assessed to corporation tax together with its other income for that accounting period. Capital gains legislation is often used as an incentive to provide tax breaks or as an anti-avoidance regulator. The main incentives and avoidance mechanisms discussed are as follows:

**Capital gains incentives**

| | |
|---|---|
| Indexation continues to be available to companies | **5.39** |
| Roll-over relief on replacement of business assets | **6.51** |
| Intra-group transfers of assets on a no-gain no loss basis | **10.21** |
| Election to treat a group asset disposal as occurring in the company with capital losses available for relief | **10.24** |
| Intra group investment asset and trading asset transfers | **10.25–10.27** |
| Relief for losses on investment in unquoted trading companies | **12.27** |
| The substantial shareholding exemption | **12.28–12.32** |
| Corporate venturing scheme | **12.41–12.42** |
| CGT on reconstructions | **15.7–15.10** |

**Capital gains anti-avoidance regulators**

| | |
|---|---|
| Companies leaving a group – crystallisation of capital gain on intra-group transfers | **10.29** |
| Depreciatory transactions | **10.31** |
| Dividend stripping | **10.32** |
| Pre-entry losses and gains | **10.33** |
| The targeted anti-avoidance rules (TAARs) | **18.16–18.23** |

## PLANNING

**20.6** A company's accounts and corporation tax computation are based on its transactions for a set period. Once that period has ended the time has passed to make any changes to the transactions. Hence all planning should ideally take place before the year end.

The minimisation of corporation tax liabilities and the maximisation of reported profits is possibly each and every company's ultimate goal. Under corporation tax self-assessment the company should be aware that planning also looks to ensuring that the company's returns are accurate and timely to avoid interest and penalties and to minimise any adverse consequences arising from an enquiry.

The following list is a summary of some of the areas that a company may wish to turn its attention to with respect to the year end. The list is by no means exhaustive:

- **Accounting dates**. If a company pays corporation tax by quarterly instalments it will pay its first instalment 6 months and 13 days after the beginning of the accounting period. If the trade is seasonal it might not have sufficient funds to pay the corporation tax. Consider changing the accounting date so that the high earning period falls at the beginning of the year rather than the end. See **3.11**.

- **Apportionment of profits**. If an accounting period is longer than 12 months, profits are normally apportioned pro rata on a time basis. However, an actual basis may be used if this gives a more accurate result. See **2.6**.
- **Assets** may be transferred to group companies without a charge to capital gains tax arising. A deemed transfer may take place to another group company prior to a disposal to a third party, in order to utilise that company's capital losses. An election must be made within two years from end of the vendor's accounting period in which the disposal is made to a third party (*TCGA 1992, s 171A*). See **10.21**.
- **Associated companies**. Associated companies eradicate the benefit of the small companies rate of corporation tax. Prepare a company structure in good time to ascertain whether the separate companies are actually necessary. See **4.32**.
- **Capital allowance** claims must be made or amended or withdrawn within 12 months after the company's return filing date. If the return is under enquiry this period may be extended to the later of 30 days after a closure notice is issued on the completion of an enquiry or 30 days after HMRC issues a notice of amendment to a return following the completion of an enquiry or 30 days after the determination of any appeal against an HMRC amendment. Enquiry does not include a restricted enquiry into an amendment to a return (restricted because the time limit for making an enquiry into the return itself has expired) (*FA 1998, Sch 18, para 82*). See Chapter 6.
- **Cars**. Instead of purchasing a standard model that will only qualify for a £3,000 writing-down allowance at the maximum, consider purchasing a low emission vehicle. Purchases made before 31 March 2008, qualify for a 100% first year allowance. See **6.17**.
- **Close investment holding company**. Where a company is making investments in land and property and that property is used by a person connected with the company, the company may be classed as a close investment holding company, liable to pay corporation tax at the full rate. See **4.23–4.26**.
- Assets eligible for capital allowances may be transferred between **connected parties** at tax written-down value. Both parties must submit an election to HMRC within two years from date of sale (*CAA 2001, s 569(1)*). See **15.2**.
- **Corporate venturing scheme**. Since 6 April 2006, the gross assets of a qualifying company issuing shares under a CVS must not exceed £7,000,000 immediately before the issue and must not exceed

£8,000,000 immediately afterwards. Group companies are included. Previously, the gross asset test was £15,000,000 and £16,000,000 (*FA 2006, Sch 14, para 3*). Similar changes have been made for the enterprise investment scheme and venture capital trusts. Companies should take note of their gross assets if considering a share issue under one of these schemes. See **12.35**.

- **Discovery assessment**. The risk of a discovery assessment may be avoided if supporting details of possible contentious items are supplied to HMRC with the corporation tax computation. This may be for instance any analysis of repairs, legal expenses or the like. If a different interpretation of the law is taken from that viewed by HMRC this should be clearly explained. The Revenue Manuals explain HMRC's interpretation of the law and working practices. See **2.26**.

- **Dividends**. Interim dividends are due and payable on the day they are declared. For this reason they may not be effective in clearing an overdue director's loan account. See **4.18**.

- **Energy saving plant and machinery** qualifies for 100% first year allowance. Consider whether it is beneficial for the company to use environmentally beneficial plant and machinery. See **6.21**.

- **Enterprise management incentives**. Ensure the company claims for any outstanding corporation tax relief on shares issued at a discount (*FA 2006, s 93*). See **5.24**.

- **Group relief** claims must be made or amended or withdrawn within 12 months after the company's return filing date. If the return is under enquiry this period may be extended to the later of 30 days after a closure notice is issued on the completion of an enquiry or 30 days after HMRC issues a notice of amendment to a return following the completion of an enquiry or 30 days after the determination of any appeal against an HMRC amendment. Enquiry does not include a restricted enquiry into an amendment to a return (restricted because the time limit for making an enquiry into the return itself has expired) (*FA 1998, Sch 18, para 74*). See Chapter 10.

- **HMRC**. A company should ensure that HMRC has been informed that the company is within the charge to corporation tax or has commenced to trade. The company should ensure that HMRC has the correct details for the company. It is the company's duty to keep HMRC informed. See **2.2**.

- **Intangible assets** allow debits and credits to follow the accounting treatment. A company might wish to ensure that its depreciation policy is suitable. See **7.10**.

- **Loans to directors**. Outstanding loans to a director at the year end attract a charge under *s 419* if not repaid within nine months of the year end. Ensure there are no outstanding loans and that they are repaid promptly. See **4.14–4.22**.

- **Long life assets**. If a company spends more than £100,000 on plant and machinery with an expected working life of at least 25 years the 6% writing-down allowance applies. The £100,000 is divided between associated companies. Consider the timing of major asset purchases. See **6.32**.

- **Minutes**. The company should ensure that it has put good board minutes in place when recommending a dividend payment and when authorising directors' bonus payments. See **5.15**.

- Relief for a **non-trading deficit** on a loan relationship must be made within two years from end of the accounting period in which a deficit arises. If the deficit is to be carried forward the claim must be made within two years from the end of the accounting period following the deficit period, or within such further period as the Board may allow (*FA 1996, s 83*(*6*), (*7*)). See **11.17–11.22**.

- **Pension contributions**. A small company may consider making additional pension contributions on behalf of its director/shareholders. New spreading rules apply from 6 April 2006 and the company should be aware of the possible business purpose test restriction. See **5.28**.

- **Plant and machinery** qualifies for capital allowances. Small companies may claim a 50% first year allowance in the period commencing 1 April 2006. A company may wish to ensure that any purchases of plant and machinery are brought in the most appropriate accounting period. See **6.19**.

- **Profits**. The corporation tax computation is based on the reported profits. Certain items of expenditure may be accelerated in order to minimise profits in a period. This may simply be placing orders to meet the company's requirements or considering additional directors' and staff bonuses. See **5.15** regarding bonus payments.

  Similarly income may be deferred if sales transactions near the year end may be postponed to the subsequent accounting period.

- **Research and development**. The development of new processes may qualify for R & D enhanced revenue deduction if of a revenue nature or a 100% allowance if capital expenditure. The company would be well advised to review its plans in this area. Claims must be made within the normal corporation tax timescale two years after the end of the accounting period. As regards the enhanced deduction, claims for accounting periods ended on or after 31 March 2006 must be made on the earlier of six years from the end of the relevant accounting period or 31 March 2008 (*FA 2006, Sch 3*). See Chapter 8.

- **Roll-over relief**. If a company is disposing of tangible assets or intangible assets it is well advised to consider purchasing new assets either 12 months before or within 3 years after sale to claim roll-over relief to reduce the chargeable gain. See **6.51–6.58** and **7.22**.
- **Short life assets**. If an asset on which capital allowances are to be claimed will be disposed of within four years, consider making a short life asset election to accelerate a balancing allowance. The claim must be made within two years from the end of the chargeable period in which the asset was acquired (*CAA 2001, s 85*). See **6.31**.
- If **stock** is transferred to a connected party on cessation of a trade it must be valued at the higher of cost or sales price. The election must be made within two years from the end of accounting period in which trade ceased (*ICTA 1988, s 100(1C)*). See **19.7**.
- If a **subsidiary company** with surplus funds is in liquidation it could invest in quoted shares in UK companies to avoid the 30% corporation tax rate on attaining a CIHC status. The dividends will not be taxable so the 30% CT rate cannot apply. See **4.23–4.24**.
- **Surrenderable losses** for group relief purposes may require to be set off against the company's other profits before surrender. The following is a brief summary. See **10.7** for full details.

| | *Required to be set off against claimant company's profits before used in a group relief claim* |
|---|---|
| Trading losses | No |
| Excess capital allowances | No |
| Non-trading loan relationship debits | No |
| Charges on income | Yes |
| Schedule A losses | Yes |
| Management expenses | Yes |
| Non-trading loss on a loan relationship | Yes |

- **Trade**. A trade must continue for *s 393* losses to be utilised. See **9.14**. For a carry back the trade must have been in existence at some time during the previous 12 months. For a carry forward the loss continues to be available until the trade ceases. See **9.2**.
- The company's **trading status** is important to retain loss and investment reliefs. Consideration should be given to the company's long term plans. Restructuring may be seen as necessary to separate the investment and the trading activities. See **15.7–15.24** and **16.13–16.18**.

- **Transfer pricing** rules now apply to all companies entering into transactions with associates. Ensure that documentation is in place to support the inter company arrangement. See Chapter 14. If a company with which the company trades has a transfer pricing adjustment the company should ensure that it claims the compensating relief. See **14.15.**

- A loss on disposal of shares in an **unquoted trading company** may be set against income of an investment company. The claim must be made within two years from end of accounting period in which the loss occurred (*ICTA 1988, s 573(2)*). See **12.26**.

# Appendix

## Company Tax Return form
### CT600 (2006) Version 2
**for accounting periods ending on or after 1 July 1999**

**Your company tax return**

**If we send the company a *Notice* to deliver a company tax return (form *CT603*) it has to comply by the filing date or we charge a penalty, even if there is no tax to pay. A return includes a company tax return form, any Supplementary Pages, accounts, computations and any relevant information.**
**Is this the right form for the company? Read the advice on pages 3 to 6 of the Company tax return guide (the *Guide*) before you start.**
**The forms in the CT600 series set out the information we need and provide a standard format for calculations. Use the *Guide* which contains general information you may need and box by box advice to help you complete the return form.**
**Please note that some boxes on form *CT600* are not in order, reflecting changes made since the form was first published in 2004.**

**Company information**

**Company name**

**Company registration number** | **Tax Reference as shown on the CT603** | **Type of Company**

**Registered office address**

**Postcode**

**About this return**

**This is the above company's return for the period**
from (dd/mm/yyyy) to (dd/mm/yyyy)

*Put an 'X' in the appropriate box(es) below*

A repayment is due for this return period

A repayment is due for an earlier period

Making more than one return for this company now

This return contains estimated figures

**Disclosure of tax avoidance schemes**
Notice of disclosable avoidance schemes

**Transfer pricing**
Compensating adjustment claimed

Company qualifies for SME exemption

**Accounts**
I attach accounts and computations
- for the period to which this return relates
- for a different period

If you are not attaching accounts and computations, say why not

**Supplementary Pages**
*If you are enclosing any Supplementary Pages put an 'X' in the appropriate box(es)*

Loans to participators by close companies, form *CT600A*

Controlled foreign companies, form *CT600B*

Group and Consortium, form *CT600C*

Insurance, form *CT600D*

Charities and Community Amateur Sports Clubs (CASCs), form *CT600E*

Tonnage tax, form *CT600F*

Corporate Venturing Scheme, form *CT600G*

Cross-border royalties, form *CT600H*

Supplementary charge in respect of ring fence trade, form *CT600I*

Disclosure of tax avoidance schemes, form *CT600J*

HMRC 08/06 CT600 (2006) Version 2

Page 2

## Company tax calculation

**Turnover**

1 **Total turnover from trade or profession** — box 1 £

2 **Banks, building societies, insurance companies and other financial concerns.** *Put an 'X' in this box if you do not have a recognised turnover and have not made an entry in box 1* — box 2

**Income**

3 **Trading and professional profits** — box 3 £

4 **Trading losses brought forward claimed against profits** — box 4 £

5 **Net trading and professional profits** — box 5 £ (box 3 minus box 4)

6 **Bank, building society or other interest, and profits and gains from non-trading loan relationships** — box 6 £

7 *Put an 'X' in box 7 if the figure in box 6 is net of carrying back a deficit from a later accounting period* — box 7

8 **Annuities, annual payments and discounts not arising from loan relationships and from which income tax has not been deducted** — box 8 £

9 **Overseas income within Sch D Case V** — box 9 £

10 **Income from which income tax has been deducted** — box 10 £

11 **Income from UK land and buildings** — box 11 £

12 **Non-trading gains on intangible fixed assets** — box 12 £

13 **Tonnage tax profits** — box 13 £

14 **Annual profits and gains not falling under any other heading** — box 14 £

15 **Income within Sch D Case VI** — box 15 £ (total of boxes 12, 13 and 14)

**Chargeable gains**

16 **Gross chargeable gains** — box 16 £

17 **Allowable losses including losses brought forward** — box 17 £

18 **Net chargeable gains** — box 18 £ (box 16 minus box 17)

19 **Losses brought forward against certain investment income** — box 19 £

20 **Non-trade deficits on loan relationships (including interest), and derivative contracts (financial instruments) brought forward** — box 20 £

21 **Profits before other deductions and reliefs** — box 21 £ (net sum of boxes 5, 6, 8, 9, 10, 11, 15, & 18 minus sum of boxes 19 and 20)

CT600 (2006) Version 2

## Deductions and reliefs

| | | |
|---|---|---|
| 22 CVS loss relief, and losses on unquoted shares under S573 ICTA 1988 | 22 £ | |
| 23 *Put an 'X' in box 23 if the entry in box 22 includes CVS loss relief, complete and attach form CT600G* | 23 | |
| 24 Management expenses under S75 ICTA 1988 | 24 £ | |
| 25 Interest distributions under S468L ICTA 1988 | 25 £ | |
| 26 Schedule A losses for this or previous accounting period under S392A ICTA 1988 | 26 £ | |
| 27 Capital allowances for the purposes of management of the business | 27 £ | |
| 28 Non-trade deficits for this accounting period from loan relationships and derivative contracts (financial instruments) | 28 £ | |
| 29 Non-trading losses on intangible fixed assets | 29 £ | |
| 30 Trading losses of this or a later accounting period under S393A ICTA 1988 | 30 £ | |
| 31 *Put an 'X' in box 31 if amounts carried back from later accounting periods are included in box 30* | 31 | |
| 32 Non-trade capital allowances | 32 £ | |
| 33 Total of deductions and reliefs | | total of boxes 22, 24 to 30 and 32<br>33 £ |
| 34 Profits before charges and group relief | | box 21 minus box 33<br>34 £ |
| 35 Charges paid | 35 £ | |
| 36 Group relief | 36 £ | |

| | |
|---|---|
| 37 Profits chargeable to corporation tax | box 34 minus boxes 35 and 36<br>37 £ |

**Page 4**

## Tax calculation

38 Franked investment income — 38 £

39 Number of associated companies in this period — 39
or
40 Associated companies in the first financial year — 40

41 Associated companies in the second financial year — 41

42 *Put an 'X' in box 42 if the company claims to be charged at the starting rate or the small companies' rate on any part of its profits, or is claiming marginal rate relief* — 42

**Enter how much profit has to be charged and at what rate of tax**

| Financial year *(yyyy)* | Amount of profit | Rate of tax | Tax |
|---|---|---|---|
| 43 | 44 £ | 45 | 46 £ p |
| | 47 £ | 48 | 49 £ p |
| | 50 £ | 51 | 52 £ p |
| 53 | 54 £ | 55 | 56 £ p |
| | 57 £ | 58 | 59 £ p |
| | 60 £ | 61 | 62 £ p |

63 Corporation tax — total of boxes 46, 49, 52, 56, 59 and 62 — 63 £ p

64 Marginal rate relief — 64 £ p

65 Corporation tax net of marginal rate relief — 65 £ p

66 Underlying rate of corporation tax — 66 • %

67 Profits matched with non-corporate distributions — 67 £

68 Tax at non-corporate distributions rate — 68 £ p

69 Tax at underlying rate on remaining profits — 69 £ p

70 Corporation tax chargeable — *See note for box 70 in CT600 Guide* — 70 £ p

## Reliefs and deductions in terms of tax

71 CVS investment relief — 71 £ p

72 Community investment relief — 72 £ p

73 Double taxation relief — 73 £ p

74 *Put an 'X' in box 74 if box 73 includes an Underlying Rate relief claim* — 74

75 *Put an 'X' in box 75 if box 73 includes any amount carried back from a later period* — 75

76 Advance corporation tax — 76 £ p

77 Total reliefs and deductions in terms of tax — total of boxes 71, 72, 73 and 76 — 77 £ p

CT600 (2006) Version 2

## Calculation of tax outstanding or overpaid

| | | Box |
|---|---|---|
| 78 | **Net corporation tax liability** | 78 £ p (box 70 minus box 77) |
| 79 | **Tax payable under S419 ICTA 1988** | 79 £ p |
| 80 | *Put an 'X' in box 80 if you completed box A11 in the Supplementary Pages CT600A* | 80 |
| 81 | **Tax payable under S747 ICTA 1988** | 81 £ p |
| 82 | **Tax payable under S501A ICTA 1988** | 82 £ p |
| 83 | **Tax chargeable** | 83 £ p (total of boxes 78, 79, 81 and 82) |
| 84 | **Income tax deducted from gross income included in profits** | 84 £ p |
| 85 | **Income tax repayable to the company** | 85 £ p |
| 86 | **Tax payable - this is your self-assessment of tax payable** | 86 £ p (box 83 minus box 84) |

## Tax reconciliation

| | | Box |
|---|---|---|
| 87 | **Research and Development tax credit, including any vaccines tax credit, or film tax credit** | 87 £ p |
| 88 | **Land remediation or life assurance company tax credit** | 88 £ p |
| 89 | **Research and Development tax credit payable, including any vaccines tax credit, or film tax credit payable** | 89 £ p (box 87 minus box 86) |
| 90 | **Land remediation or life assurance company tax credit payable** | 90 £ p (total of (boxes 87 + 88) minus (boxes 86 + 89)) |
| 161 | **Ring fence corporation tax included** | 161 £ p |
| 166 | **Tax under S501A ICTA 1988 included** | 166 £ p |
| 91 | **Tax already paid (and not already repaid)** | 91 £ p |
| 92 | **Tax outstanding** | 92 £ p (total of box 86 minus sum of boxes 87, 88 and 91) |
| 93 | **Tax overpaid** | 93 £ p (total sum of boxes 87, 88 and 91 minus box 86) |
| 94 | **Tax refunds surrendered to the company under S102 FA 1989** | 94 £ p |

## Indicators

*Put an 'X' in the relevant box(es) if, in the period, the company*

| | | Box |
|---|---|---|
| 95 | *should have made (whether it has or not) instalment payments under the Corporation Tax (Instalment Payments) Regulations 1998* | 95 |
| 96 | *is within a group payment arrangement for this period* | 96 |
| 97 | *has written down or sold intangible assets* | 97 |
| 98 | *has made cross-border royalty payments* | 98 |

**Page 6**

## Information about enhanced expenditure

### Research and development (R&D) or films enhanced expenditure

**167** *Put an 'X' in box 167 if the claim is for films expenditure* — 167 [ ]

**99** *Put an 'X' in box 99 if the claim is made by a small or medium-sized enterprise (SME), including a SME subcontractor to a large company* — 99 [ ]

**100** *Put an 'X' in box 100 if the claim is made by a large company* — 100 [ ]

**101 R&D or films enhanced expenditure** — 101 £

**102 R&D enhanced expenditure of a SME on work sub-contracted to it by a large company** — 102 £

**103 Vaccines research expenditure** — 103 £

### Land remediation enhanced expenditure

**104 Enter amount equal to 150% of actual expenditure** — 104 £

## Information about capital allowances and balancing charges

### Charges and allowances included in calculation of trading profits or losses

| | Capital Allowances | Balancing Charges |
|---|---|---|
| 105-106 Machinery and plant - long-life assets | 105 £ | 106 £ |
| 107-108 Machinery and plant - other (general pool) | 107 £ | 108 £ |
| 109-110 Cars outside general pool | 109 £ | 110 £ |
| 111-112 Industrial buildings and structures | 111 £ | 112 £ |
| 162-163 Business premises renovation | 162 £ | 163 £ |
| 113-114 Other charges and allowances | 113 £ | 114 £ |

### Charges and allowances not included in calculation of trading profits or losses

| | Capital Allowances | Balancing Charges |
|---|---|---|
| 164-165 Business premises renovation | 164 £ | 165 £ |
| 115-116 Other non-trading charges and allowances | 115 £ | 116 £ |

**117** *Put an 'X' in box 117 if box 115 entry includes flat conversion allowances* — 117 [ ]

### Expenditure

**118 Expenditure on machinery and plant on which first year allowance is claimed** — 118 £

**119** *Put an 'X' in box 119 if claim includes enhanced capital allowances for designated energy-saving investments* — 119 [ ]

**120 Qualifying expenditure on machinery and plant on long-life assets** — 120 £

**121 Qualifying expenditure on machinery and plant on other assets** — 121 £

CT600 (2006) Version 2

## Losses, deficits and excess amounts

| | Arising | Maximum available for surrender as group relief |
|---|---|---|
| 122-123 Trading losses Case I | calculated under S393 ICTA 1988<br>122 £ | calculated under S393A ICTA 1988<br>123 £ |
| 124 Trading losses Case V | calculated under S393 ICTA 1988<br>124 £ | |
| 125-126 Non-trade deficits on loan relationships and derivative contracts | calculated under S82 FA 1996<br>125 £ | calculated under S83 FA 1996<br>126 £ |
| 127-128 Schedule A losses | calculated under S392A ICTA 1988<br>127 £ | calculated under S403 ICTA 1988<br>128 £ |
| 129 Overseas property business losses Case V | calculated under S392B ICTA 1988<br>129 £ | |
| 130 Losses Case VI | calculated under S396 ICTA 1988<br>130 £ | |
| 131 Capital losses | calculated under S16 TCGA 1992<br>131 £ | |
| 132-133 Non-trading losses on intangible fixed assets | calculated under S29 FA 2002<br>132 £ | calculated under S403 ICTA 1988<br>133 £ |
| | Excess | |
| 134 Excess non-trade capital allowances | | calculated under S403 ICTA 1988<br>134 £ |
| 135 Excess charges | | calculated under S403 ICTA 1988<br>135 £ |
| 136-137 Excess management expenses | calculated under S75 ICTA 1988<br>136 £ | calculated under S403 ICTA 1988<br>137 £ |
| 138 Excess interest distributions | calculated under S468L(7) ICTA 1988<br>138 £ | |

## Overpayments and repayments

### Small repayments

If you do not want us to make small repayments please either put an 'X' in box 139 or complete box 140 below. 'Repayments' here include tax, interest, and late-filing penalties or any combination of them.

Do not repay £20 or less **139** ☐ Do not repay sums of **140** £ ______ or less. *Enter whole figure only*

### Repayments for the period covered by this return

| | |
|---|---|
| 141 Repayment of corporation tax | 141 £ p |
| 142 Repayment of income tax | 142 £ p |
| 143 Payable Research and Development tax credit | 143 £ p |
| 168 Payable film tax credit | 168 £ p |
| 144 Payable land remediation or life assurance company tax credit | 144 £ p |

**Surrender under S102 FA 1989 (including surrenders under Regulation 9 of the Instalments Regulations)**
*Repayments of advance corporation tax cannot be surrendered.*

145 The following amount is to be surrendered under S102 FA 1989, and either — **145** £ p

146 the joint Notice is attached — 146 ☐
or
147 will follow — 147 ☐

*(put an 'X' in either box 146 or box 147)*

148 Please stop repayment of the following amount until I send you the Notice — 148 £ p

CT600 (2006) Version 2

**Page 8**

**Bank details (for person to whom the repayment is to be made)**

**Repayment is made quickly and safely by direct credit to a bank or building society account.**
**Please complete the following details:**

**Name of bank or building society**

149

**Branch sort code**

150

**Account number**

151

**Name of account**

152

**Building society reference**

153

**Payments to a person other than the company**

**Complete the authority below if you want the repayment to be made to a person other than the company.**
**I, as** *(enter status - company secretary, treasurer, liquidator or authorised agent, etc.)*

154

**of** *(enter name of company)*

155

**authorise** *(enter name)*

156

*(enter address)*

157

**Postcode**

**Nominee reference**

158

**to receive payment on the company's behalf.**

**Signature**

159

**Name** *(in capitals)*

160

## Declaration

**Warning - Giving false information in the return, or concealing any part of the company's profits or tax payable, can lead to both the company and yourself being prosecuted.**

**Declaration**
**The information I have given in this company tax return is correct and complete to the best of my knowledge and belief.**

**Signature**

**Name** *(in capitals)*

**Date** *(dd/mm/yyyy)*

**Status**

**CT600 (2006) Version 2**

# Company - Short Tax Return form

**CT600 (Short) (2006) Version 2**

**for accounting periods ending on or after 1 July 1999**

## Your company tax return

**If we send the company a *Notice* to deliver a company tax return (form *CT603*) it has to comply by the filing date, or we charge a penalty, even if there is no tax to pay. A return includes a company tax return form, any Supplementary Pages, accounts, computations and any relevant information.**

**Is this the right form for the company? Read the advice on pages 3 to 6 of the Company tax return guide (the *Guide*) before you start.**

**The forms in the CT600 series set out the information we need and provide a standard format for calculations. Use the *Guide* which contains general information you may need and box by box advice to help you complete the return form.**

## Company information

**Company name**

**Company registration number**

**Tax Reference as shown on the CT603**

**Type of company**

**Registered office address**

**Postcode**

## About this return

**This is the above company's return for the period**

from (dd/mm/yyyy) to (dd/mm/yyyy)

*Put an 'X' in the appropriate box(es) below*

A repayment is due for this return period

A repayment is due for an earlier period

Making more than one return for this company now

This return contains estimated figures

**Disclosure of tax avoidance schemes**

Notice of disclosable avoidance schemes

**Transfer pricing**

Compensating adjustment claimed

Company qualifies for SME exemption

**Accounts**

I attach accounts and computations

for the period to which this return relates

for a different period

If you are not attaching accounts and computations, say why not

**Supplementary Pages**

*If you are enclosing any Supplementary Pages put an 'X' in the appropriate box(es)*

Loans to participators by close companies, form *CT600A*

Charities and Community Amateur Sports Clubs (CASCs), form *CT600E*

Disclosure of tax avoidance schemes, form *CT600J*

Page 2

## Company tax calculation

### Turnover

1 Total turnover from trade or profession — 1 £

### Income

3 Trading and professional profits — 3 £

4 Trading losses brought forward claimed against profits — 4 £

5 Net trading and professional profits — box 3 minus box 4 — 5 £

6 Bank, building society or other interest, and profits and gains from non-trading loan relationships — 6 £

11 Income from UK land and buildings — 11 £

14 Annual profits and gains not falling under any other heading — 14 £

### Chargeable gains

16 Gross chargeable gains — 16 £

17 Allowable losses including losses brought forward — 17 £

18 Net chargeable gains — box 16 minus box 17 — 18 £

**21 Profits before other deductions and reliefs** — sum of boxes 5, 6, 11, 14 & 18 — 21 £

### Deductions and Reliefs

24 Management expenses under S75 ICTA 1988 — 24 £

30 Trading losses of this or a later accounting period under S393A ICTA 1988 — 30 £

31 *Put an 'X' in box 31 if amounts carried back from later accounting periods are included in box 30* — 31

32 Non-trade capital allowances — 32 £

35 Charges paid — 35 £

**37 Profits chargeable to corporation tax** — box 21 minus boxes 24, 30, 32 and 35 — 37 £

### Tax calculation

38 Franked investment income — 38 £

39 Number of associated companies in this period — 39

or

40 Associated companies in the first financial year — 40

41 Associated companies in the second financial year — 41

42 *Put an 'X' in box 42 if the company claims to be charged at the starting rate or the small companies' rate on any part of its profits, or is claiming marginal rate relief* — 42

Enter how much profit has to be charged and at what rate of tax

| Financial year *(yyyy)* | Amount of profit | Rate of tax | Tax |
|---|---|---|---|
| 43 | 44 £ | 45 | 46 £ p |
| 53 | 54 £ | 55 | 56 £ p |

63 Corporation tax — total of boxes 46 and 56 — 63 £ p

64 Marginal rate relief — 64 £ p

65 Corporation tax net of marginal rate relief — 65 £ p

66 Underlying rate of corporation tax — 66 • %

67 Profits matched with non-corporate distributions — 67

68 Tax at non-corporate distributions rate — 68 £ p

69 Tax at underlying rate on remaining profits — 69 £ p

**70 Corporation tax chargeable** — *See note for box 70 in CT600 Guide* — 70 £ p

CT600 (Short) (2006) Version 2

| | | |
|---|---|---|
| 79 Tax payable under S419 ICTA 1988 | | 79 £ p |
| 80 *Put an 'X' in box 80 if you completed box A11 in the Supplementary Pages CT600A* | 80 | |
| 84 Income tax deducted from gross income included in profits | | 84 £ p |
| 85 Income tax repayable to the company | | 85 £ p |
| 86 **Tax payable - this is your self-assessment of tax payable** | | total of boxes 70 and 79 minus box 84<br>86 £ p |

## Tax reconciliation

| | |
|---|---|
| 91 Tax already paid (and not already repaid) | 91 £ p |
| 92 Tax outstanding | box 86 minus box 91<br>92 £ p |
| 93 Tax overpaid | box 91 minus box 86<br>93 £ p |

## Information about capital allowances and balancing charges

### Charges and allowances included in calculation of trading profits or losses

| | Capital allowances | Balancing charges |
|---|---|---|
| 105 - 106 Machinery and plant - long-life assets | 105 £ | 106 £ |
| 107 - 108 Machinery and plant - other (general pool) | 107 £ | 108 £ |
| 109 - 110 Cars outside general pool | 109 £ | 110 £ |
| 111 - 112 Industrial buildings and structures | 111 £ | 112 £ |
| 113 - 114 Other charges and allowances | 113 £ | 114 £ |

### Charges and allowances not included in calculation of trading profits or losses

| | Capital allowances | Balancing charges |
|---|---|---|
| 115 - 116 Non-trading charges and allowances | 115 £ | 116 £ |
| 117 *Put an 'X' in box 117 if box 115 includes flat conversion allowances* | 117 | |

### Expenditure

| | | |
|---|---|---|
| 118 Expenditure on machinery and plant on which first year allowance is claimed | | 118 £ |
| 119 *Put an 'X' in box 119 if claim includes enhanced capital allowances for designated energy-saving investments* | 119 | |
| 120 Qualifying expenditure on machinery and plant on long-life assets | | 120 £ |
| 121 Qualifying expenditure on machinery and plant on other assets | | 121 £ |

## Losses, deficits and excess amounts

| | | | |
|---|---|---|---|
| 122 Trading losses Case I | calculated under S393 ICTA 1988<br>122 £ | 124 Trading losses Case V | calculated under S393 ICTA 1988<br>124 £ |
| 125 Non-trade deficits on loan relationships and derivative contracts | calculated under S82 FA 1996<br>125 £ | 127 Schedule A losses | calculated under S392A ICTA 1988<br>127 £ |
| 129 Overseas property business losses Case V | calculated under S392B ICTA 1988<br>129 £ | 130 Losses Case VI | calculated under S396 ICTA 1988<br>130 £ |
| 131 Capital losses | calculated under S16 TCGA 1992<br>131 £ | 136 Excess management expenses | calculated under S75 ICTA 1988<br>136 £ |

Page 4

## Overpayments and repayments

### Small repayments

If you do not want us to make small repayments please either put an 'X' in box 139 or complete box 140 below. 'Repayments' here include tax, interest, and late-filing penalties or any combination of them.

Do not repay £20 or less 139 Do not repay sums of 140 £ or less. *Enter whole figure only*

### Bank details (for person to whom the repayment is to be made)

Repayment is made quickly and safely by direct credit to a bank or building society account.
Please complete the following details:

Name of bank or building society

149

Branch sort code

150

Account number

151

Name of account

152

Building society reference

153

### Payments to a person other than the company

Complete the authority below if you want the repayment to be made to a person other than the company.
I, as *(enter status - company secretary, treasurer, liquidator or authorised agent, etc.)*

154

of *(enter name of company)*

155

authorise *(enter name)*

156

*(enter address)*

157

Postcode

Nominee reference

158

to receive payment on the company's behalf.

Signature

159

Name *(in capitals)*

160

## Declaration

Warning - Giving false information in the return, or concealing any part of the company's profits or tax payable, can lead to both the company and yourself being prosecuted.

Declaration
The information I have given in this company tax return is correct and complete to the best of my knowledge and belief.

Signature

Name *(in capitals)*

Date *(dd/mm/yyyy)*

Status

CT600 (Short) (2006) Version 2

Page 1

# Company Tax Return form - Supplementary Pages
# Loans to participators by close companies
**CT600A (2006) Version 2**

**for accounting periods ending on or after 1 July 1999**

## Company information

**Company name**

**Tax reference as shown on the CT603**

**Period covered by these Supplementary Pages (*cannot exceed 12 months*)**

from (*dd/mm/yyyy*) to (*dd/mm/yyyy*)

## You need to complete these Supplementary Pages if

the company is close and has made a loan (or loans) to an individual participator, or associate of a participator, in this period which has not been repaid within the period. Tax is due under S419 ICTA 1988.

## Important points

- These Supplementary Pages, when completed, form part of the company's return.
- These Pages set out the information we need and provide a standard format.
- Complete the boxes with whole figures only, except where pence or decimals are indicated.
- The notes below will help you understand any terms that have a special meaning and notes on these Pages will help with the completion of this form.
- These Pages are covered by the Declaration you sign on back page of form *CT600*.
- The warning shown on form *CT600* about prosecution, and the advice about late and incorrect returns, and late payment of tax also apply to these Pages.

## Notes

A **'close company'** is one which is under the control of five or fewer participators, or of any number of participators who are directors (S414 ICTA 1988).

A **'loan'** within S419 ICTA 1988 includes the situation where a participator incurs a debt to the close company (S419(2)(a) ICTA 1988), for example by overdrawing a current or loan account. There are two exceptions where S419 ICTA 1988 does not apply

- a debt incurred for the supply by the close company of goods or services in the ordinary course of its trade or business, unless the credit given exceeds six months, or is longer than that normally given to the company's customers (S420(1) ICTA 1988), and
- certain loans made to full-time working directors or employees who do not have a material interest in the close company (S420(2) ICTA 1988).

A **'participator'** is a person having a share or interest in the capital or income of the company and includes any loan creditor of the company (S417(1) ICTA 1988).

An **'associate'** of a participator includes any relative or partner of the participator and the trustees of any settlement of which the participator or their relative is, or was, a settlor (S417(3)(a) and (b) ICTA 1988).

Methods by which a loan can be 'repaid' include depositing money into the company's bank account, crediting the participator's current or loan account with a dividend, director's remuneration or bonus, or book entry.

The term **'release'** refers to a formal procedure that normally takes place under seal for a consideration, whereas **'write off'** is a wider term that does not necessarily require formal arrangements and could include acceptance by the company that the loan will not be recovered and has given up attempts to recover it.

HMRC 08/06

**CT600A (2006) Version 2**

**Page 2**

## 1: Loans made during the return period

You must complete part 1 if the company is close and has made a loan to an individual participator, or associate of a participator, during the return period which has not been repaid within the return period.
Enter in the table below, details of any outstanding loans made to a participator or associate of a participator during the return period. If the participator or associate has a current or loan account with the company, enter details of each participator's or associate's account. The amount you enter in column 2 of the table is the total of all debit entries on the account, less any credit entries and less any credit balance brought forward from the previous return period. In arriving at this figure you must exclude any credit entries that represent repayment, release or write off of loans made in earlier return periods.

**A1** *Put an 'X' in this box if loans made during the period have been released, or written off before the end of the period* **A1** ☐

**A2** Information about loans made during the return period and outstanding at the end of the period

| Name of participator or associate | Amount of loan |
|---|---|
| | £ |
| | £ |
| | £ |
| | £ |
| | £ |
| Total | **A2** £ |

Total loans within S419 ICTA 1988 made during the return period which have not been repaid, released or written off before the end of the period

*If a continuation sheet is used, please put an 'X' in box A2A* **A2A** ☐

**A3** Tax chargeable on loans -
(*Tax due before any relief for loans repaid, released, or written off after the end of the period*) box A2 multiplied by 25% **A3** £ p

## 2: Relief for amounts repaid, released or written off after the end of the period but *earlier than* nine months and one day after the end of the period - for loans made during the return period

Complete part 2 to obtain relief for loans included in box A2 that were repaid, released or written off if

- the return is for the period in which the loans were made **and**
- the loan was repaid, released or written off after the end of the period but **earlier than** nine months and one day after the end of the accounting period in which the loan was **made.**

Enter in the table details for each participator or associate. If there have been a number of repayments on an account, enter only the total repayments for that account and give the date of the last repayment. **A separate entry must be made for each loan or part loan that has been released or written off.**

**Example**
A company makes a loan during the accounting period ended 31 December 2004 and it is all repaid to the company on 30 June 2005. The company's tax return for the accounting period ended 31 December 2004 is sent to HM Revenue & Customs on 1 November 2005. Part 2 should be completed because the loan was repaid after the end of the accounting period but earlier than nine months and one day after it.

**A4 & A5** Information about loans repaid, released or written off after the end of the period but ***earlier than*** nine months and one day after the end of the period

| Name of participator or associate | Amount repaid | Amount released or written off | Date of repayment, release or write off |
|---|---|---|---|
| | £ | £ | |
| | £ | £ | |
| | £ | £ | |
| | £ | £ | |
| | £ | £ | |
| | £ | £ | |
| Totals **A4** | £ | £ | **A5** |

*If a continuation sheet is used, please put an 'X' in box A5A* **A5A** ☐

A6 Total amount of loans made during the return period which have been repaid, released or written off after the end of the period but ***earlier than*** nine months and one day after the end of the period — total of boxes A4 and A5 **A6** £

A7 Relief due for loans repaid, released or written off after the end of the period but ***earlier than*** nine months and one day after the end of the period — box A6 multiplied by 25% **A7** £ p

**CT600A (2006) Version 2**

## Most companies will not need to complete part 3 below

Only complete part 3:

- where the loan was made during the return period, and
- where repayment, release or write off was more than nine months after the end of the period in which the loan was made, and
- the return is submitted after the date on which relief is due (if the return is sent in very late, at least twenty-one months after the end of the return period).

If you are unsure whether or not to complete part 3, apply the following questions to each claim.

Put an 'X' in this box if the loan was made in the return period.
If it was not, then you cannot complete part 3; if it was then go on to the next box

dd/mm/yyyy

End date of accounting period in which the loan was repaid, released or written off **a**

Enter the date 9 months after the end of that accounting period **b**

Date you are sending in the company tax return for the period in which the loan was made **c**

If the date at **c** is earlier than the date at **b** you cannot complete part 3, but can make a separate claim for the relief which is not due until the date in **b**.

If the date at **c** is later than the date at **b** you can complete part 3 below to obtain the relief now.

## 3: Relief for loans made during the return period repaid, released or written off *more than* nine months after the end of the period and *where relief is due now*

Complete part 3 only if loans made during the return period, that have not been included in part 2, have been repaid, released or written off and where relief is due now (see the notes above under 'Most companies will not need to complete part 3').

**Example**

A company makes a loan during the accounting period ended 31 December 2004 and it is all repaid on 30 November 2005. The company's return for the accounting period ended 31 December 2004 is sent to HM Revenue & Customs on 1 December 2005. Part 3 of this form **should not** be completed because, although the loan was repaid more than nine months after the end of the return period, the return is sent earlier than nine months after the end of the return period in which the loan was repaid.

Relief for the repayment cannot be given until the due date of the accounting period in which the repayment was made, in this case 1 October 2006 (Ss419(4A) and (4B) ICTA 1988). The company must make a separate claim for relief.

**Example**

Same as example above except that the return is not sent in until 3 December 2006. Relief for the repayment is due on or after 1 October 2006. In this case part 3 can be completed because the repayment was made more than nine months after the end of the accounting period in which the loan was made, and the relief is due at the time the return is sent in.

**A8 & A9** Information about loans made during the return period which have been repaid, released or written off ***more than*** nine months after the end of the period ***and relief is due now***

| Name of participator or associate | Amount repaid | Amount released or written off | Date of repayment, release or write off |
|---|---|---|---|
| | £ | £ | |
| | £ | £ | |
| | £ | £ | |
| | £ | £ | |
| | £ | £ | |
| | £ | £ | |
| Totals **A8** | £ | £ **A9** | |

*If a continuation sheet is used, please put an 'X' in box A9A* **A9A**

A10 Total amount of loans made during the return period which have been repaid, released, or written off ***more than*** nine months after the end of the period ***and relief is due now***

total of boxes A8 and A9
**A10** £

A11 Relief due now for loans repaid, released or written off ***more than*** nine months after the end of the period. ***Put an 'X' in box 80 on form CT600 if you have completed box A11***

box A10 multiplied by 25%
**A11** £ p

CT600A (2006) Version 2

**Page 4**

## 4: Other information

**A12** Total of all loans outstanding at end of return period - including all loans outstanding at the end of the return period, whether they were made in this period or an earlier one.

## 5: What S419 ICTA 1988 tax is payable?

**A13** **Tax payable under S419 ICTA 1988**
***Copy the figure in box A13 to box 79 on form CT600***

box A3 minus total of boxes A7 and A11
A13 £ p

**What to do when you have completed these Supplementary Pages**

- Copy the figure from box A13 in part 5 to box 79 of the form *CT600*.
- Put an 'X' in box 80 of form *CT600* if you have completed box A11 in part 3 of these Pages.
- Follow the advice shown under 'What to do when you have completed the return' on page 23 of the *Guide*.

# Company Tax Return form - Supplementary Pages
# Controlled foreign companies
**CT600B (2006) Version 2**

**for accounting periods ending on or after 1 July 1999**

## Company information

**Company name**

**Tax reference as shown on the CT603**

**Period covered by these Supplementary Pages** (*cannot exceed 12 months*)
from (*dd/mm/yyyy*) to (*dd/mm/yyyy*)

## You need to complete these Supplementary Pages if

at any time in this period, the company, held a relevant interest of 25% or more in a foreign company which is **controlled** from the UK. No controlled foreign company (CFC) need be included on these pages where it satisfies the **Excluded Countries Regulations**.

A UK company may also include companies which may not be CFCs but which would satisfy one of the exemptions if they were. This applies to foreign companies which may not be subject to a lower level of tax, or may not be controlled from the UK. It also applies where the UK company's relevant interest in the foreign company may be less than 25%. The purpose of this is to save UK companies the cost of working out whether a foreign company is in principle a CFC in cases where it is clear that one of the exemptions would be passed if it were.

## Important points

- These Supplementary Pages, when completed, form part of the company's return.
- These Pages set out the information we need and provide a standard format.
- Notes below will help with the completion of this form.
- These Pages are covered by the Declaration you sign on the back page of form *CT600*.
- The warning shown on form *CT600* about prosecution, and the advice about late and incorrect returns, and late payment of tax also apply to these Pages.

## Notes

The following information is required on pages 2 and 3:

- **Name of the CFC** Enter the full name of the CFC.
- **Territory of residence** If a residence election is made this should be noted and if a company is conclusively presumed to be resident in a territory in which it is subject to a lower level of tax then this should be indicated by the entry 'S749(5) ICTA 1988'.
- **Exemption due** Companies exempt under the provisions may indicate one (or more) exemptions here. Only one exemption need be noted, and not including an exemption will not prejudice whether it applies. If an exemption applies there is no need to complete page 3 of the supplementary return in respect of the CFC.
- **Percentage measure for apportionment** This will usually be the percentage of ordinary share capital held directly or indirectly by the UK company (but not by associated or connected persons). In all other circumstances the appropriate percentage should be calculated on a just and reasonable basis.
- **Chargeable profits** These are the chargeable profits (after reliefs available under Sch 25 ICTA 1988) apportioned to the UK company.
- **Tax on chargeable profits** This is the amount of tax apportioned on the basis of the company's share of chargeable profits before reliefs are given under Sch 26 ICTA 1988 or relief is given for advance corporation tax.
- **Creditable tax** This broadly represents tax already paid on the chargeable profits and is deductible.
- **Reliefs in terms of tax** Any reliefs available under Sch 26 should be shown at the appropriate rate of corporation tax.
- **ACT as restricted** Unrelieved surplus ACT to the extent not restricted should be shown here.
- **S747 tax chargeable** This is the column J total which is the sum of the figures in column F less the sum of the figures in columns G to I. The net figure should be copied to box 81 of form *CT600*.

## What to do when you have completed these Supplementary Pages

- Copy the figure from the Summary box J13 on these Pages to box 81 of form *CT600*.
- Follow the advice shown under 'What to do when you have completed the return' on page 23 of the *Guide*.

**Page 2**

| | A<br>Name of CFC | B<br>Territory of residence for S749 Purposes | C<br>Exemption due (if any) |
|---|---|---|---|
| 1 | | | |
| 2 | | | |
| 3 | | | |
| 4 | | | |
| 5 | | | |
| 6 | | | |
| 7 | | | |
| 8 | | | |
| 9 | | | |
| 10 | | | |
| 11 | | | |
| 12 | | | |

*Put an 'X' in this box if a continuation sheet is used for page 2*

**CT600B (2006) Version 2**

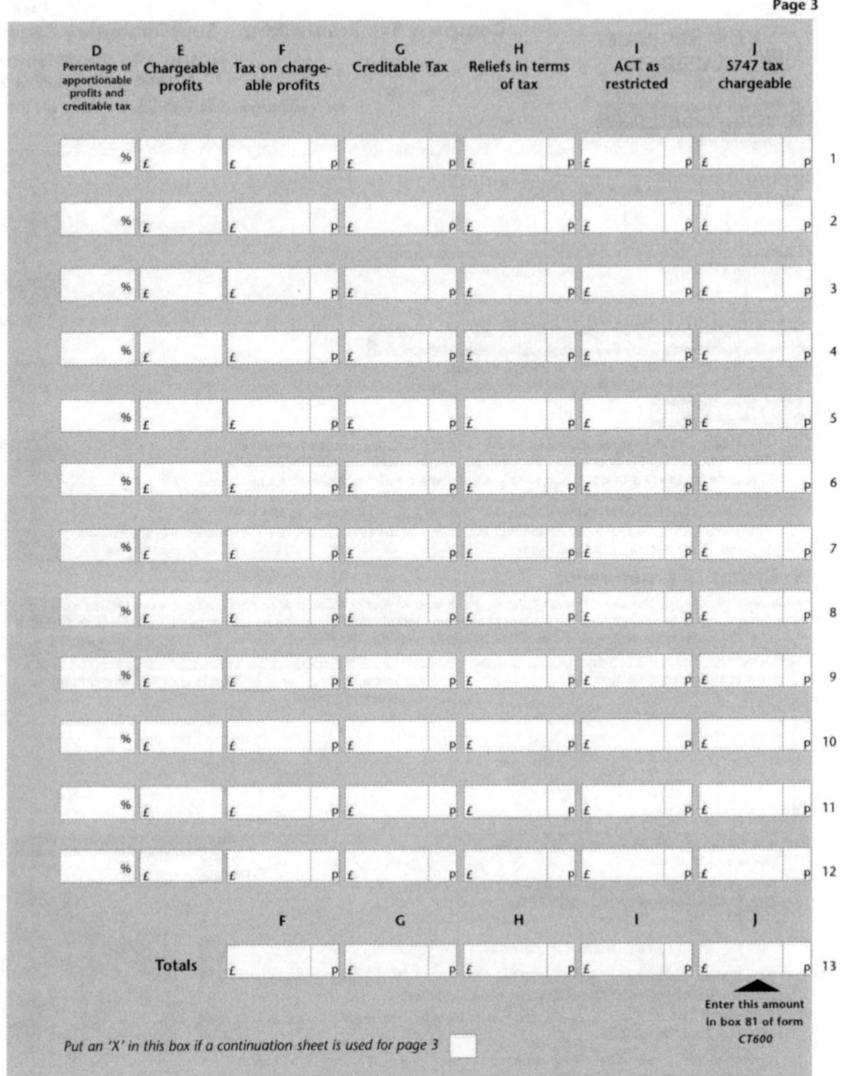

**Page 3**

| D<br>Percentage of apportionable profits and creditable tax | E<br>Chargeable profits | F<br>Tax on chargeable profits | G<br>Creditable Tax | H<br>Reliefs in terms of tax | I<br>ACT as restricted | J<br>S747 tax chargeable | |
|---|---|---|---|---|---|---|---|
| % | £ | £ p | £ p | £ p | £ p | £ p | 1 |
| % | £ | £ p | £ p | £ p | £ p | £ p | 2 |
| % | £ | £ p | £ p | £ p | £ p | £ p | 3 |
| % | £ | £ p | £ p | £ p | £ p | £ p | 4 |
| % | £ | £ p | £ p | £ p | £ p | £ p | 5 |
| % | £ | £ p | £ p | £ p | £ p | £ p | 6 |
| % | £ | £ p | £ p | £ p | £ p | £ p | 7 |
| % | £ | £ p | £ p | £ p | £ p | £ p | 8 |
| % | £ | £ p | £ p | £ p | £ p | £ p | 9 |
| % | £ | £ p | £ p | £ p | £ p | £ p | 10 |
| % | £ | £ p | £ p | £ p | £ p | £ p | 11 |
| % | £ | £ p | £ p | £ p | £ p | £ p | 12 |
| | | F | G | H | I | J | |
| | Totals | £ p | £ p | £ p | £ p | £ p | 13 |

**Enter this amount in box 81 of form *CT600*** (J, box 13)

*Put an 'X' in this box if a continuation sheet is used for page 3* ☐

**CT600B (2006) Version 2**

Page 1

HM Revenue & Customs

# Company Tax Return form - Supplementary Pages
## Group and consortium
**CT600C (2006) Version 2**

**for accounting periods ending on or after 1 July 1999**

## Company information

**Company name**

**Tax reference as shown on the CT603**

**Period covered by these Supplementary Pages (*cannot exceed 12 months*)**
from (*dd/mm/yyyy*) to (*dd/mm/yyyy*)

## You need to complete these Supplementary Pages if

- you are claiming or surrendering any amounts under the group and/or consortium relief provisions.
- you are claiming or surrendering eligible unrelieved foreign tax (for accounting periods ending on or after 31 March 2001).

## Important points

- These Supplementary Pages, when completed, form part of the company's return.
- These Pages set out the information we need and provide a standard format.
- Complete the boxes with whole figures only, except where pence or decimals are indicated.
- There are notes on these Pages to help you when you complete this form.
- These Pages are covered by the Declaration you sign on back page of form *CT600*.
- The warning shown on form *CT600* about prosecution, and the advice about late and incorrect returns, and late payment of tax also apply to these Pages.

## 1: Claims to group relief

You need to complete this part if you are claiming group relief in your calculation of corporation tax payable. Attach a copy of each surrendering company's notice of consent to the claim. Include claims made under the consortium provisions and attach a copy of the notice of consent of each member of the consortium. If a simplified arrangement is in force, the claim may be authorised below.

| Name of surrendering company | Accounting period [1] of surrendering company | Tax reference [2] | Amount claimed £ |
|---|---|---|---|
| | | | |
| | | | |
| | | | |
| | | | |
| | | | |

[1] *Enter the start and end dates of any period that is different from that covered by this return*

[2] *Enter the HM Revenue & Customs office number and taxpayer reference. If you do not know these show whatever information you can that will help us to identify the company, such as the company registration number*

enter in box 36 of form *CT600*

Total **C1** £

*Put an 'X' in box C1A if a continuation sheet is used* **C1A**

*Put an 'X' in box C1B if a group relief claim involves losses of a trade carried on in the UK through a Permanent Establishment by a non-resident company* **C1B**

*Put an 'X' in box C1C if a group relief claim involves losses of a non-resident company other than those covered by box C1B* **C1C**

A claim involves a non-resident if the claimant, the surrendering company, or any other company by reference to which their group relationship is established, is non-resident

## Claim authorisation - *complete if simplified arrangements apply and copies of notices of consent are not supplied*

**Signature** | **Name** (*in capitals*)

**Name of authorised company**

Date (*dd/mm/yyyy*)

Any person authorised to sign on behalf of the company that is authorised to act for the companies within the arrangement should sign this authorisation.

HMRC 08/06

**CT600C (2006) Version 2**

Page 2

## 2: Amounts surrendered as group relief

You need to complete this part if the company is surrendering any amount under the group (or consortium) provisions.
**Unless** a simplified arrangement is in force
- a notice of consent to each claim is needed
- this part is acceptable as a notice of consent, if the surrendering company details are entered and it is signed by an authorised person in the space below.
- send a copy of the notice of consent to the HM Revenue & Customs office dealing with the claimant company's return before or at the same time as the claimant company submits its return claiming the group relief
- the consent of all the other consortium members is needed for consortium relief.

**Surrender as group relief**

| | |
|---|---|
| Trading losses | £ |
| Excess non-trade capital allowances over income from which they are primarily deductible | £ |
| Non-trading deficit on loan relationships | £ |
| Non-trading losses on intangible fixed assets | £ |
| Excess charges over profits | £ |
| Excess of Schedule A losses over profits | £ |
| Excess of management expenses over profits | £ |
| **Total** | £ |

**Details of surrender**

| Name of claimant company | Accounting period [1] of claimant company | Tax reference [2] | Amount surrendered £ |
|---|---|---|---|
| | | | |
| | | | |
| | | | |
| | | | |
| | | | |
| | | | |
| | | **Total** C2 | £ |

[1] *Enter the start and end dates of any period that is different from that covered by this return*

[2] *Enter the HM Revenue & Customs office number and taxpayer reference. If you do not know these show whatever information you can that will help us to identify the company, such as the company registration number*

*Put an 'X' in box C2A if a continuation sheet is used.* C2A

**Details of company surrendering relief**

You must complete and sign this section if you are using this form as the notice of consent to surrender.

**Company name**

**Tax reference**

**Accounting period**

**Start date (dd/mm/yyyy)** **End date (dd/mm/yyyy)**

**I certify that all the information I have given on these pages is correct and complete to the best of my knowledge and belief.**

**Signature** *(needed if you are using this form as the notice of consent to surrender)*

**Name** *(in capitals)* **Status**

Except where a liquidator or administrator has been appointed, any person who is authorised to do so may sign on behalf of the company. A photocopy of a signature is not acceptable.

**CT600C (2006) Version 2**

## Eligible Unrelieved Foreign Tax (EUFT)

**You need to complete this part if you are claiming EUFT in your calculation of corporation tax payable, or part 4 on page 4 if the company is surrendering any amount of EUFT under the Double Taxation Relief (Surrender of Relievable Tax within a Group) Regulations. These regulations apply to income arising on or after 31 March 2001.**

**You must attach a copy of each surrendering company's notice of consent to the claim.**

**Claims to EUFT do not apply to consortium companies and, unlike the claims to and surrenders as group relief covered by parts 1 and 2 of this form, there can be no simplified arrangement for EUFT.**

## 3: Claims to EUFT

**You need to complete this part if you are claiming EUFT in your calculation of corporation tax payable.**

*Remember to include any box C3 figure in your calculation of corporation tax payable on form CT600.*

**Details of claim**

| Name of surrendering company | Accounting period [1] of surrendering company | Tax reference [2] | Amount claimed £ | p |
|---|---|---|---|---|
| | | | | |
| | | | | |
| | | | | |
| | | | | |
| | | | | |
| | | | | |
| | | | | |

*include in box 73 entry on form CT600*

**Total** C3 £ p

1 *Enter the start and end dates of any period that is different from that covered by this return*

2 *Enter the HM Revenue & Customs office number and taxpayer reference. If you do not know these show whatever information you can that will help us to identify the company, such as the company registration number*

*Put an 'X' in box C3A if a continuation sheet is used* C3A

## 4: Amounts of EUFT surrendered

You should complete this part if the company is surrendering any amount of EUFT under the Double Taxation Relief (Surrender of Relievable Tax Within a Group) Regulations.

- A notice of consent to each claim is needed.
- This part is acceptable as a notice of consent, if the surrendering company details are entered and it is signed by an authorised person in the space below.
- Send a copy of the notice of consent to the HM Revenue & Customs office dealing with the claimant company's return before or at the same time as the claimant company submits its return claiming the EUFT.

**Details of surrender**

| Name of company claiming | Accounting period [1] of claimant company | Tax reference [2] | Amount surrendered £ | p |
|---|---|---|---|---|
| | | | | |
| | | | | |
| | | | | |
| | | | | |
| | | | | |
| | | | | |
| | | Total **C4** | £ | p |

[1] *Enter the start and end dates of any period that is different from that covered by this return*

[2] *Enter the HM Revenue & Customs office number and taxpayer reference. If you do not know these show whatever information you can that will help us to identify the company, such as the company registration number*

*Put an 'X' in box C4A if a continuation sheet is used* **C4A**

**Details of company surrendering EUFT**

You must complete and sign this section if you are using this form as the notice of consent to surrender.

**Company name**

**Tax reference**

**Accounting period**
**Start date (dd/mm/yyyy)** **End date (dd/mm/yyyy)**

**I certify that all the information I have given on these pages is correct and complete to the best of my knowledge and belief.**

**Signature** *(needed if you are using this form as the notice of consent to surrender)*

**Name** *(in capitals)* **Status**

Except where a liquidator or administrator has been appointed, any person who is authorised to do so may sign on behalf of the company. A photocopy of a signature is not acceptable.

### What to do when you have completed these Supplementary Pages

- Copy any figure from box C1 in part 1 to box 36 of form *CT600*.
- Include any figure from box C3 in part 3 in box 73 of form *CT600*.
- Follow the advice shown under 'What to do when you have completed the return' on page 23 of the *Guide*.

Page 1

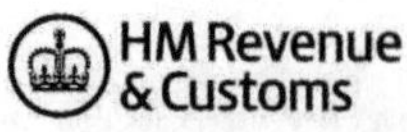


**Company Tax Return form - Supplementary Pages**
**Charities and Community Amateur Sports Clubs (CASCs)**
**CT600E (2006) Version 2**

**for accounting periods ending on or after 1 July 1999**

## Company information

**Company name**

**Tax reference as shown on the CT603**

**Period covered by these Supplementary Pages (*cannot exceed 12 months*)**
from (*dd/mm/yyyy*) to (*dd/mm/yyyy*)

## You need to complete these Supplementary Pages if

the charity/CASC claims exemption from tax on all or any part of its income and gains.

## Important points

- These Supplementary Pages will form the charity's/CASC's claim to exemption from tax on the basis that its income and gains have been applied for charitable or qualifying purposes only.
- Please use the notes on page 2 to help you complete this form.
- Please enter whole figures or '0' where appropriate.
- How often you are asked to make a return will depend on the extent and nature of your activities.
- These Pages, when completed, form part of the company's return.
- These Pages set out the information we need and provide a standard format.
- These Pages are covered by the Declaration you sign on the back page of form *CT600*.
- The warning shown on form *CT600* about prosecution, and the advice about late and incorrect returns and late payment of tax, also apply to these Pages.

## Claims to exemption

**This section should be completed in all cases**

Charity/CASC repayment reference

Charity Commission Registration number, or Scottish Charity number (if applicable)

*Put an 'X' in the relevant box if during the period covered by these Supplementary Pages:*

- the company was a charity/CASC and is claiming exemption from all tax on all or part of its income and gains.
- all income and gains are exempt from tax and have been, or will be, applied for charitable or qualifying purposes only.

If the company was a charity/CASC but had no income or gains in the period, then put an 'X' in the first box 'claiming exemption from all tax' above.

or

- some of the income and gains may not be exempt or have not been applied for charitable or qualifying purposes only, and I have completed form *CT600*.
*See the note on Restrictions of relief for non-qualifying expenditure on page 2.*

**I claim exemption from tax**

**Signature** **Date** (*dd/mm/yyyy*)

**Name (*in capitals*)**

**Status**

*Except where a liquidator or administrator has been appointed, any person who is authorised to do so may sign on behalf of the company. For CASCs the treasurer should sign. A photocopy of a signature is not acceptable.*

HMRC 08/06

**CT600E (2006) Version 2**

**Page 2**

## Notes

### *Repayments boxes E1/E1a, E2/E2b and E1a - E4d*

Transitional relief only applies on qualifying distributions made on or after 6 April 1999 and before 6 April 2004. The time limit for claims is 2 years after the end of the charity's accounting period in which the distribution was made.

In boxes E1/E1a:

- Enter the amount of income tax and transitional relief claimed on forms *R68(2000)* or *R68(CASC)* for the period covered by these Pages.
- This should relate only to income arising in the period.
- Do not include amounts claimed for earlier periods.

In Box E2/E2b enter the total amount due for income received in the period on which a charity/CASC can claim.

CASCs should leave boxes E1a to E4d blank.

### *Trading income box E5*

Enter details of the turnover of trades, the profits of which will be exempted by

a) S505(1)(e) ICTA 1988, S46 FA 2000 or ESC C4 (for charities), or

b) Schedule 18, Paragraph 4, FA 2002 (for CASCs).

If the charity/CASC has carried on a trade during the return period which falls outside the exemption, complete the *Company Tax Calculation* on form *CT600*. Do not include in the calculation sources of income which are otherwise exempt from tax. Also, complete the *About this return* section on page 1 and *Declaration* on the back page of form *CT600*.

### *Gifts boxes E11 and E12*

Include in box E11 the value of any gifts of shares or securities received under S587B ICTA 1988.

Include in box E12 the value of any gifts of real property received under S587B/S587C ICTA 1988.

### *Other sources box E13*

Enter details in box E13 of income received from sources other than those included in the boxes above where the income is exempt from tax in the hands of a charity/CASC. This will include Case VI income exempted by S505(1)(c)(iic) ICTA 1988.

### *Investments and loans within Sch 20 ICTA 1988 box E26 charities only*

Qualifying investments and loans, for the purposes of S506 ICTA 1988, are specified in Parts I and II of Sch 20 ICTA 1988.

Charities can make claims to HM Revenue & Customs for any loan or other investment not specified in Sch 20 but made for the benefit of the charity and not for avoidance of tax, to be accepted as qualifying.

Put an 'X' in box E26 only if all investments and loans are qualifying investments and loans:

- automatically, because they are specified in Sch 20, or
- because the charity has either claimed (with this return or separately) that they are under Paragraphs 9 or 10 of Sch 20 ICTA 1988, or is prepared to do so on request.

For a claim for qualifying status to succeed, the loan or investment must be made for the benefit of the charity and not for the avoidance of tax (whether by the charity or any other person). Claims should be in writing and specify

- the nature of the item (loans, or shares for example)
- the amount
- the period
- whether the claim is under Paragraph 9 or 10.

It is helpful if a claim includes full details, for example the terms of a loan.

### *Investments and loans made outside Sch 20 ICTA 1988 box E27 charities only*

If the charity has made any investments or loans which do not fall within Schedule 20 ICTA 1988, and no claim is being made with this return, enter the total of such loans or investments in box E27.

### *Restrictions of relief for non-qualifying expenditure*

Relief under S505(1) ICTA 1988 and S256 TCGA 1992 may not be available to some charities.

The charity should attach a calculation of restriction of relief under S505(3) ICTA 1988 and send it with this return.
If you need help with this calculation please telephone our helpline on **08453 020203** or email **charities@hmrc.gov.uk**

Where a CASC has incurred non-qualifying expenditure its exemptions from tax may need to be restricted. The CASC should include a calculation of the restriction of relief under Schedule 18, Paragraph 8 FA 2002 with this return.
If you need help with this calculation please telephone our helpline on **08453 020203** or email **charities@hmrc.gov.uk**

### *Further guidance*

Further guidance on the reliefs available to charities and CASCs is available on our website at **www.hmrc.gov.uk/charities**

**CT600E (2006) Version 2**

## Repayments

**Enter details of repayments of Income Tax/payments of Transitional Relief for income arising during the period covered by these Supplementary Pages**

| | | Income Tax | Transitional Relief *Charities only* |
|---|---|---|---|
| **E1/E1a** | Amount already claimed for period using form R68(2000) or R68(CASC) | E1 £ | E1a £ |
| **E2/E2b** | Total repayment/payment due | E2 £ | E2b £ |
| **and either** | | | |
| **E3/E3c** | Further repayment/payment due *Where E2/E2b is more than E1/E1a* | E3 £ | E3c £ |
| **or** | | | |
| **E4/E4d** | Amounts overclaimed for period *Where E1/E1a is more than E2/E2b* | E4 £ | E4d £ |

*If any of the amounts in boxes E3/E3c have been included in any repayment/payment claim on form R68(2000) or R68(CASC) put an 'X' in this box.* ☐

## Information required

**Enter details of any income received from the following sources, claimed as exempt from tax in the hands of the charity/CASC. Enter the figure included in the charity's/CASC's accounts for the period covered by this return**

*Do not include amounts which are not taxable. Non-exempt amounts should be entered on form CT600 in the appropriate boxes.*

| Type of income | Amount |
|---|---|
| E5 Enter total turnover from exempt trading activities | E5 £ |
| E6 Investment income - exclude any amounts included on form *CT600* | E6 £ |
| E7 UK land and buildings - exclude any amounts included on form *CT600* | E7 £ |
| E8 Deed of covenant - exclude any amounts included on form *CT600* | E8 £ |
| E9 Gift Aid or Millennium Gift Aid - exclude any amounts included on form *CT600* | E9 £ |
| E10 Other charities - exclude any amounts included on form *CT600* | E10 £ |
| E11 Gifts of shares or securities received | E11 £ |
| E12 Gifts of real property received | E12 £ |
| E13 Other sources | E13 £ |

**Enter details of expenditure as shown in the charity's/CASC's accounts for the period covered by these Supplementary Pages**

| Type of expenditure | Amount |
|---|---|
| E14 Trading costs in relation to exempt activities (in box E5) | E14 £ |
| E15 UK land and buildings in relation to exempt activities (in box E7) | E15 £ |
| E16 All general administration costs | E16 £ |
| E17 All grants and donations made within the UK | E17 £ |
| E18 All grants and donations made outside the UK | E18 £ |
| E19 Other expenditure not included above, or not used in calculating figures entered on the form *CT600* | E19 £ |

*continued on page 4*

**Page 4**

*continued from page 3*

| Charity/CASC Assets | | Disposals in period (total consideration received) | Held at the end of the period (use accounts figures) |
|---|---|---|---|
| E20/E20a | Tangible fixed assets | E20 £ | E20a £ |
| E21/E21b | UK investments (excluding controlled companies) | E21 £ | E21b £ |
| E22/E22c | Shares in, and loans to, controlled companies | E22 £ | E22c £ |
| E23/E23d | Overseas investments | E23 £ | E23d £ |
| E24e | Loans and non-trade debtors | | E24e £ |
| E25f | Other current assets | | E25f £ |
| E26 | Qualifying investments and loans. *Applies to charities only. See note on Page 2* | | E26 |
| E27 | Value of any non-qualifying investments and loans. *Applies to charities only* | | E27 £ |
| E28 | Number of subsidiary or associated companies the charity controls at the end of the period. *Exclude companies that were dormant throughout the period* | | E28 |

**What to do when you have completed these Supplementary Pages**

Follow the advice shown under 'What to do when you have completed the return' on page 23 of the *Guide*.

CT600E (2006) Version 2

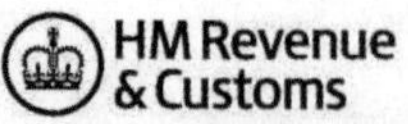

# Company Tax Return form - Supplementary Pages Corporate Venturing Scheme

**CT600G (2006) Version 2**

**for accounting periods ending on or after 1 July 1999**

## Company information

**Company name**

**Tax reference as shown on the CT603**

**Period covered by these Supplementary Pages (*cannot exceed 12 months*)**

from (*dd/mm/yyyy*) to (*dd/mm/yyyy*)

## You need to complete these Supplementary Pages if

for shares issued **on or after 1 April 2000 but before 1 April 2010** the company is claiming under the Corporate Venturing Scheme (CVS):

- investment relief on the amount subscribed for shares, **or**
- relief against income for losses on certain disposals of shares, whether effect is to be given to the claim in this period or an earlier period, **or**
- postponement of certain chargeable gains where the gains are reinvested in shares under the Corporate Venturing Scheme.

## Important points

- These Supplementary Pages, when completed, form part of the company's return.
- They set out the information we need and provide a standard format.
- They are covered by the Declaration you sign on the back page of form *CT600*.
- The warning shown on form *CT600* about prosecution, and the advice about late and incorrect returns, and late payment of tax also apply to these Pages.
- **You are advised to read the relevant notes on page 4 of this form before you complete these Pages.**

## What to do when you have completed these Supplementary Pages

- Copy the figure from box G1 to box 71 of the form *CT600*.
- Follow the advice shown under 'What to do when you have completed the return' on page 23 of the *Guide*.

## Claims

A company making a claim in its company tax return must do so using these Supplementary Pages.

If a company makes a claim later, but within the time limit for amending its return, it should make the claim on an amended return, giving the same details as are required by forms *CT600* and *CT600G*. (For instance this could be the case if the form CVS 3 to support a deferral relief claim is not received until after the return has been delivered.) No specific form is provided for an amended return, but as long as it is signed by a person authorised to do so and includes a declaration that the information is correct and complete to the best of his or her knowledge and belief, it will be accepted as an amended return.

If the time for amending a return has passed, but the claim is still in time, the company should again give the same details as are required by forms *CT600* and *CT600G*. The claim should be signed by a person authorised to do so and include a declaration that the information is correct and complete to the best of his or her knowledge and belief.

**Page 2** ***Use this page together with page 3***

***If there is not enough space in any section, please continue on a separate sheet and attach it to the form.***

**Investment Relief**

**For each issue of shares in respect of which investment relief is claimed, please enter the following details:**
*All this information, except the actual amount of investment relief claimed, is on the form CVS3 that the issuing company sent to the investing company.*

1

| Name of qualifying issuing company | Number of shares subscribed for |
|---|---|
| | |
| | |
| | |
| | |
| | |

**Relief for losses on disposals of shares**

**For each disposal in respect of which a claim is being made, please enter the following details:**

2

| Name of qualifying issuing company | Description of shares disposed of |
|---|---|
| | |
| | |
| | |
| | |

**Deferral relief**

**For claims to postpone chargeable gains or parts of gains, please enter the details below. Use a separate line for each gain or part of gain.**

3

| Name of qualifying issuing company whose shares have been disposed of, or in relation to which another chargeable event has occurred | Where the gain was previously postponed under the CVS, enter name of qualifying issuing company on which original gain arose | Date of disposal or of other chargeable event |
|---|---|---|
| | | |
| | | |
| | | |
| | | |
| | | |
| | | |

**CT600G (2006) Version 2**

***Use this page together with page 2*** **Page 3**

***If there is not enough space in any section, please continue on a separate sheet and attach it to the form.***

1

| Nominal value of shares subscribed for £ | Date of issue (given on form CVS 3) | Amount subscribed for the shares £ | Amount of investment relief claimed net of any reduction for value received £ | Small Company Enterprise Centre reference |
|---|---|---|---|---|
| | | | | |
| | | | | |
| | | | | |
| | | | | |
| | | | | |

**Total investment relief claimed** *Copy the figure in box G1 to box 71 of form CT600* **G1** £

2

| Number of shares disposed of | Date of issue of shares | Date of disposal of shares | Accounting period(s) of claim, and amount of loss relief claimed for (each) period | | |
|---|---|---|---|---|---|
| | | | From | To | £ |
| | | | | | |
| | | | | | |
| | | | | | |
| | | | | | |

3

| Amount of chargeable gain (or of part of chargeable gain) matched against unused qualifying expenditure on new qualifying shares £ | Name of qualifying issuing company that issued the new qualifying shares | Date of issue of new qualifying shares |
|---|---|---|
| | | |
| | | |
| | | |
| | | |
| | | |
| | | |

**CT600G (2006) Version 2**

**Notes**

**These notes do not provide a full explanation of the Corporate Venturing Scheme.**
**More guidance is available on our website at www.hmrc.gov.uk/guidance.htm**

**Investment relief**

A company must not claim the relief on any investment unless it has received a compliance certificate on form CVS 3. You may be asked to produce the certificate relating to that investment.

Investment relief takes the form of a reduction in the investing company's corporation tax liability for the accounting period in which the shares were issued. Except as mentioned below, the amount of that reduction is 20% of the amount of any subscriptions (excluding any associated costs) or, if that would exceed the corporation tax liability, such an amount as will reduce that liability to nil. The amount subscribed will be shown on form CVS 3.

Where the investing company (or any person connected with it) has received value from the issuing company (or from any person connected with that company) so that paragraph 47 of Sch 15 FA 2000 applies, the amount of relief is reduced. The amount of the reduction is usually 20% of the amount of value received, but it will be less where paragraph 51 or 52 of Sch 15 FA 2000 apply. Any amount of value received by the investing company from the issuing company (or any connected person) that was known to the issuing company at the time the form CVS 3 was issued should be shown on that form.

**Loss relief**

A claim to set an allowable loss on a share disposal against income may be made under the CVS only if

- investment relief was attributable to the shares disposed of at the time of the disposal, **and**
- the investment relief is not withdrawn in full as a result of the disposal, **and**
- the shares were held continuously from the date the shares were issued until disposal, **and**
- the disposal is
  - a disposal by way of a bargain at arm's length for full consideration, **or**
  - by way of a distribution in the course of dissolving or winding up the issuing company, **or**
  - a disposal within S24(1) TCGA 1992, **or**
  - a deemed disposal following a claim under S24(2) TCGA 1992, **and**
- the disposal does not occur in consequence of any company reconstruction or amalgamation for the purposes of tax avoidance.

CVS loss relief may be claimed against income of the accounting period in which the loss arises. Any loss not so relieved may be claimed against income of accounting periods ending in the previous 12 months, subject to the apportionment provision in paragraph 69(2) of Sch 15 FA 2000. To the extent that the loss is not set off against income it may be deducted from chargeable gains in the usual way.

The amount of an allowable loss is calculated according to the rules in TCGA 1992, as modified by paragraph 94, Sch 15 FA 2000.

**Deferral relief**

A claim may be made to postpone

- a chargeable gain accruing on a disposal of shares to which investment relief was attributable immediately before the disposal, provided that the shares were held continuously from the date they were issued until the disposal, **or**
- a chargeable gain previously postponed under the CVS in respect of an investment in shares which is revived because of a 'chargeable event' (that is a disposal or an event other than a disposal which causes any investment relief attributable to the shares to be reduced or withdrawn).

To be eligible for the relief the company must have subscribed - during the period starting one year before and ending three years after the date on which the gain accrued - for shares to which investment relief is attributable. Before deferral relief can be claimed a form CVS 3 must be held in respect of those shares. If those shares were issued before the gain accrued, the company must have held the shares continuously from the date they were issued until the gain accrued **and** investment relief must be attributable to them at the time the gain accrued.

However, deferral relief is not available where the gain to be deferred accrues on a disposal of shares and the shares subscribed for are in the same company or in any member of its group. Similarly, deferral relief is not available where the gain to be deferred has been revived because of a chargeable event and the shares subscribed for are in the company whose shares were involved in that event, or in any member of its group.

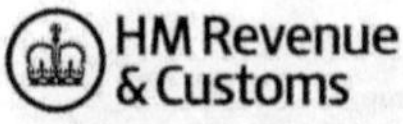

# Company Tax Return form - Supplementary Pages
## Cross-border Royalties
**CT600H (2006) Version 2**

**for accounting periods ending on or after 1 July 1999**

## Company information

**Company name**

**Tax reference as shown on the CT603**

**Period covered by these Supplementary Pages (*cannot exceed 12 months*)**
from (*dd/mm/yyyy*) to (*dd/mm/yyyy*)

## You need to complete these Supplementary Pages if

- the company is a UK company and made cross-border royalty payments after 1 October 2002, and reasonably believed that the recipient of the royalties would be entitled to treaty relief on any tax deducted. The company is entitled to make such payments without deduction of tax or at the rate specified by reference to the double taxation treaty appropriate to the country of residence of the payee. Further information about countries or territories that have double taxation agreements with the UK can be found on our website at **www.hmrc.gov.uk**

**and/or**

- the company is a UK company or UK permanent establishment of an EU company, and made royalty payments to an associated company in another Member State of the EU on or after 1 January 2004 (1 May 2004 for States joining the EU on that date) and reasonably believed that the beneficial owner of the royalties is exempt from UK income tax on those payments following the implementation of the Interest and Royalties Directive. Such payments should be made without deduction of tax.

In this context 'permanent establishment' is a fixed place of business situated in a Member State through which the business of a company of another Member State is wholly or partly carried on.

## Important points

- These Supplementary Pages, when completed, form part of the company's return.
- These Pages set out the information we need and provide a standard format.
- Complete the boxes with whole figures only, except where pence or decimals are indicated.
- These Pages are covered by the Declaration you sign on the back page of form *CT600.*
- The warning shown on form *CT600* about prosecution, and the advice about late and incorrect returns, and late payment of tax also apply to these Pages.
- There are additional penalty provisions for failure to observe the law regarding royalty payments. Details are contained in S349E(1)(7) ICTA 1988, S98(4D) TMA 1970 and S98(4DA) TMA 1970 and there is provision for a Direction to be issued under S349E(1)(3) ICTA 1988 or S96(3) FA 2004, as appropriate.

## What to do when you have completed these Supplementary Pages

- Complete box 98 of form *CT600* to show that you have made cross-border royalty payments under reasonable belief.
- Follow the advice shown under 'What to do when you have completed the return' on page 23 of the *Guide.*

HMRC 08/06

CT600H (2006) Version 2

Page 2

## Details of payments made

| | Name of recipient of the royalty | Full address of recipient of the royalty | Type of royalty payment made |
|---|---|---|---|
| 1 | | | |
| 2 | | | |
| 3 | | | |
| 4 | | | |
| 5 | | | |
| 6 | | | |
| 7 | | | |
| 8 | | | |
| 9 | | | |
| 10 | | | |
| 11 | | | |
| 12 | | | |

*Put an 'X' in this box if a continuation sheet is used.* ☐

CT600H (2006) Version 2

| Gross amount of royalty paid £ | Agreement under which relief claimed: (a) Interest and Royalties Directive ***or*** (b) country with double taxation agreement with UK | Rate of tax deducted from payment % | Amount of tax deducted from payment £ p | Additional notes | |
|---|---|---|---|---|---|
| | (a)<br>(b) | | | | 1 |
| | (a)<br>(b) | | | | 2 |
| | (a)<br>(b) | | | | 3 |
| | (a)<br>(b) | | | | 4 |
| | (a)<br>(b) | | | | 5 |
| | (a)<br>(b) | | | | 6 |
| | (a)<br>(b) | | | | 7 |
| | (a)<br>(b) | | | | 8 |
| | (a)<br>(b) | | | | 9 |
| | (a)<br>(b) | | | | 10 |
| | (a)<br>(b) | | | | 11 |
| | (a)<br>(b) | | | | 12 |

**CT600H (2006) Version 2**

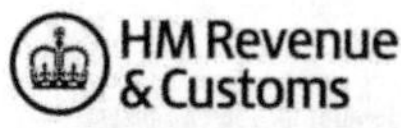

Page 1

**Company Tax Return form - Supplementary Pages**
**Disclosure of tax avoidance schemes**
**CT600J (2006) Version 2**

**for notifiable arrangements on or after 18 March 2004**

## Company information

**Company name**

**Tax reference as shown on the CT603**

**Period covered by these Supplementary Pages (*cannot exceed 12 months*)**
from (*dd/mm/yyyy*) to (*dd/mm/yyyy*)

## You need to complete these Supplementary Pages if

you are a party to any notifiable arrangements under S308, 309, 310 Finance Act 2004 (FA 2004) and you have received a reference number.

Under S313(1) FA 2004 you are required to provide HM Revenue & Customs with

- any reference number notified to you in the accounting period covered by this return, **and**
- the time when you obtain or expect to obtain a tax advantage from the notifiable arrangements either in the accounting period covered by this return or in a period covered by a future return.

**You should not use this form if**

- you are an employer and the notifiable arrangements concerned are arrangements connected with employment. A scheme reference number for employment products should be notified separately using form AIU4.
- you are a party to any notifiable arrangements in the accounting period covered by this return that have not otherwise been notified to HM Revenue & Customs you should do so now by completing form AIU3.

Forms AIU3 and AIU4 are available on our website at **www.hmrc.gov.uk/aiu/index.htm** or from the Orderline by telephoning **0845 300 6555.**

## Important points

- These Supplementary Pages, when completed, form part of the company's return.
- These Pages set out the information we need and provide a standard format.
- These Pages are covered by the Declaration you sign on back page of form *CT600*.
- The warning on form *CT600* about prosecution and the advice about late returns and late payment of tax also apply to these Pages. Other penalties that apply are shown overleaf.

## Disclosable tax avoidance schemes

*See notes overleaf before completing these boxes.*

| Scheme Reference Number | Accounting period in which the expected advantage arises (*dd/mm/yyyy*) |
|---|---|
| J1 | J1A |
| J2 | J2A |
| J3 | J3A |
| J4 | J4A |
| J5 | J5A |
| J6 | J6A |
| J7 | J7A |
| J8 | J8A |
| J9 | J9A |
| J10 | J10A |

HMRC 08/06

CT600J (2006) Version 2

**Page 2**

## Scheme Reference Number

Enter the reference number given to you by the promoter or by HM Revenue & Customs (as appropriate) for each notifiable proposal or notifiable arrangement if you

- have received the scheme reference number in the accounting period covered by this return, or
- expect to obtain a tax advantage in the accounting period covered by this return, or
- expect to obtain a tax advantage in an accounting period covered by a later return.

You should enter the reference number even if you have already entered the number on a return covering an earlier period, unless you no longer expect any tax advantage to arise from the notifiable arrangements either in this accounting period or in any later accounting period.

## Accounting period in which the expected advantage arises

You should enter the last day of the accounting period in which you currently expect any tax advantage resulting from the notifiable arrangements to arise, using the format *dd/mm/yyyy*. If you expect the tax advantage to cover more than one accounting period, enter the earliest.

## Penalties

If the company fails
- to provide any reference number given to it by the promoter or by HM Revenue & Customs for any notifiable proposal or arrangement, **or**
- to report the last day of the accounting period in which you first expect any tax advantage to arise, as required by S313(1) FA 2004,

the company may be liable to a penalty under S98C(3) Taxes Management Act 1970.

The amount of the penalty will vary as follows:
- £100 for each scheme to which the failure relates unless either of the bullets below applies -
  - £500 for each scheme where the company has previously failed to comply on one and only one occasion during the period of 36 months ending with the date of the current failure, whether or not the failure relates to the same scheme.
  - £1000 for each scheme where the company has previously failed to comply on two or more occasions during the period of 36 months ending with the date of the current failure, whether or not the failure relates to the same scheme.

## Glossary

**Tax advantage** here means
- relief or increased relief from, or repayment or increased repayment of corporation tax, or the avoidance or reduction of a charge to that tax, or an assessment to that tax, or the avoidance of a possible assessment to that tax
- the deferral of any payment of tax or the advancement of any repayment of tax, or
- the avoidance of any obligation to deduct or account for any tax.

**Arrangements connected with employment** means any notifiable proposal or arrangements which are disclosable under S308, 309, or 310 FA 2004 by virtue of Part 1 of the Schedule to the Tax Avoidance Schemes (Prescribed Descriptions of Arrangements) Regulations 2004 (as amended). A copy of the Regulations giving the prescribed descriptions of arrangements can be seen at **www.hmrc.gov.uk/aiu/index.htm**

**Notifiable proposal** and **Notifiable arrangements** have the meanings given in S306 FA 2004.

**Reference number** in relation to the notifiable arrangements, has the meaning given by S311(3) FA 2004.

## What to do when you have completed these Supplementary Pages

Follow the advice shown under 'What to do when you have completed the return' on page 23 of the *Guide*.

**CT600J (2006) Version 2**

# Index

[*all references are to paragraph number*]

**B**



**C**

## D

## G

**H**

## S

## U



## V



## W



## Y